234

Non-State Actors
and Authority in the
Global System

Traditionally in International Relations, power and authority were considered to rest with states. But recently, in the light of changes associated with globalisation, this assumption has come under scrutiny both empirically and theoretically. This book analyses the continuing but changing role of states in the international arena and their relationships with a wide range of non-state actors, which possess increasingly salient capabilities to structure global politics and economies.

This book identifies two principal types of non-state actors. First, there are private sector corporate actors, which can be further divided into transnational corporations and multinational corporations. Second, there are non-governmental organisations – either societally-sponsored or state-sponsored – which play an increasingly important role at the global level. The degree of importance attached to non-state actors depends to a great extent upon one's definition of globalisation. This book offers four different definitions: the global neo-liberal discourse, the hegemony of American values, a confluence of economic phenomena along the lines of liberal interdependence, and globalisation as one historical epoch of many. Each of the chapters concentrates on empirical case studies and therefore highlights the usefulness of the definitions.

While a range of non-state actors have acquired authority at the international level, understanding the state in all its sophistication and complexity remains a crucial question in contemporary political economy. The individual contributions in this volume offer ways of understanding the nature of relationships between states and non-state actors – sometimes conflicting but often symbiotic – in an evolving economic order.

Richard A. Higgott is Professor and Director of the ESRC Centre for the Study of Globalisation and Regionalisation, University of Warwick, and is the editor of the *Pacific Review*. **Geoffrey R. D. Underhill** is Professor of International Governance at the University of Amsterdam; his most recent books include *Industrial Crisis and the Open Economy*, and *The New World Order in International Finance*. **Andreas Bieler** is College Lecturer and Director of Studies in Social and Political Sciences at Selwyn and Newnham College, University of Cambridge.

Routledge/Warwick Studies in Globalisation

Edited by Richard Higgott and published in association with the Centre for the Study of Globalisation and Regionalisation, University of Warwick.

What is globalisation and does it matter? How can we measure it? What are its policy implications? The Centre for the Study of Globalisation and Regionalisation at the University of Warwick is an international site for the study of key questions such as these in the theory and practice of globalisation and regionalisation. Its agenda is avowedly interdisciplinarian. The work of the Centre will be showcased in this new series.

This series comprises two strands:

Routledge/Warwick Studies in Globalisation is a forum for innovative new research intended for a high-level specialist readership, and the titles will be available in hardback only. Titles include:

1. Non-state Actors and Authority in the Global System
Edited by Richard A. Higgott, Geoffrey R. D. Underhill and Andreas Bieler

Warwick Studies in Globalisation addresses the needs of students and teachers, and the titles will be published in hardback and paperback. Titles include:

1. Globalisation and the Asia-Pacific
Contested territories
Edited by Kris Olds, Peter Dicken, Philip F. Kelly, Lily Kong and Henry Wai-chung Yeung

Non-State Actors and Authority in the Global System

**Edited by Richard A. Higgott,
Geoffrey R. D. Underhill and
Andreas Bieler**

London and New York

First published 2000
by Routledge
11 New Fetter Lane, London EC4P 4EE

Simultaneously published in the USA and Canada
by Routledge
29 West 35th Street, New York, NY 10001

Transferred to Digital Printing 2002

Routledge is an imprint of the Taylor & Francis Group

Typeset in Times by
Curran Publishing Services Ltd
Printed and bound in Great Britain by
Intype London Ltd

British Library Cataloguing in Publication Data
A catalogue record for this book is available
from the British Library

Library of Congress Cataloging in Publication Data
Non-state actors and authority in the global system / edited by
    Richard A. Higgott, Geoffrey R. D. Underhill and Andreas Bieler.
    320 pp. 15.6 x 23.4 cm
    Includes bibliographical references and index.
    1. International economic relations. 2. International economic
    integration. 3. International business enterprises. 4. Non-governmental
    organizations.
    I. Higgott, Richard A. II. Underhill, Geoffrey R. D. III. Bieler,
    Andreas.
    HF 1359.N662 1999
    337–dc21
                                                        99-34775
                                                        CIP

ISBN 0–415–22085–8

Contents

Figures

Tables

Acronyms

ACTN	Advisory Committee for Trade Negotiations
ACTPN	Advisory Committee on Trade Policy Negotiations
AGBM	Ad-hoc Group on the Berlin Mandate
AIC	Apparel Industry Coalition
ANSI	American National Standards Institute
APEC	Asia-Pacific Economic Cooperation
ASEAN-ISIS	Association of South East Asian Nations' Institute for Strategic and International Studies
ASME	American Society of Mechanical Engineers
BCSD	Business Council for Sustainable Development
BIAC	Business and Industry Advisory Committee
BITs	Bilateral Investment Treaties
BRIE	Berkeley Roundtable of International Economics
CAFC	Court of Appeals for the Federal Circuit
CAN	Climate Action Network
CEO	Chief Executive Officer
CIEL	Centre for International Environmental Law
CIME	Committee on Investment and Multilateral Enterprises
CIS	Commonwealth of Independent States
CMIT	Committee on Capital Movements and Invisible Transactions
COP	Conference of the Parties
CPMP	Committee for Proprietary Medicinal Products
CPNs	Cross-National Production Networks
CPR	Common Pool Resources
CSCAP	Council for Security Cooperation in Asia-Pacific
CSE	Centre for Science and Environment
CSGR	Centre for the Study of Globalisation and Regionalisation
CSI	Coalition of Service Industries
CTE	Commitee on Trade and Environment
CVDs	Countervailing Duties

DAFFE	Directorate on Financial Fiscal and Enterprise Affairs
DRAM	Dynamic Random Access Memory
DSB	Dispute Settlement Body
DSU	Dispute Settlement Understanding
EAs	Environmental Assessments
EC	European Community
ECOSOC	United Nations Economic and Social Council
ECSCAP	European Council for Security and Cooperation in Asia-Pacific
ED	Executive Director
EDF	Environmental Defence Fund
EECA	European Electronics Components Association
EIAJ	Electronic Industry Association of Japan
EMEA	European Medicines Evaluation Agency
ENGOs	Environmental Non-Governmental Organisations
EPZs	Export Processing Zones
ESM	Environmental Social Movement
EU	European Union
EURODAD	European Network on Debt and Development
FCCC	Framework Convention on Climate Change
FDA	Food and Drug Administration
FDI	Foreign Direct Investment
FOE-US	Friends of the Earth, United States
FTA	Free Trade Agreement
GAP	Group for Alternative Policies
GATS	General Agreement on Trade in Services
GATT	General Agreement on Tariffs and Trade
GCC	Global Climate Coalition
GEIs	global economic institutions
GEMIT	Group on Environmental Measures and International Trade
GEP	Global Environmental Politics
GONGOs	Governmentally Organised Non-Governmental Organisations
GRINGOs	Governmentally Regulated and Initiated Non-Governmental Organisations
GROs	grass roots organisations
GSMs	global social movement
GSP	Generalised System of Preference
GSS	General Social Survey
HIPC	Highly Indebted Poor Countries
ICA	International Corporation Alliance
ICC	International Chamber of Commerce
ICCA	International Council of Chemical Associations
ICCP	International Climate Change Partnership
ICE	Information Council for Environment
ICFTU	International Confederation of Free Trade Unions

ICTSD	International Centre for Trade and Sustainable Development
IDI	Inward Direct Investment
IEA	Internet Energy Agency
IFCS	Inter-governmental Forum on Chemical Safety
IGIDR	Indira Gandhi Institute for Development Research
IGOs	International Governmental Organisations
IIE	Institute for International Economics
IISS	International Institute of Strategic Studies
ILO	International Labour Organisation
INC	Inter-Governmental Negotiating Committee
IMF	International Monetary Fund
INC	Inter-Governmental Negotiating Committee
INGOs	Inter-Governmental Organisations or International Non-Governmental Organisations
INSPAC	Investment and Services Policy Advisory Committee
IOE	International Organisation of Employers
IP	Intellectual Property
IPC	Intellectual Property Committee
IPCC	Inter-Governmental Panel on Climate Change
IPR	Intellectual Property Rights
IR	International Relations
ISEAS	Institute of South East Asian Studies
ISO	International Organisation for Standardisation
ISSP	International Social Survey Program
ITC	International Trade Commission
ITO	International Trade Organisation
IUCN	International Union for the Conservation of Nature
JCIF	Japan Centre for International Finance
JUSCANZ	Japan, US, Canada and New Zealand
KSIA	Korean Semiconductor Industry Association
LDCs	less developed countries
MAI	Multilateral Agreement on Investment
MANGOs	Manipulated Non-Governmental Organisations
MCA	Medicines Control Agency
MD	managing director
MDBs	Multilateral Development Banks
MFA	MultiFibre Arrangement
MFNs	Most Favoured Nations
MITI	Ministry of International Trade and Industry
MNCs	Multinational Corporations
MNEs	multinational enterprises
MOEF	Ministry of Environment and Forests
NAFTA	North American Free Trade Agreement
NAM	National Association of Manufacturers
NGOs	non-governmental organisations

NIESR	National Institute of Economic and Social Research
NUMMI	New United Motor Manufacturing Inc.
ODC	Overseas Development Council
ODI	Overseas Development Institute
OECD	Organisation of Economic Co-operation and Development
OFII	Organisation for International Investment
OPEC	Organisation of Petroleum Exporting Countries
PICS	platform for Internet content selection
POPS	persisstent organic products
PTO	Patent and Trademark Office
REIOs	Regional Economic Integration Organisations
RUSEL	Research Unit for the International Study of Economic Liberal-isation and its Social and Political Effects
SDR	special drawing right
SET	secure electronic transaction
SIA	Security Industry Association or Semiconductor Industry Association
SIPRI	Stockholm International Peace Research Institute
STA	Semiconductor Trade Agreement
TERI	Tata Energy Research Institute
THM	transnational historical materialism
TNCs	transnational corporations
TRIMs	Trade Related Investment Measures
TRIPs	Trade Related Intellectual Property Rights
TUAC	Trade Union Advisory Committee
UAW	Union of Automotive Workers
UNCED	United Nations Conference on Environment and Development
UNCTAD	United Nations Conference on Trade and Development
UNDP	United Nations Development Programme
UNEP	United Nations Environmental Programme
UNFCCC	United Nations Framework Convention on Climate Change
UNICE	Union of Industrial and Employers Confederations of Europe
UNICEF	United Nations International Children's Emergency Fund
URRA	Uruguay Round Agreements Act
USCIB	US Council for International Business
USTR	United States Trade Representative
VERs	voluntary export restraints
WIDE	Women in Development Europe
WRI	World Resources Institute
WSC	World Semiconductor Council
WTO	World Trade Organisation
WWF	World Wide Fund for Nature

Contributors

Andreas Bieler: Lecturer at Selwyn and Newnham Colleges, University of Cambridge, UK.

Daniel Egan: Assistant Professor, University of Massachusetts, Lowell, USA.

Ann M. Florini: Resident Associate, Carnegie Endowment for International Peace, Washington D.C., USA.

Gilbert Gagné: Sessional Lecturer, Concordia University College of Alberta, Canada and McGill University, Canada.

Virginia Haufler: Associate Professor, University of Maryland, USA.

Richard A. Higgott: Professor and Director, Centre for the Study of Globalisation and Regionalisation, University of Warwick, UK.

Susanne Jakobsen: Ph.D. candidate, University of Copenhagen, Denmark.

David L. Levy: Assistant Professor, University of Massachusetts, Boston, USA.

Jochen Lorentzen: Lecturer, John Hopkins University Bologna Centre, Italy.

Duncan Matthews: Research Fellow, Centre for the Study of Globalisation and Regionalisation, University of Warwick, UK.

John F. Pickering: Professor of Business Strategy, School of Management, University of Bath.

Brian Portnoy: Ph.D. candidate, University of Chicago, USA.

Jan Aart Scholte: Reader, University of Warwick, UK.

Susan K. Sell: Associate Professor, George Washington University, Washington D.C., USA.

Elizabeth Smythe: Assistant Professor, Concordia University College of Alberta, Canada.

Kendall W. Stiles: Associate Professor, Loyola University, Chicago, USA.

Diane Stone: Lecturer, University of Warwick, UK.

Maria Isabel Studer Noguez: Associate Professor, Instituto Tecnológico Autónomo de México.

Geoffrey R. D. Underhill: Professor, Department of Political Science, University of Amsterdam, The Netherlands.

Andrew Walter: Senior Lecturer, London School of Economics, UK.

Marc Williams: Professor of International Politics, University of New South Wales, Sydney, Australia.

Preface

This volume represents the best of the papers from the inaugural conference of the Centre for the Study of Globalisation and Regionialisation (CSGR) at Warwick University. Funded by the Economic and Social Research Council of the UK with an initial grant of over £2.5 million, the Centre is rapidly becoming an international site for the study of key issues in the theory and practice of globalisation and regionalisation. As the papers in this volume demonstrate, the Centre's agenda is avowedly inter-disciplinary. Research staff in the CSGR are drawn from international relations, political science, economics, law and sociology. The Centre is committed to scholarly excellence but also strives to be problem-solving in methodological orientation.

Three broad categories of activity inform and underwrite the research programme of the Centre. First, what is globalisation? Second, can we measure its impacts, and if so, how? Third, what are its policy implications? Understandings of globalisation are seen to be multi-dimensional – political, economic, cultural, ideological – so the CSGR sees globalisation in at least two broad ways: first, as the emergence of a set of sequences and processes that are increasingly unhindered by territorial or jurisdictional barriers and that enhance the spread of trans-border practices in economic, political, cultural and social domains; and second, as a discourse of political and economic knowledge offering one view of how to make the post-modern world manageable. For many, globalisation as 'knowledge' constitutes a new reality. Centre research will ask what kinds of constraints globalisation poses for independent policy initiatives on the part of national policy-makers and under what conditions these constraints are enhanced or mitigated.

Within these broad contexts empirical work at the CSGR focuses on: first, particular regional projects in Europe, North America and the Asia-Pacific; second, the enhancement of international institutions, rules and policy competence on questions of trade competition and international finance and investment; third, normative questions about governance, sovereignty, democratisation and policy-making under constraints of globalisation.

Indeed, Centre research is sensitive to the wider normative nature of many of these questions, especially in research into the counter-tendencies towards, or sites of resistance to, globalisation at regional and local levels that give rise to different understandings of the importance of space and territoriality.

Routledge/Warwick Studies in Globalisation will provide an avenue for the publication of scholarly research monographs, policy-oriented studies and collections of original themed essays in the area of the research agenda of the CSGR. In this context, *Non-State Actors and Authority in the Global System,* the second volume in the series, addresses several of the key themes of the CSGR's research, notably the shifting relationship between state authority and market power under conditions of globalisation and the relationship between states and non-state actors in that process in a number of crucial policy areas.

The editors would like to thank Jill Southam and Denise Butler for their assistance in the production of the manuscript and Siwon Jin for his invaluble assistance producing the index.

Anyone interested in knowing more about CSGR is invited to visit our website at www.csgr.org.

Richard Higgott
Director, CSGR

Introduction

Globalisation and non-state actors

Richard A. Higgott,
Geoffrey R. D. Underhill
and Andreas Bieler

Traditionally, in International Relations (IR), power and authority were considered to rest with states. This has recently come under scrutiny empirically and theoretically due to the changes associated with 'globalisation'. Globalisation is a complex concept. Two extreme versions oppose each other. Globalists, especially prior to the economic meltdown of 1997–8, regard globalisation as moving inevitably to a borderless world and economic 'level playing field', on which truly global companies are the primary actors. There is little or no role left to states beyond the provision of infrastructure and public goods required by business (Ohmae 1990 and 1995). In more nuanced fashion, Strange talks about an increasing hollowness of state authority or a 'retreat of the state' (Strange 1996). Conversely, internationalists consider states to be still the main actors in international economics and politics. Hirst and Thompson argue that the economy is predominantly international, not global, and that therefore states, although in a slightly different way, still play a central role in its governance (Hirst and Thompson 1996: 178–89). The changes are called internationalisation, not globalisation, and are defined as a drastic increase in cross-border flows of goods, services and capital (Keohane and Milner 1996).

This collection of original essays demonstrates that neither of the two extreme positions adequately conceptualises the role of states and non-state actors under conditions of globalisation. The state has been strengthened in some areas, while it has clearly lost power in others. The role of the state has not diminished, but it has changed. The state has been and continues to be restructured (Weiss 1998). Although states retain a significant degree of importance, a wide range of non-state actors possess increasingly salient capabilities to structure global politics and economics.

Two principal types of non-state actors can be identified. Firstly, there are private sector corporate actors, which we further divide into transnational corporations (TNCs) and multinational corporations (MNCs). While TNCs strive for a world-wide intra-firm division of labour, MNCs attempt to replicate production within a number of regions in order to avoid the risks of trade blocs.[1] Secondly, non-governmental organisations (NGOs) play an increasingly important role at the international level, partly thanks to new technologies such as the Internet. Some larger and more active NGOs are now also referred to as global social movements (GSMs). The second group we divide into societally-sponsored NGOs, to be found mainly in the Western world, and state-sponsored NGOs, often referred to as

GONGOs (Governmentally Organised Non-Governmental Organisations), MANGOs (Manipulated Non-Governmental Organisations) or even GRINGOs (Governmentally Regulated and Initiated Non-Governmental Organisations), which are, for example, present in East Asia. In short, instead of investigating the world either as a purely state-dominated arena or a place without state authority, the main theme of this book is the study of both state and the large variety of non-state authorities and their relation with each other.

Contextually, we see globalisation as a technological and social revolution that has until recently been progressing towards a globally integrated production structure with specialised but interdependent labour markets, the privatisation of state assets, and the linkage of technology across borders.[2] Crucially, this production structure is underpinned by a pattern of transnational financial markets and monetary relations which provide the key infrastructure for investment, production, and trade in goods and services (Underhill 1997). This understanding represents the neo-liberal discourse, focusing on the deregulation and liberalisation of markets, the dismantling of state functions, the organisation of production on a transnational scale and the emergence of a global world financial market. Within this discourse, the transfer of authority from the state to the market is not only deemed inevitable, but also beneficial. Prior to the 1997–8 financial market meltdown, it was a clearly optimistic view of globalisation, considered to lead to the improvement of everybody's living conditions, provided the neo-liberal path was pursued. The new powerful actors within this discourse are TNCs, which enjoy a predominant role in universalised market structures and consider consumers, not states, as the representatives of civil society. Nevertheless, the TNC component of this discourse is doubtful (Higgott and Reich 1998). As Doremus *et al.* (1998) outline, the majority of firms are MNCs with clearly anchored national bases. Corporations in big countries, especially, still treasure their home bases. In short, the extent to which there is actually a fully global production structure may be more limited than much globalisation literature assumes. In chapter 10 of this book, Maria Isabel Studer Noguez outlines how Ford's original global strategy, exemplified in its world car projects since the 1970s, has failed and been replaced with regional production structures, in particular in Europe and North America. But most TNCs stem from small countries, most importantly the Netherlands, Sweden and Switzerland. This raises the question of whether it is not simply due to the particular domestic context of these corporations that they transnationalised their production. Small home markets, additionally characterised by high labour costs and limited research facilities, may make it imperative for them to expand abroad in times of weakened national trade and investment barriers.

Undoubtedly, TNCs and MNCs play an increasingly important role in the governing of the global economy. Susan K. Sell in chapter 5 shows how it was the initiative by the Intellectual Property Committee (IPC), formed by twelve Chief Executives of US based MNCs, which was at least partly responsible for the coming about of the Trade Related Aspects of Intellectual Property (TRIPs) agreement. In chapter 6, Duncan Matthews and John F. Pickering draw a similar picture of the influence of MNCs on the rule-making within some sectors of the

Single Market of the European Community. Virginia Haufler outlines in chapter 7 the importance of private sector international regimes, established through the cross-border cooperation of firms, in pursuing product standardisation and guaranteeing the security of transactions.

The rising importance of TNCs and MNCs does not imply that states decline in significance, as the neo-liberal global discourse *pace* Ohmae *et al.* argues. The setting-up of private sector regimes, for example, often involves negotiations between firms, governments and NGOs. Moreover, Andrew Walter shows in chapter 3 that the structural power of TNCs and MNCs due to increased capital mobility is overestimated. Important developing countries such as China, Indonesia and Brazil continue to receive FDI despite the lack of a liberal investment regime. Their good economic prospects make them attractive to TNCs and it is they that have to comply with these countries' conditions rather than the other way round. This argument is underlined by Elizabeth Smythe's conclusion in chapter 4 that MNCs were unable to obtain sweeping liberalisation principles and clear restrictions on state authority in the Multilateral Agreement on Investment (MAI) negotiations within the Organisation of Economic Co-operation and Development (OECD). David L. Levy and Daniel Egan support this view in their study of the climate change negotiations by pointing out in chapter 8 that capital is strongly contested within the international institutions for the negotiations of social and environmental policies. Hence, it still relies on state support in the face of adverse regulations. Finally, Jochen Lorentzen in his study of industrial restructuring in Central Europe (chapter 11) demonstrates how the power of TNCs *vis-à-vis* host countries of their FDI depends on the particular arrangements and, therefore, is not necessarily predominant. In short, while TNCs and MNCs are important sources of authority in the global system, they share it with states and other non-state actors.

A different reading of globalisation views it as the hegemony of American values. It is the triumph of a particular ideology consisting of the 'characteristic features of a limited state apparatus, representative government and a liberal concept of freedom and choice' (Higgott and Reich 1998: 8). Associated with earlier theories of modernisation (see Higgott 1983), this view argues that we are seeing a gradual international convergence towards liberal democracy and modernity, defined as industrialised economic development. This view of globalisation assumes a positive relationship between democracy and development and regards it as a moral failure not to follow this path. Important international actors carry the banner of this approach. Firstly, Inter-Governmental Organisations (INGOs) such as the World Bank and the International Monetary Fund (IMF) appear to act as vehicles to establish the American variant of capitalist liberal democracy in former Communist countries and countries with a different variant of capitalism such as in East Asia (Bhagwati 1998; Higgott 1998). Gilbert Gagné (chapter 13) shows how the World Trade Organisation (WTO) was strengthened in the Uruguay Round to arbitrate in international conflicts over trade related matters along a coherent neo-liberal, American line. Nevertheless, the spread of capitalist liberal democracy is, and will continue to be, contested by NGOs.

At one level, this struggle can be described as a contest between the old multilateralism, constituted by the interaction of states, and a new multilateralism, which attempts to 'reconstitute civil societies and political authorities on a global scale, building a system of global governance from the bottom up' (Cox 1997: XXXVII). The strategies of the two types of multilateralism differ significantly. On the one hand, INGOs attempt to extend their area of influence incrementally: 'geographically, by universalising their membership; functionally, by coverage of more issues; inclusively, by the cooption of erstwhile recalcitrant actors, thus securing their socialisation into the dominant market liberal ideological mode' (Higgott 1999). GSMs, on the other hand, pursue a highly politicised, normative approach. It is a working assumption of many GSMs that INGOs are instruments if not necessarily of US hegemony, at least of an OECD dominance of the existing world economic order. Through their interaction with INGOs, GSMs attempt to alter the prevailing assumptions of this order and thereby change policy outcomes. They push for transparency and demand democratic accountability at the international level. Marc Williams and Jan Aart Scholte in chapters 14 and 15 respectively discuss to what extent GSMs to date have been able to democratise global governance through participation in the decision-making of the IMF, the World Bank and the WTO. Although traditional multilateralism has not been replaced by a new multilateralism from below, a change in the practice of the INGOs due to the need to accommodate to GSMs is identified. Moreover, governments increasingly become aware of the fact that the support or neutralisation of social movements is as important for the development of international policies as it is for the development and implementation of policies within the domestic context. Finally, international NGOs/GSMs can be regarded as vehicles to empower domestic NGOs via their capacity to facilitate the transfer of policy advice across borders. Think tanks play an increasingly important role in this respect, as Diane Stone in chapter 12 demonstrates. And as Kendall W. Stiles in chapter 2 shows, they make it possible to challenge governmental policy from the outside as well as the inside. Thus, international NGOs strengthen local groups *vis-à-vis* their government through 'civil society empowerment' projects. Susanne Jakobsen offers an empirical demonstration in chapter 16 of how foreign NGOs put pressure on the Brazilian government via their transnational networks to review its policy on Amazonian deforestation and how domestic non-state actors in India gained direct access to the government policy-making on climate change thanks to their transnationally derived knowledge.

There is perhaps a third way of looking at globalisation: as a confluence of economic phenomena, an aggregation and acceleration of change across a range of areas of modern economic life along the lines initially expressed in the liberal interdependence literature (for example, Keohane and Nye 1977). In contrast to our two earlier understandings of globalisation, this approach does not argue that capitalist systems are converging. 'Capitalism' and 'democracy' remain different in practice. National sovereignty may have been eroded, but states still continue to set the rules for the international economy. This understanding of globalisation represents a dialectical discussion with regionalism, in which regionalism is viewed as a way of maintaining separate forms of capitalism within the global economy on the one hand (Johnson 1991) or even as a manifestation of globalisation on the other. The three most important instances of regionalism in North America, Western Europe and the Asia Pacific, while showing clear differences in the degree of institutional integration, demonstrate a commitment to the removal of trade barriers within a region without the establishment of new ones to the outside. Thus, the phenomenon of regionalism is part and parcel of globalisation, not a contradiction (Gamble and Payne 1996: 251–3). In this regional understanding, MNCs are often as important actors as states. They represent the basic institutional characteristics and values of the countries from which they emanate and pursue more a regional than global strategy. Again, Studer Noguez's study of Ford's regional production structures in chapter 10 serves as a good example. Authors within this understanding of globalisation also point to the increasing number of (both regional and global) strategic alliances and joint ventures of firms. The importance of these strategic alliances and their networks as a source of governance is outlined by Brian Portnoy in chapter 9. He also demonstrates how the increasing importance of MNCs does not necessarily imply the retreat of the state. Instead, their interaction is only one side of 'triangular diplomacy' (Stopford and Strange 1991) with state–state and state–firm interaction as the two other sides.

A final understanding of globalisation is to see it simply as but one historical epoch, starting from about the beginning of the détente at the end of the 1960s and the end of the Cold War in 1989 (Higgott and Reich 1998). It is closely associated with the breakdown of the 'embedded liberal compromise' (Ruggie 1982) and the rise of neo-liberal economics. It falls clearly within the realist tradition of IR theory. Thus, globalisation implies a shift in the economic and political relationship between the former superpowers at the international level and between capital and labour at the national level. This approach recognises that the structural constraints of globalisation are rooted in agency and that there is, therefore, room for actors to make a difference and change the policy outcomes, in particular in the area of redistribution between the beneficiaries and the losers of globalisation. The state itself is not deemed to be at its end. It is the end of a particular state, the Keynesian welfare state, which has to be dealt with. This understanding is useful in the identification of sites of resistance to global liberalism. Resistance emanates, for example, from old style labour unions in those industries which are negatively affected by global structural change. In addition, other particularistic groups, often related to a specific ethnicity, are key actors in this process of resistance, as they often understand globalisation as a threat to national identity and culture, giving rise to both conservative nationalist and progressive internationalist responses.

Depending on the particular understanding of globalisation adopted, the exact distribution of authority between actors differs. Different definitions provide different insights in this highly complex understanding of authority in international relations. This does not automatically need to be expressed in terms of some actors gaining authority at the expense of others. All four perspectives outlined above have one feature in common. They accept states and markets as two distinct entities and take this as their starting-point of investigation. As Burnham (1994) makes clear, this distinction overlooks the fact that states and markets appear only as two different entities in a particular epoch of capitalist development.

What should be clear from the above discussion is that the various categories of non-state actors are closely integrated into the processes of governance which revolve around states. This is most marked in the case of business associations and firms, domestic or transnational, even where inter-state bargaining is concerned (see Sell in chapter 5). State policies are effectively inconceivable without the input of these powerful (corporate) particularistic interests. Markets are structured as much by state policy processes, often directly reflecting the preferences of powerful corporate elites, as they are by the process of inter-firm competition itself (Underhill 1998).

It is equally difficult, in the face of the empirical evidence in this volume, to view NGOs, INGOs, or other categories of non-state actors as genuinely distinct from states and state policy processes. Some NGOs were clearly created or encouraged by states or the INGO extensions of states; at the very least, state and by implication INGO policy is the object of their efforts and their *raison d'être*. The distinction between 'state' and 'non-state' is useful, as our discussion reveals, but it needs to be employed carefully and understood as an abstraction, not representative of a much more subtle reality.

In order to assess the internal relationship between the two, states and markets have to be understood as two different expressions of the same configuration of social forces. States and markets are integrated ensembles of governance involving firms, the NGOs of 'civil society', and traditional INGOs. A neo-Gramscian concept of an 'historic bloc' throws light on this communality. Various social forces may attempt to form an historic bloc in order to establish an order preferable to them. 'The historic bloc is the term applied to the particular configuration of social classes and ideology that gives content to a historical state' (Cox 1987: 409) and, thus, consists of structure and superstructure. As a consequence, rather than treating states and non-state actors as different entities, we can alternatively view forces of both as being part of the very same historic bloc. In other words, managers of TNCs and MNCs can be as much part of the ruling historic bloc as officials in state ministries. The fact that state authority is passed on to firms, INGOs and NGOs does not mean that states lose and non-state actors gain authority. Rather, it signifies a new way of sustaining capitalist accumulation in an era of global structural change. What appears at first sight as a competition for authority turns out to be a strategy for the continuation of the same system of economic production, only under new conditions. Understanding the state in all its sophistication and complexity remains the central question in contemporary political economy (Underhill 1999), and the rhetoric of the extremes only serves to obscure. The chapters of this book, we suggest, offer the opportunity to understand the nature of these relationships between states and non-state actors – sometimes conflicting but often symbiotic – in an evolving global economic order.

Outline of the book

The first part of the book deals with the changing role of authority relations in the world order. In chapter 1, Ann M. Florini takes up the question of diminishing state authority and discusses which collectivities will provide which collective goods in the emerging world order. She concentrates on the developments in information technology and their impact on authority in the world order. Although broad empirical evidence is not available yet, technological innovation and related shifts in identity formation have altered the role of states and non-state actors in providing collective goods and shifted patterns of identification from national to other categories of group identity. The corresponding shift of authority from state to non-state actors, Florini concludes, is likely to increase in the future.

In his contribution in chapter 2, Kendall W. Stiles investigates the shift from state-centred development schemes to projects carried out by international NGOs in cooperation with local grass-roots organisations, an approach labelled 'civil society empowerment'. Theoretically, Stiles uses a 'pluralist global model', which focuses on the effects of structural changes, most importantly the end of the Cold War and the third world debt crisis, on the relative strength of the various actors in development policy. The impact on states' role in the new world order is not as clear cut for Stiles as in Florini's contribution, where states lose authority in general. On the one hand, Stiles asserts that the debt crisis weakened developing states to such an extent that they have been unable to reject the involvement of international NGOs, which undermine their sovereignty and thus authority. On the other hand, developed donor countries regard the new way of development policy as a good way of first, saving money and second, being able to re-direct assistance to Central and Eastern Europe, Central Asia and the Middle East, the new objectives after the end of the Cold War. Considering that grand security strategies are no longer necessary after the fall of the Soviet Union, the 'civil society empowerment' approach implies no risks for donor states. In short, the shift from state to non-state actors in development policy does not mean that donor states' authority declined. Rather, it was one way for these countries of off-loading responsibility for a potentially costly policy area by sub-contracting it to NGOs and to ensure a cost-effective, human-rights and capitalist-oriented development policy at the same time.

The contributions in the second part of the book concentrate on the role played by TNCs and MNCs in the establishment of international rules. In chapter 3, Andrew Walter analyses the 'convergence hypothesis', linked to the neo-liberal discourse of globalisation, which claims that 'the enhanced mobility of TNCs in the world economy confers structural power upon such firms, resulting in a process of convergence of national policy regimes upon TNC policy preferences'. The results of his investigation, however, severely qualify the validity of the neo-liberal discourse. There is little evidence that there has been a convergence of states around a liberal investment regime or that a policy change towards convergence is currently taking place. China, Malaysia, Brazil, Indonesia and Thailand, for example, which are important FDI recipients, still show medium to high levels of restrictiveness towards FDI. Thus, FDI does not necessarily go to those countries, which adopt investment regimes corresponding to TNCs' preferences. Rather, TNCs invest in countries such as China and Indonesia despite the lack of liberal investment regimes, because these countries enjoy generally good economic prospects. Consequently, the major developing host countries in East Asia and Latin America are under considerably less pressure to adapt to the TNCs' preferences than is assumed by the neo-liberal discourse. Overall, Walter concludes that the degree of mobility and concomitant structural power of TNCs in the global economy is frequently overestimated as is the pressure TNCs are alleged to put on states to comply with their preferences.

Elizabeth Smythe (chapter 4) continues the theme with an in-depth analysis of the MAI negotiations. She too concludes that TNCs and MNCs, despite their assumed structural power, were unable to obtain sweeping liberalisation principles and clear restrictions and binding of state authority. She most interestingly shows how labour and environmental NGOs were successful in influencing the inter-state negotiations by lobbying individual member countries and the OECD itself. As a result, binding commitments to environmental and labour standards are most likely going to be part of the MAI, should it ever come about.

Based on the theoretical insights of the agency-structure debate in IR theory, Susan K. Sell in chapter 5 examines in full the role of the IPC, formed by twelve CEOs of US based MNCs, in the coming-about of the TRIPs accord. She stresses the fact that while the IPC was *structurally* advantaged within the domestic US and international context, it was nevertheless unlikely that TRIPs would have come about without *active agency*. She points to the IPC's activities at the domestic and international level and emphasises its transnational leadership expressed in the formation of ties with its European and Japanese counterparts.

Duncan Matthews and John F. Pickering in chapter 6 concentrate on the impact of MNCs on the rule-making within the Single Market of the European Community. Their contribution explores the influence of firms in the legislative process and examines corporate responses in rule-governed conditions within the Single Market across six different industrial sectors. Interestingly in view of the previous chapters, although not surprisingly, the conclusion demonstrates a wide variety of responses differing from sector to sector. For example, the rules of the Single Market are less important for those firms which operate in a global market such as machine tools and pharmaceuticals. Furthermore, while the Single Market has been completed in some sectors, it may still take some time in others. In the leasing sector, companies successfully lobbied against a Single Market, which would have implied a loss of profitable leasing arrangements based on highly segmented national markets.

In chapter 7, Virginia Haufler outlines how firms, in response to the globalisation of economic activity and the lack of governance at the global level, cooperate across national borders in the establishment of private sector international regimes in order to increase their efficiency, stability and power. In particular, Haufler provides examples of product standardisation, the establishment of 'codes of conduct' in areas of social concern and the security of transactions and information. These regimes are legitimated by public authorities due to budgetary constraints, lack of capabilities in view of complex technological developments, ideological commitment, the difficulty of negotiating international agreements and through simple neglect. The setting-up of these regimes often involves negotiations between firms and governments and NGOs, which indicates that global governance is nowadays of a shared and multifaceted nature and that there is a variety of actors playing an increasingly important role in addition to states.

In chapter 8, David Levy and Daniel Egan contest the claim of the globalisation thesis that capital dominates international organisations without constraints. While this may be the case in relation to some (financial) institutions attempting to advance a neo-liberal international economic order, capital is strongly contested within the institutions for the negotiations of social and environmental policies. The authors analyse the international climate change negotiations and conclude that the relevant international organisations are removed from the impact of capital's structural power. As a consequence, capital attempts to influence indirectly the international negotiations on climate change via pressure on the decision-making process at the national level, where it is much more likely to make its power felt. In short, capital still relies on states' support in promoting its interests instead of taking away states' authority in the global economy.

The third part of the book looks at the role of MNCs in the international restructuring of production. Brian Portnoy opens the debate in chapter 9 with an investigation of the phenomenon of the simultaneous cooperation and competition between major companies in the same sector. He argues that these new international strategic alliances set up networks which are an increasingly important source of governance in the global economy and thus continues the theme of the previous part in this book. In a wider sense, the discussion is linked to the notion of 'triangular diplomacy' (Stopford and Strange 1991) and attempts to fill the analytical gap in International Political Economy of firm–firm interaction. Concentrating on state–state and state–firm interactions so far, the discussion of strategic alliances is supported by an important case study of the semiconductor industry. While competition among firms has continued on the world market, cooperation has become more frequent and deeper since the early 1990s. It culminated in the establishment of the World Semiconductor Council (WSC) in 1996, which is now responsible for the formation of a consensus on matters facing the industry. Although the WSC was a private initiative, governments remain important in their role as enforcers, indicating the importance of the other two sides of the 'triangular diplomacy'.

Rather than looking at firm–firm interaction, Studer Noguez focuses on Ford's strategies of industrial restructuring between 1960 and 1993 in chapter 10 in order to assess the assumption that global integration strategies of companies create a genuine global system of production. She concludes that Ford's original global strategy, exemplified in the failure of its world car projects since the 1970s, was unsuccessful due partly to the need of geographic proximity between production site and consumers and partly to different consumer tastes across the Atlantic. As a consequence, the global strategy was successfully replaced by regional production structures, in particular in Europe and North America. The incorporation of Mexico in the North American system of production was the most important development in the latter case. The chapter qualifies the frequently made claim of the inexorable stabilisation of global production structures and the predominant role of TNCs in that process and points to the existence of regional production structures within the global market.

In the final chapter of part III of the book, Jochen Lorentzen (chapter 11) addresses the question of whether the advanced countries or newcomers benefit from the emergence of a global economy. In particular, he asks how the role of the domestic firm *vis-à-vis* the foreign investor determines the distribution of benefits between home and host country. With reference to the industrial restructuring of Central Europe, Lorentzen concludes, firstly, that affiliated companies in advanced countries are in a stronger position *vis-à-vis* their parent company than affiliated companies in transition countries. Secondly, it is difficult to draw general conclusions about a particular region, country, firm or sector. Investments in Central Europe take place in labour-intensive and capital-intensive sectors and the produced goods are both standard and highly specialised. In short, the impact of FDI on the host economy has to be examined case by case.

The fourth part of this volume is dedicated to INGOs and NGOs. In chapter 12, Diane Stone assesses the significance of think tanks at the international level. They have, she argues, mobilised expertise to contribute to policy thinking on issues of international affairs and act as policy entrepreneurs at the domestic and international level, advocating particular policies in order to influence the agenda-setting process. In particular, think tanks play an important role as fora for 'informal diplomacy'. Their status as independent expert organisations and their image of neutrality frequently facilitate political dialogue between opponents, which would be impossible at the official level. Overall, Stone concludes that think tanks are not significant non-state actors. Nevertheless, they perform service roles for states and non-state actors alike, providing research and analysis, ideas and argumentation.

In chapter 13, Gilbert Gagné outlines how the Uruguay Round of multilateral trade negotiations, and in particular the strengthened rules on dispute settlement, provided the World Trade Organisation (WTO) with a greater authority in cases of international conflicts over trade related matters. Nevertheless, Gagné also reminds us that big states can and do sometimes disregard the decisions of INGOs and pursue unilateral strategies instead. While the history of US trade policy is a potential problem in this respect (Nivola 1986), it has during the first four years of the WTO's existence mostly complied with the rules. The adoption of trade notions along US lines by the WTO was one reason why this was the case, the fear of reciprocity by other countries against US products another. In short, this chapter demonstrates how an INGO such as the WTO takes on authority in the international arena, the rules of which even the most powerful state will more often than not have to comply with.

In chapters 14 and 15, the interaction between INGOs, also labelled Global Economic Institutions (GEIs), such as the WTO, the World Bank and the IMF on the one hand, and GSMs on the other, are discussed. Marc Williams (chapter 14) specifically examines the evolving relationship between the World Bank and the WTO and the environmental social movement. On the one hand, the World Bank has increased its contacts with social movements and seems to have at least partially responded to demands for changed policies. For example it introduced a new information disclosure policy in January 1994 in response to complaints about a lack of transparency. On the other, the WTO has remained more or less closed to

GSMs. Williams concludes that the agenda and culture of a particular organisation and not a general trend is responsible for the development or non-development of global democratic politics. The increasing contacts between the environmental social movement and the GEIs can be traced, but the *significance* of these links is not easily established at this stage.

Jan Aart Scholte (chapter 15) investigates the increasing contacts between GSMs, considered to be part of an international civil society, and the IMF and asks whether steps towards further democratisation of global governance have been achieved. Like Williams, his conclusions are cautious. While the increasing exchanges have led to some attention to the social dimension of structural adjustment programmes and to some democratisation of the Fund's policy in the form of greater transparency, there is still a long way to go towards a fully democratic dialogue. The chapter ends with a range of suggestions of how this could be achieved. Overall, while there has been a change in the political practice of INGOs due to the need to accommodate to increasingly articulate GSMs, states are still the most important actors in these domains.

Susanne Jakobsen (chapter 16) provides an excellent summary of the theme of this book: the complex nature of global authority. She paints a rich picture of how transnational NGO links, scientific knowledge and global structural factors such as the media and public sentiment have affected the formation of India's and Brazil's position for international negotiations on climate change. In the case of Brazil, international media and public sentiment together with the efforts by foreign NGOs to create international attention via their transnational networking were crucial in making Brazil review its policy on Amazonian deforestation. In India domestic NGOs, thanks to their superior, transnationally-derived expert knowledge, were a key factor in the formulation of India's negotiation position. At the theoretical level, Jacobsen demonstrates that one has to go beyond state-centric approaches and include domestic and transnational politics in order to account for national policy-making in relation to issues of global environmental politics such as climate change. Otherwise, the range of domestic and transnational NGOs and diffuse forces of media and public sentiment are overlooked.

Taken collectively, the essays in this volume offer us both rich *empirical* insights into the interaction between states and non-state actors under conditions of globalisation at the end of the twentieth century. They also provide insights into how we need to continually rethink this relationship *theoretically*. Strict divisions between their roles, aspirations and policies cannot be allowed to remain. The evolving relationship between states and non-state actors constitutes one of the fastest moving dimensions of contemporary international politics. This volume represents an early word on this process. It will not be the last one.

Notes

1 This definition of TNCs and MNCs is based on Ruigrok's and Van Tulder's distinction between globalising and glocalising firms (Ruigrok and Van Tulder 1995: 9–10).
2 We cannot review the voluminous literature on globalisation here. For a taxonomy of this literature, see Higgott and Reich (1998).

References

Bhagwati, Jagdish (1998) 'The capital myth: the difference between trade in widgets and trade in dollars', *Foreign Affairs* 77(3): 7–12.

Burnham, Peter (1994) 'Open Marxism and vulgar international political economy', *Review of International Political Economy* 1(2): 221–31.

Cox, Robert W. (1987) *Production, Power and World Order: Social Forces in the Making of History*, New York: Columbia University Press.

Cox, Robert W. (ed.) (1997) *The New Realism: Perspectives on Multilateral and World Order,* Basingstoke: Macmillan.

Doremus, Paul N., William W. Keller, Louis W. Pauly and Simon Reich (1998) *The Myth of the Global Corporation*, Princeton, N.J.: Princeton University Press.

Gamble, Andrew and Anthony Payne (1996) 'Conclusion: the new regionalism', in Andrew Gamble and Anthony Payne (eds) *Regionalism and World Order,*   Basingstoke: Macmillan: 247–64.

Higgott, Richard (1983) *Political Development Theory*, London and New York: Routledge.

—— (1998) 'The Asian economic crisis: a study in the politics of resentment', *New Political Economy* 3(3): 33–56.

—— (1999) 'Economics, politics and (international) political economy: the need for a balanced diet in an era of globalisation', *New Political Economy* 4(1):23–36.

Higgott, Richard and Simon Reich (1998) 'Globalisation and sites of conflict: towards definition and taxonomy', *CSGR Working Paper* no. 01/98.

Hirst, Paul and Grahame Thompson (1996) *Globalization in Question: The International Economy and the Possibilities of Governance*, Cambridge: Polity Press.

Johnson, Hazel (1991) *Dispelling the Myth of Globalisation: A Case for Regionalisation*, New York: Praeger.

Keohane, Robert O. and Helen V. Milner (eds) (1996) *Internationalization and Domestic Politics*, Cambridge: Cambridge University Press.

Keohane, Robert O. and Joseph S. Nye (1977) *Power and Interdependence: World Politics in Transition*, Boston and Toronto: Little, Brown.

Nivola, P. S. (1986) 'The new protectionism: US trade policy in historical perspective', *Political Science Quarterly* 101(4): 576–600.

Ohmae, Kenichi (1990) *The Borderless World: Power and Strategy in the Interlinked Economy*, London: Collins.

—— (1995) *The End of the Nation State: The Rise of Regional Economies*, London: Harper Collins.

Ruggie, John Gerard (1982) 'International regimes, transactions, and change: embedded liberalism in the postwar economic order', *International Organization* 36 (2): 379–415.

Ruigrok, Winfried and Rob van Tulder (1995) *The Logic of International Restructuring*, London and New York: Routledge.

Stopford, J. and S. Strange (1991) *Rival States, Rival Firms: Competition for World Market Shares*, Cambridge: Cambridge University Press.

Strange, Susan (1996) *The Retreat of the State*, Cambridge: Cambridge University Press.

Underhill, Geoffrey R. D. (ed.) (1997) *The New World Order in International Finance*, Basingstoke: Macmillan.

—— (1998) *Industrial Crisis and the Open Economy*, Basingstoke: Macmillan.

—— (1999) 'Conceptualising the changing global order', in R. Stubbs and G. Underhill (eds) *Political Economy and the Changing Global Order* (second edition), Oxford: Oxford University Press.

Weiss, Linda (1998) *The Myth of the Powerless State*, Ithaca: Cornell University Press.

Part I

Theoretical considerations

The changing nature of authority relations

1 Who does what?

Collective action and the changing nature of authority

Ann M. Florini

Introduction

With a little translation into the appropriate theoretical terms, the debate over the form of the emergent world order boils down to disagreements over which collectivities will provide which collective goods to whom. Huntington's (1996) clash-of-civilisations thesis contends that civilisations, rather than states, will provide such collective goods as defence (from other civilisations) and cultural belonging. Kaplan's (1996) prediction of *The Coming Anarchy* asserts that many collective goods will not be provided at all because poverty and environmental degradation will overwhelm the capacity of states to undertake collective action. Mathews' (1997) *Power Shift* analysis argues that the information revolution has rendered a whole host of non-state actors increasingly capable of undertaking collective action and is thus undermining the power of the state.

As these and many other authors show in very different ways, the tendency in international relations studies to see states as the sole providers of collective goods has become an increasingly inappropriate over-simplification. States cannot solve all, or even most, of humanity's most important collective action problems, nor can all these collective goods be converted by the magic of property rights into private goods to be provided by the market. This is true in part because state capacity is being undermined even at the domestic level by everything from the globalisation of the economy to environmental degradation (for the debate, see *inter alia* Ayoob 1995; Barber 1995; Guehenno 1995; Hirst 1997; Hirst and Thompson 1996; Homer-Dixon (forthcoming), Horsman and Marshall 1995; Ohmae 1995; Sassen 1996; Strange 1996). Even more significant is the growing importance of transnational issues and actors: many of the most pressing collective action problems cannot be resolved by individual states acting alone, and the world is awash with actors whose interests and capacities span national borders (Hammond 1998; Mathews 1989 and 1997).

At a time when the supply of and demand for collective action seem increasingly out of balance, it is useful to review what theory can tell us about when and why people do contribute to the provision of collective goods, that is, when and why collective goods, especially transnational collective goods, are provided (or underprovided). The first section provides an overview of the literature on collective action. The next addresses the effect of the information revolution on the various bases for collective action. Then follows a look at the sketchy empirical evidence about where and why people actually are making contributions to the provision of collective goods. The conclusion suggests that while broad evidence is not yet available about the shifts in provision of collective goods or in group identity, both theory and the likely developments in information technology give strong reasons to believe that the shift in authority from state to non-state actors will continue and intensify.

Theory of collective action

The essence of the collective action problem is the lack of congruence between individual incentives and desired outcomes for the group. The problem is clearest with the most famous category of collective goods: public goods. These are goods that are non-excludable and non-rival in consumption: that is to say, if any amount of a public good is provided by anyone, no one can be prevented from consuming it, and no one's consumption reduces anyone else's consumption.

The classic example is national defence: if a state defends its boundaries, everyone within those boundaries gets defended, whether or not they contribute to the defence, and the defence of one person does not detract from the defence of another. Climate protection offers another example: everyone 'consumes' the same climate, and no one's 'consumption' uses it up. Thus, preventing climate change benefits everyone, whether or not they contribute to that prevention, and my enjoyment of that benefit does not detract from yours. Under these conditions, no individual has an economically rational incentive to contribute to the provision of public goods, because everyone would rather free-ride on the contributions of others. Thus, public goods are not adequately provided by market forces.

In reality few pure public goods exist. Non-excludability is usually a matter of feasibility rather than impossibility: a country could, for example, choose not to defend a region that fails to pay taxes. Non-rivalry of consumption is often subject to 'crowding' effects; that is, rivalry sets in as more and more people try to consume a good. National parks with few visitors are public goods. National parks with a million visitors on the Fourth of July weekend suffer serious rivalry of consumption. Yet such goods and services have some degree of non-excludability and non-rivalry, and thus pure market forces cannot be relied on to match demand and supply.

Accordingly, collective action theory has cast a wider net beyond public goods, incorporating the broader range of goods whose provision is made difficult by the collective action problem. Although Olson's famous 1965 book was entitled *The Logic of Collective Action: Public Goods and the Theory of Groups*, in fact the book addressed primarily non-excludable, not non-rival, goods (Olson 1965: 14). And as Hardin (1982) has pointed out, the important issue in analysing the supply and demand of collective goods is not whether consumption has the demanding technical characteristics of pure public goods, but whether provision of the good requires collective action and thus requires overcoming the collective action problem. Collective action theory thus applies to a broad range of goods and services that have some degree of one or both of the defining characteristics of non-excludability and non-rivalry.

Despite the tendency to underprovision, collective goods do get provided, often at levels that are less than socially optimal, but still far more than can be explained by motives of economic individual self-interest. Government, organised into territorially based states, has long been the primary means by which collective goods are provided, and governments have compelled contributions through legally mandated taxes. Beyond this, several additional motivations (often overlapping rather than mutually exclusive) can explain why people do often contribute to the provision of collective goods.

Olson suggests that two factors – small size and selective incentives – can overcome the free-rider problem. Achieving common ends is easier in small groups than large ones, says Olson, because the costs of organising grow with size.[1] It is also easier in 'privileged' groups, assumed to be small, where members are of unequal size and the bigger ones benefit enough from their own contributions to be willing to carry the smaller members as free-riders. These conditions aside, provision of collective goods is likely to require selective incentives, that is, rewards available only to contributors. Sandler (1992: 60) gives examples of selective incentives such as journals provided to members of a learned society or concert tickets given to supporters of a symphony orchestra. Social incentives also exist, but, says Olson, these usually require face to face contact: yet another reason small groups do better than large ones. Overcoming collective irrationality in larger groups thus may require designing institutions that make large groups function like small ones, for example by dividing themselves into federations of smaller sub-groups.

Ostrom (1990) has examined a sub-catagory of collective goods called *common pool resources* (CPR), which are fully rival in consumption but not excludable, such as open-access fisheries or some irrigation systems. She shows that groups can organise themselves without governmental intervention to ensure optimal, and sustainable, exploitation of such resources. As she notes, 'communities of individuals have relied on institutions resembling neither the state nor the market to govern some resource systems with reasonable degrees of success over long periods of time' (Ostrom 1990: 1). To do so, they need to solve several problems: to determine the capacity of the resource (so that they do not use it up beyond sustainable levels); to agree on a system of allocating usage (for example, who gets to fish where when); to monitor compliance with that system; and to enforce adherence to the agreement. Although these are difficult things to do, Ostrom argues, what is striking is that these non-state and non-market institutions are often more successful at organising collective action with regard to CPR than are the governmental and market actors on which analysts normally concentrate. Communities that actually use CPR are more likely to have the necessary information to come up with workable systems than are external governmental officials, and because many of the resources (fish, water) are not stationary, it can be impossible to devise workable ways of assigning, and enforcing, private property rights. But success in managing CPR through non-state and non-market mechanisms has its own difficulties. Above all, it requires time to evolve workable institutions and long time horizons on the part of participants so that reputational concerns and diffuse reciprocity can maintain cooperation.

The large literature in international relations theory on regimes or institutions (Krasner 1983; Rittberger 1993; Keohane 1989) essentially addresses the collective action problem as it applies among states. Because much of the difficulty of achieving collective action lies in the cost of negotiating, monitoring and enforcing agreements, these theorists argue, institutions that can lower such costs should raise the likelihood that collective action will occur. But this literature has predominately focused on regimes and institutions that result from state-to-state cooperation. Only recently are we beginning to see the emergence of studies that examine non-state actors as integral components of such regimes (Chayes and Chayes 1996: chapter 11). While states remain important actors, their role is increasingly circumscribed. As is discussed below, the identity basis on which state power largely rests is giving way to new forms of identity, and the powerful advances in information technology are transforming the bases of power.

The preceding literature largely assumes that groups have and recognise common interests, and that motivations for contributing to the realisation of those common interests are economically rational.[2] Olson, for example, deliberately and explicitly limited his analysis to a sub-set of collective goods and motivations for collective action. He discussed only groups whose purpose is to further their members' economic interests, primarily labour unions, not philanthropic or religious organisations, nor communal groups, nor other groups motivated by non-economic considerations (Olson 1965: 6). We need to turn now to the identification of group interests and 'extra-rational' – that is, social and moral rather than material – motivations.

Once we get beyond the sub-set of interests that are economic in nature, the question of how groups become groups and identify their interests becomes a crucial consideration. One of the major puzzles of human affairs is what makes a group a coherent entity. In the words of *Webster's Dictionary*, a group is 'a social unit comprising individuals in continuous contact through intercommunications and shared participation toward some commonly accepted end' (*Third New International Dictionary* 1976: 1004). This suggests that ongoing contact, shared experience and a common goal are all necessary elements of being a group. But it is possible to feel part of a group while never having communicated at all with most of its members nor having agreed on any particular goals: large kin groups and nation-states are united by something more.

The drive to form groups seems inherent in human nature. Given the need to belong to a group in order to survive, it is not surprising that the need for community feeling seems to be bred into humanity. When we have the sense of belonging to a group, we feel secure and purposeful in life. When we lack it, we feel uneasy, alienated, insecure. Fukuyama based his famous end-of-history thesis on the Hegelian assumption that human behaviour is motivated by a deep-rooted drive for recognition by other humans, a drive as fundamental as any material interest (Fukuyama 1993).

But the need to belong somewhere says little about *where* people will end up feeling they belong. Once humanity moved beyond the small kin groups of pre-historic times, the bases of 'groupness' became rather more complex. Mere contiguity is not enough to form a coherent group, as the long and difficult process of nation-building shows (Tilly 1975; Hobsbawm and Ranger 1983; Gellner 1983). People may live near each other, and may share similar conditions and concerns, but if they act individually rather than collectively, they are not a group.

Two types of bonds can unite groups sufficiently to motivate individual action: cultural and associational. In the 'cultural' category are characteristics such as shared language, religion, social practices, and kinship (real or imagined). Associational groups, by contrast, share specific interests and goals. The former are generally seen to be the more powerful motivator of collective action. Huntington argues that 'what ultimately counts for people is not political ideology or economic interest. Faith and family, blood and belief, are what people identify with and what they will fight and die for' (Huntington 1993: 194). Along the same lines, Gurr has noted that 'it is seriously misleading to interpret the Zapatistas as just a peasants' movement or the Bosnian Serbs as the equivalent of a political party: they draw their strength from cultural bonds, not associational ones' (Gurr 1996: 53).

But this is too simplistic. People are part of a large and growing number of systems and collectivities, each of which may recognise, or require, a different identity from the same individual. Identities have always been social constructions, but increasingly, the constructors are individuals rather than societies and the weight of tradition. As noted sociologist Anthony Giddens puts it, in modern, 'post-traditional' societies, individuals must *choose* personal, professional, and religious identities (Boynton 1997: 74). Civil society greatly increases the number of such choices. Even so-called 'ascriptive' characteristics – identities that others ascribe to an individual based on ostensibly unalterable characteristics – are becoming optional in many cases, depending on what the individual in question chooses to emphasise. Thus, what types of groups exist and are able to carry out collective action is becoming a question to be explored, not a starting assumption, even in the field of international relations where scholars have long assumed that the only significant group identity comes from belonging to a nation-state.

The information revolution

The most important driver of change in the nature of groups able to carry out collective action flows from the information revolution. It usually takes a generation or two for the social impacts of technological innovations to reveal themselves, so it is not surprising that only recently has a plausible picture begun to appear (Grubler 1996). That emerging picture suggests a growing pattern: information technology is changing authority relations between states and non-state actors.

The information revolution incorporates three types of technologies: those that observe; those that process; and those that communicate. Among the observers, two categories of technology matter: data-gathering systems and surveillance systems. The most impressive data-gatherers are remote-sensing satellites, which have been around for decades, but for several reasons their capabilities are improving rapidly. The dramatic changes expected in the next few years in remote-sensing satellite capabilities are emblematic of the types of changes to be expected in other data-gathering systems. By the turn of the century, the remote-sensing data that are publicly available will rival that of US spy satellites, with several private companies competing to sell imagery with resolution as fine as one metre, and scores of firms popping up to interpret and enhance the imagery to the customer's satisfaction.[3] Already civil analysts are using satellite imagery to make public arguments on everything from tropical rainforest deforestation to territorial disputes over the South China Seas.

The new eyes are not only in the sky. On the ground, video surveillance systems are proliferating. In Britain, dozens of cities have installed more than 250,000 remote-controlled video cameras, linked directly to police headquarters, in trouble spots around town to reduce crime. They have been wildly successful, reducing crime in some areas to one-seventieth the pre-surveillance levels (Brin 1998: 5). Around San Francisco, video cameras are extensively used to monitor traffic and issue tickets, with the operators making occasional reports to the police about suspicious activities they observe along the way (Learmonth 1997). These cameras are at least visible, if you know where to look. But the same faster-cheaper-smaller technological imperative that is making satellite systems ever more commercially feasible is leading to microcameras that will be all but invisible to those they observe (Stentz 1997).

This growing transparency at all levels, from the most local to global, provides a significant new content to the data-processing technologies more commonly associated with the information revolution, which are undergoing similarly rapid transformations. Computing power has increased 25,000 times over the past twenty-five years, and shows every sign of continuing to improve at least as rapidly for some time to come (Patterson 1995). Data storage and processing capacity is already sufficient that vast databases exist on an enormous range of subjects, raising as yet unresolved dilemmas over personal privacy and intellectual property rights that will only be compounded as the technology advances. Improved software is taking advantage of the increased power to squeeze ever more useful information out of the raw data. For example, geographic information systems that layer digitised economic, social, environmental and other data on computer-based maps can allow users to discover correlations between seemingly unrelated phenomena, and these systems are rapidly increasing in power and usability.

All these technologies are significant in their own right, but what renders them politically transformative is their connection to the communications revolution. Communications technology includes everything from phone systems (both wired and cellular) to cable and broadcast television to the Internet to communications satellites. As these advance, it becomes ever easier and cheaper to create networks that can make shared use of the information provided by the data-collection and information-processing technologies. The connections are increasing rapidly: the number of Internet hosts is doubling annually, and the number of phone lines in the world has nearly doubled in the past decade (Cane 1997: 1). With the current dismantling of scores of government monopolies in national telecommunications systems around the world, competition is likely to drive prices down and accelerate the process of wiring the world together.

Much of this 'wiring' will actually be wireless, using sophisticated computer systems to locate 'roaming' customers and to customise the services they receive. By 2001, it is expected that some 75 per cent of US households and close to 500 million people around the world will subscribe to some sort of wireless service (Zysman 1995: 68–9). Wireless faxes will probably be common within a few years, and video mail (both wired and wireless) may be close behind (Zysman 1995: 70).

How comprehensive this revolution is depends on whom you ask. One fairly typical enthusiast claims that technological and commercial forces are driving the world toward creation of a Meganet, which within a few decades will connect virtually everyone on earth in a network of phones, computers, fax machines, and data banks (Dizard 1997). More cautious voices warn that the market-driven diffusion of information technology is leaving gaping holes in the net, particularly wherever the world's growing number of the absolutely destitute are to be found (Wresch 1996). The favourite statistic of the latter perspective points out that half the world's population has never made a phone call.

Implications for collective action

These developments have two types of implications for collective action. First, they substantially increase the number of collective action problems to be solved. Second, they alter the relative capabilities of different types of actors to solve those and other collective action problems, in particular increasing the capacity of non-state actors relative to states and creating a much larger number of players in the international system.

The information revolution increases the need for governance: in other words, it adds a large number of new or exacerbated collective action problems to the world's already significant supply. The most commented upon of these is the need to create human capital: to educate people so that they can effectively participate in the 'knowledge society'. Beyond this major demand for collective action, the information revolution creates or complicates a number of additional areas where governance is needed: regulating content; assuring the security of the information infrastructure; combating organised crime and terrorism; fostering legitimate commerce; and promoting equity.

Content Despite the claims by the more extreme proponents of unrestricted information flows, a good case can be made for some regulation of the content of information flowing through electronic systems, just as content is regulated in older informational systems from the printing press to radio and TV. On the Net, for example, anything that can appear in the form of words or pictures can be found: images of Mars, the *New York Times*, conspiracy theories, pornography, wild rumours and outright lies. No one currently plays the role of gatekeeper to sort through the mishmash. Garbage circulates unrestricted. And it is very easy to alter digital information undetectably. How, and whether, to regulate the cacophony presents a major challenge to global governance, with policy options ranging from restrictions on access to selective screening to *laissez-faire*.

The content issues include privacy, intellectual property rights, and what might be called 'anti-social' information. On privacy, there is no global (or US) system for ensuring that personal data are protected. On intellectual property rights, debate rages over the meaning of ownership in a medium that combines the functions of personal communication and publication, and on which unlimited copying is virtually free. The category of 'anti-social' information includes such things as pornography, libel, and incitement to group hatred.

Information assurance The growing dependence of many economies (and in the US the military) on information technology has created new vulnerabilities, sparking concern about the integrity of the information systems that support the information infrastructure. Hackers have repeatedly demonstrated the ease with which computer systems can be penetrated and disrupted. To date, these disruptions have largely reflected more the efforts of individuals concerned with demonstrating their prowess than any systematic effort to do real damage, but they have caused enough trouble to make it apparent that assuring information system integrity is a significant problem requiring a coordinated response within and across borders.

Crime The capacity to network globally benefits not only principled advocacy groups like Amnesty International, but anyone with a non-governmental agenda to pursue, including organised crime. Perhaps the most significant criminal use of information technology is the growing capacity for money laundering, with sums in the several hundred billion dollar range being laundered each year, camouflaged in the far larger set of legitimate transactions (*Economist* 1997a). Crime on this scale threatens political stability and possibly the ability to carry out macro-economic policy. Yet information technology promises to make money laundering much easier through potentially untraceable electronic transfers of electronic money (*Economist* 1997b).

Commerce A key function of governments in market societies is to create confidence in commerce by making contracts enforceable and transactions safe. Both are rendered more difficult by information technology. Enforcing contracts requires jurisdiction, and territorially based national jurisdiction does not fit well with the characteristics of cyberspace. The security of transactions in cyberspace requires encryption, so that no one but the intended recipient can read such data as credit card numbers. Over the past several years, governments and industry have fought over just how secret secrets should be on the Internet. The US government, concerned about the increasing use being made by organised crime of global information technology as well as about its capacity to monitor overseas developments, has insisted that export controls be placed on encryption codes (Americans are committing a felony if the laptops they take overseas have a moderately good encryption system), and that it should be given the key to any truly effective encryption systems. The private sector has strongly opposed the government's proposals, and it seems unlikely that the US will long find it useful to maintain export controls on technology that is already globally available.

Equity and adequacy The information revolution is incomplete. Although vast quantities of data are newly available, most of the world lacks access to much of it, and much potentially important information is left out. Wresch (1996) points out the degree to which much of the world's population is excluded not only from the Net and the Web but from newspapers, television, and books. Information important to public policy often lacks market value, and pressures on even rich-country budgets increasingly take their toll on this quintessential public good. A long-standing and still valid complaint of many developing countries is that no one gathers much information about them. And some environmentalists have long decried the gaps in needed environmental data and knowledge (Rodenburg 1992).

The changing roles of actors

While many people will be left out of or on the margins of the information revo-lution, others will find – and are already finding – ways to use the technologies to pursue collective action of all kinds. The information revolution affects the supply side of collective action even more strongly than the demand side. It changes both which actors have the capacity to determine what gets counted as a collective action problem and which are able to carry out collective action. The actors affected range from the state to formal non-governmental organisations to ethnic communities to the private sector.

The changing role of the state

The state has dominated collective action for the past several centuries because it has provided certain collective goods more effectively than other actors could (Mann 1993: 137). In virtually all parts of the world it has provided defence/war-making capability and basic communications and transportation infrastructure. Among democracies it has provided the primary channel for political representation and the primary means of defending human rights, while in some other states it has effectively prevented any actor from fulfilling those functions. In the twentieth century, its functions have expanded to include macro-economic planning and a social safety net of increasingly lavish proportions. It has been able to carry out these functions in large part because of its ability to compel contributions from many of the inhabitants of the territory under its control.

State capacity is affected by the information revolution in three ways: states have all these new and old collective action problems at their doorstep; their capacity to gather the resources necessary to fulfill their functions is being under-mined; and their freedom of action is increasingly constrained due to competition from other actors. How capable of responding is the state? A recent *Economist* survey trumpeted the claim that the state is as strong as ever because there has been no decrease in the state's share of GDP (Crook 1997). But a closer look reveals a different picture: a huge and growing share of state revenues goes to transfer payments and interest, not on provision of collective goods.

There are three reasons to believe that the state will be in greater trouble in the future, all related to the information revolution. As capital flows ever more freely around the world and as more and more commerce is conducted over the Internet, governments may find it difficult to collect many of the taxes that constitute their lifeblood (see Froomkin 1997 on the capacity to conduct business through the Net anonymously). Second, state power is, of course, based much more on voluntary (or quasi-voluntary) compliance than on sheer coercion, and such compliance stems in large part from perceptions of shared national identity. Now, however, all states face increased competition for people's loyalties, as information technology connects people across borders, uniting dispersed identities and interests.

Third, new forms of political organisation are emerging. Information technology is altering the nature of social organisations, in a transformation as fundamental as the emergence of hierarchical governments or competitive markets (Mathews 1997; Ronfeldt 1996). In facilitating the organisation of all kinds of groups, the information revolution particularly increases the effectiveness of network forms of social organisation relative to the hierarchy familiar in government and the competitive exchange system emblematic of the private sector (Ronfeldt 1996). Dispersed groups can so readily share information and coordinate their efforts that the advantages of centralised control over information are slipping away. These networks can be ephemeral and yet effective, as parts of different organisations come together as needed in cyberspace.

In collective action theory terms, these networks are empowered by the reduction in the transactions costs inherent in collective action. Much of the difficulty in achieving successful collective action lies in determining how to pay for the negotiation, implementation, monitoring and enforcement of collective agreements. Information technologies can lower such costs, often dramatically. Negotiations can take place in cyberspace, rather than requiring the time and cost of travel. Indeed, the participants can be people who have never met. The vast array of increasingly sophisticated monitoring technologies is making it ever easier to see who is doing what where, thus reducing monitoring costs. Even enforcement may become easier, as the awareness that violations of agreements are likely to become public knowledge may shame potential violators into stricter adherence, or at least persuade them that they are likely to have to bear whatever costs non-compliance entails if they fail to stick to the terms of the agreement.

The new capacity to network is not necessarily good. By drastically reducing the costs of communicating and organising, the information revolution may lead to an excess of civil society: too many competing interest groups with little common space. In theory terms, it may make sustained community harder to achieve by decreasing the prospects that people will encounter one another repeatedly, thus changing the effectiveness of norms of diffuse reciprocity and altering the bases on which loyalties form. It may alter the criteria on which people choose identities, although the net effect remains unpredictable: will people be overwhelmed by information and fall back on ascriptive criteria for their own identification as well as to label others, or will they increasingly pick and choose among possible identities to serve their interests of the moment?

In short, the information revolution is both making collective action easier across the board and increasing the *potential* for a wide variety of institutional innovations for carrying out collective action. But to what extent are these innovations happening? Do they represent a significant change in global patterns of authority or merely the greater ability of non-state actors to draw public and scholarly attention, and how can we know? The next section examines the extremely sketchy evidence currently available.

The empirical evidence

The discussion so far argues that technological innovation and related shifts in identity formation have altered the role of states and non-state actors in providing collective goods. If it is true, as so often asserted, that the global capacity for collective action is undergoing a period of transition, we should see evidence that goes beyond the amassing of case studies. Much of the discussion to date on the changing nature of authority in the international system is based on anecdotal evidence and case studies. While case studies and observations are interesting and can be invaluable, it is necessary to at least attempt an empirical overview of whether and to what degree the world is already seeing changes in who is providing collective goods and why. The evidence should indicate the rising role of non-state actors in two respects: changing resource allocation from state to non-state actors and shifting patterns of identification from national to other categories of group identity.

A preliminary effort to gather such empirical evidence suggests that measuring changes in the contribution of each sector (state, private sector, and civil society) to the provision of collective goods and evaluating the survey data on which collectivities elicit loyalty will be no easy task. Researchers are just beginning to gather hard data on civil society, for instance, especially for developing countries. The Institute for Policy Studies at John Hopkins University has launched the Comparative Nonprofit Sector Project, which to date has gathered comprehensive empirical evidence on the third sector for only seven countries. Although the project is in the process of expanding, for the foreseeable future scholars will have data on only a small number of countries. The surveys by Civicus (1997) cover many more countries, but provide broad descriptions rather than quantitative detail.

The problem of measuring relative contributions goes beyond the paucity of efforts to gather data. Conceptually, it may be impossible to produce meaningful numbers about who is contributing what share of the collective good. The issue of environmental protection exemplifies the problem. Some sources have tried to divide up expenditures on environmental protection among public, private, and 'other' or 'third sector' payers, but these sources are replete with 'information not available' notations (see, for example, Wilkie 1994; *Social Portrait of Europe* 1995;

The Environment in Europe and North American Annotated Statistics 1992; Salamon *et al.* 1996). The scarcity of figures reflects more than the relatively recent emergence of environmental protection as a recognised collective good in many parts of the world. Rather, it highlights the lack of consensus on how to value non-market 'goods' and 'bads'. It may simply be impossible to get an accurate sense of who pays for collective goods of this sort and whether the contributions have indeed been shifting over time.

Third, undertaking broad, cross-national statistical analyses introduces the danger of drawing unjust comparisons. Often, data are presented in each country's national currency. Conversions into a common currency by means of the official exchange rate do not always reflect the real costs of the expenditure. Similarly, since no single resource exists that tracks the expenditure distribution on all of the selected collective goods, a variety of sources needs to be referenced. Each source defines both the actors (the public sector, the private sector and which types of institutions are included as part of the third sector) and the issues differently (see, for example, the differing approaches on 'social security' and 'welfare' used by the IMF's *Government Finance Statistics Yearbook* 1996; the OECD in *Figures: Statistics in OECD Member Countries* 1997; and Salamon *et al.* 1996). Moreover, it is well known that the data for some countries are at best suspect.

Despite all these problems, it is still possible to draw some conclusions. Most importantly, governments remain the largest providers of many collective goods. In a few countries, such as South Africa and France, general government expenditure has grown by as much as a third over the last quarter century. Governments have maintained a near monopoly in providing certain collective goods, such as national defence, and the last thirty years are marked by increased public expenditures in nearly every country for a number of issue areas such as education and health (Sivard 1996: 45–7). In short, while important shifts in the state's provision of collective goods may indeed be underway, the numbers are not yet available to support the rhetoric.

Identity

While an analysis of expenditures on collective goods is important, where the money is spent and by whom addresses only commodifiable goods and services and thus tells only part of the story. Even if governments are the major implementors of collective action, increasingly non-state actors are usurping the state's role in the other stages of collective action: agenda-setting, negotiation, monitoring, and even (through the mobilisation of public opinion to shame non-compliers) enforcement. A growing number of case studies have addressed these new non-state roles in collective action, but it is no easy task to come up with a useful measure for the extent of this shift. A useful proxy is to measure changes in self-perceived identity, on the theory that what you identify with most strongly motivates your contributions to collective action. A second investigation is needed, therefore, on what is known about people's self-perceptions of identity and whether those notions have been changing over time.

Unfortunately, the evidence here is as sparse as the expenditure data. Despite the large number of social surveys on the questions of identity and how closely aligned one feels with their nation versus their ethnic group, these studies tend to cover a specific group or country and a single time period. Finding comparisons that either span the entire global community or record trends over time proves difficult, and no surveys do both. Even in the US, the General Social Survey (GSS), which consciously repeats questions in order to enable time trend comparisons, began only in the 1970s. Furthermore, such relevant questions as 'When you think of social and political issues, do you think of yourself mainly as a member of a particular ethnic, racial or nationality group or do you think of yourself as mainly just an American?' did not appear on the survey until 1994.

Recognising the lack of available data, a number of international efforts have recently been made to gather information on the identity questions. For example, the International Social Survey Program (ISSP) was launched in 1985 in the hopes of coordinating the methods and questions of social survey institutions from around the world. Its modules change yearly, making comparisons over time difficult. However, one promising development is the ISSP's 1995 Survey on National Identity which examines such themes as nationalism, localism, patriotism and globalism. The integrated data file for this survey became available in late 1997 through the National Opinion Research Center at the University of Chicago. A few additional surveys, such as the World Values Survey under the auspices of the World Values Study Group, aims to enable crossnational comparisons of basic values and norms. In its two trials, one in the early 1980s and the other in the early 1990s, the World Values Survey asked the participant which groups he or she belonged to and which group the participant identified with most closely. While this data may prove useful, it is very limited in scope. In general, concrete figures on the shifting perceptions of identity remain inconclusive.

In short, the huge holes in the data mean that empirical answers to the questions of who provides global society's collective goods and how identities are changing are unavailable. Although some data are now being gathered, until much more is available we will continue to rely on theory, anecdote and case studies.

Conclusion

This variegated story comes down to three simple themes. First, collective action theory helps provide understanding of how the world might overcome the free-rider problem to redress the growing needs for collective action. By breaking the literature down into the various bases for overcoming the free-rider problem, it is easier to think logically about what affects each. This requires thinking about what constitutes an actor (i.e. an entity capable of carrying out collective action), and what is changing around the world that is altering the relative capabilities of actors. The most important changes are those engendered by the information revolution, which is altering the nature of social organisation.

Second, despite all the hoopla about new actors and changing patterns of authority, the evidence is still at the anecdote and case study stage. The data does not yet allow us to paint a broad picture of collective action and changing patterns of authority.

Third, nonetheless, an analysis of the impact of the information revolution gives strong reason to believe that the shift in authority is just beginning. As outlined in the introduction of this book, states increasingly have to share authority in the international arena with a range of different non-state actors. The information revolution increases the capacity of non-state actors relative to states by making it possible for ephemeral networks to lower transactions costs, just as more permanent institutions have always done. It may in the future undermine state capacity to extract contributions to the provision of collective goods. Because of the pace of technological change and the unpredictability of human adaptation to it, the ultimate impacts of the information revolution on global governance remain murky.

But at least we can know what the major questions are. There are three:

*   How much do people need direct human interaction to form sustainable collectivities, and to what degree can technologically mediated interactions substitute, especially as the latter become more and more 'lifelike'? Information technology has the potential to alter the very nature of 'groupness', raising broad sociological issues about communities, nationalism, identity, and social cohesion. The debate is essentially about an 's': is information technology creating a kind of universalism – the 'global village' – or is it contributing to the creation of intensely parochial 'global villages,' with all the narrow-mindedness of small village life but focused around single issues rather than geographic contiguity?
*   How widely accessible will the various technologies become around the world? The answer will depend on whether the technology becomes so much cheaper that people whose incomes are a few dollars a day can make use of them, how rapidly development ensues in poor countries and regions, and whether the private sector works to develop markets in poor areas. All are unpredictable, even to the people who have most to gain from getting it right. As Intel co-founder Andy Grove has noted 'On any given day, those of us who work in the high-tech industry make decisions that are basically educated guesses about the future of technology and – equally important – about future market trends' (Auletta 1997: 140).
*   How will individuals and groups cope with information overload? Will a 'tipping point' phenomenon dominate as the decrease in transactions costs increases the number of collectivities? Will the reaction be to increase the rewards disproportionately to groups that can stand out even a little bit, or will the cacophony prove sustainable?

Notes

I wish to acknowledge the excellent research assistance of Wynne Rumpeltin on this paper.

1 Hardin (1982) points out that the costs of organising collective action do not necessarily grow with size, as economies of scale may apply.
2 New literature is emerging that applies rational choice collective action theory more broadly, notably Hardin 1995.
3 Spatial resolution – how much detail an image shows – is only one of the many characteristics that determine how useful a satellite's data is. For a discussion of satellite capabilities, see Florini 1988.
4 These include France, Germany, Hungary, Italy, Japan, the United Kingdom and the United States.

References

Auletta, K. (1997) 'The next frontier: only the fast survive', *New Yorker* 73(32):140–2.
Ayoob, Mohammed (1995) *The Third World Security Predicament: State Making, Regional Conflict and the International System*, Boulder: Lynne Rienner.
Barber, Benjamin (1995) *Jihad vs. McWorld: How the Planet is Both Falling Apart and Coming Together and What This Means for Democracy*, New York: Times Books.
Boynton, Robert (1997) 'The two Tonys', *New Yorker* 6 October: 66–73.
Brin, David (1998) *The Transparent Society: Will Technology Force Us to Choose between Privacy and Freedom?*, Reading: Addison-Wesley.
Cane, Alan (1997) 'Innovation key in fight for survival', *Financial Times Review of the Telecommunications Industry*, September 1997.
Chayes, Abram and Antonia Handler Chayes (1995) *The New Sovereignty: Compliance with International Regulatory Agreements*, Cambridge: Harvard University Press.
Civicus, *The New Civic Atlas: Profiles of Civil Society in 60 Countries,* Washington, D.C.: Civicus.
Crook, Clive (1997) 'The future of the state', *Economist* 20 September: 7.
Dizard, Wilson (1997) *Meganet*, Boulder: Westview Press.
'The fear of foreign cash,' *Economist*, 26 July 1997: 15.
'Next, cyberlaundering?' *Economist*, 26 July 1997: 2.
The Environment in Europe and North America: Annotated Statistics (1992) New York: United Nations.
Florini, Ann (1988) 'The opening skies: third party imaging satellites and US security', *International Security* 13: 91–123.
Froomkin, A. Michael (1997) 'The Internet as a source of regulatory arbitrage', in Kahin and Nesson (eds) *Borders in Cyberspace*, Cambridge, Mass.: MIT Press.
Fukuyama, Francis (1992) *The End of History and the Last Man*, New York: Free Press.
Gellner, Ernest (1983) *Nations and Nationalism*, Ithaca: Cornell University Press.
Government Finance Statistics Yearbook (1996) Washington, D.C.: International Monetary Fund.
Grubler, Arnulf (1996) 'Time for a change: on the patterns of diffusion of innovation', *Daedalus* 125: 3.
Guehenno, Jean-Marie (1995) *The End of the Nation-State*, Minneapolis: University of Minnesota Press.
Gurr, T. R. (1996) 'Minorities, nationalists and ethnopolitical conflict', in Chester A. Crocker, Fen Osler Hampson and Pamela Aall (eds), *Managing Global Chaos: Sources of and Responses to International Conflict,* Washington, D.C.: US Institute of Peace.
Hammond, Allan (1998) *2050: Scenarios for a New Century*, Washington, D.C.: Island Press.

Hardin, Russell (1982) *Collective Action*, Baltimore: Johns Hopkins University Press for Resources for the Future.

—— (1995) *One for All: The Logic of Group Conflict*, Princeton: Princeton University Press.

Hirst, Paul (1997) 'Myths and realities', *International Affairs* 73(3): 409–25.

Hirst, Paul and Grahame Thompson (1996) *Globalisation in Question: The International Economy and the Possibilities of Governance*, Cambridge: Polity Press.

Hobsbawm, E. and T. Ranger (eds) (1983) *The Invention of Tradition*, Cambridge: Cambridge University Press.

Homer-Dixon, Thomas (forthcoming) *Environment, Scarcity and Violence*, Princeton, N.J.: Princeton University Press.

Horsman, Mathew and Andrew Marshall (1995) *After the Nation-State: Citizens, Tribalism and the New World Disorder*, London: Harper Collins.

Huntington, Samuel P. (1996) *The Clash of Civilizations and the Remaking of World Order*, New York: Simon and Schuster.

—— (1993) 'If not civilizations, what? Paradigms of the post-cold war world,' *Foreign Affairs* 72(5): 186–94.

Kaplan, Robert D (1996) *The Ends of the Earth: A Journey at the Dawn of the 21st Century*, New York: Random House.

Keohane, Robert (1989) *International Institutions and State Power: Essays in International Relations Theory*, Boulder: Westview Press.

Krasner, Stephen D (1983) *International Regimes*, Ithaca, N.Y.: Cornell University Press.

Learmonth, Michael (1997) 'Say cheese', *Metro* 6–12 February. http://www.metroactive.com/papers/

Mann, M. (1993) 'Nation-states in Europe and other continents: diversifying, developing, not dying', *Daedalus* 122(3):115–40.

Mathews, Jessica (1989) 'Redefining Security', *Foreign Affairs* 68(2): 162–77

—— (1997) 'Power shift: the rise of global civil society', *Foreign Affairs* 76(1): 50–66.

OECD (1997a) *National Accounts 1983–1995*, Paris: OECD.

—— (1997b) *The OECD in Figures: Statistics in OECD Member Countries 1997*, Paris: OECD.

Ohmae, Kenichi (1995) *The End of the Nation State: The Rise of Regional Economies*, New York: Simon and Schuster.

Olson, Mancur (1965) *The Logic of Collective Action: Public Goods and the Theory of Groups*, Cambridge, Mass.: Harvard University Press.

Ostrom, Elinor (1990) *Governing the Commons: The Evolution of Institutions for Collective Action*, Cambridge: Cambridge University Press.

Patterson, David 'Microprocessors in 2020', *Scientific American* 273(3): 62–7.

Reddy, Marlita (ed.) (1994) *Statistical Abstract of the World*, Detroit: Gale.

Rittberger, Volker (1993) *Regime Theory and International Relations*, Oxford: Clarendon Press.

Rodenburg, Eric (1992) *Eyeless in Gaia: The State of Global Environmental Monitoring*, Washington, D.C.: World Resources Institute.

Ronfeldt, David (1996) *Tribes, Institutions, Markets, Networks: A Framework About Societal Evolution*, Santa Monica, Calif.: RAND.

Salamon, Lester *et al.* (1996) *The Emerging Sector: A Statistical Supplement*, Baltimore: Johns Hopkins Institute for Policy Studies.

Sandler, Todd (1992) *Collective Action: Theory and Applications*, Ann Arbor: University of Michigan Press.

Sassen, Saskia (1996) *Losing Control: Sovereignty in an Age of Globalization*, New York: Columbia University Press.

Sivard, Ruth (1996) *World Military and Social Expenditures*, Washington, D.C.: World Priorities.

Social Portrait of Europe (1995) Luxembourg: Statistical Office of the European Communities.

Stentz, Zack (1997) 'Unmarked society', *Metro*, 6–12 February. http://www.metroactive.com/papers

Strange, Susan (1996) *The Retreat of the State: The Diffusion of Power in the World Economy*, Cambridge: Cambridge University Press.

Tilly, Charles (ed.) (1975) *The Formation of National States in Western Europe*, Princeton, N.J.: Princeton University Press.

Wilkie, James (1994) *Statistical Abstract of Latin America*, Los Angeles, CA. : UCLA Latin American Center Publications.

Wresch, William (1996) *Disconnected: Haves and Have-nots in the Information Age*, New Brunswick, N.J.: Rutgers University Press.

Zysman, George (1995) 'Wireless networks', *Scientific American* 273(3): 68–71.

2 Grassroots empowerment

States, non-state actors and global policy formulation

Kendall W. Stiles

Introduction

During the decade of the 1980s, a new approach to development emerged and came to dominate the policies of many donors, both national and multilateral. What can best be described as the 'civil society empowerment' approach (Stiles 1998) involves an emphasis on indigenous, grassroots development. The model is based mostly on the successful experiences of international non-governmental organisations (INGOs) such as Oxfam in promoting small scale locally-managed cooperative enterprises in rural areas of Latin America and Asia. Nurtured by local non-governmental organisations (NGOs) in developing countries such as the Grameen Bank, these grassroots organisations (GROs) have proved capable of significantly improving the living conditions of their members, opening public space for women and the poor, and diminishing the need for constant flows of aid from national and international public agencies (Korten 1990).

This model (see Table 2.1) departed from traditional approaches prevalent in the 1970s, through which funds were channelled to states for the purpose of promoting countrywide social welfare programmes aimed at addressing the 'basic needs' of the poor, such as establishing a network of health clinics, conducting a national immunisation programme, or launching a latrine-building campaign. While both approaches emphasise relief of poverty, Hyden sees the gradual move away from state-centred development schemes as a natural evolution away from an emphasis on management towards participation on the one hand, and away from equity for its own sake towards growth-with-equity (Hyden 1991: 135).

While originally conceived as a relatively cautious approach which was intended to be applicable in societies with a wide range of government structures and legal frameworks, the civil society empowerment model has been incorporated in the 'good governance' strategy of the World Bank as well as the push towards democratisation by Western powers. Conversely, some have embraced the principles of civil society empowerment as a means to achieving widespread social justice and human rights. Perhaps the most intriguing thing about this approach is its appeal to both the left and the right:

Table 2.1 The civil society empowerment model

Origins of model:

Philosophical Roots:
- Classical Western liberal economic and political ideology (especially Scottish Enlightenment and Alexis de Tocqueville).
- Social Democratic egalitarianism.
- Liberation Theology.
- Schumacher's 'small is beautiful' economic models.

Policy Experience:
- Successes experienced by Peace Corps and other volunteer workers, in both the developing and developed worlds.
- Success of international NGO community in relief work.
- Successful record of Third World NGO efforts, including cooperatives, women's clubs, micro-lending banks and welfare agencies.
- Frustration with failed large scale, state-centred projects.
- Frustration with shrinking public development budgets, among both donors and developing countries.

Objectives of model:

Starting Premises:
- Ultimate recipients of aid generally understand their own needs and circumstances best.
- Development projects are more likely to be implemented by recipients if they provide input in designing the project.
- Projects will be more sustainable if they are the result of participant input.

Secondary Considerations:
- Grassroots actors will develop greater organisational and managerial experience as a result of participating in designing and implementing projects.
- With their enhanced abilities, grassroots organisations will be in a strong position to make demands on state agencies, thereby increasing state accountability and responsiveness.
- As grassroots organisations practice democratic governance, their members will press for democracy at all levels of government.

Neo-populist development theorists and practitioners extol the virtues of grassroots NGOs as paradigms of social participation and the potential building blocks of democracy; economic liberals bolster their case for deregulation and privatization by emphasizing how these measures contribute to the emergence of a business class to counter-balance and discipline wayward states; treasury-based cost-cutters see devolution of governmental functions to voluntary organisations as an ideologically palatable way of reducing traditional social solidarities in the face of the disruption caused by markets; and radical socialists zero in on the potential role of social organisations based on community, group or issue in transforming society or providing an alternative form of social governance.

(White 1994: 378)

The model has become the object of an intense political struggle at the highest levels of policy with implications for international relations and domestic politics across the globe.

This paper will offer a 'pluralist global model' for why the civil society empowerment model became a popular alternative to the basic needs model at the time it did by considering the relative power and interests of the major participants in the policy process, and by showing how changes in global economic and political conditions altered relationships between these participants. By understanding the effects of structural changes on the relative strength of the various players in development policy, it is possible to explain, *post hoc*, why the civil society model emerged in the form it did at the time it did. Further, I argue that by exploring scenarios of systemic change, it is possible to anticipate how this development model will evolve in the future.

This perspective borrows loosely from the various pluralist models of domestic government (Dahl 1971) as well as some of the 'global governance', 'neo-liberal institutionalist' and 'epistemic community' literature (Rosenau and Czempiel 1992; Ruggie 1993, 1996; Haas 1990) by emphasising the importance of non-state actors in the determination of international policy preferences. This contrasts with the more idealistic and hopeful tone of much of the recent work on global civil society however, and pulls us back into the language of interests and power. It also contrasts with the 'learning' and 'constructivist' schools (Haas 1977, Onuf 1989), in that I argue that the interests and identities of major players tend not to change over time, only their strategies and tactics depending on the general distribution of power and resources. States continue to care deeply about security, relative power, autonomy and internal control. International organisations care about securing the support and resources of donors, the cooperation of all members, and enough policy space to carve out a unique niche. INGOs, NGOs and GROs all seek resources to serve their members while preserving the autonomy to chart their own destiny. The policies each player promotes reflect these long-standing interests, although the overall policy outcome will depend on the relative power and influence of the players at particular moments. Ultimately, the international economic and political context provides the parameters of the debate and helps to determine which resources will be most effective.

I will now move into a discussion of the major players and their basic interests. I will then review the nature of the changes in international economic and political conditions between 1980 and 1990 which were key to the emergence of the civil society empowerment model. Finally, I will review the way each of the major players was affected by these global changes and how they approached the new model. In so doing it will become clear that the debt crisis and the end of the Cold War contributed to a strengthening of those actors which had an interest in promoting the civil society empowerment model while at the same time they weakened its opponents and made them unable to prevent its implementation. I will then add a word of epilogue which explores possible future scenarios as they relate to the long-term potential of the new development model.

The key players

Any attempt at explaining the emergence of the model based on the rational behaviour of actors requires that we take a moment to identify them and describe their goals and resources. Table 2.2 summarises this information with respect to the present study. The actors can be distinguished by whether they are governmental or non-governmental, local or transnational, and Northern or Southern.

As can be seen, I assume all states have certain common interests and resources by virtue of their international and domestic roles. As put by Bratton, 'The basic function of any state is to impose and maintain political order . . . Even if a government professes a developmentalist ideology, its first responsibility is to guard the integrity and security of the territorial realm' (Bratton 1989: 573). In addition, states seek to create a more secure international climate, to the extent that their resources allow. 'Grassroots empowerment' can be seen as both a threat and an opportunity from the point of view of both the Northern and Southern state. In the case of third world states – particularly those which lack legitimacy – it can represent a direct threat to their survival (Harbeson 1994, Kilby 1997).

Table 2.2 Players in the civil society empowerment model

Player	Interests	Resources
Donor states	Global influence Maintaining liberal order Electoral success Domestic fiscal restraint	Considerable funds Policy access for INGOs Votes in IGOs Networks of development workers in LDCs
Developing states	Domestic stability Domestic influence Attraction of funds Political legitimacy	Policy access for IGOs, INGOs Regulation of NGOs Expertise on conditions in local areas

Multilateral donor organisations	Financial stability
	Policy influence
	Measurable achievements
	Maintain confidence of
	    member states
		Moderate funding
		Policy coordination
		Policy expertise
		Networks of field
		    workers in LDCs

International NGOs	Financial stability
	Policy influence
	Comparative achievement
	Maintain confidence of
	    private/public donors
		Limited funding
		Policy expertise
		Networks of field
		    workers in LDCs
		Reputation/authenticity

National NGOs and GROs	Financial stability Membership services Access to policy circles Membership representation	Access to grassroots in LDCs Mobilisation skills Policy expertise Reputation/authenticity

In the case of donor states, it can serve as an inexpensive and convenient tool of foreign policy. Both sets of states must consider the possibility that providing NGOs with additional resources may significantly increase their influence on policy.

Non-state actors share a preoccupation with both flexibility and visibility in the context of intense competition for scarce resources (Fowler 1992: 17–19). While some transnational NGOs form close ties with states (Smillie 1993: 27), others have kept them at arm's length (Hellinger *et al.* 1988: 148). NGOs and GROs in the developing world are under even more severe financial constraints, not to mention even more ambiguous relations with governments (see the state-in-society literature: Harbeson 1994). While many of them have developed a strong identity and considerable autonomy (note the Grameen Bank in Bangladesh: Huque 1988: 47) they are sometimes merely extensions of Northern NGOs (Clark 1991: 83, Bornstein 1996: 178) or the local elites (UNDP 1993: 89–90). Many are on the fence (note Sarvodaya Shramadana in Sri Lanka: Lean 1995: 38, Perera 1997). Nearly all NGOs, both in the North and South, seek to influence public policy, but on their terms and with as much control over funding as possible.

International governmental organisations share many of the characteristics of both states and non-state actors. They are deeply enmeshed in the state system and must consider issues of legality and sovereignty when designing programmes and choosing aid recipients (Coate, Alger and Lipschutz 1996: 95–6, Stiles 1998). On the other hand, the staff of these agencies often have considerable first-hand experience with development issues and have generated original and progressive strategies which often conflict with state priorities. In many cases, tensions emerge between the staff, the IGO leadership and the member-states (Helleiner, Cornea and Jolly 1991).

A decade of crisis

Between 1982 and 1992 a string of shocks beset the international system which dramatically changed the relative weights of the major players listed above. Specifically, the debt crisis undermined Third World development and state autonomy relative to donors and IGOs; the 'structural adjustment' strategy undermined LDC states and created openings for non-state actors; the end of the Cold War and the denigration of Marxist socialism strengthened the hand of liberal donors and IGOs; and the renewed interest in human rights and democratisation and the general weakening of sovereignty norms weakened LDC states in the short term relative to civil society actors. To this list could be added 'donor fatigue' and the end of Soviet aid to the members of the Non-Aligned Movement. I will consider first the economic questions.

Economic upheaval

The story of the debt crisis is well known and need not be laboured here (Kahler 1986). Suffice it to say that the debt–service ratio of all developing countries increased from 13.3 per cent of export earnings in 1970 to 23 per cent in 1980 and remained at 21 per cent in 1990, while total debt relative to GNP increased from 26.2 per cent in 1980 to 42.3 per cent in 1991 (for sub-Saharan Africa the increase was from 28.6 per cent to 107.9 per cent). As result of devoting more and more resources to debt repayment, incomes stagnated. GNP per capita in 1982 stood at $2,010 on average for 'intermediate income countries' (as defined by UNDP) which were hardest hit by the debt crisis. By 1985 that figure had dropped to $1,800 and did not return to its 1982 level until 1987 (World Bank 1995; UNDP 1996). Over the course of the period 1982 to 1993, GNP per capita for these countries grew only 21 per cent overall. Least developed countries' GNP per capita grew only 18 per cent over twelve years while OECD countries' GNP per capita grew 111 per cent (World Bank 1995). As more and more developing countries found themselves owing more and more to industrialised countries, both in official and private debt, they recognised that their ability to secure development assistance was severely constrained. While many nations negotiated generous debt rescheduling arrangements (Stiles 1991), little of this new money went towards social services or infrastructure. By the late 1980s, the proportion of aid going to social services was a scant 16.9 per cent of the total (UNDP 1996).

In this context, donor states increased their pressure on LDC governments to ensure accountability and cost savings while at the same time providing enough capital to allow debtors to maintain interest payments in order to preserve the stability of the international financial system. Long-term development goals were largely irrelevant to this effort at crisis management. Perhaps most important to debtor nations was the decision on the part of donors to address their problems on a case by case basis rather than address structural issues. Several of the most dramatic reschedulings were timed to prevent the consolidation of a 'debtor cartel' (Stiles 1987). As a consequence, the solidarity which had emerged between developing states during the 1970s was largely dissolved (Rothstein 1979, Krasner 1985).

The roles of the International Monetary Fund and later the World Bank were dramatically expanded as they served as intermediaries between creditors and debtors. Because of the disproportionate weight of creditor member states and the orthodox economic training of the staff, the policy of structural adjustment came to prevail. The policy aimed at 'getting prices right', focusing on what the Fund considered fiscal imprudence and monetary irresponsibility. Policy instruments included reduction of state subsidies for food and fuel, reduction of social services, privatisation of state-owned firms, currency devaluation, reduction of trade and investment barriers and interest rate increases to stifle consumption.

The result was to significantly alter the state–society relationship across the Third World. As put by Harbeson:

> The campaigns for structural adjustment are in part responsible for the reemergence of the idea of civil society, in that the concept grew out of a faith in the vitality and indispensability of the private sector to a country's political and economic health. Moreover, civil society is ingrained in the very classical liberal philosophy upon which the structural adjustment discourse has been founded.
>
> (Harbeson 1994: 9)

The reduction of state-funded public welfare created important opportunities for non-profit charities to intervene, albeit without having been adequately prepared. As put by Reilly:

> Austerity politics, sometimes enjoined on national governments by external actors (particularly the International Monetary Fund and the World Bank), contribute to the *de facto* decentralization trends and to the breaking down of traditional, corporatist-clientelist patterns of interaction. The populist handouts of the past are quite impossible today.
>
> (Reilly 1995: 249)

The debt crisis coincided with a shift in the mood of many donor states, described in the literature as 'donor fatigue.' The discouragement many in the West felt regarding the effectiveness of aid put pressure on governments (usually through the legislature) to reduce development assistance in favour of domestic priorities. Annual aid levels in the United States, for example, averaged 0.24 per cent of US GNP from 1980 to 1985, but slipped to 0.19 per cent between 1987 to 1993. In Britain, aid levels fell from an annual rate of 0.37 per cent of GNP in 1980–5 to 0.3 per cent in 1987–93 (World Bank 1995). Whether manifested as opposition to UN programmes by the US Congress or ambivalence about continuing generous aid policies in Sweden and the Netherlands, there were clear signals being sent to developing countries across the Third World that they would be expected to rely on private rather than public capital in the future. Furthermore, the end of the Cold War and the Gulf War and subsequent peace process in the Middle East created new objects of assistance. Aid to Europe and Central Asia increased from $200 million in 1989 to $1.3 billion in 1990 and $1.9 billion in 1991. Aid to the Middle East increased from $3.5 billion in 1989 to $9.7 billion in 1990 and stayed at $9.3 billion in 1991 (World Bank 1995). While data are inconclusive as to whether these increases in aid came at the expense of traditional aid recipients (note that aid to sub-Saharan Africa increased somewhat during the same period), it became clear that the latter should not expect any dramatic new development initiatives in the near future.

Donor states came to the realisation that they could achieve some cost savings in the area of humanitarian and development assistance by sub-contracting to INGOs. Beginning in the mid-1980s, major donors began to funnel a significant portion of their aid through INGOs. By 1990, roughly $750 million in public aid went through INGOs, a figure which increased to $800 million by 1994, or 10 per cent of all public development assistance (Van Rooy 1997: 3; Gordenker and Weiss 1996: 25). UNDP began tracking NGO public assistance and reported that in 1994 9 per cent of Canadian, 10 per cent of Dutch and over 10 per cent of Swiss net development aid went through NGOs (UNDP 1996: 199). The US in 1995 pledged to increase the share of its aid going through NGOs from roughly 25 per cent to nearly half by 2000 (Gordenker and Weiss 1996: 25). Overall, '[t]he increase of donor-funded NGO relief operations and Western disengagement from poor countries are two sides of the same coin' (Gordenker and Weiss 1996: 25). Increased authority of INGOs does not necessarily signify a loss of authority by states. In this case, it was a new strategy by donor states to get rid of the responsibility for a possibly costly policy area. The interest in INGOs ultimately spread to IGOs as well and the World Bank began to integrate INGOs and eventually NGOs into project implementation while at the same time tolerating INGO criticism of past projects for the first time in the late-1980s (Conca 1996: 109).

The net effect was a strong stimulus for INGO growth in the context of a generally stagnant aid pool for developing countries. This has proved to be a mixed blessing for these agencies, since the receipt of public funds increases INGOs' accountability to states, contrary to their goals of autonomy and independence. In addition, the prospect of public funding has prompted the formation of new INGOs, so that competition has increased. One result is what Smillie calls the 'homogenisation' of mature INGOs so that they resemble each other more and more in function, outlook and structure (Smillie 1993: 23).

Political restructuring

Coinciding with and often related to these significant changes in economic conditions between donors and recipients of aid were a number of political developments. First was the undermining of authoritarian and populist regimes. As alluded to earlier, traditional patronage was no longer possible in the context of structural adjustment. One could add that austerity measures, while often accompanied by an increase in repression over the short term, tend to undermine large-scale internal security institutions over the medium and long term. '[P]articipation is being grudgingly offered [to NGOs and GROs] as an alternative to patronage that governments can no longer finance, and repression they can no longer indulge as aid agencies become increasingly preoccupied with human rights and good governance' (Bebbington and Farrington 1993: 204). The 'third wave' of democratisation is closely linked to the dismantling of strong states through structural adjustment (Huntington 1991; Haggard and Webb 1994). While the process has often resulted in greater democracy and civil liberties, it has also led to social disintegration, polarisation and the creation of parallel state institutions (Zartman 1995). In Chile and much of Latin America, the dismantling of state services galvanized civil society associations and precipitated a generally peaceful democratic transition (Zuniga 1989: 197). In parts of Africa, 'societal groups responded to state decline by establishing new institutions outside of the formal structures of state' (Rothchild 1994: 202), including black markets, NGO and GRO service provision and even informal local security arrangements such as the Sungu Sungu activities in Tanzania. Manifestations of weakened states abound, whether in the constructive political parties of the Czech Republic, organised crime in Russia, ethnic warfare in Bosnia or warlords in Somalia, and can often be attributed to transitions from authoritarian or patronage systems.

The collapse of strong states in the Third World coincided with the demise of command economies in Eastern Europe. Culminating in the end of central planning and authoritarianism, the shift made possible the end of Cold War hostilities. This change dramatically altered the place of the Third World in world affairs and directly influenced the prevailing development strategy. To begin, Western powers, and especially the US, no longer needed the strategic benefits of authoritarian states and could gain more politically at home by severing ties with the most egregious human rights violators. West-leaning hardline regimes in South Africa, Zaire, Chile, Haiti, the Philippines and elsewhere were each in turn either cut off or put under severe pressure to halt massive human rights abuses. The West could also afford the political cost of demanding greater accountability from aid recipients and became less tolerant of the graft and corruption that so often accompanied international aid. Given the lack of alternative sources of development assistance with the end of Soviet largesse, few regimes were able to resist Western policies.

Western powers, yielding to domestic concerns and in the hope of creating a more hospitable international environment, made human rights a high priority. Whether on the political left or the right, 'political conditionality' for aid has become extremely popular (Farrington *et al.* 1993: 10). This spirit has been advanced in multilateral agencies as well, and the Security Council, World Bank and other IGOs have promoted more activist policies aimed at liberalising authoritarian regimes. Extreme actions include the surrendering of sovereignty to the UN by Somalia and Cambodia as well as the direct military engagement of authoritarian forces in Haiti and Bosnia. In general, the notion of sovereignty is under question (Weber 1995; Lapidoth 1992). With respect to the question of 'civil society empowerment', the World Bank's 'good governance' initiative of 1988 is perhaps the most dramatic (World Bank 1989: 60). The approach called on states not only to restructure their economic systems and reorder their fiscal and monetary priorities, but to improve performance through improved bureaucratic accountability, increased decentralisation of policy and enhanced popular partic- ipation in policy. While not officially a 'democratisation' programme, 'good governance' was seen by LDC states and Bank opponents as a purely political initiative (Nelson 1995: 9).

> Governance provides a new tool-kit, an instrument of control, an additional conditionality for the time when the traditional blame-the-victim defence again becomes necessary. It further offers the opportunity both to instil Western political values in borrowing countries and to fault them if things go wrong.
>
> (George and Sabelli 1994: 142)

Use of NGOs became integral to Bank efforts to circumvent bloated, corrupt central governments in practice while promoting their importance in principle (compare Fonseca 1995: 66 with World Bank 1997).

Other IGOs, in support of donor and INGO initiatives, more directly supported NGOs and GROs in the developing world. The Global Environmental Facility's Small Grants Program – an outgrowth of the 1992 UN Conference on the Environment and Development – provides resources directly to NGOs and GROs for local environmental protection and is designed to be distributed by local NGOs themselves. While state representatives may sit on allocation committees, they may not veto majority decisions (Work 1996). When Nigeria objected to this arrangement, which it considered an infringement on its sovereignty, the administering IGO simply waited it out. The government eventually relented and accepted the funds along with the procedures. UNICEF has taken to engaging local organisations directly in the name of the Convention on the Rights of the Child and routinely brings together state and NGO officials for joint policy and planning meetings (Nelson 1996). The World Health Organisation, stymied by reluctant states with respect to implementing its Global AIDS Strategy in 1988, simply invited NGOs and INGOs to create a parallel service-delivery structure called the International Council of AIDS Service Organisations (Coate, Alger and Lipschutz 1996: 108). IGOs now actively promote the recognition by states of NGO rights:

> One big challenge is establishing the legal framework in a country to permit NGOs to work in partnership with governments. To this end, the public and governments need to be educated about the nature and function of civil society organizations. Governments need to be helped to understand that giving up some control is not necessarily only a loss. UNICEF and other UN agencies clearly have a role to play in establishing a more enabling legal and administrative environment.
>
> (UNICEF 1995)

In short, INGOs may strengthen local NGOs in their position *vis-à-vis* their government. The inclusion of community groups in development projects has moved beyond a mere cost-saving strategy. 'Viewed as an end in itself, participation is endowed with normative qualities: it becomes tantamount to a human right.' (Marsden 1991: 3). As put by Bebbington and Thiele:

> Different donors have . . . been promoting NGO participation for more explicitly political ends: to strengthen civil society and the process of social participation in the new democracies. During the last few years, these financing agencies have become increasingly explicit in acknowledging that democratisation is both necessary for the development process and a desirable goal in and of itself.
>
> (Bebbington and Thiele 1993: 55)

LDC states have therefore been put on the defensive and held to account for their human rights records. Some observers have gone so far as to suggest that the new 'civil society empowerment' model is merely a front for an effort which aims at reducing the LDC state to the status of donor 'franchisee', replacing public officials with private actors unaccountable to the public (Wood 1997: 84).

The results have not been entirely beneficial for the NGOs and GROs themselves. Although they have enjoyed increased funding, they have been forced to adopt more sophisticated accounting techniques and in many cases have adjusted their programmatic focus to accommodate IGO, INGO and bilateral donor priorities. In some cases, this has led to serious disruptions within the organisation, as we saw in the case of the Sarvodaya Shramadana Movement mentioned earlier (Lean 1995: 42). Oxfam UK and UNICEF were impressed with a national nurse training programme established by an NGO in Malawi and decided to support it, only to find a few years later that it was the organisation's energetic improvisation and pioneering spirit which were the keys to its success, and which were destroyed by donor support (Clark 1991: 110–16).

NGOs have also been injured by being excluded from the civil society empowerment model. The World Bank is heavily biased against NGOs with an 'agenda' and even UNICEF steers clear of overt ties to secessionist groups, no matter how effective at delivering services to their members (Nelson 1995: 130–2, 1996). A bias in favour of mainstream agencies willing to work with the state has emerged, especially at the behest of the Scandinavian donors and INGOs. At the same time, US and British agencies have pressed for entrepreneurial NGOs. The net result is that many technical NGOs have received considerable funding and are therefore multiplying in number. Whether this trend is healthy for the promotion of equitable and just development is highly questionable. In fact, the nurturing of these technical NGOs is likely to exacerbate social divisions (Boyle 1997).

Aftermath and implications

What has 'civil society empowerment' become in the wake of these upheavals and conflicting pressures? Given the overwhelming dominance of donors, the stronger presence of IGOs and INGOs, and the relative weakness of LDC governments, it is not surprising that the civil society model has emerged as the dominant approach to development. It satisfies the need for economical human rights and capitalist-oriented development on the part of donors which no longer need worry about grand security strategy and maintaining competing spheres of influence. It allows IGOs to promote principles to which the staff and leadership have long been committed, namely democratic development. It provides resources for INGOs in their struggle to survive in a competitive market-place for charity and relieves some of the pressure to collect private funds. The policy has almost no risks for the donors, although there is always the danger that IGOs may alienate less developed member states if they push too hard. INGOs and other voluntary associations have found some risks involved in allowing public agencies to dominate their funding, but have generally taken the money anyway.

Developing country governments, on the other hand, have seen much of their authority and sovereignty come under fire, sometimes in rather subtle ways. Although IGOs tend, more than other donor agencies, to respect the authority of states in principle – the World Bank's 1997 World Development Report stresses the fact that there is no substitute for effective state programmes – in practice they and other donors have done much to undermine it. NGOs and GROs often find themselves caught up in a global power struggle in which they are ill-prepared to participate. There exists a real danger for them of co-option by external players bent on promoting participation and democratisation for their own sakes.

The image presented here is less appealing than many advocates of civil society and empowerment have presented, but I believe it gives us a more accurate picture of the policy's nature and its sources. The image also points to some important theoretical and policy implications.

First, the policy implications. The civil society empowerment model will flourish so long as the donors remain uncontested and unmolested and the recipients have no alternatives to their aid. Several items on the horizon might change this situation. If the debt burden of developing states becomes manageable and their economies begin to expand, they will become less dependent on donor support and will be able to adopt their own development strategies and define state–society relations more autonomously. They may still have to cater to the needs of foreign investors and creditors, but these will tend not to have political agendas. We already see evidence of this pattern in Malaysia, Chile, Mexico and Poland. Second, if alternative sources of aid become available, we are likely to see a turning away from the civil society empowerment approach. I note that the Japanese tend to place little emphasis on NGO participation; as of 1994 only 1 per cent of their net development aid was channelled through non-governmental organisations. Should the oil exporting nations or China emerge as major aid givers in the years to come, I would expect that the emphasis on civil society would diminish. Most importantly, if the global strategic situation changed in such a way that it became important once again for the West to court Third World leaders, the stress on civil society empowerment would likely be the first thing to go. Western donors have already made exceptions for Bosnian Muslims and the regimes in Kuwait and Jordan which are far more important as strategic allies than models of democracy.

It is also possible that we are building towards a Third World backlash with respect to the civil society programme. Already we have seen several important global Western initiatives flounder on the rocks of sovereignty and Third World solidarity. Malaysia, Egypt and other states are drawing the line on human rights and seem to have stymied progress on this front. And, of course, Iraq, Libya, Cuba and other pariah states have loudly lamented the general erosion of sovereignty, although with much less effect. It is not unreasonable to expect a backlash against the civil society empowerment programme if power shifts even slightly. In this regard, recent nuclear tests by Pakistan and India might be enough.

This said, there is a possibility of 'frontlash' as well. If GROs, NGOs and INGOs continue to receive considerable support, and especially if they are able to become self-sustaining, it is possible that they will continue to constrain the actions of states and preserve the liberal economic and political principles which have been introduced. This is unlikely, however, unless the non-governmental actors can secure their own independent sources of income rather than remaining largely dependent on outside funds. Synergos and Civitas have promoted the creation of autonomous, locally-managed foundations, begun with both internally and externally generated funds from which local GROs received grants and loans indefinitely (Synergos 1996, Jacqz 1996). Such autonomous non-profits offer the promise of the sort of civil society maturation described in Tarrow which is more logically related to the consolidation of democratic institutions (Tarrow 1977).

In theoretical terms, the image presented here helps to put the role of non-governmental organisations in proper perspective. Lacking the resources of donor states, these agencies cannot expect to have unilateral influence on policy. However, given a change in power relations, it is possible that these INGOs and NGOs can be invited into policy circles and have genuine impact.

By the same token, the discussion puts the role of states in proper perspective since it illustrates the capacity of non-state and multilateral actors to influence the implementation of policies and, to some extent, the delineation of the range of policy options. By using INGOs and NGOs, donors found they could not entirely control outcomes and were forced to accept some of the priorities and practices of these agencies. Their experience with Grameen Bank, for example, taught donors that they could not force an NGO to take their money unless they accommodated the organisation's priorities to some extent.

Most important, the image presented here helps to clarify the linkages across levels of analysis and across issues in ways most approaches do not. While the state–society relationship is central to the story, it cannot be understood without considering the broader donor–recipient relations. And while the donor–recipient relationship is central, it also cannot be fully understood without considering the broader systemic context. While economic forces are crucial to the dynamic, they cannot be fully understood without the political context. And while legal questions enter into the mix, they need to be understood in the context of political and ideational forces.

References

Bebbington, Anthony and John Farrington (1993) 'Governments, NGOs and agricultural development: perspectives on changing inter-organizational relationships', *Journal of Development Studies* 29(2): 199–219.

Bebbington, Anthony and Graham Thiele (eds) (1993) *Non-Governmental Organisations and the State in Latin America: Rethinking Role in Sustainable Agricultural Development*, New York: Routledge.

Bornstein, David (1996) *The Price of a Dream: The Story of the Grameen Bank and the Idea That Is Helping the Poor to Change Their Lives*, New York: Simon and Schuster.

Boyle, Patrick (1997) 'Parents, private schools, and the politics of an emerging civil society in Cameroon', *Journal of Modern African Studies* 34: 609–22.

Bratton, Michael (1989) 'The politics of government–NGO relations in Africa', *World Development* 17(4): 569–87.

Clark, John (1991) *Democratizing Development: The Role of Voluntary Organisations*, West Hartford, Conn.: Kumarian Press.

Coate, Roger, Chadwick Alger and Ronnie Lipschutz (1996) 'The United Nations and civil society: creative partnerships for sustainable development', *Alternatives* 21: 93–122.

Conca, Ken (1996) 'Greening the UN: environmental organisations and the UN system', in Thomas Weiss and Leon Gordenker (eds) *NGOs, the UN and Global Governance*, Boulder: Lynne Rienner: 103–20.

Dahl, Robert A. (1971) *Polyarchy: Participation and Opposition*, New Haven: Yale University Press.

Farrington, John, Anthony Bebbington, Kate Wellard and David J.Lewis (1993) *Reluctant Partners: Non-Governmental Organizations, the State and Sustainable Agricultural Development*, New York: Routledge.

Fisher, Julie (1993) *The Road From Rio: Sustainable Development and the Nongovernmental Movement in the Third World*, Westport, Conn.: Praeger.

Fonseca, Chandler de (1995) 'Challenges and future directions for Asian NGOs', in Noeleen Heyzer, James V. Riker and Antonio Quizon (eds) *Government–NGO Relations in Asia: Prospects and Challenges for People-Centered Development*, New York: St. Martin's Press: 57–76.

Fowler, Alan (1992) 'Building partnerships between Northern and Southern development NGOs: issues for the nineties', *Development* 1: 16–23.

George, Susan and Fabrizio Sabelli (1994) *Faith and Credit: The World Bank's Secular Empire*, Boulder: Westview Press.

Gordenker, Leon and Thomas G. Weiss (1996) 'Pluralizing global governance: analytical approaches and dimensions', in Thomas Weiss and Leon Gordenker (eds) *NGOs, the UN and Global Governance*, Boulder: Lynne Rienner: 17–47.

Haas, Ernst (1977) *Scientists and World Order: The Uses of Technical Knowledge in International Organizations*, Berkeley: University of California Press.

Haas, Peter M. (1990) *Saving the Mediterranean: The Politics of International Environmental Cooperation*, New York: Columbia University Press.

Haggard, Stephen and Steven Webb (1994) *Voting for Reform: Democracy, Political Liberalization, and Economic Adjustment*, New York: Oxford University Press.

Harbeson, John W. (1994) 'Civil society and political renaissance in Africa', in John Harbeson, Donald Rothchild and Naomi Chazan (eds) *Civil Society and the State in Africa*, Boulder: Lynne Rienner: 1–29.

Helleiner, Gerald, G. A. Cornea and Richard Jolly (1991) 'IMF adjustment policies and approaches and the needs of children', *World Development* 19(12): 1823–34.

Hellinger, Stephen, Douglas Helinger and Fred O'Regan (1988) *Aid for Just Development*, Boulder: Lynne Rienner.

Huntington, Samuel P. (1991) *The Third Wave: Democratization in the Late Twentieth Century*, Norman: University of Oklahoma Press.

Huque, Ahmed Shafiqul (1988) *Politics and Administration in Bangladesh: Problems of Participation*, Dhaka: University Press.

Hyden, Goran (1991) 'The role of aid and research in the political restructuring of Africa', in Richard Crook and Alf Morten (eds) *Government and Participation: Institutional Development, Decentralization and Democracy in the Third World*, Fantoft, Norway: Michelson Institute: 132–43.

Jacqz, Jane (1996) Interview with the author at UNDP headquarters, March 6.

Kahler, Miles (1986) *The Politics of International Debt*, Ithaca: Cornell University Press.

Kilby, Christopher (1997) 'Sovereignty and NGOs', paper presented at the annual meeting of the International Studies Association, Toronto, Canada.

Korten, David C. (1990) *Getting to the Twenty-First Century: Voluntary Action and the Global Agenda*, West Hartford, Conn.: Kumarian Press.

Krasner, Stephen D. (1985) *Structural Conflict: The Third World Against Global Liberalism*, Berkeley: University of California Press.

Lapidoth, Ruth (1992) 'Sovereignty in transition', *Journal of International Affairs* 45: 325–46.

Lean, Henry (1995) *Bread, Bricks and Beliefs: Communities in Charge of Their Future*, West Hartford: Kumarian Press.

Marsden, David (1991) 'What is community participation?', in Richard Crook and Alf Morten (eds) *Government and Participation: Institutional Development, Decentralization and Democracy in the Third World*, Fantoft, Norway: Michelson Institute.

Nelson, Janet (1996) Interview with the author at UNICEF House, March 3.

Nelson, Paul (1995) *The World Bank and Non-Governmental Organizations*, New York: St. Martin's Press.

Onuf, Nicholas G. (1989) *World of Our Making: Rules and Rule in Social Theory and International Relations*, Columbia: University of South Carolina Press.

Perera, Jehan (1997) 'In unequal dialogue with donors: the experience of the Sarvodaya Shramadana Movement', in David Hulme and Michael Edwards (eds) *NGOs, States and Donors: Too Close for Comfort?*, New York: St. Martin's Press: 156–67.

Rahman, Atiur and Abu N. M. Wahid (1992) 'The Grameen Bank and the changing patron-client relationship in Bangladesh', *Journal of Contemporary Asia* 22(3): 303–21.

Reilly, Charles A. (ed.) (1995) *New Paths to Democratic Development in Latin America: The Rise of NGO-Municipal Collaboration*, Boulder: Lynne Rienner.

Rosenau, James N. and Ernst-Otto Czempiel (eds) (1992) *Governance Without Government: Order and Change in World Politics*, New York: Cambridge University Press.

Rothchild, Donald (1994) 'Structuring state-society relations in Africa: toward an enabling political environment', in Jennifer Widner (ed.) *Economic Change and Political Liberalization in Sub-Saharan Africa*, Baltimore: Johns Hopkins University Press: 201–29.

Rothstein, Robert L. (1979) *Global Bargaining: UNCTAD and the Quest for a New International Economic Order*, Princeton: Princeton University Press.

Ruggie, John Gerard (ed.) (1993) *Multilateralism Matters: The Theory and Praxis of an Institutional Form*, New York: Columbia University Press.

—— (1996) *Winning the Peace: America and World Order in the New Era*, New York: Columbia University Press.

Smillie, Ian (1993) 'Changing partners: northern NGOs, northern governments', in Smillie, Ian and Henny Helmich (eds) *Non-Governmental Organizations and Governments: Stakeholders for Development*, Paris: OECD: 13–43.

Stiles, Kendall W. (1987) 'Argentina's bargaining with the IMF', *Journal of Inter-American Studies and World Affairs* 29(3): 55–85.

—— (1991) Negotiating Debt: *The IMF Lending Process*, Boulder: Westview Press.

—— (1998) 'Civil society empowerment and multilateral donors: the centrality of international institutions in the translation of new international norms', *Global Governance* 4(2): 199–216.

Synergos Institute (1996) 'Global action research to strengthen the role of communities in development', paper presented to the World Bank, Washington, D.C., March.

Tarrow, Sidney (1977) *Between Center and Periphery: Grassroots Politicians in Italy and France*, New Haven: Yale University Press.

UNDP (1993) *Human Development Report 1993*, New York: Oxford University Press.

—— (1996) *Human Development Report 1996*, New York: Oxford University Press.

UNICEF (1995) 'A renewed UNICEF/NGO partnership: building blocks', Workshop held at UNICEF House, 12–13 June.

Van Rooy, Alison (1997) 'The civil society agenda: switching gears in the post Cold War world', paper presented at the annual meetings of the International Studies Association, Toronto, Canada.

Weber, Cynthia (1995) *Simulating Sovereignty: Intervention, the State, and Symbiotic Exchange*, New York: Cambridge University Press.

White, Gordon (1994) 'Civil society, democratization and development (i): clearing the analytical ground', *Democratization* 1(3): 375–90.

Wood, G. (1997) 'States without citizens: the problem of the franchise state', in David Hulme and Michael Edwards (eds) *NGOs, States and Donors: Too Close for Comfort?*, New York: St. Martin's Press: 79–92.

Work, Robertson (1996) Interview with the author at UNDP Headquarters, March 7.

World Bank (1989) *Sub-Saharan Africa: From Crisis to Sustainable Growth, a Long-Term Perspective Study*, Washington, D.C.: World Bank.

—— (1993) *World Development Report 1993*, Washington, D.C.: World Bank.

—— (1995) *World Tables 1995*, Washington, D.C.: World Bank.

—— (1997) *World Development Report 1997*, Washington, D.C.: World Bank.

Zartman, I. William (ed.) (1995) *Collapsed States: The Disintegration and Restoration of Legitimate Aucthority*, Boulder, Colo.: Lynne Rienner.

Zuniga, Luis (1989) 'Self-sufficiency and ways to strengthen institutional aspects of social projects in the non-governmental sector', in Charles Downs, Giorgio Solimano, Carlos Vergara and Luis Zuniga (eds) *Social Policy from the Grassroots: Non-governmental Organisations in Chile*, Boulder: Westview: 191–7.

Part II

Multinational companies and the establishment of international rules

3 Globalisation and policy convergence

The case of direct investment rules

Andrew Walter

Globalisation and direct investment rules

It is commonly claimed that increasing capital mobility, an important aspect of globalisation in the world political economy, has eroded the ability of governments to make policies that constrain the activities of transnational corporations (TNCs) within their jurisdictions.[1] This view is widespread amongst both critics and supporters of globalisation and, as outlined in the introduction of this book, represents the currently dominant neo-liberal discourse. As in the early 1970s, there is today a thriving populist literature on the growing power of TNCs in the world economy and the associated loss of power on the part of states and communities.[2] Such critics fear a 'race to the bottom' in real wages and in labour and environmental standards, as well as lower corporate taxes and higher subsidies to mobile firms. Supporters of globalisation also often argue that the competition for foreign direct investment (FDI) between states explains the trend towards the liberalisation of inward FDI rules. For them, globalisation produces a beneficial 'race to the top' in regulatory and policy standards. For example, the *Financial Times* recently editorialised that 'fierce worldwide competition for capital means that countries that discriminate unfairly against foreign investors risk severe market sanctions. That is a powerful incentive for host governments to stick to the straight and narrow' (*Financial Times* 1998a). From both sides of the debate, there is agreement that TNCs enjoy increasing amounts of influence or 'structural power' over national policies.

This chapter asks how much evidence there is for this claim, which I term the 'convergence hypothesis'. This hypothesis claims that the *enhanced mobility of TNCs in the world economy confers structural power upon such firms, resulting in a process of convergence of national policy regimes upon TNC policy preferences.* Specifically, is the apparent trend towards the liberalisation of rules and policies towards TNCs a product of their increasing structural power in the world economy? Do TNCs 'arbitrage' policy regimes, compelling states to compete for 'footloose' capital through such liberalisation?

The chapter leaves aside, among others, two related questions. The first is the extent to which the structural power enjoyed by TNCs produces policy convergence in the broad range of macro-economic, micro-economic and other regulatory policies that affect business and investment, or in factor market prices and conditions across countries. The focus of this paper is only upon rules relating to the regulation of inward FDI. It leaves aside questions such as whether globalisation is responsible for eroding real wages or higher unemployment in unskilled sectors, for the claimed erosion of environmental or labour standards, or for declining capital taxation rates.[3] The assumption made here is that if the convergence hypothesis is true, we ought to find a clear link between actual FDI inflows and policy liberalisation in capital-importing states.

The second issue largely left aside is the political lobbying role of TNCs in the setting of policies in both home and host countries.[4] Many environmental, development and consumer NGO critics argue that recent OECD negotiations on a Multilateral Agreement on Investment (MAI) reflect a shift in power away from governments and citizens towards global firms.[5] Space considerations are one reason, but there are other grounds to think it secondary. First, while globalisation theorists often suggest that structural power 'may be supplemented by direct lobbying, and gentlemanly arm-twisting' (Gill and Law 1988: 87), they tend to argue that the structural power of TNCs is primary.[6] Second, while some argue that the threat of exit associated with TNC mobility enhances their direct political voice, the literature is unclear on how to separate the effects of mobility from the effects of political lobbying (Sklair 1998). Third, if the structural power deriving from mobility is as strong as many claim, it is unclear why TNCs need bear the costs of substantial political lobbying. Even in home countries, political lobbying is time-consuming and costly for business; we would expect the transaction costs (and the potential damage which may result from 'politicising' their preferences) of lobbying to be even higher for firms operating in foreign political jurisdictions. This implies that exit and voice are largely substitutes, so that significant political lobbying activities by TNCs would be evidence in favour of the weakness of structural power.[7]

The chapter has the following structure and argument. First, the convergence hypothesis is outlined, and a strong and weak version are distinguished. A second section asks if TNC preferences relating to FDI rules are coherent and consistent, as is required for the convergence process to work. Focusing upon the policy preferences of US-based TNCs, it argues that there is an identifiable and largely consistent set of international business preferences relating to FDI policy. A third section focuses on the evidence of FDI regime change in developing countries, since it is here that most convergence should occur.[8] I suggest that the empirical evidence is inconsistent with the claims of the convergence hypothesis in both its strong and weak forms. In particular, many of the most important developing host countries have attracted large amounts of FDI while maintaining policy regimes at odds with TNC preferences. This suggests that structural power (or, for that matter, the effects of political lobbying by TNCs) is weaker than claimed in the globalisation literature.

A final section asks why this is so. It argues that this literature has exaggerated the actual mobility of most FDI. Even for relatively mobile projects, the degree of competition between firms tends to limit the loss of power suffered by many host states. Globalisation literature has underestimated the collective action dilemma that confronts firms in oligopolistic sectors; the evidence suggests that globalisation often increases rather than reduces the ability of host states to maintain policies at odds with TNC preferences. A conclusion suggests this remains true even in the midst of financial crises. I also conclude that the structural weakness of TNCs reduces the ability of governments in advanced countries to negotiate stronger investment treaties with important developing countries.

The convergence hypothesis

Globalisation as a fact and an explanation of change in the international political economy is much in dispute, and it is difficult to locate a narrow set of hypotheses associated with it (Hirst and Thompson 1996; Boyer and Drache 1996; Keohane and Milner 1996). However, a core element of 'globalisation theory' is that enhanced capital mobility in a world divided into separate states constitutes a structural constraint upon national economic policy. The 'convergence hypothesis' goes further to assert that this constraint upon policy has increasing bite: *policies at odds with the preferences of mobile capital agents are undermined by the actuality or threat of exit.* While this claim is most often made with regard to portfolio capital flows (Andrews 1994), it is now commonly made with respect to FDI flows as well. For example, Scholte argues that '[global] firms can . . . with relative ease relocate production facilities and sales outlets to other jurisdictions if they find a particular state's regulations overly burdensome. Usually this threat alone is sufficient to make a state amenable to, *inter alia,* privatization and liberalization' (Scholte 1997: 443). Korten also argues the result of increased mobility has been a regulatory race to the bottom: 'The dream of the corporate empire-builders is being realized. The global system is harmonizing standards across country after country – down towards the lowest common denominator' (Korten 1995: 237).

The hypothesis can be divided into the following two propositions. First, the policy preferences of TNCs as a group are coherent, and these firms act in ways consistent with their preferences. Second, states suffer from a collective action problem that constrains them to converge upon TNC policy preferences through a process of regulatory and subsidy-based competition.

The first proposition is usually implicit rather than explicitly stated. Claims about the 'power of transnational capital' imply an ability of internationally mobile capital agents to achieve a set of coherent preferences. Those who regard the 'competition state' as a response to capital mobility assume that TNC preferences are widely known, and that entrepreneurial politicians respond directly to them (Cerny 1995: 610). Rarely is this assumption explored in the literature; nor is it asked if the preferences of owners and managers, or those of parent-based managers and affiliate-based managers, differ. The main argument is that 'capital agents', presumably managers acting according to the wishes of shareholders, favour policies that enhance profit opportunities, including those now commonly associated with the term 'liberalisation'. Fewer regulatory constraints upon business of all kinds, such as lower tax rates and fewer trade and capital account restrictions, are associated with a 'retreat of the state' in accord with international business preferences (Strange 1996).

Unfortunately, 'liberalisation' (like 'state retreat') is ambiguous, and in certain respects TNC preferences are likely to diverge from what are commonly understood as liberal policies and institutions. If firms are assumed to maximise profits and lower the costs of business in and across different political jurisdictions, they will prefer certain aspects associated with 'strong states', such as transparent and enforceable rules. A weak and corrupt judicial and political system clearly raises the costs of doing business, particularly for 'outsiders'. At the same time, however, they are likely to favour states open to business influence, rather than those where other social groups such as labour have entrenched influence. It also follows that TNCs will prefer jurisdictions that invest in productivity-enhancing infrastructure (including both physical and human capital), though they ought to prefer that immobile taxpayers bear the cost of its provision. They are also likely to prefer subsidies (such as investment incentives) funded by sources other than business taxation. Thus, when we talk of 'policy convergence', it should be defined in reference to the actual preferences of TNCs.

The second proposition, that state competition for mobile investments results in regime convergence, builds on the first. Productivity is often said to be increasingly firm-specific, so that TNCs in effect are minimising costs across different countries (Cerny 1995). In this view, TNCs prefer to invest in countries that offer the most favourable operating conditions at lowest cost. As Rodrik argues, globalisation exacerbates this tension, and the real question is not whether such institutional differences between countries matter, but how much (Rodrik 1997). Restrictions on the entry and exit and the operational flexibility of TNCs by political authorities raise the cost of doing business, and mobile corporations will 'vote with their feet'.

Why states may value mobile investment projects so highly is related. Most authors emphasise the firm-specific advantages TNCs provide to host states, particularly the technological and managerial assets necessary to compete in world markets (Dunning 1993: 557–8). The debt crisis was also important in changing attitudes towards FDI in many developing countries. More generally, the perceived failure of state-led development in many parts of the developing and former communist world is seen as having enhanced the ability of business to achieve its policy preferences. Radical scholars argue that a key element of the structural power of global capital is the dominance of the new liberal orthodoxy itself, which asserts the bankruptcy of such developmental strategies (Gill 1995; Scholte 1997). For a variety of reasons, states compete aggressively for FDI via unilateral policy liberalisation and the provision of various incentives for mobile firms. While in principle states could cooperate to prevent such policy arbitrage, in practice the competitive international political system means that there is an acute collective action problem preventing such regulatory coordination (Gill and Law 1988: 92; Gill 1995: 399; Stopford and Strange 1991: 215). The exit option of TNCs provides them with an enormous advantage over immobile states and relatively immobile labour and small business, and it provides states with a powerful incentive to defect from a coordination coalition.

What remains unclear, however, is the degree of convergence predicted by the hypothesis. A strong form, apparently put forward by Korten (quoted above), is that *the degree of existing convergence is great and policies increasingly reflect TNC preferences*. Policies inconsistent with TNC preferences are rendered unsustainable by the threat or actuality of capital flight. Other authors are vague on this question. As noted above, Scholte suggests the threat of exit by TNCs has made states 'amenable to privatization and liberalization'. I take this as a weak form of the hypothesis, which claims only that the direction of policy change is towards convergence, without suggesting the process to be complete. This makes it more difficult to test empirically. However, it does appear to claim at least that *FDI flows will be increasingly biased towards countries where the degree of policy convergence is greatest*.

TNC preferences

Are the investment policy preferences of TNCs coherent, as the convergence hypothesis assumes? For reasons of space, I concentrate here upon US TNC preferences, as revealed by their stance on the MAI negotiations, one of the key policy issues for American firms in the last few years. Some qualifications follow from this. Clearly, it would be wrong to generalise on the basis of TNCs from one major host country. However, the importance of US TNCs as a 'national' group means that they are the obvious first point of reference. The openness of the American political process and the high degree of political organisation of business in the US may also be exceptional, but this also makes it easier to identify the relevant policy preferences of TNCs.

Broad business coalitions

'Preferences' relating to many complex policy issues are more often the province of the industry organisation and the legal specialist than the senior executive. The result is that most firms in the US, as elsewhere, tend to rely upon general sectoral or broad industry organisations to formulate detailed policy preferences and lobbying strategies. As Bauer *et al.* found in their major study on the role of business in US trade politics, the function of pressure groups was often precisely 'to define the interests of its partisans' (Bauer *et al.* 1963: 339).

Broad overlapping US business associations have been the lead lobbies on international investment rules, at home and abroad. The most relevant here is the US Council for International Business (USCIB), the American affiliate of the International Chamber of Commerce (ICC), of the Business and Industry Advisory Committee (BIAC) to the OECD, and of the International Organization of Employers (IOE). Its main task is representing international business interests in US government and intergovernmental organisations, and accordingly it has taken the lead on investment issues, including the MAI negotiations (USCIB 1996a; Williamson 1998). A USCIB Investment Policy Committee has led delegations on MAI to Japan, and to US regional centres, state governments, and governors' associations. USCIB also has overlapping memberships with other business umbrella organisations such as the US Business Roundtable (BR), which led in lobbying on the Uruguay Round (Freeman 1996).

Another important forum is one of eight US Trade Representative Policy Advisory Committees, the Investment and Services Policy Advisory Committee (INSPAC), which provides USTR with specific advice in this area. The broader Advisory Committee on Trade Policy Negotiations (ACTPN) comprises forty-five members from representative parts of the US economy with international commercial interests, devised to provide broad guidance from the private sector to the administration on trade (and now investment) policy. In a report released in September 1996 (USTR 1996b), it argued that investment is probably 'the most important post-Uruguay Round new issue', bemoaning the lack of international discipline on governments' investment policies and supporting the US MAI strategy.

One other broad US business organisation worth mentioning for its stance on investment rules is the Organization for International Investment (OFII).[9] OFII represents over fifty US affiliates of major foreign TNCs in the US. Most are European and Japanese manufacturing firms, but there are some general services and insurance firms in the organisation. While OFII's main concern has been US adherence to international investment regimes, it liaises closely with other groups such as the BR and USCIB, since these latter groups are able to take a higher profile on MAI in Washington than can OFII. Also, firms such as Unilever, BASF and Sony are all active on MAI in both OFII and in USCIB (USCIB 1996b). OFII shares the objective of the other main US business organisations of prioritising the binding of developing and transition economies to 'high-standard' investment rules.

Sectoral coalitions

Given the crucial importance of FDI in the global strategies of services firms, it is not surprising that many services industry associations also tend to have clear stated positions on MAI. The Coalition of Service Industries (CSI) is a strong supporter of MAI, as it was of the GATS in the Uruguay Round. Support for MAI was pushed in 1996 by the Securities Industry Association (SIA), which chaired the CSI and wished to use the broader forum to push its views. The SIA/CSI lobbied especially hard to include portfolio as well as direct investment within the scope of the agreement, but the overall differences with the broader coalition positions are unimportant. The commercial banking industry appears to have been less vocal than the securities industry in its support of the MAI, though individual banks such as Citicorp have been major supporters. This may partly reflect the relative competitiveness of the US securities industry compared to commercial banks. Asia has been the biggest problem for many US financial services firms, as for US TNCs in general. Initially, the SIA supported the APEC process in the hope that it might make progress in this area, but the lack of progress led it to shift its attention to the MAI (SIA 1996). Over 1997 the SIA again shifted its attention to the ultimately successful WTO financial services negotiations, given the more direct relevance of these negotiations to the industry and their overlap with MAI on the issue of investment access.

The US manufacturing sector lobbies have appeared less vocal on the issue than the services sector. However, the National Association of Manufacturers (NAM) has been broadly positive, and there are individual firms which are highly globalised, such as IBM and Procter and Gamble, which have been supportive in various organisations mentioned above. The US electronics and automobile industries, which have increasingly globalised in recent years, are strong supporters, not least because they are among the most affected by restrictions such as performance requirements.

US business preferences on investment regimes

Despite some differences across the groups identified above, US business speaks with a fairly consistent voice on the question of international investment regimes. The key objectives are consistently enunciated by different business organisations, from active individual firms through sectoral organisations such as SIA to the broad umbrella groups such as USCIB and OFII. Broadly speaking, US business preferences amount to the desire for standard, consistent and enforceable rules which secure their access and property rights, and maximise their operating flexibility.

Specifically, these preferences are as follows. First, non-discriminatory treatment (the better of national and MFN treatment) for US investors and their international investments, with limited and specified exceptions. This demand includes, importantly, pre-establishment as well as post-establishment treatment, which amounts to a 'right of establishment' clause. Second, high standard investor protection, which include clear limits to expropriation and the right of the investor to due legal process and compensation. This includes the demand that investors have the right to impartial international arbitration in the event of a dispute with a host government ('investor–state dispute settlement'). Third, full operating freedom for investors, including the right to all investment-related financial transfers, prohibitions upon the imposition of performance requirements, and the right to transfer managerial personnel.

To summarise, US international business organisations have formulated clear preferences relating to international investment rules, in part because they have been in a position to influence government policy and negotiation strategies in the US and elsewhere in the OECD.[10] The clear priority of all groups is to bind the main developing and transition countries to high-standard investment rules, as these countries are seen as the main problems for US (and other) investors. While US TNCs have specific complaints about investment policy in the main OECD countries, which still account for over 90 per cent of the total stock of US FDI abroad, these are not the main targets of US business pressure. Groups such as USCIB see the establishment of a binding international investment regime to which all countries would adhere as the ultimate objective, and have put most of their lobbying effort into the MAI negotiations. Again, East Asia has generally been seen as the hardest nut to crack on the investment regime issue, and is identified as the main US international business concern by lobbies (USCIB 1996b; USTR 1996b).

Measuring convergence in developing countries

If TNCs have reasonably clear preferences relating to FDI policies in host countries, are these increasingly reflected in national policy practice? And if so, is the strong or the weak version of the convergence hypothesis valid? Inward investment policy regimes in developing countries are the focus of this section for the following reasons. First, developing countries attitudes towards inward FDI in the 1960s and 1970s were often hostile, and we could interpret the broad shift towards a more positive stance since then as supporting the convergence hypothesis. Second, as developing countries as a group are large net recipients of FDI, their FDI policy regimes are comparatively uncomplicated by the politics of outward investment. Finally, developing countries have not been as constrained by international investment-related agreements and norms developed in bodies such as the OECD, EU or GATT/WTO. For these reasons, they ought to provide the best case for the convergence hypothesis.

There is considerable evidence that policies in the developing world have moved towards a more positive stance towards inward FDI in recent years. The UN *World Investment Report* provides evidence for this in Table 3.1.

These aggregate figures do not separate the adoption and enforcement of liberal rules on inward FDI from the various incentive measures, such as direct subsidies or tax breaks. In fact, fully 29 per cent of the total changes in investment regimes in 1996 involved net new incentives for inward investors, slightly more than the 27 per cent accounted for by more liberal operational conditions for TNCs (UN 1997: 18). A further 9 per cent of changes were new promotional measures other than incentives. Overall, 33 per cent of the total changes for 1996 provided for net liberalisation of operating conditions and of ownership and sectoral restrictions. This appears consistent with TNC preferences and the convergence hypothesis.

However, these figures do not show how these trends and the remaining differences in the absolute levels of restrictiveness differ across countries. Most high-income countries have had relatively liberal inward investment regimes for some time, though they too have moved in the direction of liberalisation in recent years. This is presumably in part a matter of reciprocity, since these countries are large outward investors as well as having the largest inward flows. The OECD accounts for about 85 per cent of total world FDI outflows (and about 65 per cent

Table 3.1 Changes in inward investment regimes, all countries, 1991–6

Item	1991	1992	1993	1994	1995	1996
Number of countries introducing changes in their investment regimes	35	43	57	49	64	65
Number of changes	82	79	102	110	112	114
Of which:						
In the direction of liberalisation/promotion[a]	80	79	101	108	106	98
In the direction of control[b]	2	–	1	2	6	16

Source: UN, *World Investment Report*, 1997: 18.

Notes:

a Including measures aimed at strengthening market supervision, as well as incentives.

b Including measures aimed at reducing incentives.

of total world inflows) today, and the other biggest investors include Hong Kong and Singapore. Many developing countries, however, remain wary towards FDI and considerably more restrictive than Western Europe and North America, even if they have moved in the same direction. Most of the newly industrialising countries of East Asia fall into this category, though as we shall see this has not prevented them from enjoying high rates of FDI inflow.

Attitudes in Taiwan and particularly South Korea are considerably less liberal than the OECD average because of strong nationalist and developmental traditions, despite the fact that these countries are becoming significant outward investors themselves. Others such as Indonesia, Thailand, China and Malaysia are major host countries, but are also heavy users of performance requirements, sectoral prohibitions, screening, equity requirements, and other restrictive measures (see Table 3.2). In Thailand, for example, the Alien Business Law of 1972, still unrepealed, requires every registered business in Thailand to have majority Thai ownership, and prohibits minority foreign ownership in up to sixty-eight specific industries (*Financial Times* 1998d).[11] While most developing countries have moved away from the traditional dependency view of unrestricted foreign investment as a form of imperialism, some such as India retain remnants of this position. Others, like Brazil and especially Argentina, which traditionally fell into the same category, have moved in recent years to liberalise substantially their inward investment regime. Nevertheless, Brazil also remains considerably more restrictive than the OECD average.

To get an idea of the outstanding levels of restrictiveness in the major developing countries, Table 3.2 provides a rough qualitative assessment of the relative restrictiveness of their inward investment regimes for US investors in 1995–6, based upon reports from US embassies in host countries. This annual source, supplemented by reports by the USTR, is one of the most consistent assessments of individual countries' investment regimes available. The table shows key aspects of the investment regimes of the top fifteen developing and transition economies in terms of US FDI inflows in the 1991–5 period. These countries accounted for almost 20 per cent of total US FDI flows in this period, and received more than the rest of the developing/transition world combined.

It would be wrong to take the overall measure of restrictiveness for each country too seriously. First, measures have been ranked according to high, medium and low levels of relative restrictiveness, with 'low' approximating average practice in the advanced industrial countries. Second, policies and practice have been evolving in recent years in a number of developing and transition countries, and this provides an indication of the position in 1995–6. Finally, the source of the data is concerned with restrictiveness for US TNCs rather than TNCs in general. However, non-US TNCs usually enjoy lower standards of protection and liberalisation in host countries than US firms.

Nevertheless, Table 3.2 shows that despite significant liberalisation in a number of countries, FDI policy regimes remain very restrictive in some. China is the most conspicuous case. Despite the *ad hoc* opening of particular sectors to foreign investment since 1978 and the boom in inward FDI which began in the late 1980s, it remains highly restrictive on almost all measures. Across the Asian region in

Table 3.2 Restrictiveness of investment policy regimes for US investors:
top fifteen low- and middle-income recipients of US FDI 1991–5

Country/region	Cumulative US FDI flows, 1991–5	% Total US FDI flows 1991–5	Inward investment regime characteristics		
			Important sectoral prohibitions	Restrictive equity requirements in other sectors	Non-transparent/ arbitrary screening
Brazil	14,106	4.7%	M	M	L
Mexico	11,597	3.9%	M	M	L
Argentina	5,530	1.8%	L	L	L
Panama	3,826	1.3%	L	L	L
Venezuela	3,801	1.3%	M	M	L
Chile	3,018	1.0%	L	L	L
Thailand	2,689	0.9%	M	M	L
Indonesia	2,620	0.9%	H	M	H
South Korea	2,038	0.7%	M	M	M
Taiwan	2,011	0.7%	M	M	L
Malaysia	1,981	0.7%	M	H	M
China	1,851	0.6%	H	H	H
Hungary	1,758	0.6%	L	L	L
Saudi Arabia	1,339	0.4%	H	M	H
Philippines	1,135	0.4%	M	H	L
Top fifteen low- and middle-income countries	59,300	19.9%	1.9	1.9	1.6
World	299,074	100.0%			

Sources: US Department of State, *Country Commercial Guides* (various);
USTR, *National Trade Estimate* (various);
Report of the Commission on United States-Pacific Trade and Investment Policy,
Building American Prosperity in the 21st Century (Washington, April 1997).

general, as has been highlighted in the recent crisis, important sectors such as
financial services have remained much more closed than average, and as compared
to Latin America (OECD 1998: 45–50). Also, while many have liberalised (though
hardly completely) entry and exit restrictions on TNCs, the use of operating restrictions in the relatively interventionist states in East Asia remains high on average.
This is consistent with evidence of a general shift in developing countries in the
1970s and 1980s away from entry and exit restrictions towards the use of performance requirements aimed at enhancing the contribution of FDI to the host
economy.[12]

Another indication of relative restrictiveness in a different group of countries
is given in Table 3.3. This shows countries with which the US has negotiated a
'high-standard' BIT, which provides formal rules of the kind US TNCs prefer.[13]
By 1998, the US had concluded forty-two BITs since 1982 (the first was with

Table 3.2 cont.

Discrimin- atory treatment	Investment incentives	Performance requirements	Poor intellectual property protection	Difficulties in repatriating profits	Inadequate arbitration mechanisms	Overall score
M	M	H	M	M	M	18
L	L	L	M	L	L	15
L	M	L	M	L	L	11
L	M	L	M	L	L	11
L	M	M	M	M	M	16
L	L	L	M	M	M	14
L	M	M	M	L	M	15
H	M	H	M	L	H	22
M	L	M	M	M	M	19
L	M	L	L	L	L	12
M	M	M	L	L	L	16
H	H	H	H	M	H	24
L	M	L	L	L	L	10
H	M	M	M	L	M	20
L	M	L	M	L	M	15
1.6	2.1	1.7	1.9	1.3	1.7	16

Notes:
H = high restrictiveness (= 3); M = medium restrictiveness (=2);
L = low restrictiveness (= 1). The scores are reversed for investment incentives.

Panama), of which thirty-one were in force (Bureau of Economic and Business Affairs 1998a). There are only two countries in the top fifteen (Argentina and Panama) identified in Table 3.2, though Mexico provides approximately similar treatment through NAFTA. The other forty countries with which the US has negotiated BITs are not important recipients of US FDI flows.

This must be interpreted cautiously. There is inevitably a big difference between formal investment rules and the actual treatment of foreign investors. Focusing only upon formal FDI policies might provide a misleading picture if on the ground these rules are ignored (Haggard 1990: 214). However, the categories in Table 3.2 take into account both formal rules and actual practice, since US embassy reports take note of the practical difficulties raised by American businesses investing in the host country. Also, in sectors where FDI is prohibited or severely restricted by formal rules, individual TNCs cannot begin to bargain for better

Table 3.3 US bilateral investment treaties

	Country	Date of signature	Date entered into force
1	Albania	January 11, 1995	January 4, 1998
2	Argentina	November 14, 1991	October 20, 1994
3	Armenia	September 23, 1992	March 29, 1996
4	**Azerbaijan**	August 1, 1997	(See note 2)
5	Bangladesh	March 12, 1986	July 25, 1989
6	Belarus	January 15, 1994	(See note 4)
7	**Bolivia**	April 17, 1998	(See note 1)
8	Bulgaria	September 23, 1992	June 2, 1994
9	Cameroon	February 26, 1986	April 6, 1989
10	Congo, Democratic Republic[6]	August 3, 1984	July 28, 1989
11	Congo, Republic (Brazzaville)	February 12, 1990	August 13, 1994
12	Croatia	July 13, 1996	(See note 1)
13	Czech Republic[5]	October 22, 1991	December 19, 1992
14	Ecuador	August 27, 1993	May 11, 1997
15	Egypt	March 11, 1986	June 27, 1992
16	**Estonia**	April 19, 1994	February 16, 1997
17	Georgia	March 7, 1994	August 17, 1997
18	Grenada	May 2, 1986	March 3, 1989
19	Haiti	December 13, 1983	(See note 1)
20	Honduras	July 1, 1995	(See note 1)
21	Jamaica	February 4, 1994	March 7, 1997
22	**Jordan**	July 2, 1997	(See note 1)
23	Kazakhstan	May 19, 1992	January 12, 1994
24	Kyrgyzstan	January 19, 1993	January 12, 1994
25	**Latvia**	January 13, 1995	December 26, 1996
26	**Lithuania**	January 14, 1998	(See note 1)
27	Moldova	April 21, 1993	November 25, 1994
28	Mongolia	October 6, 1994	January 1, 1997
29	Morocco	July 22, 1985	May 29, 1991
30	Nicaragua	July 1, 1995	(See note 1)
31	Panama	October 27, 1982	May 30, 1991
32	Poland	March 21, 1990	August 6, 1994
33	Romania	May 28, 1992	January 15, 1994
34	Russia	June 17, 1992	(See note 3)
35	Senegal	December 6, 1983	October 25, 1990
36	Slovakia[5]	October 22, 1991	December 19, 1992
37	Sri Lanka	September 20, 1991	May 1, 1993
38	Trinidad and Tobago	September 26, 1994	December 26, 1996
39	Tunisia	May 15, 1990	February 7, 1993
40	Turkey	December 3, 1985	May 18, 1990
41	Ukraine	March 4, 1994	November 16, 1996
42	Uzbekistan	December 16, 1994	(See note 2)

Source: Bureau of Economic and Business Affairs, US Department of State, *US Bilateral Investment Treaties* (BITs), mimeo, 27 April 1998.

Notes:
1   Entry into force pending ratification by both parties and exchange of instruments of ratification.
2   Entry into force pending US ratification and exchange of instruments of ratification.
3   Entry into force pending other Party's ratification and exchange of instruments of ratification.
4   Entry into force pending exchange of instruments of ratification.
5   Treaty signed on 22 October 1991, with the Czech and Slovak Federal Republic and has been in force for the Czech Republic and Slovakia as separate states since 1 January 1993.
6   Formerly Zaire.
7   US investment in Canada and Mexico is covered by Chapter Eleven of the North American Free Trade Agreement (NAFTA) which contains provisions similar to BIT obligations, though with more exceptions and reservations.

treatment. Finally, it is unlikely that growing divergence between formal FDI regimes and state policy in individual cases can be sustained over long periods of time; liberalisation is often due to a recognition that formal rules were being undermined by increasing numbers of specific deals.[14]

Is the liberalisation that has occurred consistent with either version of the convergence hypothesis? It is clearly at odds with the strong version, since it is evident that convergence of policies upon TNC preferences is lacking, even in the most 'liberal' developing countries. More interestingly, the evidence also casts doubt upon the weaker version. There are conspicuous exceptions to the prediction that FDI flows favour countries with liberal FDI regimes. This appears to be true not just for US FDI. Table 3.4 ranks the major host country recipients of world FDI inflows over the period 1990–6. China, which has a highly restrictive FDI regime compared to most middle income developing countries, received more FDI in the 1990s than any other country except the (much more liberal) US, and about a third of total non-OECD FDI inflows. Even leaving aside China as an exceptional case, there are at least four of the next six most important developing country recipients that exhibit medium to high levels of restrictiveness towards FDI: Malaysia, Brazil, Indonesia, and Thailand. This is consistent with the strongly stated concerns of TNCs and business lobbies that key developing country investment regimes, particularly in East Asia, remain a major problem for international firms. It is contrary to the predictions of both the strong and weak forms of the convergence hypothesis.

We would expect a negative correlation between the levels of FDI inflows and the score of restrictiveness in Table 3.2. In fact, it is -0.35, which provides limited support for the weak form of the convergence hypothesis. However, this low negative correlation should be interpreted cautiously, due to the likelihood of omitted variable bias and the low number of observations, not to mention the dubious nature of the restrictiveness scores. Only a multivariate regression analysis, which controls for other variables that determine the geographic pattern of FDI flows, could estimate the marginal influence of FDI policy regimes on such flows. This line of enquiry is plagued with difficulties and is pursued elsewhere rather than here.[15]

The larger group of countries with which the US has BITs provides less support for the convergence hypothesis. Of the twenty-two developing countries whose cumulative FDI inflows from the US over 1991–6 exceeded $1 billion, only three had negotiated BITs (Panama, Argentina, and Jamaica) and a further three belonged to NAFTA (Mexico) or joined the OECD (Korea and Hungary). For the other 112 developing countries for which figures are available, cumulative US FDI inflows over this period were less than $1 billion for each, but thirty-one of these had negotiated BITs with the US. In other words, using $1 billion as the cut-off point, the conditional probability that the host country has a high standard investment regime is approximately the same above and below this point. Indeed, twenty-four of the thirty-one countries with BITs each received less than $100 million in cumulative FDI inflows over this period. Overall, US BITs cover only about one-seventh of the total US FDI stock in developing and transition

Table 3.4 Total FDI inflows by principal host country, 1990–6

	Host country	Cumulative FDI inflows, 1990–6 ($ million)
1	*US*	327,074
2	**China**	158,462
3	*UK*	146,671
4	*France*	124,850
5	*Belgium-Luxembourg*	68,526
6	*Spain*	62,737
7	*Netherlands*	47,881
8	*Canada*	44,921
9	*Australia*	44,468
10	**Mexico**	40,222
11	*Singapore*	39,176
12	*Sweden*	38,188
13	**Malaysia**	31,967
14	*Italy*	26,534
15	**Brazil**	22,876
16	**Argentina**	22,409
17	*Germany*	21,663
18	**Indonesia**	20,773
19	*Denmark*	15,810
20	*New Zealand*	15,286
21	*Switzerland*	15,170
22	**Thailand**	14,238
23	**Hungary**	12,508
24	*Hong Kong*	11,639
25	*Portugal*	11,081
26	**Poland**	11,075
27	*Norway*	10,720
28	**Chile**	10,152
29	**Colombia**	9,814
30	**Peru**	9,540
	Top 30 total	1,436,431
	World	1,659,092

Source: OECD, *Foreign Direct Investment and Economic Development: Lessons from Six Emerging Economies* (OECD, 1998): 16, Table 2; UN, *World Investment Report* 1997.

Note:
High income countries in italics, others in bold.

economies. If Panama (2.3 per cent of total US FDI stock in 1996) is excluded, BITs' coverage is even more negligible.

In sum, although there are some examples of considerable convergence over the past decade, there is little evidence of a systematic bias of FDI flows towards countries with investment regimes favoured by TNCs. This means that the nature of this convergence is inconsistent with both strong and weak versions of globalisation theory. It is more accurate to say that FDI has been rising rapidly in some important developing countries in spite of, rather than because of, liberalisation of the regulations on inward FDI. An immediate and obvious implication is that much globalisation theory has exaggerated TNC power over host states.

Explaining outcomes: the limits of structural power

Mobility and structural power

Why is the evidence at odds with the convergence hypothesis? One possible explanation is that policies and policy-makers exhibit inertia and do not respond rapidly to market signals. As Frieden and Rogowski have shown, one can predict liberalisation as a rational policy response to globalisation using standard neo-classical assumptions (Frieden and Rogowski 1996). As the costs of closure increase with international economic integration, economic pressures to move towards more *laissez faire* policies should increase. In this view, the main explanation for the asymmetrical pattern of liberalisation across countries noted above is that domestic institutions block or channel the responses of interest groups to inter-national price signals in ways which inhibit such policy reform (Milner and Keohane 1996). However, one problem with this line of argument is that neo-classical assumptions may be misleading in the case of FDI. As economists have emphasised, FDI can only be explained and understood in the context of highly imperfect markets (Dunning 1993; Caves 1982). Thus, the high costs of closure assumed in neoclassical political economy models no longer follow, and countries may be able to sustain restrictive policies over long periods of time (Lall 1997).

This line of reasoning is unconvincing. Even if restrictions are optimal from a national economic standpoint, they are not from the point of view of global firms.[16] If performance requirements impose higher operating costs on TNC affiliates, such countries could still be shunned by mobile investors, as many developmentalists fear. The only likely explanation of the ability of some countries to resist policy convergence upon TNC preferences, therefore, is that TNCs themselves do not base their location decisions (entirely) upon host country investment regimes. This is supported by much survey evidence, which has asked firms their reasons for making (country) investment location decisions. Most such studies, as well as statistical research, have shown that market size, growth prospects, geographical location, access to large regional markets, local infrastructure, human capital, and political stability are more important factors in attracting investment than the nature of the FDI policy regime. Many of these factors are beyond the policy control of governments. Nor has this evidence suggested that incentives have a significant impact on the investment location decision across countries. Some survey data does suggest that after the initial country location decision has been made, factors such as incentives and policy differences between sub-state regions may influence the final location decision, but such factors are apparently of marginal importance at the initial stage (Dunning 1993: 139–48).

Of course, degrees of mobility vary considerably by sector and by project, and so therefore should host country bargaining power. Domestic market-seeking and resource-based FDI is mainly affected by domestic resources and market prospects. Large countries will enjoy greater bargaining power, *ceteris paribus*, for projects which are domestic-market oriented. For countries like China or Brazil, if one firm dislikes the conditions of entry imposed by the host country there are usually others eager to take its place. The evidence shows that historically the great majority of FDI projects is aimed at improving access to the domestic market rather than international markets (Table 3.5, and OECD 1998: 21–2). In Argentina and a number of other developing countries in the last decade, a large proportion of FDI inflows have been privatisation-related, often in utilities and infrastructure and hence particularly immobile (OECD 1998: 27–32). This suggests that the claim of Scholte (1997) that TNC mobility makes states amenable to policies of privatisation is back to front.

Export-oriented or 'efficiency-seeking' FDI, on the other hand, should be more sensitive to the national FDI policy regime, as confirmed by various studies (Haggard 1990: 221–2; Kobrin 1987). Table 3.5 shows the sales pattern of US affiliates in 1994 by country of location for all industries and for the manufacturing sector. Manufacturing FDI in East Asia, by comparison with Latin America, has been more export-oriented, with a wide range of variation. Countries like China, India, Indonesia, and Korea follow the Latin American pattern, partly because of their domestic market size and partly because of import substitution policies. Singapore, Malaysia and Thailand stand out as countries that have successfully attracted export-oriented manufacturing FDI, particularly in electronic and automobile components. Yet Malaysia and Thailand have done so while maintaining comparatively restrictive inward FDI regimes. It is true that they have often relieved export-oriented FDI projects of some restrictions, providing some support for the weak version of the convergence hypothesis. Malaysia, for example, often exempts export-oriented FDI from the otherwise onerous restrictions on equity ownership, and many developing countries have created Export Processing Zones (EPZs) for precisely this reason.

However, EPZs tend to be isolated from the rest of the economy. By offering better deals to some, host countries prevent the emergence of concerted action by a unified group of investors by giving individual mobile firms an incentive to defect. Also, even in sectors in which technology is crucial and mobility may be high, the high levels of competition between US, Japanese, and European firms has reduced the arbitrage pressure on host countries' policy regimes (Lipson 1985: 161–82; Moran 1985: 8–9; Oman *et al.* 1997: 210–12). Another point is that technological change, often seen as shifting power away from states towards firms, has often reduced the minimum efficient plant scale in many industries, increasing the bargaining power of smaller countries in the process (Bartlett and Seleny 1998). Overall, even for relatively mobile export-oriented industry, attractions other than FDI policy (such as geographic position, regional trade liberalisation, physical infrastructure and human capital) are probably more important in location decisions of TNCs (Dunning 1993: 144). Countries like Malaysia, which have often waived equity restrictions and provided tax incentives to export-oriented projects, have also required substantive local content requirements in

Table 3.5 Sales by US MNC affiliates by selected country/region of affiliate, 1994 ($MM)

	All industries				Manufacturing affiliates			
	Total sales	*Local sales*	*Exports*	*Exports/ total*	*Total sales*	*Local sales*	*Exports*	*Exports/ total*
All countries	1,435,901	963,779	472,122	33%	697,554	413,873	283,681	41%
Canada	194,004	134,197	59,807	31%	108,969	57,823	51,146	47%
Europe	796,816	516,754	280,062	35%	396,154	223,925	172,229	43%
Latin America	134,808	91,832	42,976	32%	76,287	57,595	18,692	25%
Argentina	11,545	10,086	1,459	13%	7,182	6,084	1,098	15%
Brazil	33,232	29,238	3,994	12%	25,445	21,726	3,719	15%
Chile	4,937	3,551	1,386	28%	1,789	1,150	639	36%
Colombia	6,501	5,620	881	14%	3,125	2,774	351	11%
Ecuador	795	564	231	29%	300	241	59	20%
Venezuela	5,431	4,955	476	9%	3,622	3,178	444	12%
Mexico	39,420	27,022	12,398	31%	30,873	20,033	10,840	35%
Panama	NA	NA	NA	NA	218	198	20	9%
Africa	14,866	9,485	5,381	36%	3,532	2,807	725	21%
Nigeria	3,141	810	2,331	74%	NA	NA	NA	NA
South Africa	3,629	3,308	321	9%	1,871	1,792	79	4%
Middle East	8,070	4,688	3,382	42%	1,769	988	781	44%
Israel	2,351	1,519	832	35%	1,561	863	698	45%
Saudi Arabia	887	670	217	24%	4	49	1	25%
Asia/Pacific	281,081	204,301	76,780	27%	110,841	70,734	40,107	36%
Australia	42,552	36,349	6,203	15%	17,367	14,303	3,064	18%
China	3,225	2,520	705	22%	1,921	1,450	471	25%
Hong Kong	29,729	16,769	12,960	44%	5,686	3,193	2,493	44%
India	983	934	49	5%	724	681	43	6%
Indonesia	8,229	3,012	5,217	63%	1,727	1,549	178	10%
Japan	97,604	88,280	9,324	10%	37,361	31,941	5,420	15%
S. Korea	5,553	4,883	670	12%	2,961	2,500	461	16%
Malaysia	11,579	6,700	4,879	42%	6,684	2,524	4,160	62%
New Zealand	4,685	4,279	406	9%	NA	1,054	NA	NA
Philippines	5,211	3,884	1,327	25%	3,053	1,921	1,132	37%
Singapore	46,871	17,808	29,063	62%	21,512	4,234	17,278	80%
Taiwan	13,690	10,701	2,989	22%	6,394	3,649	2,745	43%
Thailand	9,627	7,019	2,608	27%	3,838	1,451	2,387	62%

Source: Bureau of Economic Analysis, US Department of Commerce, *US Foreign Direct Investment Abroad: 1994 Benchmark Survey* (BEA, 1998).

turn (OECD 1998: 80). Other studies have found manufacturing TNCs tend to remain in host countries even when tax holidays and other incentives expire or are removed (Stopford and Strange 1991: 101,147).

Hence, mobility appears to make some difference, and truly 'footloose' FDI is likely to receive more liberal treatment. Overall, however, other factors predominate in the location decisions of TNCs, and the bulk of FDI is domestic market-seeking.

East Asia has been highly attractive over the past decade or more, primarily because of its growth prospects, allowing such countries to maintain policy regimes that diverge significantly from TNC preferences. In contrast, many African and former communist countries now have very liberal policy regimes in comparison with most of East Asia and Latin America but receive a fraction of the inward investment. The convergence hypothesis might plausibly be turned on its head: the major developing host countries in East Asia and Latin America attract FDI because of their economic prospects and are accordingly under considerably less pressure to adopt policies which favour inward investors.

Ideology and structural power

Even if mobility is substantially less than globalisation theorists suggest, does a *perception* by states that FDI policies matter for location decisions by firms promote a competitive liberalisation process? If true, this would attest to the power of ideas, as suggested in Gramscian accounts of the structural power of capital, and it might also limit the effects of rivalry among firms for dominant positions in key emerging markets. However, the evidence is also inconsistent with this view. First, as noted above, the extent of policy competition among states for FDI has been exaggerated, with important developing countries maintaining restrictive policies over long periods. Second, the argument that change is ideologically-driven is inconsistent with the differentiated pattern of opening across sectors and over different aspects of FDI policy in the developing world in recent years. If policy change were ideological in nature, we would expect an across-the-board liberalisation pattern. While this appears to be true for some countries (e.g. Argentina or the Czech Republic), most countries in East Asia and Latin America have embraced very *ad hoc* liberalisation.[17]

The Gramscian view portrays liberalisation in zero-sum terms and as a gain largely for capital, whereas developing countries have often felt able to regulate inward investment to their benefit. For countries like China and Malaysia, liberalising entry restrictions in particular has been seen as enhancing national development opportunities (Xiaoqiang 1997). More liberal rules can also enhance host country bargaining power. As Bartlett and Seleny point out for the case of automobile TNC investment in central Europe, the adherence to liberal FDI rules by the transition economies enabled host governments to resist TNC demands for preferential concessions which departed from the rules (Bartlett and Seleny 1998). The recent shift in thinking in developing countries is better described as pragmatic rather than ideologically blinkered: governments recognise that FDI can contribute to development, but only if certain restrictions are placed upon their affiliate operations to enhance their contribution to the local economy. The ideology of neo-liberalism is no match for the ideology of economic nationalism when the two conflict. As a recent OECD study on investment policy in emerging economies concluded:

> While there has been a growing acknowledgment of the role that direct investment can play in stimulating economic growth and development, there

remains a tremendous diversity in approaches of countries in their policies towards FDI, as well as a lingering scepticism in certain spheres as to the inevitability or universality of the benefits from FDI . . . As a result, many countries screen incoming investment and retain extensive controls on foreign participation in particular sectors. Performance requirements on investment are sometimes still considered necessary or desirable to ensure that the activities of foreign multinationals are consonant with host country development strategies.

(OECD 1998: 7–8)

Conclusion

Globalisation theory has exaggerated the degree of mobility and structural power enjoyed by TNCs in the world political economy. The claim that states suffer from a collective action problem *vis-à-vis* TNCs is also misleading. It appears to be firms rather than states that have suffered from collective action problems, since there has been no strong tendency on the part of TNCs to avoid China, Indonesia or Malaysia simply because they dislike aspects of these countries' investment regimes. While TNCs investing in countries like China or Indonesia would prefer these countries to provide a strong liberal investment regime, the sheer attractiveness of these economies for most investors has prevented them from wielding power over the host government to force such liberalisation.

Will the current financial crisis in Asia and elsewhere change this? Haggard and Maxfield have argued that private capital agents may be able to overcome the collective action problem during balance of payments crises, when herd behaviour predominates (Haggard and Maxfield 1996). However, even if this is true for portfolio capital, the exercise of the exit option by long term capital is less credible given the relative immobility and illiquidity of fixed assets. The much lower volatility of direct investment flows in balance of payments financing compared to portfolio flows reduces the incentive for states to liberalise treatment of FDI in crises. Yet there is some evidence of a link. For example, in 1976, Peru reversed a ban on new oil contracts with foreign firms in the wake of a foreign exchange crisis (Stepan 1978. 286–9). More recently, due to its payments and domestic financial crisis, Thailand has removed some important constraints on inward investment in the Thai financial sector (*Financial Times* 1998f). Since the Asian crisis began in mid-1997, there have been a series of further FDI liberalisation measures in most of the affected countries, often as part of IMF packages. According to a recent ICC/UNCTAD survey, most East Asian countries affected have relaxed or removed limits on foreign shareholding limits, particularly with the view to promote inward FDI in the troubled domestic financial sector (ICC/UNCTAD 1998: annex).

However, there is a difference between announcements of relaxations made in the heat of a crisis and actual policy change. It was initially thought that Thailand would allow foreign investors to bid for the estimated $19 billion in assets of the fifty-six finance companies that were shut down in 1997 (much of which is property), to help restore confidence and improve sale values. However, the return of confidence in early 1998 led the government to backtrack on this pledge, and to shelve plans to increase the number of years foreigners may hold property lease-holds and to remove foreign ownership restrictions on most businesses. Actual foreign takeovers have been rarer than first expected; Citibank's deal to take over First Bangkok City Bank collapsed in mid-February 1998 (*Financial Times* 1998c). A Thai government proposal to remove most restrictions on inward investment was approved by cabinet in August 1998, a year after the onset of the crisis, but this law still required passage by Parliament (*Financial Times* 1998d).

The ratification of such proposals can be difficult. There is great sensitivity and political resistance in the region to a 'fire-sale' of domestically-owned assets to foreign firms in a crisis. The *Financial Times* recently noted of Malaysia that in spite of the severity of the crisis, 'they are not prepared to sacrifice the sacred cow of majority control of significant banking institutions' (*Financial Times* 1998b). The ICC/UNCTAD study which looked at this question also noted con-tinuing restrictions on hostile takeovers across the region (ICC/UNCTAD 1998: 6). One could add that much of the pressure for policy liberalisation has come from the IMF rather than the market itself, consistent with a more traditional view of power in the international system than with that provided in globalisation theories. Finally, Malaysia's decision to impose extremely strict capital controls in September 1998 is at odds with both the Haggard-Maxfield model and the preferences of TNCs, showing that crises can produce severe backlashes against globalisation in all its forms (*Financial Times* 1998e).

A final implication of the argument presented here is that the structural weakness of global firms also weakens attempts by home country governments to negotiate stronger international investment regimes with developing host coun-tries. USTR representatives admit that obtaining BITs with East Asia will probably involve making concessions on some of the basic principles of the US model BIT, because these countries are so attractive to investors that they have little incentive to sign up to strong rules (USTR 1996a). In other words, US business objectives are likely to be compromised ultimately because firms find it difficult not to invest in the key target countries. This also makes it unlikely that US firms would support a tough retaliatory policy on developing countries that did not agree to bilateral investment negotiations or any future MAI treaty (which now looks very unlikely). In the end, the main hope of government negotiators and business lobbies seems to be that if developing countries do not sign, they will be denied FDI (Malan 1996). As we have seen, evidence for this optimistic assumption is hard to find. If anything, globalisation has strengthened the ability of key host countries to pursue policies at odds with the interests of TNCs and Western governments. Thus, market power is not likely to provide a substitute for tough intergovernmental negotiations on investment issues for some time to come.

Notes

I wish to thank the generous support of two institutions: the Pacific Council on International Policy, Los Angeles, where I was a research fellow in 1996, and Oxford University, for allowing me a year's leave. Thanks are also due to Peter Muchlinski,

Charles Oman, Jan Aart Scholte, Susan Strange, and Chris Wilkie for comments on an earlier draft of this paper, and to panel participants at a conference on Non-State Actors and Authority in the Global System, 31 October to 1 November 1997, Warwick University (UK). Remaining errors are the responsibility of the author.

1 For simplicity, I use the term 'TNCs' throughout, but take no position on the issue of whether such firms are in practice transnational, multinational, or merely international in character.
2 See Korten (1995), and for an earlier example, Barnet and Müller (1974).
3 For sceptical views on these questions, see Lawrence (1996) and Garrett (1998).
4 See the contribution by Elizabeth Smythe to this volume.
5 See testimony by Wallach (1998).
6 A statement by the environmental NGO, Friends of the Earth, is representative: '[T]he need for an [MAI] agreement liberalizing foreign investment rules seems questionable *since foreign investors can largely dictate the terms of their investment already*' (Durbin 1997; italics added).
7 See in general Hirschman (1970), and Rodrik (1997: 70).
8 This point is argued later.
9 Most of what follows is from an interview with Todd Malan (1996).
10 One likely divergence between expressed and real preferences occurs with incentives. Although TNC lobbies avoid mentioning the maximisation of incentives as one of their policy objectives, they are the main beneficiaries of the incentives some governments and local authorities provide to attract FDI.
11 It should be noted that the US–Thai Treaty of Amity and Economic Relations of 1966 exempts US investors from many of the restrictions imposed by the 1972 law.
12 For a general overview, see Lipson (1985) and Oman (1989). See also Stopford and Strange (1991: 101,147).
13 'US Model BIT', mimeo, USTR. See also Bureau of Economic and Business Affairs (1998b).
14 Another problem is that embassy reports provide only a general description of a country's treatment of foreign investors, whereas individual TNCs may be able to strike better (or worse) bargains. This question requires research on individual state-firm bargains, but it is not pursued here.
15 See Walter (1999). For an overview of the existing empirical literature, see Dunning (1993: chapter 6).
16 A possible exception being trade protection that favours inward investors.
17 Even in the paradigm case of the neo-liberal Czech government, policy has been more nationalistic and restrictive in practice. See Muchlinski 1996: 662.

References

Andrews, David M. (1994) 'Capital mobility and state autonomy', *International Studies Quarterly* 38: 193–218.
Barnet, Richard J. and Ronald E. Müller (1974) *Global Reach: The Power of the Multinational Corporations*, New York: Simon and Shuster.
Bartlett, David and Anna Seleny (1998) 'The political enforcement of liberalism: bargaining, institutions, and auto multinationals in Hungary', *International Studies Quarterly* 42: 319–38.
Bauer, Raymond A., Ithiel de Sola Pool, and Lewis A. Dexter (1963) *American Business and Public Policy: The Politics of Foreign Trade*, New York: Atherton.
Boyer, Robert and Daniel Drache (eds) (1996) *States Against Markets: The Limits of Globalization*, London: Routledge.
Bureau of Economic and Business Affairs (1998a), US Department of State, *Multilateral Agreement on Investment: The Facts*, mimeo, 23 March.

—— (1998b), US Department of State, *U.S. Bilateral Investment Treaties (BITs)*, mimeo, April 27.

Caves, Richard E. (1982) *Multinational Enterprise and Economic Analysis*, Cambridge: Cambridge University Press.

Cerny, Philip G. (1995) 'Globalization and the changing logic of collective action', *International Organization* 49(4): 595–625.

Chakwin, Naomi and Naved Hamid (1997) 'Economic environment in Asia for investment', in Oman *et al.* (eds) (1997), *Investing in Asia*, Paris: OECD Development Centre: 208–23.

Dunning, John H. (1993) *Multinational Enterprises and the Global Economy*, Wokingham: Addison-Wesley.

Durbin, Andrea (1997) 'Transnational bill of rights: negotiations for a multilateral agreement on investment', *Tools for Change Newsletter* 1(2).

Financial Times (1998a) 'Bye-bye, MAI?', 19 February.

—— (1998b) 'Malaysia banks feel the strain as merger efforts go ahead', 18 February.

—— (1998c) 'First in, first out?', 25 February.

—— (1998d) 'Thailand to end curbs on foreign ownership', 20 August.

—— (1998e) 'Controlling capital flows', 2 September.

—— (1998f) 'Thai rules relaxed for foreigners', 15 October.

Freeman, Harry (1996), Business Roundtable lobbyist, interview 6 June, Washington D.C.

Frieden, Jeffry and Ronald Rogowski (1996) 'The impact of the international economy on national policies: an overview', in Keohane and Milner (eds) *Internationalization and Domestic Politics*, Cambridge: Cambridge University Press: 25–47.

Garrett, Geoffrey (1998) *Partisan Politics in the Global Economy*, Cambridge: Cambridge University Press.

Gill, Stephen (1995) 'Globalisation, market civilisation, and disciplinary neoliberalism', *Millennium,* 24(3): 399–423.

Gill, Stephen and David Law (1988) *The Global Political Economy*, Hemel Hempstead: Harvester-Wheatsheaf.

Haggard, Stephan (1990) *Pathways from the Periphery*, Ithaca: Cornell University Press.

Haggard, Stephan and Sylvia Maxfield (1996) 'The political economy of financial internationalization in the developing world', *International Organization* 50(1): 35–68.

Hirschman, Albert O. (1970) *Exit, Voice, and Loyalty: Responses to Decline in Firms, Organizations and States*, Cambridge, Mass.: Harvard University Press.

Hirst, Paul and Grahame Thompson (1996) *Globalization in Question*, Cambridge: Polity Press.

ICC/UNCTAD (1998) *The Financial Crisis in Asia and Foreign Direct Investment*, mimeo, February.

Keohane, Robert O. and Helen V. Milner (eds) (1996) *Internationalization and Domestic Politics*, Cambridge: Cambridge University Press.

Kobrin, Stephen J. (1987) 'Testing the bargaining hypothesis in the manufacturing sector in developing countries', *International Organization* 41(4): 609–38.

Korten, David (1995) *When Corporations Rule the World*, West Hartford: Berrett-Koehler.

Lall, Sanjaya (1997) 'East Asia', in John H. Dunning (ed.) (1997) *Governments, Globalization, and International Business*, Oxford: Oxford University Press: 414–23.

Lawrence, Robert Z. (1996) *Single World, Divided Nations? International Trade and OECD Labor Markets*, Paris/Washington: OECD/Brookings.

Lindblom, Charles E. (1977) *Politics and Markets: The World's Political and Economic Systems*, New York: Basic Books.

Lipson, Charles (1985) *Standing Guard: Protecting Foreign Capital in the Nineteenth and Twentieth Centuries*, Berkeley: University of California Press.

Malan, Todd (1996), Director, OFII, interview 24 June, Washington, D.C.

Milner, Helen V. and Robert O. Keohane (1996) 'Internationalization and domestic politics: a conclusion', in Keohane and Milner (eds) *Internationalization and Domestic Politics*, Cambridge: Cambridge University Press: 243–58.

Moran, Theodore H. (ed.) (1985) *Multinational Corporations : the Political Economy of Foreign Direct Investment*, Lexington: D.C. Heath.

Muchlinski, P. T. (1996) 'A case of Czech beer: competition and competitiveness in the transitional economies', *Modern Law Review* 59(5): 658–74.

OECD (1998) *Foreign Direct Investment and Economic Development: Lessons from Six Emerging Economies*, Paris: OECD.

Oman, Charles (1989) *New Forms of International Investing in Developing Countries*, Paris: OECD.

Oman, Charles P., Douglas H. Brooks and Colm Foy (eds) (1997) *Investing in Asia*, Paris: OECD Development Centre.

Rodrik, Dani (1997) *Has Globalization Gone Too Far?*, Washington, D.C.: Institute for International Economics.

Scholte, Jan Aart (1997) 'Global capitalism and the state', *International Affairs* 73(3): 427–52.

SIA. (1996) *Asia-Pacific Economic Cooperation Forum Finance Ministers Meeting*, mimeo, March.

Sklair, Leslie (1998) 'Transnational corporations as political actors', *New Political Economy*, 3(2): 284–7.

Stepan, Alfred C. (1978) *The State and Society*, Princeton: Princeton University Press.

Stopford, John M. and Susan Strange (1991) *Rival States, Rival Firms: Competition for World Market Shares*, Cambridge: Cambridge University Press.

Strange, Susan (1996) *The Retreat of the State: The Diffusion of Power in the World Economy*, Cambridge: Cambridge University Press.

UN (1997) *World Investment Report*, Geneva: United Nations.

USCIB (1996a), interview 6 June, Washington, D.C.

—— (1996b), interview 14 June, Washington, D.C.

USTR (1996a), interview 25 July, Washington, D.C.

—— (1996b) *ACTPN Discussion Draft on Investment*, mimeo, September.

Wallach, Lori (1998), Director, Public Citizen's Global Trade Watch, testimony to Congressional hearing on the MAI, House International Relations Committee, Subcommittee on International Economic Policy and Trade, Thursday, March 5.

Walter, Andrew (1999) 'Capital mobility and policy arbitrage: the case of inward investment policies', unpublished paper.

Williamson, Edwin D. (1998), Vice Chairman of the Committee on Multinational Enterprises and International Investment of the US Council for International Business, testimony before the House Committee on International Relations, Subcommittee on International Economic Policy and Trade, March 5.

Xiaoqiang, Zhang (1997) 'Investment in China's Future', in Oman *et al.* (eds) (1997), *Investing in Asia*, Paris: OECD Development Centre: 41–3.

4   State authority and investment security

Non-state actors and the negotiation of the Multilateral Agreement on Investment at the OECD

Elizabeth Smythe

Introduction

This chapter examines the impact of globalisation on the development of international investment rules through a case study of the role of non-governmental actors in the negotiation of the Multilateral Agreement on Investment (MAI) at the Organisation for Economic Cooperation and Development (OECD). It argues that globalisation has reshaped the interests, ideas and influence of both state and non-state actors in the development of an international investment regime increasingly in the direction of rules designed to restrain the authority of states over multinational capital. Globalisation has had an impact on the way in which states have redefined their investment interests, as a result of the shifting balance of inward and outward investment, and a perceived loss of state bargaining power *vis-à-vis* firms (Bartlett and Seleny 1998: 322). Despite the enhanced power of increasingly mobile capital, multinational corporations have not had free rein in the writing of investment rules. The process has not gone unchallenged for several reasons. First, it is states which negotiate these rules within interstate organisations where multinational capital still has limited access. Second, a variety of other non-state actors have sought to influence the process, both at the national and the transnational level. This has been part of a process of questioning the impact of globalisation which OECD officials themselves refer to as a 'backlash'. This chapter argues that, in the case of the MAI, the direct influence of multinational capital in the negotiations has not been successful and that, as the negotiations dragged on, non-governmental organisations (NGOs), opposed to limiting state authority, gained ground. This has occurred largely as a result of intensive NGO lobbying of several OECD members states. In addition globalisation has also facilitated the development of a global network, opposed to these limits on state authority and the MAI, as a result of the development of new technology, such as the Internet.

The first part of the chapter examines globalisation and the changing patterns of post-war foreign direct investment and how these have been viewed by states. The second section examines the interests of labour and multinational capital regarding international investment rules and then outlines the role of other

NGOs, especially environmental groups, that have taken an active role in trying to influence global trade and investment rules. The third section traces the origins of the MAI negotiations at the OECD and the special status of representation that labour and capital have enjoyed since the creation of the organisation. The fourth section examines the preferences of non-state actors, especially capital and labour, and their attempts to influence the negotiation process. It also analyses the activities of other non-state actors that have become increasingly involved in trying to influence the MAI negotiations, despite not having any formal standing at the OECD. The final section discusses how successful these non-state actors have been. The case of the MAI indicates that, despite the enhanced power of global capital and in contrast to the assertions of the neo-liberal global discourse (see Introduction of this book), the attempt to roll back state authority has not gone uncontested and that this opposition has had an impact on the negotiations. The extent of state authority over capital has become an arena of struggle between capital, labour, environmental and other groups, both at the national and the transnational level, at the same time that the negotiations of these international investment rules, which are intended to limit state authority, are themselves the subject of inter-state bargaining.

Globalisation and the redefinition of investment interests

For many observers the most significant development in the global economy in the post-war period has been the increased mobility of capital in the form of longer- and shorter-term flows. In the case of longer-term flows, foreign direct investment (FDI) has been seen as the key factor in reshaping the global economy, influencing trade flows and ultimately challenging state sovereignty. Increasingly the treatment of foreign investors by host states has become the subject of regional and multilateral agreements among states, which have taken the form of defining principles, seeking to limit the discretionary authority of states over foreign capital. The aim is to increase the security of these investments for foreign investors by ensuring the predictability and transparency of state investment policy and by giving foreign investors recourse to international dispute settlement mechanisms in their conflicts with states. These changes, it can be argued, have their roots in changing post-war patterns of investment and ideas about FDI, as well as in the changing interests of state and non-state actors in investment rules.

Investment outflows in the early post-war period were dominated by the United States while many of the OECD members were host to net inflows of FDI. In many cases the inflows, by the 1960s, had led to large and growing stocks of FDI which raised concerns on the part of domestically-based capital and host states. A series of measures was designed in a number of countries to either limit or bar FDI from key sectors, pre-empt FDI by creating strong national firms, or screen incoming investment to maximise the spin-off of local economic benefits in the form of performance requirements in return for the state granting access.

Over time, however, the sources of FDI within the OECD became more diversified as the US share of outflows dropped to about one quarter of flows (from almost half) while those of Japan, Germany and a number of other countries increased. By the 1980s the United States itself had become the major host to significant flows of FDI while remaining the largest home, a position it still retains. (UN 1997: 4) Thus outward FDI increased rapidly in many OECD countries which had previously been primarily hosts to FDI.

Along with changes to FDI flows in the early 1980s went a series of other economic changes. These included slower economic growth and increased competitive trade pressures in OECD countries as a number of industrialising countries expanded exports as well as increasing FDI in new sectors such as services.

The response on the part of many host countries to such changes was to liberalise investment regulations, particularly by removing some of the sectoral limits on FDI and abandoning the effort to generally control access and use it to bargain with incoming investors. In the case of a number of developing countries this liberalisation was tied to the debt crisis, the need for new capital and the requirement to liberalise imposed as a condition of debt relief. This trend to investment deregulation was selective, however, and many forms of less transparent, discriminatory regulation of foreign investors remained, especially in the service sector.

At the same time attempts to bargain over incoming investment and to influence the behaviour of investors were increasingly viewed by the United States, and ultimately by the GATT, as having trade-related consequences as illustrated by the 1983 dispute regarding the operation of Canada's Foreign Investment Review Agency. Thus trade and investment became linked both in US trade legislation and international trade rules.

The removal of barriers to FDI which had followed the lowering of barriers to trade, along with technological changes, ushered in an era of increasingly intensified linkages among OECD economies and a group of ten of the larger non-OECD economies, which attracted the bulk of the investment not going to the OECD countries. As a result intra-firm trade became a growing proportion of OECD trade. A series of domestic changes that have reduced the role of the state in many OECD countries and deregulated various sectors of the economy have accompanied the global changes and further served to enhance capital mobility.

As a result of these processes the roles of host or home economies among the OECD member countries are less clear. Trade and investment are now viewed as closely linked and investment liberalisation has been seen by member countries as a positive measure to attract new investment and as a means to ensure the competitive position of existing firms. This trend is also reflected in the dramatic increase in both bilateral investment treaties and trade agreements that address investment (UN 1997:19).

Investment rules: the interests of capital and labour

How have these changes affected the views of multinational capital and domestically based, and largely immobile, labour? In the case of multinational capital investment liberalisation has lessened the preoccupation of the 1960s and 1970s with expropriation and the denial of access to national markets in favour of demands for the removal of those sectoral barriers to FDI, especially in services, and attacks on any state regulation which could systematically disadvantage a foreign investor once established within a national market. The focus of multinational firms and organisations has been increasingly on rules which would secure an investment from state regulatory measures which would in any way limit its capacity to compete within a market. The establishment of binding international agreements with dispute resolution mechanisms thus becomes a way for investors to have legal recourse against states which may attempt to alter or increase regulation of firms, even if that is in response to public demand. Thus multinational capital seeks to limit state discretion to regulate in any way that would disadvantage it. There is no interest, however, in limiting the competitive bidding among states to attract investment, either through fiscal incentives, or through competitive deregulation.

Labour, in contrast to capital, is largely immobile and has both benefited from the expansion of economic activity which new, incoming capital can bring, but has also been disadvantaged by the ability of capital to relocate investment and jobs to other economies. In the case of host countries like Canada, trade unions in the early 1970s were not strong champions of limiting FDI inflows. As capital became more mobile, however, and investment outflows have increased, many labour organisations have seen this as a loss of bargaining power. The trade unions of the OECD member countries recognise the reality that 'member countries no longer view discriminatory controls against multinationals or foreign investors, as a practical policy tool in general. On the contrary countries and regions appear to be competing to attract foreign investment through a range of incentives' (TUAC 1997a: 1). Labour is thus interested in international rules which would limit the capacity of multinational firms to play states off competitively and provide protection for the interests of labour as capital mobility is enhanced. Labour has also sought policy space which would permit states the discretion of using national regulation and social programmes to provide compensation and facilitate adjustment, thus counterbalancing the enhanced power of capital.

An important part of the OECD process has been the representation from early on of the views of capital and labour through the Trade Union Advisory Committee (TUAC), which was founded in 1948, and the Business and Industry Advisory Committee (BIAC), founded in 1962. Both organisations include the members of business or labour federations from the twenty-nine OECD countries and put the views of their members before the OECD on a regular basis through meetings with the various OECD committees, national delegations and members of the Secretariat. These two organisations have had a formal channel through which to communicate their investment interests and tried to influence the first major agreement on FDI negotiated in the mid-1970s.

In the early 1970s the United States pushed hard at the OECD to get an agreement on national treatment of investors in order to generate a stronger consensus among capital-exporting countries and stop the growing momentum at the United Nations to negotiate a code on transnational corporations which would have been much more hostile to the interests of investors. National treatment, at that time, had been a principle which generated strong disagreement within the OECD. The resulting agreement committed the OECD members to national treatment of foreign firms, but was not binding. This agreement was accompanied by a set of voluntary guidelines on the behaviour of multinational corporations within national economies which reflected a number of labour's concerns. At that time BIAC and TUAC were virtually the only non-state actors seeking to influence the OECD process.

In recent years, however, additional non-state organisations have sought to influence the negotiation of international investment rules on trade and investment at the OECD and the World Trade Organisation (WTO). The negotiation of international environmental agreements and treaties spawned the development of transnational environmental organisations. The spectre of enhanced capital mobility undermining state and international environmental regulation has led these organisations to turn their attention to international trade and investment rules. At the domestic level in many OECD countries these groups have lobbied successfully to increase state environmental regulation, conserve resources and promote sustainable development. This struggle has often pitted these groups against business organisations which have sought to limit state regulation. It has also, at least in North America, sometimes pitted them against labour organisations, especially on issues involving resource conservation or wilderness preservation. Enhanced capital mobility, however, has generated an increasingly cooperative relationship between labour and environmental groups at the international and regional level as both seek to limit the incentives or capacity of capital to exit national economies to avoid regulation. Environmental groups and labour organisations cooperated in their opposition to North American Free Trade (Audley 1997) and built networks which have also facilitated coordinated action opposing similar investment rules at the WTO as well as the MAI at the OECD. In the case of the OECD however these groups, unlike labour and capital, have not had official standing.

In North America organisations like the Sierra Club have formed a common front against the MAI with labour and social justice groups and the Washington office of the Friends of the Earth, and have lobbied member countries in opposition to the agreement and to alert other organisations to its potential implications. How successful have capital, labour and environmental groups been in influencing the negotiations? To answer this question we first need to understand the origins and process of the negotiations.

Negotiating the MAI at the OECD

The United States had called on the OECD to initiate discussion on a wider investment instrument which OECD ministers in June 1991 agreed to study. The Business and Industry Advisory Committee (BIAC) of the OECD expressed the view in 1992 that such an agreement was necessary (BIAC 1994). The United States wanted a much tighter, more comprehensive and binding agreement than what was provided in the 1976 code and the national treatment instrument. It had been increasingly frustrated by the slow process of trying to strengthen aspects of the national treatment instrument and make it binding. The difficult process of negotiating even the very limited trade-related investment measures at the Uruguay Round of the GATT, and the opposition within the Asia-Pacific Economic Cooperation Forum (APEC) to binding investment rules there, influenced the US decision to look to the OECD. In December 1991 the United States began the push to launch a full-scale negotiation at the OECD of a comprehensive, binding investment treaty which would have high standards of liberalisation, protection of investors and a dispute resolution process (United States 1991: 1).

Despite the strong consensus among OECD members on the need for such a set of rules and the desire for investment liberalisation, there was no consensus that the OECD was the preferred venue for such negotiations, or that there was an urgent need to proceed quickly.[1] Arguments for and against the OECD as the venue for such negotiations put forward by OECD members over the next three years centred around two aspects of the organisation: its restricted membership and the strengths and weaknesses of the organisation and its Secretariat.

The OECD membership, up until 1991, reflected its roots in post-war cooperation among industrialised market economies. Since that time Mexico, Poland, Hungary and the Czech Republic have become members, along with Korea. But their admission has not substantively altered the organisation even though it has added four more, primarily host, countries. Admission came only after their adoption of sufficiently liberal values and economic policies, including adherence to the various OECD investment and capital movement codes. Clearly for some OECD countries the restricted nature of the membership was seen to be an advantage in future negotiations. The United States identified a large degree of consensus on many aspects of the treatment of FDI, making ultimate agreement on a strong treaty with high standards of liberalisation quite likely. Other members, however, saw restricted membership differently. Any agreement negotiated by OECD members would not include the very countries where investors had complained of discrimination. When Canada and a number of other European countries canvassed their own business communities they found few or no complaints about the treatment of FDI within other OECD countries. All members recognised that the ultimate target for new discipline on the treatment of FDI were countries outside the OECD. The advantage of the OECD from the US view was that agreement there would both 'prevent backsliding within the OECD and promote the adoption of these standards outside the OECD' (United States 1991: 3) reflecting the view of the OECD as a forum for consensus among the largest market economies and as a missionary for values of liberalisation. The real targets for an MAI were the observer countries, those Asian economies which were attracting investment, and countries such as Brazil and India which had led efforts to resist investment liberalisation in organisations such as the GATT/WTO.

Concerns over the limits of the OECD as a negotiating venue were reflected in the report on the MAI which was adopted in May 1995. The communiqué from the 24 May meeting and the appended report on an MAI (OECD 1995) reflected the compromises required by members in order to gain acceptance of the agreement to launch negotiations at the OECD. The ministers agreed to the start of negotiations aimed at reaching an agreement by May 1997. The agreement would:

> provide a broad multilateral framework for international investment with high standards for the liberalisation of investment regimes and investment protection and with effective dispute settlement procedures; be a free-standing international treaty open to all OECD Members and the European Communities, and to accession by non-OECD Member countries, which will be consulted as the negotiations progress.
>
> (OECD 1995: 1)

The communiqué also called for increased cooperation with the WTO on investment issues. WTO observers were present at meetings of the MAI negotiating group, reflecting the desire of some OECD members to ultimately have the agreement migrate to the WTO (Canada 1998).

The report outlined the need for an MAI which arose from the 'dramatic growth and transformation of Foreign Direct Investment which has been spurred by widespread liberalisation and increased competition for investment capital,' and the fact that foreign investors still encountered 'investment barriers, discriminatory treatment and uncertainty.' The MAI would set a high standard for the treatment of investors with 'clear, consistent rules on liberalisation, dispute settlement and investor protection'. Most importantly it would create pressure on the non-OECD investment dissidents because 'the MAI would provide a benchmark against which potential investors would assess the openness and legal security offered by countries as investment locations. This would in turn act as a spur to further liberalisation' (OECD 1995: 3). Both the report and the communiqué made a commitment to consult with non-members. This later took the form of workshops in various locations, such as Hong Kong and Brazil, where selected non-member economies were invited to discuss the MAI along with sponsoring OECD members and officials of other organisations, such as the WTO and UNCTAD, and regional organisations like the Organisation of American States (OAS). As the Brazilian workshops in 1996 and 1997 indicated, the invited countries would consider 'how high standards of multilateral agreement on investment can make a contribution to economic development in Latin America' (OECD 1997c: 1).

Although there was a high degree of consensus on principles at the outset the negotiations proved frustrating and slow to reach the point of key political compromises necessary to forge an agreement, making it impossible to reach agreement by the original May 1997 deadline and ultimately resulting in a six-month suspension of negotiations in April, 1998 (OECD 1998b). This was followed by a collapse of the negotiations in October after the withdrawal of the French government.

To understand some of the negotiating difficulties and the process itself we need to understand the way in which the OECD has generally dealt with investment issues. Much of the work on investment issues has been undertaken within the context of two committees, the Committee on Capital Movements and Invisibles Transactions (CMIT) and the Committee on Investment and Multinational Enterprises (CIME). These committees monitor and oversee the compliance of member countries with the OECD codes dealing with capital movements, national treatment and the guidelines for multinational enterprises. Only the capital movements code, however, is binding on members. The committees issue reports, direct research programmes and oversee the various reporting obligations of member countries, all with the assistance of the staff of the Directorate on Financial Fiscal and Enterprise Affairs (DAFFE). Member countries are represented equally on committees which operate on the basis of consensus, as does the OECD as a whole. The OECD itself, however, has been affected by global changes. The emergence of the WTO and a broader trade agenda including investment, along with a declining need to organise the cooperation of Western market economies with the end of the Cold War, has thrown the future of the OECD into question, something that the Secretary-General, Don Johnston, has had to address. Moreover, unilateral reductions in US financial support in recent years have forced budget cuts and put constraints on the 1,800 staff at the organisation. The decision to negotiate a binding MAI was thus embraced enthusiastically by DAFFE and the Secretary-General as a way to demonstrate the importance of the organisation and the directorate which deals with investment issues.

Representation on the over 200 committees and special bodies of the OECD has been the purview of various departments and agencies within national bureaucracies in member countries. In the case of the CIME and CMIT representation has, in some member countries, been the role of foreign ministries and diplomatic departments, while in others it has involved economic department or agencies. Thus the level of negotiating expertise and experience in matters such as services, intellectual property and the process of creating binding enforceable investment rules varied widely among representatives. Moreover, the work of committees has reflected, in the view of some observers, a corporate culture of extensive research, consensus building, an old boys' network, and the tendency to opt for the lowest common denominator, thus producing weak agreements. As a result, a number of member countries which championed the negotiations, like the US, were unwilling to use the existing CIME and CMIT committee structures to negotiate the MAI. A number of countries, and the Commission of the EC, which is also involved, wanted a negotiating group and chair separate from the existing committee structure.

Non-state actors' influence on the negotiations

Both BIAC and TUAC have had long-established organisations and structures to communicate their views to the OECD. In the case of BIAC the organisation is structured as a federation of business organisations of the twenty-nine member countries. Much of the work is carried out by the five-member executive board which represents the larger members in Europe, the United States and Japan, assisted by a small permanent staff in Paris. The various subject areas of OECD work are covered by committees. The chair of BIAC and policy committee chairs are executives of some of the largest multinational corporations based in the member countries (BIAC 1996a).

Members of the organisation are themselves typically umbrella business organisations within their national economies, such as the Keidanren in Japan. Most observers agree that the United States Council for International Business is one of the most influential and vocal members of BIAC and enjoys good access to US decision-makers, staffed as it is by former US Treasury and United States Trade Representative (USTR) officials, along with links to the major business organisations in the United States. Internationally the BIAC works closely with the International Chamber of Commerce, also headquartered in Paris.

Despite its small staff in Paris, BIAC has access to major resources in its efforts to influence OECD decisions, especially via the corporate legal staff of large multinationals on which it can draw. At the beginning of the MAI negotiations BIAC assembled a high-powered Experts Group of mostly corporate legal staff specialising in trade and investment issues and in the employ of some of the largest firms. The normal processes of consultation were, however, somewhat disrupted by the special arrangements for negotiating the MAI.[2] BIAC's high-powered group of experts on the MAI (primarily corporate legal counsel), ready to provide detailed input on aspects of the MAI to negotiators at short notice, was frustrated that its veritable 'swat team' had not been called upon with any frequency. There was concern about the limited access to negotiators and the limited flow of information about the negotiations. Its views, along with those of TUAC, have been communicated by meetings with the negotiating group or the chair and often through letters to the chair. Even the draft text on the MAI from early 1997 on which BIAC made detailed comment (BIAC 1997) had to be obtained via 'informal' channels of a member country because the secretariat and the negotiating group had initially closely guarded such documents.

The Trade Union Advisory Committee is also composed of union federations from the member countries and maintains links with the international umbrella labour organisations such as the International Confederation of Free Trade Unions (ICFTU). All the affiliated organisations meet twice a year in plenary session to make key policy decisions, set priorities and approve the budget. A smaller administrative committee of representatives (president and several vice-presidents) from the larger members in Europe, North American and Japan run the organisation, assisted by a permanent staff of six people in Paris. In contrast to BIAC, the staff are expected by their union affiliates to provide expertise and advice out of the small operation in Paris and do not have the sort of broader resources to draw on that BIAC does.

In recent years TUAC has begun to include environmental issues as a priority along with other issues such as social and economic policy, training and labour standards. TUAC also has regular consultations with CMIT and CIME and is present as an observer at many routine meetings and conferences similar to BIAC.

For TUAC one area of focus has been on strengthening the implementation and follow up to ensure that the Guidelines on Multinational Enterprises are being adhered to in member countries.

Much of TUAC's work regarding FDI has been focused on building an acceptance of, and a commitment to, core labour standards within the OECD member countries. This is part of a broader movement to generate global acceptance of labour standards that has been pursued at the UN Social Summit and the ministerial meeting of the WTO in Singapore. TUAC has pushed for OECD research studies and sponsored a conference (OECD 1996) designed to demonstrate that adherence to labour standards will not deter investors. It has sought to make adherence to core labour standards, defined as 'freedom of association, right to collective bargaining, freedom from forced or compulsory labour, freedom from child labour and freedom from discrimination in respect of employment and equal remuneration of men and women' (OECD 1996), a central commitment shared by all OECD members.

This issue has taken an even greater salience with the admission of new OECD members in the 1990s, especially Korea, and the prospects of broadening membership down the road. Enhanced capital mobility without adherence to core labour standards, in TUAC's view, raises the possibility of states seeking to attract FDI by suppressing labour rights and putting downward pressure on labour standards elsewhere. TUAC has cited a number of state Sponsored Export Processing Zones (EPZs) in Asia as evidence of this practice.

It was clear that TUAC faced a challenge at the outset of the negotiation since it is evident in the initial report to ministers recommending the launching of the MAI negotiations that the central preoccupation of the negotiations was the business agenda, that is, liberalisation of investment regulations and improving the treatment of foreign investors. Neither labour standards nor environmental issues received much attention in the initial report.

TUAC's demands regarding the MAI included stronger support for core labour standards in the preamble of the agreement. TUAC also called for the annexation of the Guidelines on Multinational Enterprises, a set of non-binding principles which outline socially responsible good corporate citizenship. In addition TUAC asked for a commitment of signatories to the MAI to pledge not to lower labour or environmental standards in order to attract investment (TUAC 1997a).

The annexing of the Guidelines, the environmental standards and the inclusion of core labour standards were demands for changes to which BIAC had been most vocal in its opposition. In several documents and legal opinions presented to the negotiating group BIAC argued against any linking of the agreement to the Guidelines, which they claimed would render the currently voluntary guidelines obligatory and therefore depress investment flows (BIAC 1997). The claim that any provisions of the agreement would depress investment flows, a threat that MNCs can make because of their control of, and ability to move, capital, provided a strategic advantage in lobbying member countries.

On the issue of labour standards, however, BIAC had problems maintaining a unified opposition and faced the embarrassment of having the Belgian and French business organisations publicly dissent from the official BIAC position. (BIAC 1996b). The labour standards issue has had an even higher profile since the admission of Korea to the OECD and unrest there as a result of labour law changes.

By the spring of 1997 capital and labour were not the only groups being heard on the investment issue, both in member countries and at the OECD. When information on the nature of the agreement being negotiated became public through a leak of the first draft of the negotiating text, quickly distributed on the Internet, others, including environmental groups such as the World Wide Fund for Nature and the Sierra Club, began disseminating critical information on the MAI, in cooperation with various other labour and social justice organisations across North America and Europe . Much of this information was distributed on the Internet. Several groups asked to be heard at the OECD and then met with the chair of the negotiating group in November 1996 to express their concerns regarding the potential erosion of environmental standards. As this is an inter-governmental treaty-making process, with a separate negotiating group of state representatives, other transnational, non-governmental organisations have had limited access to the negotiations. As a consequence many of these groups have had to focus simultaneously on key member countries, particularly those where they can find easier access to decision-makers.

Part of the alarm which the draft text raised among opponents was a reaction to the way in which the OECD secretariat and the chair of the negotiating group had sought to forge an early consensus on the agreement. The secretariat, especially DAFFE, had a strong interest in an early and successful outcome. At the outset they characterised the agreement as one that would be 'state of the art' and would lead to sweeping liberalisation. Creating a consolidated draft text as rapidly as possible became an important goal. The text, which emerged in early 1997, was one which codified all of the major principles of investment agreements. It included a broad definition of investor, a commitment to national treatment of all investors, obligations to protect foreign investors from arbitrary actions, such as expropriation, which are standard in many bilateral investment treaties, and a strong dispute settlement mechanism available to investors in disputes with states. Objections of single countries to various provisions or wording of the text, whether major substantive ones or narrow technical ones, were relegated to footnotes to the basic text. By beginning with broad principles that all aspired to or shared and leaving the issue of what sectors or countries these provisions would apply to until the end left an impression that a sweeping agreement, based on a high level of consensus and a wholesale acceptance of the corporate agenda, was already a *fait accompli*, and that all of the reservations and exemptions, which in March 1997 were yet to be negotiated, were simply minor details. The reality was, however, that there were much more diverse views on the scope and applicability of the agreement than was reflected in the draft text. These differences were apparent once countries began lodging their draft reservations with the chair in March 1997. Some countries, such as the NAFTA partners, Canada, the US and Mexico, listed over eighty non-conforming measures, largely replicating their annexes from chapter 11 of that agreement, while other countries listed very few reservations.

Such disparities hardly provided a basis of negotiation. It quickly became clear that delegates, at that point, had no shared meaning of what constituted a reservation, resulting in a the creation of a set of guidelines to ensure some consistency in the process. Moreover, negotiators had not even begun the process of resolving the major disagreements among some of the key actors.

At that point, in March 1997, the process began to bog down and it became clear that the negotiators would be unable to meet their original two-year deadline of May 1997. A new deadline to finish the negotiations by the May 1998 was agreed, despite the chair and the secretariat's preference for December 1997. The leaking of the draft agreement, combined with the extension of the deadline, provided momentum to opponents of the agreement. It also provided time for political events to have an impact, such as the change in governments in Britain and France. The shift in the British position was reflected in the fall of 1997 when the British negotiator, speaking at a meeting with representatives of non-OECD countries, talked of a 'pendulum swinging back. Concern for labour standards and more strikingly, environmental protection is stronger than in the 1980s' and went on to outline how these concerns were being addressed in the negotiations and the like-lihood that the guidelines on multinationals would be attached to the agreement, although they remained voluntary (Bridge 1997). In the case of the US Administration, moves to accommodate concerns other than those of business reflected the fierce political battle over fast track legislation, which was ultimately to fail. The growing willingness of some member countries to hear the concerns of labour and other NGOs met with a hostile reaction on the part of BIAC, even as it moved very reluctantly on the issue of the guidelines. One of BIAC's most influential members, the United States Council on International Business, wrote to the United States Trade Representative in July 1997 protesting against the intention of the US to table additional proposals on the environment and new language on labour standards which would prove 'troublesome' to business (Katz 1997).

In recognition of the growing NGO opposition and their sustained lobbying, the OECD scheduled further meetings of the whole negotiating group with environmental and other critics of the MAI on 27 October 1997. Groups gathered for a strategy session prior to the meeting to share information, establish networks and further develop their campaign of opposition in cooperation with TUAC. The NGOs made a case for a suspension of negotiations until a comprehensive assessment of the social, environmental and developmental impact of the MAI could be undertaken. The twenty-seven organisations demanded a strengthening of labour, human rights and environmental commitments in the agreement and elimination of the investor-state dispute resolution process. They also called for greater transparency of the negotiation process and wider public consultation. After calling for a suspension of negotiations, which the OECD refused, groups made a commitment to country by country campaign to block ratification (Sierra Club, 1997). This included a series of protests in various member countries in February and March 1998 coinciding with a key point in the negotiations and the expansion of their international network to over 600 groups in more than fifty countries.

Over all, the OECD has been rather unsure in how to deal with the other

NGOs. Partly because they had been shut out of the process in Paris, these groups have forged loose international coalitions and focused on cultivating opposition to the MAI within a number of key member countries. In Canada opposition in the form of a public information campaign with town hall meetings across the country was designed to counter the behind the scenes, low-key access of business to decision-makers and the fact that the popular media was initially uninterested in the MAI, while the business press totally dismissed concerns. The Canadian coalition of labour, environmental, cultural and nationalist groups took out an advertisement in the *Globe and Mail* national newspaper attacking the MAI in the midst of the June 1997 election campaign. Charges of a secretive government agenda hit home in the fall of 1997 when the Canadian Trade Minister responded by asking a parliamentary committee to review the negotiations (Canada 1997), providing NGOs with another opportunity to criticize the agreement. A similar process occurred later in the winter of 1998 in Australia where the press criticism of opposition politicians and well known individuals also led to a parliamentary review of the negotiations (Australia, 1998).

In Britain the change in government and the presence of opponents to the MAI within Labour ranks has ensured a steady flow of debate in the House of Commons since the spring of 1997 and questions about the impact of the MAI have been raised in the context of a policy review of British international development assistance. Labour ministers have had to defend Britain's continued participation in the negotiations in the media and Parliament and before various NGOs, even as they have championed a review of the environmental impact of FDI at the OECD (OECD 1997b) and pushed for stronger wording on labour and environmental standards.

Opposition in France also began to increase in the fall of 1997 and the winter of 1998 and took the form of attacks on the agreement in the press and a series of demonstrations. The French government has had to reiterate its commitment to the cultural exemption (France 1998) and in the spring of 1998 took a position at the OECD that negotiations should cease. However, the EU Commission and other EU members supported a continuation of the negotiations.

In the case of the United States, environmental and social justice NGOs, such as Ralph Nader's Public Citizen, took a lead role in opposing the MAI and have had some support from a group of members of the House of Representatives. A brief one-day hearing on the MAI was held in March 1998. More important, in the US case, has been the battle over fast track authorisation for trade talks in the Americas, the trade protectionist sentiments in Congress, and the division and disagreements within the Administration over the merits of pushing for an MAI. This has resulted in a loss of momentum on the US side which led to their support for a hiatus in negotiations. US multinationals, aware of the waning momentum, wrote to the US Trade Representative in April 1998 reaffirming their support for the agreement. But no real progress was expected until the congressional elections in November 1998. By that point, however, France had withdrawn leading to a formal cessation of negotiations in December 1998. These developments must be contrasted to the launching of the negotiations in 1995 with the rhetoric

of the US, BIAC and the OECD Secretariat which talked of significant liberalisation of investment regulations with scarcely a mention of the social
responsibility of corporations.

Conclusion: non-state actors, state authority and global investment rules

The case study of the MAI raises a number of questions about the extent to which
capital mobility and globalised production have reshaped or limited state authority.
The changing balance of inward and outward flows of capital in a number of
OECD countries and increased capital mobility have led states to abandon a
number of regulatory instruments in dealing with foreign investors. In the interests
of attracting investment OECD member states were willing to respond, at least
partially, to the desire of investors for security by embracing the idea of investment liberalisation, investor protection and national treatment in the form of a
binding agreement designed to limit state authority and ratchet it ever downward.
For its own reasons the OECD put itself forward as the best forum in which to
achieve such a goal.

If we examine BIAC's initial preferences for an investment agreement we would
see that many of them are reflected in the first draft agreement, including a broad
and inclusive definition of investor, a commitment to national treatment, and
recourse to a dispute resolution process when dealing with states. However, the
scope and extent of the applicability of national treatment was left unclear because
of the inability to resolve conflicts over members' reservations. In other areas there
was even less success for BIAC. Taxation measures were not covered by the draft
agreement largely because of intra-state bureaucratic battles. Commitments to environmental and labour standards, although they may not have been strong enough to
suit environmental groups or TUAC, were going to be part of the agreement and
binding, along with the attachment of the guidelines, all of which BIAC strongly
opposed at the outset. Even investor protection, an area of broad consensus initially,
came under reassessment as a result of the concerns which environmental NGOs
had raised arguing that the broad definition of investor, coupled with the loose
wording on expropriation, and the investor-state dispute resolution process, would
unleash a plethora of corporate attacks on state environmental regulations (Sierra
Club 1997). A number of states were seeking partial exemptions of existing regulations from the dispute settlement, standstill and rollback commitments.

Can the changes in the positions of countries, the defeat of the agreement
itself and changes to the wording of the draft text be explained solely by the
activities and influence of NGOs? Clearly they cannot. Major disagreements
emerged during the negotiations among states over issues such as the US
investment embargo contained in the Helms-Burton Act, the insistence of the
EU on an exemption from national treatment for Regional Economic
Integration Organisations (REIO) and the problems of binding sub-national
entities (such as US states and Canadian provinces) along with the cultural
exemptions demanded by France and Canada. These proved difficult to resolve

within the OECD context and the exigencies of domestic politics, especially in the US and France. These disagreements, however, did slow down the process and provide the capacity for NGO intervention. In the case of the issues of labour and environmental standards and national regulations which may be affected by the MAI, NGOs, in conjunction with changes in governments, reshaped the priorities of a number of member countries and forced both the OECD and member countries to provide much more information about the negotiations and defend the process of liberalisation (OECD 1998c). At the same time work has continued on the part of actors such as the Commission of the EU at the WTO to move the issue of investment rules on to the agenda of any future round of trade negotiations. Thus even though the NGOs were successful in their opposition to the process at the OECD, the issue of an MAI type agreement will likely re-emerge at some point. However, the MAI case suggests that any future such agreement will have to do a better job of balancing the concerns of global capital with those of the environment, labour and cultural identity.

Labour and environmental organisations, as the case study shows, have a shared interest in preventing mobile capital from further eroding state regulatory sovereignty through encouraging competitive deregulation. In this instance they too, however, wish to limit state discretion by ensuring a regulatory floor for labour and environmental standards, either at the state level or by binding commitments at the international level, to remove the incentives and capability of capital to exit or to challenge such regulations. Given their weaker bargaining position and limited resources in comparison to global capital, they have been surprisingly successful and have made real advances since the beginning of the negotiating process. The case of the MAI also suggests that there may be limits to globalisation and that the 'backlash' the OECD Secretary-General has alluded to in speeches is real (OECD 1998c). Given the association of globalisation with a reduced role for the state and costly adjustment burdens in the form of cutbacks and job dislocation now in the minds of citizens in many member countries, the apparent scope of the draft agreement may have itself aroused opposition. Opponents have been able to use the context of inter-state negotiations to begin to redress the shifting imbalance of power between citizens and capital either through shoring up national authority or through transferring it to the global level via international regulation which reflects more than the interests of multinational capital.

Notes

The author wishes to acknowledge the support of the Canadian Social Sciences and Humanities Research Council in funding this research, as well as the cooperation of the Department of Foreign Affairs and International Trade and the research assistance of Carolyn Hawryluk. An earlier version of this article was presented at the conference on Non-State Actors and Authority in the Global System, University of Warwick, 31 October to 1 November 1997.

1   This analysis is based in on interviews conducted in May 1996, and February–April 1997 with negotiators in the Canadian Departments of Foreign Affairs and International

Trade and other negotiators and officials at the OECD in Paris in April 1997 along with documents obtained under the Canadian Access to Information Act.
2   Based on interviews in Paris, in April 1997 with representative of TUAC and BIAC and members of the DAFFE Directorate of the OECD.

References

Audley, John (1997) *Green Politics and Global Trade: NAFTA and the Future of Environmental Politics*, Washington: Georgetown University Press.

Australia (1998) Joint Standing Committee on Treaties of the Parliament of the Commonwealth of Australia, *Multilateral Agreement on Investment;. 14th report*, May.

Bartlett, David and Anna Seleny (1998) 'The political enforcement of liberalism: bargaining, institutions and auto multinationals in Hungary', *International Studies Quarterly* 42(2): 319–38.

BIAC (1994) *Linking Labour Standards With International Commerce*, Paris.

—— (1996a) *Annual Report*, Paris.

—— (1996b) *The Multilateral Agreement on Investment and the OECD Guidelines: Environment, Labour and Consumer Matters*, Paris.

—— (1997) Letter to Mr. Franz Engering, 24 March.

Bridge, Charles (1997) 'The OECD Guidelines and the MAI' presented at MAI briefing for Non-OECD Countries', 17 September.

Britain (1997) House of Commons, *Proceedings of the Select Committee on International Development*, 22 December.

—— (1998) House of Commons, *Hansard* (various issues) January–April.

Canada (1997) House of Commons Standing Committee on Foreign Affairs and International Trade Subcommittee on Trade, Trade Disputes and Investment, *Canada and the MAI: First Report of the Subcommittee*, Ottawa, 11 December.

Canada (1998) Statement of the Minister of International Trade, Paris, 27 April.

France (1998) *Négociation de l'accord multilatéral sur l'investissement*, Paris: Ministère de L'Économie, 12 February.

Katz, Abraham (1997) Letter to the US Administration: USCIB Concerns with Environmental Provisions of the MAI, 11 July.

Le Monde Diplomatique (1998) 'The dangers of the multilateral agreement on investment', Paris: March.

OECD (1995) *Meeting of the OECD Council at Ministerial Level, May 24, 1995 and a Multilateral Agreement on Investment Report by the Committee on International Investment and Multinational Enterprise and the Committee on Capital Movements and Invisibles Transactions*, Paris: OECD.

—— (1996) *Labour Standards in the Global Trade and Investment System*, Paris: November.

—— (1997a) *Foreign Direct Investment and the Environment: A Overview of the Literature*, Paris: September.

—— (1997b) *Meeting of the Council at the Ministerial Level*, Paris, 26–27 May, Communiqué.

—— (1997c) *Second Workshop on Multilateral Rules on Investment*, Brasilia, Brazil, 4–5 February, Paris: OECD Press Release, 3 February.

—— (1998a) 'Environment and labour in the MAI' speaking notes for Press Seminar, William Wetherill, Director of DAFFE, Paris: 26 March.

—— (1998b) *Ministerial Statement on the Multilateral Agreement on Investment*, Paris: 27 April.

—— (1998c) *Open Markets Matter: The Benefits of Trade and Investment Liberalization*, Paris.

Sierra Club of Canada (1997) *Presentation to the House of Commons Committee on Foreign Affairs and International Trade Subcommittee on Trade, Trade Disputes and Investment*, 27 November, 1997, Appendix 1, 'Joint NGO Statement on the Multilateral Agreement on Investment, Paris: 27 October.

Smythe, Elizabeth (1998) 'The Multilateral Agreement on Investment: A Charter of Rights for Global Investors or Just Another Agreement?', in Fen Osler Hampson and Maureen Appel Molot (eds) *Canada Among Nations 1998: Leadership and Dialogue*, Toronto: Oxford University Press: 239–66.

Trade Union Advisory Committee (TUAC) (1997a) *The Multilateral Agreement on Investment: The Treatment of Labour Issues*, Briefing Notes for Affiliates, Paris: February.

—— (1997b) *Working Group on Global Trade and Investment: Update on Developments in the MAI*, Paris: March.

—— (1998a) *The OECD Multilateral Agreement on Investment: Key Concepts and the Trade Union Response*, Paris: January.

—— (1998b) TUAC Note on the Ministerial Statement on the Multilateral Agreement on Investment, Paris: 28 April.

United Nations Conference on Trade and Development (1997) *World Investment Report: Transnational Corporations Market Structure and Competition Policy*.

United States (1991) 'New OECD Investment Instrument', 6 December: 1.

United States Council for International Business (USCIB) (1998) 'CEO letter reaffirming business support for a high standard MAI', Washington, 20 April.

5 Structures, agents and institutions

Private corporate power and the globalisation of intellectual property rights

Susan K. Sell

The Trade-Related Aspects of Intellectual Property (TRIPs) agreement, enshrined in the World Trade Organisation (WTO), dramatically expands the global protection of intellectual property (IP; i.e. patents, trademarks, copyright) rights. In this chapter, I argue that a small handful of US-based multinational corporation (MNC) executives and their advisors succeeded in amplifying its private interests into public international law. This is a case of particular MNCs wanting, and getting, their kind of international regulation of intellectual property. My argument combines structural, institutional, and agent-based explanations with a focus on contingency and concrete problems that decision-makers at various levels sought to solve. Agents' interests are refracted by the state and projected on to the international system. If the US state were not so structurally powerful, its domestic agents would have had less impact. If US policy-makers had not been facing new challenges arising from the changing structure of global capitalism, they would not have been so receptive to the MNCs' efforts. If the particular agents pressing for a tough multilateral agreement were not so powerful within the US, their actions would have been less effective. The MNC IP activists were structurally privileged in terms of having structural power in US and global markets, but more centrally were successful in converting this latent power into purposeful action.

The chapter begins by briefly describing the TRIPs agreement. The second section addresses the agent-structure debate and presents the argument. Section three introduces the agents and their interests. Section four describes the changing structure of global capitalism and its effects on US policy-making. Section five analyses the direct and indirect power of the activist MNCs, and TRIPs as an example of structural power, and section six presents conclusions about this case.

The TRIPS agreement

The TRIPs agreement provides intellectual property owners with a twenty-year monopoly right. TRIPs binds signatory states, requires them to pass implementing domestic legislation, adopt enforcement measures, and face the threat of trade sanctions if they fail to comply with the TRIPs provisions. The TRIPs agreement is striking on many levels. First, the US-based proposal to globalise a commitment to stronger IP enforcement was surprising, given the fact that domestically the US enforcement of IP rights was relatively lax until about 1982 (Whipple 1987). In a very short time period, the US changed its domestic approach to IP, then sought to globalise this commitment by incorporating IP into its trade policy instruments in both 1984 and 1988 amendments to domestic trade laws. This redefinition of US interest requires an explanation. Second, the TRIPs accord closely mirrors the expressed wishes of the twelve CEOs who spearheaded this effort. Third, it is based on a very specific notion of IP, which privileges protection over diffusion, that is far from consensual. Fourth, in a departure from GATT precedent, the TRIPs accord does not merely circumscribe the range of acceptable policies governments may practice, but 'obliges governments to take positive action to protect intellectual property rights' (Hoekman and Kostecki 1995: 156). Fifth, the stated rationale for the IP agreement – that it will promote economic development worldwide – has virtually no empirical support. Sixth, it has important implications for innovation, economic development, the future location of industry, and the global division of labour.

TRIPs is not merely an incremental change in international regulation, but rather the embodiment of a new 'constitutive principle' in so far as it creates new international property rights that create or define new forms of behaviour and generate structures (Dessler 1989: 455; Burch 1994: 37–59). Like the enclosure movement, it empowers the 'haves' at the expense of the 'have nots' by freezing a status quo and closing a gate for up-and-comers. The redistributive implications of TRIPs are not yet fully understood; however, the short-term impact of stronger global IP protection will be a significant transfer of resources from developing country consumers and firms to industrialised country firms. In short, it reconstitutes both agents and structures, reproducing and transforming them, and thereby redefines winners and losers.

Agents, structures and institutions

As Wendt suggests:

> agents are inseparable from social structures in the sense that their action is possible in virtue of those structures, and social structures cannot have causal significance except in so far as they are instantiated by agents. Social action, then, is 'co-determined' by the properties of both agents and social structures.
>
> (Wendt 1987: 365)

The challenge facing social scientists is to provide explanations that acknowledge and encompass both structure and agency.

The TRIPs outcome constitutes structural power, the power to shape the environment and redefine options for others (Palan and Abbott 1996:138; Strange 1996). TRIPs was a product of structured agency. The actions of the agents were necessary but not sufficient conditions for the TRIPs outcome. The changing structure of global capitalism provided a permissive condition for the TRIPs agreement. The institution of the US state, embedded in this broader structure, mediated between domestic private sector actors and international institutions. The efficacy of the activist MNCs was conjunctural and context-dependent. As Wilks points out, 'economic arrangements are established by social bargains and perpetuated through social institutions, they are neither natural nor inevitable and must therefore be analysed in a contingent social setting' (Wilks 1996: 40).

One can consider the agent as the proximate or immediate cause, who is embedded in larger and larger structures, including material causes, state institutions and the structure of global capitalism, that both constrain and empower. Regarding the structures relevant to TRIPs, only a relatively small handful of agents was powerful. Structural power is 'the power to choose and to shape the structures of the global political economy within which other states, their political institutions, their economic enterprises, and (not least) their professional people have to operate' (Strange 1987: 565). If we examined migrant farm-workers or American textile workers as agents in the context of the Uruguay Round we would be telling a story of powerful constraints and powerless agents. The story to be told here emphasises the empowering features of structure that made *these* corporate agents particularly efficacious. According to Granovetter, actors' 'attempts at purposive action are . . . embedded in concrete, ongoing systems of social relations' (Granovetter 1985: 487). Therefore, it is necessary to illuminate the relationships between agents and structures and the mediating role of the state as an institution.

As Palan and Abbott point out, 'capitalist enterprises need the state to provide . . . the political and social conditions of accumulation' (Palan and Abbott 1996: 36). The state structures private sector participation and access to decision-makers; 'it is within options set out by the state that interest groups organize and influence policies and their implementation' (Woods 1995: 170). Some actors are more privileged than others, and state institutions often favour particular interests. Corporate actors employ both direct power by lobbying, and indirect power, establishing the normative context, in pursuing their aims. In order to reveal the process by which private interests become public one must examine the substance and power of discourse, and the 'fit' between the message and the audience. Complementarity between state and private interests is ultimately constructed. There is nothing automatic about this process.

The agents and their interests

The agents are a group of twelve like-minded CEOs of US-based multinational corporations and their advisors.[1] These CEOs formed the *ad hoc* Intellectual Property Committee (IPC) in March 1986, just prior to the Punta del Este meeting that launched the Uruguay Round. In 1986 the members of the IPC were: Bristol-Myers; CBS; Du Pont; General Electric; General Motors; Hewlett-Packard; IBM; Johnson & Johnson; Merck; Monsanto; and Pfizer. These companies represent a broad spectrum of US intellectual property interests, including chemical, computer, entertainment, pharmaceutical, and software industries.

The IPC sought a multilateral agreement to strengthen global protection of its members' intellectual property. As technological prowess increasingly has become diffused throughout the world economy, the capacity for others to inexpensively reproduce expensively produced goods has grown; certain types of technology have become easy and relatively inexpensive to appropriate. Some of the leading US industries' (e.g. electronic instruments and equipment, pharmaceuticals, software) competitive edge is reliant upon easily appropriated IP. The American-based firms have comparative advantage in these products, but felt they faced losing that advantage without government help. 'As the US economy became more internationalized, many firms saw government as a potential ally against foreign companies . . . Firms became politically active because the government had influence on critical uncertainties in the firm's environment' (Yoffie 1987: 45). In particular, they were uncertain about the extent to which foreign governments would protect US-held IP. They began their quest by seeking US government support in pressuring foreign governments to adopt and enforce more stringent IP protection. They sought, and won, changes in US domestic laws, most notably Sections 301 and 337 of the US trade laws. They urged the US government to get tough on foreign violators of US-held IP rights. The IPC lobbied the government to support and promote a multilateral IP agreement through the GATT, eschewing the traditional venue, the World Intellectual Property Organisation, because of its lack of enforcement powers and dominance by less developed countries. Transnationally, the IPC member executives by-passed their industry associations and directly engaged their European and Japanese private sector counterparts to press for a TRIPs agreement in the GATT. The transnational leadership of these US-based corporations was decisive in the achievement of the TRIPs accord. The transnational private sector coalition seeking to globalise its preferred conception of IP policy needed GATT to further and legitimise its goals, monitor compliance, and enforce policy.

The agents in this case operated at multiple levels in pursuit of their goals. They were active at the domestic level, pushing for changes in US legislation (Sell 1995). Transnationally, they mobilised a private sector coalition supportive of their vision of a trade-based IP regime. They actively pressed their case in international organisations prior to and during the Uruguay Round. They visited government and private sector representatives in countries known for lax IP protection and enforcement. They pleaded their case for a tough multilateral IP instrument to governmental officials in other industrialised states. In short, they used every available access channel to make their views known and champion their cause.

However, to stop there and conclude that agency tells the whole story begs important questions. How did *these particular* agents become so powerful? Why were they so successful? Why *now*? In order to answer these questions one must incorporate structural and institutional factors as well.

The changing structure of global capitalism

Four important aspects of globalisation that have altered market structure include, 'the globalization of finance, the internationalization of production, the changing role of technology, and the politics of de-regulation' (Palan and Abbott 1996: 20). These changes led to the rise of a competitive state strategy - 'a set of policies that are explicitly aimed at improving the climate for business . . . and hence at enhancing the "competitive" advantage of such countries in the global economy' (Palan and Abbott 1996: 6). Competitiveness concerns in the US animated a number of significant policy changes relevant to the politics of IP. US policy-makers were preoccupied by US 'decline', as reflected in both trade and budget deficits. The US sought to enhance the ability of its corporations to compete in global markets.

The globalisation of finance facilitated market expansion, and market access became the clarion call of US competitiveness. Worries over US trade deficits elevated the importance of trade in US policy-making. Domestically, the US shifted to supply side economics to provide the conditions for generating growth (Palan and Abbott 1996: 4). Attendant policies included the relaxation of antitrust enforcement, which paved the way for reinvigorated domestic IP protection. In so far as patents confer temporary monopoly privileges, a natural tension exists between IP protection and antitrust. 'Antitrust rules that once sharply restricted the commercial exploitation of patents have been greatly liberalized' (Silverstein 1991: 313–14). The increasing importance of high technology sectors in the global economy heightened US interest in IP as an important element of competitive advantage. In recent years, beginning in 1982 with the establishment of the Court of Appeals for the Federal Circuit (CAFC), the so-called 'patent court', the US has dramatically improved the legal environment for patent holders. The CAFC vigorously upholds patent holders' rights against infringers, and other US policies have extended the definition of patentable subject matter, and the scope and duration of patent rights.

The post-war US commitment to 'free trade' came under stress in the early and mid-1980s and was eclipsed by the concept of 'free-but-fair trade.' Proponents of this position argued it was necessary to 'level the playing field,' or to reduce distortions emanating from other countries' trade practices, implying that in a perfect world the US could continue to practise free trade, but others are preventing it from doing so. In principle, the fair trade policy is designed to promote freer trade worldwide by opposing protectionism at home, enforcing individual cases brought under US trade law to counter 'unfair' foreign practices, and negotiating bilateral and multilateral agreements to reduce trade barriers (Greenwald 1987: 234). IP activists redefined inadequate IP protection abroad as a barrier to legitimate trade.

Adding inadequate enforcement of US IP rights abroad as actionable under existing trade statutes, such as 301, brought IP under the normative umbrella of trade policy. Private sector IP activists effectively cast intellectual property rights as equivalent to general property rights, hence essential to free trade. Behaviour that once was tolerated was now redefined as objectionable and unfair. Linking IP to trade and advocating this conception for the multilateral trading order, the IPC was able to appeal to an existing international institution, GATT, and emphasise the benefits of the new approach not just for the IPC but for the world trading system as a whole. As one member of the IPC remarked:

> We in industry need to articulate the important market access and domestic growth aspects of intellectual property protection. . . . It is critical that US companies work to stress the importance in public policy debates of intellectual property protection to the health of the international trading system.
>
> (Bale in Walker and Bloomfield 1988: 123)

The IPC offered an agenda that advocated expanding global economic integration. The IPC exuded confidence about its industries' abilities to compete in the new global economy, and urged policy-makers to get on board with the winners. The IPC packaged its prescriptions as being good for America as a whole and good for the health of the global trading system.

The internationalisation of production, characterised by a 'post-Fordist' regime of accumulation, empowered a new set of domestic corporate actors.[2] Post-Fordism implies reduced political power for high wage labour, and reduced bargaining power for industries still based on the Fordist model in industrialised countries. Industries in decline as a result of aggressive import competition from low-wage labour sites enjoyed reduced political power. High technology IP-based industries eclipsed formerly powerful sectors, such as steel, agriculture, and textiles.

In the Uruguay Round so-called 'sunset industries', such as textiles, lost out to those industries that presented themselves as the leaders of the next wave. These industries of the IPC – e.g. pharmaceutical, entertainment, computer software – were in a good position in so far as they were vigorous exporters that enjoyed positive trade balances. While the US economy was hurting, these US businesses were prospering abroad:

> The decline of the US economy was accompanied by a wave of internationalization of US business abroad. Thus, while the US economy appears to have lost its relative position, US business, in particular in the strategic sectors [such as pharmaceuticals, telecommunications, computer technology, and banking] have been able to maintain their position.
>
> (Palan and Abbott 1996: 138)

To secure a TRIPs agreement, the negotiators had to make trade-offs with other parts of the Uruguay Round agenda. For example, the MultiFibre Arrangement (MFA), which for years had provided US textile producers some import protection from low wage producers, will now be phased out. According to Hoekman and Kostecki, there was 'a recognition that without a deal on TRIPs, ratification of the Uruguay Round package in the US Congress was unlikely given the political weight of the US industries supporting strong IPR discipline' (Hoekman and Kostecki 1995: 157; Mowrey 1993: 369).

Thus far, I have identified the agents, relevant structures, and the changing institutional context of the US that produced expectations regarding the promotion of a dramatically strengthened multilateral IP regime as embodied in the TRIPs accord. However, what remains to be explained is the process by which private actors constructed complementarity between state and private interests, and how private interests became enshrined in public international law. Despite the facilitating conditions described in previous sections, there was nothing automatic about this process. While the member corporations of the IPC were structurally privileged by virtue of their role in the US and the global economy, their potential for influence had 'to be made a reality by conscious political action' (Augelli and Murphy 1993: 132).

Direct and indirect power of the IPC

In capitalist economies, two types of corporate power are noteworthy: direct and indirect power. Corporations exercise direct, instrumental, power when they mobilise resources and pressure. Their provision of information and expertise, their lobbying activities, and institutional access reflect direct power. A second, equally important, type of power is indirect and normative. Their 'mobilization of bias' and construction of actors' meanings and interests reflect indirect power (Wilks 1996). Indirect power rests on the general societal acceptance of the corporation as 'the dominant and essentially beneficial institution of economic life. That acceptance is manifest in the political weight given to the view of business groups . . . and the economic weight given to the market performance of such companies' (Wilks 1996: 45). I will discuss each of these in turn.

Direct power

The government relies on information provided by corporations. Large transnational corporations are able to provide government officials with potentially useful information about foreign countries; 'not all rivals can compete politically on these terms' (Yoffie 1987: 49). In IP, multinational corporations and their industry associations consistently have provided detailed information about foreign governments' failures to provide adequate IP protection. Corporations have committed considerable resources to the exposure of piracy of IP abroad. Furthermore, to determine the scale and scope of foreign piracy, the government has had to rely on loss estimates provided by affected firms. For example, the first official quantitative estimates of distortions in US trade stemming from inadequate IP protection abroad were based on data collected by the International Trade Commission (ITC), which sent out questionnaires to affected industries. Firms interested in a trade-based approach to IP had plenty of incentive to overestimate the losses, especially 'knowing that the ITC report would be used by politicians and economists in Washington when they debated whether or not IP protection should become a major issue in international trade negotiations' (Emmert 1990: 1324–5). Subsequent independent estimates suggested that the ITC figures were wildly inflated (Gadbaw and Richards 1988).

The private sector can provide expertise in issue areas not well understood by government. In this regard, IP is especially unusual. Unlike other attorneys, most IP lawyers possess highly technical backgrounds in science, engineering, chemistry, or biochemistry. IP lawyers are privileged purveyors of expertise. The government had to rely on IP experts, typically corporate counsel, who were also advocates, to translate the complexities into political discourse and make clear the connection between IP and international trade.

The IPC member corporations and their industry associations waged an extensive lobbying campaign. They pressed the Congress and Administration to recognise the

> critical importance to the United States of trade in goods and services dependent upon intellectual property protection worldwide, and . . . to help forge the necessary legal tools enabling our trade negotiators to convince foreign nations to take action against massive and debilitating piracy and counterfeiting of US . . . products.
>
> (US Senate 1986: 162–4)

They packaged their ideas as problem-solvers, arguing that support for their robust export industries would help the US out of its perceived economic decline. They successfully pressed for changes in US trade laws that would institutionalise their desired link between trade and IP. Amendments to the trade acts in 1979, 1984 and 1988 progressively responded to the demands of the IP lobby, and strengthened the link between IP protection and trade. As Gorlin commented, 'the transformation of intellectual property into a trade issue and the development of a trade-based approach to improving the protection of intellectual property could not have occurred had the US government and the US private sector not worked closely together' (Gorlin in Walker and Bloomfield 1988: 172). The consensus-building process drew upon expertise (identifying the problem, providing information and loss estimates), discursive elements (translating arcane IP issues into new instruments of trade policy), and the cognitive appeal of the solutions advocated.

Another important manifestation of the IP activists' direct power was their institutional access. A particularly important advisory body, constituted by the Executive Branch to solicit private sector views on trade policy, is the Advisory Committee for Trade Negotiations (ACTN). It is the top of the private sector pyramid in terms of government representation. The President appoints its members, who played a major role in devising a trade-based IP strategy. The ACTN proved to be an important vehicle for the globalisation of the private interests of its member corporations. Throughout the 1980s, the increasingly vocal IP lobby played a large role in the formation of US trade policy. Two corporate executives, Edmund Pratt of Pfizer Pharmaceutical and John Opel of IBM, had long been lobbying the US government to get serious about IP violators abroad. Both Pratt and Opel participated in the US-based International Anti-Counterfeiting Coalition (to protect trademarked high fashion and luxury goods) at the end of the Tokyo Round of GATT negotiations. Pratt's focus was patent protection for pharmaceuticals, whereas Opel was primarily concerned about copyright protection and computer software.

Beginning in 1981, Pratt chaired the ACTN. Pratt and Opel pursued parallel efforts during 1983 and 1984 to advance their specific IP concerns to the administration. Largely as a result of their input, the President's Commission on Competitiveness report of 1983–4 included an addendum on IP protection as a competitiveness issue. In 1984, the United States Trade Representative (USTR) requested private sector input on including IP in the upcoming GATT Round. Opel commissioned Jacques Gorlin, an economist who served as a consultant to ACTN and subsequently the IPC, to draft a paper for the USTR outlining a trade-based approach for IP. Gorlin's paper (Gorlin 1985) became the basis for the multilateral IP strategy that corporations soon pursued. It provided concrete proposals for a multilateral IP agreement, emphasising minimum standards of protection, dispute settlement, and enforcement, and suggested strategies for consensus building. ACTN created an eight-member Task Force on Intellectual Property Rights, which included Opel, Fritz Attaway, vice president and counsel of the Motion Picture Association, and Abraham Cohen, president of the International Division of Merck & Company, Inc. (at that time America's largest pharmaceutical corporation). In October 1985, this task force presented its report to ACTN and its recommendations appeared to be lifted wholesale out of Gorlin's paper (USTR 1985 and 1986).

Significantly, Edmund Pratt, CEO of Pfizer, was the Business Roundtable's leader in 1988 as trade and intellectual property dominated the US agenda. Pratt was selected to represent the private sector at the Uruguay Round trade talks. He was an advisor to the US Official Delegation at the Uruguay Round in his capacity as chairman of ACTN. This was auspicious because the private sector has no official standing at GATT. Thus the state, through ACTN, conferred power upon particular agents to advance their IP agenda in multilateral negotiations.

Indirect power

Corporations also pursue normative power, or the construction of the normative context. This normative context defines right and wrong, and distinguishes fair from unfair practices. It also points to which sets of competing ideas are likely to find favour. As Sikkink (1991) has pointed out, particular economic ideas are more likely to prevail – that is, to be supported, adopted, and implemented by policy-makers – if they resonate with the broader culture and are considered to be legitimate. The IPC's policy advocacy responded to concrete problems facing policy-makers in a contingent social context in which US policy-makers were trying to respond to changes in the structure of global capitalism.

In cognitive terms, economic ideas perform four basic functions: a cathartic function, which apportions blame; a morale function, which provides a vision of the future; a solidarity function, which provides a rallying device or a basis for coalitional politics; and an advocacy function, which stresses empowerment (Woods 1995: 173–4). The particular ideas promoted by the IPC laid the blame for the United States' growing trade deficit elsewhere by identifying an enemy (foreign pirates). Placing the blame for America's trade woes on foreign countries' unfair practices helped to sharpen policy options in a way that an extended round of introspection could not. Policy-makers were spared the arduous task of evaluating the extent to which US trade problems were the products of either its or its firms' bad choices. The morale functions of the IPC's policy advocacy were apparent in as much as the IPC promised a more robust future for US competitiveness and promoted their member corporations as viable and vibrant industries capable of leading the United States out of its economic doldrums. The IPC agenda also included a solidarity function; the IPC industries united behind a trade-based conception of IP protection, which became a rallying device for mobilising a powerful group of industries that could present themselves as part of the solution to America's trade woes. They elevated intellectual property to the top tier of the US trade agenda in a way that would permit the United States to maximise its leverage via access to its huge domestic market. Promoting the instrument of trade leverage for resolving disputes over intellectual property protection, the IPC was able to emphasise an avenue that gave the United States a clear advantage, especially *vis-à-vis* developing countries whose access to the US market is imperative for their long-term economic development. Therefore, the ideas and solutions promoted by the IPC captured the imagination of US policy-makers as both feasible and politically beneficial.

In fact, the TRIPs accord stood out in the Uruguay Round agenda because it was not about freeing trade, but extending more protection (Hoekman and Kostecki 1995: 152). Borrus has characterised the US approach to IP as 'quite defensive, trying to hold ground by increasing intellectual property protection' (Borrus 1993: 376). It is ironic in the context of both competitiveness and IP debates that extending monopoly privileges could be marketed as 'freer trade.' But conditions of uncertainty create new opportunities to redefine interests, despite the fact that some versions seem to defy logic and come from the wrong side of Alice in Wonderland's Looking Glass. Indeed, the international public policy manager for the Hewlett-Packard Company defended his quest as follows:

> Intellectual property protection is the only valid type of 'protectionism' being pushed in Washington now because it is really not traditional protectionism at all. Instead, it is at the heart of an open trading system, and those companies that support the strengthening of the trading system and oppose protectionist approaches are the same ones that need and support better intellectual property protection.
>
> (Bale in Walker and Bloomfield 1988: 123)

One of the most crucial aspects of the IPC's indirect power, was its ability to mobilise an inter-sectoral transnational private sector consensus on substantive norms for international IP protection. In Wilks' terms, substantive norms 'represent an understanding between the major actors about the main content of agreements or policies' (Wilks 1996: 49). As Lou Clemente, VP General-Counsel of Pfizer, Inc. and founding member of the IPC remarked:

I think the overriding significance of [the IPC] is that it has been able to join together with our colleagues in electronics, in the traditional copyright fields, the chemical industry, and so on, to present a united front on behalf of strong intellectual property protection.

(Clemente in Walker and Bloomfield 1988: 134)

From the time of its formation in March 1986, the IPC only had six months before the upcoming September Punta del Este meeting. IPC members immediately contacted their counterparts in European and Japanese industry. In June 1986, the IPC met with the Confederation of British Industries, the BDI in Germany, the French *Patronat,* and through them, with the Union of Industrial and Employers' Confederations of Europe (UNICE). UNICE is the official representative of European business and industry in European institutions; it is composed of thirty-three member federations from twenty-two countries. In July, the IPC went to Japan and met with the Japan Federation of Economic Organisations (Keidanren hereafter). Keidanren is a private, non-profit economic organisation representing virtually all branches of economic activity in Japan. In these meetings, the IPC stressed that the issue of IP was too important to leave to governments.[3] The group argued that industry needed to decide upon the best course of action and then tell governments what to do. The IPC convinced their European and Japanese counterparts of the merits of a trade-based approach by emphasising their shared experience and common plight. The IPC stressed the high costs of IP piracy, and the successes that it had achieved through bilateral trade negotiations. The IPC succeeded in forging an industry consensus with its European and Japanese counterparts, who agreed to work on it and pledged to present these views to their respective governments in time for the launching of the Uruguay Round. As Pratt noted, this joint action by the US, European and Japanese business communities represented 'a significant breakthrough in the involvement of the international business community in trade negotiations' (quoted in Drahos 1995: 13). UNICE and Keidanren successfully advanced their new cause to their governments. By the launching of the new trade round in September, the US, Japan, and Europe were united behind the inclusion of an IP code in the GATT.

The IPC, UNICE, and Keidanren agreed to continue to work together to devise a consensual approach to an IP code at the GATT. Industry representatives met in October and November 1986, and worked on producing a consensus document to present to their respective governments and the GATT Secretariat. Participants made a concerted effort to 'honestly represent all forms of intellectual property and all industries concerned' (Enyart 1990: 55). In June 1988, this 'trilateral group' released its 'Basic Framework of GATT Provisions on Intellectual Property' (IPC, Keidanren, and UNICE 1988). This document was strikingly similar to Gorlin's 1985 paper, covering minimum standards of protection, enforcement and dispute settlement provisions, and became the basis of the eventual TRIPs agreement. It was a consensus document that included compromises. For instance, the US research-based pharmaceutical industry was not completely satisfied with the compulsory licensing provisions, but the IPC conceded the issue to keep the Europeans and Japanese on board. Having produced this consensus proposal, the IPC, Keidranen, and UNICE had to go home and sell the approach to other companies and industries (Enyart, 1990: 55). This process was not at all difficult for the IPC, which faced a very receptive home government. In fact, the US government sent out the June 1988 proposal as reflecting its own views.[4]

The private sector's normative power was consolidated and institutionalised in so far as it 'elevated its own self-interest to the status of a substantive norm' and established 'understandings about what is proper, natural and legitimate' that reflected 'the interests of the big corporate players' (Wilks 1996: 49–50).

Structural power

In the TRIPs negotiations the IPC had a potent ally at the Uruguay Round in Edmund Pratt of Pfizer, who was an advisor to the US Official Delegation at the Round in his capacity as chairman of ACTN. The IPC worked closely with the USTR, the Commerce Department, and the Patent and Trademark Office (PTO). A 1988 IPC report stated that 'this close relationship with USTR and Commerce has permitted the IPC to shape the US proposals and negotiating positions during the course of the negotiations' (Drahos 1995: 13).

Expressing satisfaction with the final 1994 TRIPs agreement Gorlin, advisor to the IPC, said that the IPC got 95 per cent of what it wanted.[5] Formerly intransigent developing countries went along for several reasons. First of all, they faced escalating pressure from the US via Section 301 and GSP (generalised system of preference) actions (Sell 1998). In May 1988 the US officially dropped the East Asian NICs from its list of countries eligible for GSP benefits. Many developing countries hoped that cooperation on TRIPs would ease the 301 pressure. India had received considerable bilateral pressure from the US to drop its opposition. Also, the US, Canada, and Mexico had successfully negotiated NAFTA, which included stiff IP requirements. Many Latin American countries, hoping eventually to join NAFTA, considered IP commitments as 'part of the price of admission' (Drahos 1995: 15). For smaller countries that had not been targeted by 301 actions, NAFTA and the proliferation of similar regional trading blocs posed a different set of concerns that led them to support TRIPs and the Round as a whole. Not being parties to any preferential regional agreements, they came to endorse a strong liberalising outcome to counter discriminatory trade practices emanating from the regional blocs (Whalley in Martin and Winters 1995: 305–26).[6]

The triumph of the IPC was the triumph of a small fraction of the private sector. Structural factors tipped the scale in the direction of the privileged agents and their preferred policies, but it took the actions of agents to ensure this outcome. This case demonstrates how agents reproduce and transform the structure through their actions. The TRIPs accord redefines winners and losers and the WTO institutionalises a more aggressively liberal world trading order. As Murphy points out:

> once GATT liberalizations are in effect, they shape government perceptions of the national interests, biasing them in a liberal direction. Moreover, the

liberalizations negotiated under GATT have come to shape the perceptions of business, becoming a predictable part of the business environment.

(Murphy 1994: 198–9)

This expanded approach is now a structural feature that may either constrain or empower the agents. The TRIPs component of the WTO empowers the IPC.

Conclusion

The TRIPs accord was a product of structured agency. The IPC was structurally privileged in terms of having structural power in US and global markets. Although the IPC had many advantages, its triumph was not a foregone conclusion. Examining elements of agency, direct and indirect power, highlights the importance of the IPC's activities in marshalling support for a comprehensive, trade-based IP code. With so many structural factors weighing in favour of these particular agents, one might argue that this explanation is overdetermined. One might wonder, 'who needs agency?' Yet, considering the counterfactual case – that is, if the IPC had not exerted itself in this arena – it is highly unlikely that there would be a TRIPs accord. The most likely outcome would have been a much narrower, resuscitated Anticounterfeiting Code, if that. Until the IPC began lobbying its European and Japanese private sector counterparts, there was very little enthusiasm or even interest in a comprehensive IP code. The IPC itself was surprised by how much it achieved. The TRIPs accord far surpassed the IPC's initial expectations. It is an example of the neo-liberal global discourse, which claims that TNCs and MNCs have gained significant authority against the background of an emerging global economy (see introduction of this book).

Yet the mediating role of the US state was also critically important. The IPC's activities notwithstanding, there would be no TRIPs accord if the US had not changed its domestic attitudes towards strong IP protection. The US state, embedded in the context of the changing structure of global capitalism, redefined its interests and adopted a competitive strategy that made it particularly receptive to the IPC's policy advocacy.

My argument draws upon insights from the agent-structure debate to explain the adoption of the TRIPs accord. This discussion has highlighted the structured nature of agency, as mediated by institutions, which is neglected in interest group, rational choice, and liberal pluralist accounts of similar processes. Furthermore, accounts of this process that confine their focus to the activities of states alone obscure more than they reveal. State-centric analyses, that treat states as unitary, rational actors, render a misleading portrayal of the driving forces behind the TRIPs agreement. Such analyses are ill-equipped to explain the process whereby private interests become public law. The TRIPs accord is the social construction of privileged agents whose interests were mediated through the US state. The knowledge and ideas promoted by the IPC were powerful elements in this process. The IPC's technical expertise, the discourse of the IPC's advocates, and the cognitive appeal of the IPC's diagnosis and pre-scriptions help to provide the explanatory link between agents and structures.

The argument presented here inquires critically about the origin of the demand for new rules of international commerce, takes structural context seriously, and incorporates both institutional and intersubjective aspects of politics. Yet even more broadly, this analysis underscores the importance of integrating private actors into explanations of the global political economy and provides a useful prism for understanding what is at stake in the ongoing debates over globalisation.

Notes

1 Throughout the decade from 1986–96, the IPC's membership has fluctuated from eleven to fourteen. In 1994 the IPC represented the following corporations: Bristol-Myers Squibb; Digital Equipment Corporation; FMC; General Electric; Hewlett-Packard; IBM; Johnson & Johnson; Merck; Pfizer; Procter & Gamble; Rockwell International; and Time Warner.
2 Post-Fordism is a term popularised by the French Regulation School of political econ-omy, and describes

> the decline of the old manufacturing base and the growth of 'sunrise,' computer-based industries . . . an economy dominated by multinationals, with their new international division of labour and their greater autonomy from nation–state con-trol; and the 'globalisation' of the new financial markets, linked by the communications revolution.
>
> (Hall, 1988; quoted in Amin 1994: 4)

See also Bernard in Stubbs and Underhill, 1994: 216–29; Cox, 1993.
3 This paragraph based on author's interview with Gorlin, 22 January 1996, Washington, D.C.
4 Author's interview with Gorlin.
5 Author's interview with Gorlin.
6 For an account of the devastating effects of NAFTA on the economies of the Caribbean. See, 'Backlash from NAFTA batters economies of the Caribbean,' 30 January 1997, *New York Times* A1 and A8.

References

Amin, A. (ed.) (1994) *Post-Fordism: A Reader,* Oxford: Blackwell.

Augelli, E. and C. Murphy (1993) 'Gramsci and international relations: a general perspective with examples from recent US policy toward the third world', in S. Gill (ed.) *Gramsci, Historical Materialism and International Relations*, Cambridge: Cambridge University Press:127–47.

Bernard, M. (1994) 'Post-Fordism, transnational production, and the changing global political economy', in R. Stubbs and G. Underhill (eds) *Political Economy and the Changing Global Order*, New York: St. Martin's Press: 216–29.

Borrus, M. (1993) 'Global intellectual property rights in perspective: a concluding panel discussion', in M. Wallerstein, M. Mogee, and R. Schoen (eds) *Global Dimensions of Intellectual Property Rights in Science and Technology*, Washington, D.C.: National Academy Press: 373–7.

Burch, K. (1994) 'The "properties" of the state system and global capitalism', in S. Rosow, N. Inayatullah and M. Rupert (eds) *The Global Economy as Political Space*, Boulder, CO.: Lynne Rienner: 37–59.

Cox, R. (1993) 'Structural issues of global governance: implications for Europe', in S. Gill (ed.) *Gramsci, Historical Materialism and International Relations*, Cambridge: Cambridge University Press: 259–89.

Dessler, D. (1989) 'What's at stake in the agent-structure debate?', *International Organization* 43(3): 441–73.

Drahos, P. (1995) 'Global property rights in information: the story of TRIPs at the GATT,' *Prometheus* 13(1): 6–19.

Emmert, F. (1990) 'Intellectual property in the Uruguay Round - negotiating strategies of the Western industrialized countries', *Michigan Journal of International Law* 11: 1317–99.

Enyart, J. (1990) 'A GATT intellectual property code', *Les Nouvelles* 25: 53–6.

Gadbaw M. and Richards, T. (1988) *Intellectual Property Rights: Global Consensus, Global Conflict?,* Boulder: Westview Press.

Gorlin, J. (1985) 'A trade-based approach for the international copyright protection for computer software', unpublished.

Granovetter, M. (1985) 'Economic action and social structure: the problem of embeddedness', *American Journal of Sociology* 91(3): 481–510.

Greenwald, J. (1987) 'Protectionism in US economic policy', *Stanford Journal of International Law* Spring: 233–61.

Hoekman, B. and M. Kostecki (1995) *The Political Economy of the World Trading System: From GATT to the WTO*, Oxford: Oxford University Press.

Intellectual Property Committee, Keidranen, and UNICE (1988) *Basic Framework of GATT Provisions on Intellectual Property*, The Intellectual Property Committee, Keidranen, UNICE.

Martin, W. and L. Winters (eds) (1995) *The Uruguay Round and the Developing Countries*, Washington, D.C.: World Bank.

Mowrey, D. (1993) 'Global intellectual property rights issues in perspective: a concluding panel discussion', in M. Wallerstein, M. Mogee and R. Schoen (eds) *Global Dimensions of Intellectual Property Rights in Science and Technology*, Washington, D.C.: National Academy Press: 368–72.

Murphy, C. (1994) *International Organization and Industrial Change: Global Governance since 1850*, New York: Oxford University Press.

Palan, R. and J. Abbott with P. Deans (1996) *State Strategies in the Global Political Economy*, London: Pinter.

Rodrik, D. (1994) 'Comments on Maskus and Eby-Konan', in A. Deardorff and R. Stern (eds) *Analytic and Negotiating Issues in the Global Trading System*, Ann Arbor: University of Michigan Press: 447–50.

Sell, S. (1995) 'The origins of a trade-based approach to intellectual property protection: the role of industry associations', *Science Communication* 17(2): 163–85.

—— (1998) *Power and Ideas: The North–South Politics of Intellectual Property and Antitrust*, Albany: State University of New York Press.

Sikkink, K. (1991) *Ideas and Institutions*, Ithaca: Cornell University Press.

Silverstein, D. (1991) 'Patents, science and innovation: historical linkages and implications for global technological competitiveness', *Rutgers Computer and Technology Law Journal* 17(2): 261–319.

Strange, S. (1987) 'The persistent myth of "lost" hegemony', *International Organization* 41: 551–74.

—— (1996) *The Retreat of the State: The Diffusion of Power in the World Economy*, Cambridge: Cambridge University Press.

Stubbs, R. and G. Underhill (1994) *Political Economy and the Changing Global Order*,

New York: St Martin's Press.

US Senate, Senate Finance Committee (1986) *Intellectual Property Rights: Hearings Before the Subcommittee on International Trade of the Senate Finance Committee*, 99th Cong., 2nd. sess. 14 May.

US Trade Representative, Task Force on Intellectual Property (1985) *Summary of Phase I: Recommendations of the Task Force on Intellectual Property to the Advisory Committee for Trade Negotiations*, unpublished report.

US Trade Representative, Advisory Committee for Trade Negotiations' Task Force on Intellectual Property Rights (1986) *Summary of Phase II: Recommendations of the Task Force*, unpublished report.

Walker, C. and M. Bloomfield (eds) (1988) *Intellectual Property Rights and Capital Formation in the Next Decade*, Lanham, Md.: University Press of America.

Wallerstein, M., M. Mogee and R. Schoen (eds) (1993) *Global Dimensions of Intellectual Property Rights in Science and Technology*, Washington, D.C.: National Academy Press.

Wendt, A. (1987) 'The agent-structure problem in international relations theory', *International Organization* 41(3): 335–70.

Whipple, R. (1987) 'A new era in licensing', *Les Nouvelles* (22)3: 109–10.

Wilks, S. (1996) 'Comparative capitalism and the political power of business', in S. Strange (ed.) *Globalisation and Capitalist Diversity: Experiences on the Asian Mainland*, Florence: European University Institute: 31–63.

Woods, N. (1995) 'Economic ideas and international relations: beyond rational neglect', *International Studies Quarterly* 39: 161–80.

Yoffie, D. (1987) 'Corporate strategies for political action: a rational model', in A. Marcus, A. Kaufman and D. Bean (eds) *Business Strategy and Public Policy: Perspectives from Industry and Academia*, NY: Quorum: 43–60.

6 Business strategy and evolving rules in the Single European Market

Duncan Matthews and
John F. Pickering

Introduction

Rules in the Single Market can take a number of forms. Rules may be formal or informal; imposed or negotiated; prescriptive or discretionary in the manner of their implementation; evolving over time (e.g. see Wilks 1992) or rigorously specified from the beginning; they may be interpreted and developed through case law in the European Court; they may depend on the efforts and actions of professional bodies (Brazier *et al.* 1992) or standard setting bodies and national regulatory agencies for their implementation. They may constitute elements of 'hard law' where rules are imposed and enforced through formal regulation or take the form of 'soft law', including elements of self-regulation, where a more flexible and interpretative approach is adopted. Whatever the format, the overriding purpose is the opening up of the Single Market and the emphasis on allowing continuing evolution in rule-making and, through the process of competition among rules driven by the corporate sector, the convergence upon best practice.

The economic benefits of the Single Market were extolled in the Cecchini Report (1988) (see also Jacquemin and Wright 1993). In particular, it was argued that there would be transaction cost savings, enhanced productive efficiency as a result of a larger market, improved resource allocation and manpower savings.

In the context of the present research (Matthews and Pickering 1997) it is possible to identify likely effects of steps to create a Single European Market in terms of actions and responses within key industry sectors. Within this tradition, we may adopt a stimulus-response paradigm, in which the way firms respond to changes in the regulatory environment is seen as depending on their perception of that environment and of the market, the organisational characteristics of the company, the scope for coordination of responses with other firms and the credibility of the rule-making process and expectations as to the commitment to its enforcement.

By adapting to the external rule changes in ways that are to their own advantage, firms will drive the development of the Single Market. As outlined in the introduction of this book, multinational and transnational corporations are thus powerful actors in the rule-setting at the international level. Corporate responses to the external rule-making may be: unilateral and/or collaborative (i.e. in conjunction with other firms in the industry); through internal (organisational) change and/or through response in the external market place; based upon an 'inertial' approach (minimising the differences between the old and the new rules) and/or dynamic in response to new opportunities and challenges; collusive or competitive. Where the benefits of coop-eration exceed those of competition, firms may seek to lay down new procedures, e.g. in the form of self-regulation akin to 'soft law' coordination to stabilise the market. Firms may attempt to lobby or indeed 'capture' regulators before the rule change takes place (Neven *et al.* 1993), to influence its implementation at the national level (Majone 1996), or to encourage a second round of changes as part of a process of on-going regulatory review (Matthews and Pickering 1997).

The research that is reported in this paper explores the nature of rule-making and response in the light of Single Market developments. The work focused on different industry sectors, including leasing, machine tools, construction, insurance, retailing, and pharmaceuticals. In each case, different types of rule-making in support of the Single Market Programme and/or wider socio-economic consider-ations had been pursued.

In the next section we assess the different EC regulatory approaches by sector, explaining where Single Market harmonisation has been kept at bay and where the EC has intervened particularly prescriptively. The detailed findings from each industry study are set out elsewhere in separate papers, referenced in the text. We then review the contributions that these case studies make to our understanding of the process of rule-making and response. We then draw out the main implications of this study in the concluding section.

Industry studies

Leasing

Corporate strategies may have the objective of encouraging the achievement of a Single Market, or may be designed to maintain the *status quo* where the existence of segmented markets is profit-enhancing for the industry involved. The leasing industry in Europe is based upon a series of separate national markets with a significant diversity of rule systems (see Leaseurope/Arthur Andersen 1992, Soper *et al.* 1992, Matthews and Mayes 1994a).

The lack of harmonisation in relation to economic policy instruments (accounting provisions, banking regulations and taxation measures) is a serious hindrance to the creation of a Single Market in the sector. The continued existence of these barriers to a Single Market can be attributed to a number of factors. First, there has been no coordinated attempt by the various Directorates General of the European Commission to systematically remove trade disparities in leasing. Where progress has been made the initiative has come from particular Directorates General with their own policy objectives, not from the European Commission as a whole acting as a collegiate body. There has been a problem in coherence of approach because leasing does not readily fall within the remit of any one of the Commission's Directorates General.

Second, in the policy process the Commission has lacked much of the technical expertise needed to deal with the complex regulatory matters at hand and, in common with the classic model of Community policy-making (Mazey and Richardson 1993), has turned to leasing industry experts for advice. This is the 'low politics' of technical committees which is often so important in the policy process (Weale and Williams 1992). The evidence is that the representatives of the leasing industry, on whom the EC relied for guidance and advice, have not favoured a move to a Single Market. Their preference has been for the preservation of differences between the national markets, the causes of which, they advised, would be too complex for the European Commission to address.

The reasons why the Commission was advised by the industry that it should not act to harmonise standards for the leasing industry are twofold. On the one hand the advice was due to the European industry trade association, Leaseurope, facing a conflict of different national interests among its member associations. This reduced the coherence of Leaseurope's approach and left it without a clear mandate as to the preferred direction of developments. On the other hand, there were significant commercial advantages for the industry in ensuring that national markets remained highly segmented so that the tax efficiencies inherent in cross-border leasing transactions could be maintained. Many profitable leasing arrangements actually rely on disparities between national accounting and tax provisions for their success. As a result of these factors, convergence of national rules has been slow.

Thus the leasing industry remains heavily segmented on a national basis, to the benefit of the firms in the industry who see little advantage in achieving a Single Market. It is clear that the various national leasing industries wish to retain their separateness and avoid a coordinated European Commission effort to accelerate the convergence process. Their advice to the Commission in various technical committees reflects this approach.

Machine tools

Where a Single Market, or indeed a global market, already exists there can be no presumption that firms see advantage from further regulatory change. In machine tools, the EC has constituted a Single Market for a significant period of time (see Boston Consulting Group 1985, Buigues *et al.* 1990, Matthews and Mayes 1992). This is attributable to the overall economic significance of the EC in world demand and supply of machine tools, with major international manufacturers treating the EC as one important sector of their world market and hence their global market strategy. This has been reflected by inward investment into the EC by both Japanese and US companies. A factor encouraging inward investment by non-EC companies has been to avoid any adverse consequences which might have arisen from a 'fortress Europe' approach, raising entry barriers at the external frontiers of the EC to products from third countries.

Given the overall openness and competitiveness within the EC market for machine tools, the Single Market Programme has not had a significant impact on the industry in relation to the removal of physical barriers at borders, fiscal barriers or technical barriers, such as the provisions of the Machinery Directive. Initiatives to enhance the free movement of labour, particularly as a consequence of the mutual recognition of qualifications, may have a more significant impact on the machine tool industry in the longer term. However, language considerations may well continue to create an effective barrier to the movement of skilled workers. It has also been noted that many member states were slow to transpose the first General Directive on the recognition of professional qualifications into national legislation, thus hindering the availability of qualified operatives from other member states.

Construction

Where national regulation differs markedly from EC rules, a lack of regulatory 'fit' may have a significant impact on corporate strategy. Although harmonisation of technical standards (Woolcock *et al.* 1991) and EC rules on public procurement (Cox 1993, Fernandez Martin 1996) have their own important implications for the construction industry, this case study looked at social policy legislation that might impact upon the economic and competitive activities of the sector. Since social and employment policy in the United Kingdom traditionally differs from that in Continental Europe (Teague 1989, Gold 1993, Gold and Matthews 1996), the focus of this discussion is on the implications of EC social policy rules for the UK construction industry (see Spencer Chapman *et al.* 1991, Matthews and Pickering 1995).

The construction industry has been very directly affected by a number of legislative initiatives by the European Commission with general applicability, particularly aimed at influencing labour market conditions and providing social protection to workers. While much of this has not been specifically directed at the construction sector, because of the industry's particular characteristics the impact of new rules has potentially been significant. Production tends to occur at the point of consumption (on building sites), much of the activity is subject to climatic conditions and the availability of daylight and much of the employment in major construction activities derives from sub-contracting, self-employment and use of itinerant workers.

It is apparent that the approach traditionally adopted by the Employment, Industrial Relations and Social Affairs Directorate General (Directorate General V) of the European Commission has been very much to follow a Continental European model of labour market regulation (perhaps particularly drawing upon that of Germany and France). This has tended to rely on a prescriptive approach of a formal and rigid nature, specifying the precise actions that are to be taken. This contrasts markedly with the UK's approach which has tended to be more pragmatic with an emphasis on achieving a desired end result (namely better labour market and safety protection for consumers), rather than over-emphasis on the particular means to be adopted to achieve this outcome. The action of the European Commission in choosing to harmonise standards on the basis of prescriptive provisions may be interpreted as reflecting a fear of a 'race to the bottom' in employment standards if less prescriptive and coercive provisions were introduced.

However, while the Continental model of labour market regulation does not 'fit' with UK practice, the actual impact of the social policy rules may not be as serious as feared since many adverse implications of the social policy measures were negotiated out during the rule-making process. On occasion, the likely adverse impact of new social policy measures may also have been exaggerated by the industry. Thus far, EC social policy rules have not resulted in the loss of competitiveness or recruitment of workers that had earlier been predicted by the UK construction industry.

Insurance

Where national regulation is later followed by equivalent EC regulation, firms may benefit from their earlier adaptation to equivalent rules since they will have prior knowledge and experience of that regulatory regime (a 'first mover' opportunity). The path to liberalisation and creation of a Single Market in insurance is a case in point. In many member states there have historically been very detailed and restrictive national regulatory controls, justified as being necessary to protect the consumer interest. These controls were the cause of significant barriers to cross-border trade in insurance and have been subject to a long programme of EC regulatory activity (see Boleat 1995, Weidenfeld 1996, Matthews and Pickering 1997). The UK and the Netherlands, in contrast, have traditionally been more liberalised markets. In the UK this was reinforced by the Financial Services Act 1986.

The UK's own liberal approach has been consonant with that pursued by the European Commission and in many respects appears to have served as the template for EC-level regulation rather than the much more constrained and regulated approaches adopted in such countries as France and Germany. This approach by the European Commission we have called 'regulatory emulation'.

Explanations for the adoption of the UK model may be found in the evidence of earlier British success in liberalising its insurance industry while retaining high level supervision of companies' financial reserves and the suitability of those in senior positions in the industry. The clarity of view among British firms, trade associations and Government departments as to the direction in which the EC should be encouraged to move was also no doubt helpful.

In addition, the fact that UK nationals (and more recently also the supportive Dutch) are in senior positions within the Commission Directorate General responsible for financial services (Directorate General XV) is significant. Since the UK and Dutch experiences have provided the only substantive examples of successful liberalisation of insurance markets in an otherwise heavily regulated EC financial services sector, it is perhaps not surprising that officials within Directorate General XV have turned to the UK as a model of good practice. Since the 'regulatory fit' between UK and EC rules for the insurance industry has been achieved so well, UK firms have been largely satisfied with the outcome of the progress of EC legislation to liberalise insurance markets. Regulatory emulation which has looked to the UK model as its starting point has had the effect of requiring little change in regulatory compliance or in market behaviour on the part of insurance companies with their head offices established within the United Kingdom.

Retailing

While some corporate strategies will be in response to a change in the regulatory environment, other aspects of corporate strategy may be a response to self-imposed rules created by the industry itself. Self-regulatory industry behaviour can then itself require a regulatory response from EC rule-setters.

Analysis of German retail sector strategies (see Matthews and Mayes 1994b) allows an exploration of the ways in which 'soft law' has been adopted as a response to, and a stimulus for, 'hard law' (Tammes 1983; Chinkin 1989). In this context, the concept of hard law is used to refer to formal legislative rule-making by the European Commission or by member state governments (Wellens and Borchardt 1989), while soft law is used to describe the adoption of self-regulation or other behavioural responses pursued on the initiative of the companies within an industry (Gruchalla-Wesierski 1984). The response of German retail firms to the 1991 Packaging Ordinance is perhaps the clearest example of industry-led soft law rules subsequently requiring action from EC regulators. The response of German firms to the Ordinance had the effect of distorting intra-Community trade and required further EC legislation to ensure the proper functioning of the Single Market.

Under the German Packaging Ordinance, retailers are required to take back and recycle pre-determined volumes of packaging materials (see Klepper and Michaelis 1993). In response to these new rules, a consortium of German retailers, manufacturers and waste disposal companies set up the *Duales System Deutschland* (DSD), a private company to organise a voluntary network for waste collection and its recycling. This led to the introduction of a green dot (the Grüner Punkt) on the packaging of manufacturers that were paying a fee to participate in the scheme with a view to sharing the cost burden of complying with the Packaging Ordinance. German retailers then collectively announced their intention to stock only products that bore the green dot, in effect excluding from the market companies that were not participating in the DSD scheme. While the introduction of industry-led 'soft law' rules more stringent than the legislation originally intended may not have had a significant impact upon firms who supplied the bulk of their products to the German market, the effects were serious for companies based in other member states.

Firms that exported only small proportions of their output to Germany would be compelled to join the 'voluntary' DSD scheme in order to gain access to retail outlets. This in itself might have been sufficient reason for the European Commission to intervene in response what amounted to a distortion of trade and a barrier to the free movement of goods in the Single Market. However, the intervention of the Commission instead came via another route. The large amounts of waste recovered by the efficient German collection system and the obligation on DSD to recycle waste returned by consumers led to a distortion of the EC recycling market. Recycling companies in other parts of the European Community were unable to meet domestic demand because waste collected by DSD, which was anxious to comply with the provisions of German legislation, was being exported across the Community and recycled or disposed of in other member states.

In response to the coordinated, collusive behaviour of German firms, in December 1994 the European Parliament and the Council of Ministers adopted a Directive on packaging and packaging waste. The aims of the Directive are to prevent any impact on the environment that might result from differing national measures on packaging waste and to remove any obstacles to the Single Market that might result from those national measures. The introduction of EC-level recovery and recycling targets were therefore a direct response to market distortions brought about by events in Germany. The Directive was not, however, the direct result of domestic German legislation *per se*. Rather it was a response to the enthusiasm with which German firms had complied with the national rules by setting up their own 'voluntary' recycling system. In this instance, corporate behavioural (soft law) responses to (hard law) regulatory initiatives were far in excess of what the regulators had originally intended. It was this unanticipated behaviour of firms, not the legislation in Germany itself, which then provided the stimulus for far-reaching EC-wide legislation on recycling packaging waste.

Pharmaceuticals

The growth in EC-level regulatory agencies raises issues for a new level of interaction between institutional and corporate actors in the Single European Market. In the pharmaceutical sector the European Medicines Evaluation Agency was established as an EC-level regulatory agency in 1995 specifically to oversee a new EC-wide system of drug authorisations to facilitate a Single Market. The EMEA is located in London.

The pharmaceutical sector has a long history of EC regulation dating back to 1965 (Thompson 1994, Evers 1995, Wilson and Matthews 1997) but drug authorisation had traditionally remained the preserve of national agencies. The latest round of EC regulatory activity culminated in 1995 when, under the 'future systems' initiative, two new procedures – the decentralised and the centralised routes – were introduced to improve earlier attempts to achieve EC-wide drug approval. The arrangements within these systems apply to new drug authorisation, monitoring and pharmacovigilance.

The decentralised system (which is not available to some biotechnology and some high technology products: 'List A' products) is based upon the principle of mutual recognition between member states. Under this, an application is made for authorisation to one member state that has 210 days to evaluate and report to other member states who then have ninety days to recognise the authorisation. The only ground on which these member states may object is a risk to public health. In the event of such an objection the Committee for Proprietary Medicinal Products (CPMP) arbitrates.

The choice of the national authority to which the application is initially made (the reference member state) is left to the drug producer. This is considered to have benefits since it allows some national authorities, such as the UK Medicines Control Agency (MCA), to continue to draw upon their strong scientific resources. This arrangement also has the effect of creating a degree of competition between national authorities (see Woolcock 1994) which will be encouraged to endeavour to demonstrate that they are well equipped to take on this work on behalf of the Community. The benefits this offers are that it reduces the pressure to achieve consensus and hence helps to avoid delay. It is also considered that this system will be helpful to smaller businesses that may wish to obtain drug authorisations not for the whole of the European Community but simply for a subset of member states.

The centralised procedure is mandatory for biotechnology and other high technology products. It is optional for 'innovative products' ('List B' products). An application for authorisation is made direct to the EMEA. Upon receipt of an application the EMEA appoints a rapporteur and co-rapporteur from among the CPMP member countries. The rapporteurs then report to CPMP, which reaches an opinion on the proposed authorisation. This opinion is then passed on for final approval of the drug by the European Commission.

The establishment of the dual, centralised and decentralised, system of drug authorisations, reflects the wish of the pharmaceutical industry to avoid what it perceives to be the unduly bureaucratic and ponderous authorisation procedure available in the USA via the Food and Drug Administration (FDA). The availability of an alternative, competing system was strongly advocated by the UK pharmaceutical industry.

So far, there has been only limited use of either of the new systems, especially in relation to new drug authorisations. While companies have made positive choices to use the centralised system for 'List B' products, thereby suggesting confidence in the procedure, neither system has yet been fully tested. The existence of the two systems inevitably gives rise to the possibility of competition among rule systems. Not only is there industry-driven competition between the alternative systems for 'List B' products, there is also competition between the different national authorities to win a sufficient volume of work to enable them to retain a strong scientific and evaluation base which will then assist them in gaining further work.

At the present time, the pharmaceutical industry is still coming to terms with the new systems and the implications to which they give rise. It appears that some companies which are risk-averse are continuing to make use of the multiple applications routes, while others are testing their experiences with the decentralised and centralised systems under the 'future systems initiative'.

Review and interpretation

The industries that formed the focus of the case studies reviewed in the previous section offer a wide range of different characteristics and experiences in relation to the effects of Single Market activities. This section seeks to draw out of the case studies common themes and interpretations that may have more general application.

Competition among rules

One of the benefits of Single Market legislation is that it allows a process of regulatory evolution to take place through time as a result of competition between rules (Woolcock 1994, Majone 1996). In examining this proposition, it is helpful to have in mind three different possible arenas for competition between rules:

- Competition in rule-making, in the selection of systems to be emulated and others to be rejected.
- Competition between alternative rule systems in a market economy, where the actions of firms in moving between alternative systems may indicate market preferences and hence lead to the strengthening of one at the expense of the other.
- Competition between agencies under different rule systems.

As we have already noted, some of the industries studied (e.g. construction and insurance) have been the subject of specific choices by the European Commission as to the type of rule system it wished to adopt. Construction has resulted in a prescriptive rule system. In this case, the Commission seems to have chosen to emulate a Continental approach rather than the more liberal approach adopted by the UK, although the UK's style of regulation was emulated by the Commission in insurance.

In other cases, a less prescriptive approach to law-making leaves open the possibility of continuing competition between rule systems. This applies particularly in the case of pharmaceuticals where a deliberate choice between a centralised and a decentralised procedure has been retained, other than for biotech and high-technology products that have to be authorised under the centralised procedure. In the case of insurance and leasing it would appear that multiple systems of supervisory control may continue: home country control or host country control under the Second Banking and Insurance Directives. Whether, in the case of insurance, there is sufficiently strong pressure to sustain competition rather than merely collaboration remains to be seen. What does seem likely is that there will be continuing efforts to prevent a weakening of supervisory standards.

In the case of pharmaceuticals, not only is choice between alternative rule systems provided for many authorisations, but there is also provision for competition between national drug authorisation agencies. In the decentralised system, the drug company has the opportunity to choose the national agency it wishes to undertake the main authorisation review. In the centralised system, the EMEA has the opportunity to allocate rapporteur work to the various national agencies without any commitment to considerations of equity, equality of opportunity or transparency. The effect of the exercise of choice under each of these systems is likely to encourage national agencies to behave competitively, especially in terms of the quality and speed of their work, in an effort to attract contracts and the funding that goes with them. By so doing, they will be able to sustain their scientific base and hence attract further work. They may also, as a result, be able to obtain work from other national agencies on a subcontract basis.

Steps to the Single Market: corporate responses

While it is possible to remove barriers to the creation of a single, liberalised market, it is more difficult to ensure that all available steps will be taken by firms to achieve the potential. As a general economic proposition, one may suggest that firms will respond to new opportunities or challenges offered by the Single European Market in ways that best suit their own operational and strategic interests. However, while the EC represents a significant economic grouping, it would appear that for some industries (e.g. machine tools) that are operating in a largely global market, a more liberalised European market may not present sufficient a change to give rise to a variation in internal rule-making or new strategic choices within a firm or industry sector.

In some cases, industries and groups of firms may develop their own responses through soft law and self-regulation (retailing) and EC rules may then be required in response. Market expansion into other parts of the European Community, together with new product development and lower prices, appear to have occurred, especially in insurance and perhaps also in machine tools. Some companies (e.g. insurance and leasing) have particularly developed their business across contiguous boundaries where similarities of language, culture and economic well-being have offered particular incentives and attractions. Location decisions within the European Community may well have been influenced, perhaps especially for non-EC companies such as Japanese and American corporations (machine tools), who may have been motivated by a general concern to avoid any risk of a 'shut-out' from the EC.

Hindrances to the Single Market

Even among those industries that have been subject to liberalising instruments, there are still hindrances to the creation of the Single Market. A number of factors can be identified which tend to apply across several of the products and industries studied. Initial reluctance on the part of governments or firms to support, and give effect to, the Single Market account for several such instances. This is said to have applied in leasing and machine tools. A number of states have been slow in implementing European Community Directives into national policy.

The problems of market asymmetry have also been a factor mentioned in almost all the case studies. Culture and language difference may make some products less acceptable in particular parts of the Community, and language barriers may hinder the free movement of staff and hence the ability of firms to establish operations in other countries (Butt and Porter 1995). In several industries, such as leasing and insurance, references were also made to the difficulties experienced in achieving a Single Market while there was a lack of harmonisation in tax, accounting and banking rules and in the absence of a common currency, or at least stable exchange.

Of the cases investigated, regulation of construction appears to have been driven by considerations that did not primarily relate to the creation of a Single Market but were rather influenced by other (social and environmental) considerations. It should not therefore necessarily be expected that they would have effects that were supportive of a single economic market, but it is relevant briefly to review the consequences of those rules against the Single Market model.

The construction industry has been particularly exposed to various Directives that were intended to protect workers within the European Community. The essence of these measures also appears to lack an economic rationale and to be likely to run counter to the objectives of Single Market policy. In particular, the legislation, especially given the prescriptive way in which it has been formulated, has added to the degree of risk and uncertainty faced by the construction industry.

Conclusions

The regulatory programme envisaged for the European Community in pursuit of the Single European Market has been largely accomplished. Our research on external regulatory environments and internal, or behavioural, responses by firms, suggests the following conclusions:

- Important developments towards a Single Market may well take a considerable time to achieve as part of an evolutionary process of change and require two or more successive rounds of legislative refinement (insurance, pharmaceuticals). In such circumstances, feedback and review of the impact of particular rules becomes especially important. Mutual recognition of national authorities and the establishment of a 'single passport' are important steps to the Single Market for some industries (leasing, insurance).
- Prescriptive legislation is likely to constrain the scope for strategic responses to Single Market rules by firms or national governmental agencies (construction). More liberal approaches to rule-making are more likely to encourage and allow competition among rules as an aid to the evolutionary process of change in a Single Market (insurance, pharmaceuticals).
- In their responses to external regulatory developments, firms are driven by their perceptions of that regulatory environment and their view as to the likely commercial benefits to them of alternative courses of action. The history and experience of the firm and the industry of which it is a part are also important influences. In the industries studied, major uncertainties and instabilities do not appear to have arisen as a result of external rule-making. An explanation for this seems to lie partly in the ability of firms to organise and

respond effectively and also to the role of national governments in protecting their member firms from adverse effects.

- Analysis of strategic responses by firms needs to recognise the effect of a global market in some industries which reduces the significance and impact of the Single European Market so far as the conduct of firms is concerned and the significance of Single Market policy on non-European Community firms, who may be influenced to vary locational and trading strategies as a result of external rule-making (machine tools, pharmaceuticals).
- The development of self-regulation and other collective corporate initiatives in response to Single Market and national rules that has some of the characteristics of soft law conduct interacts directly with hard regulatory law (retailing). In some cases this is a response and in other cases an attempt to avoid or mitigate EC rule-making, to the benefit of participating firms.
- Within the industries studied, the impact of external rules has varied from small (because the market was already open, as in the case of machine tools), to negligible (because the market has successfully been kept segmented, as in the case of leasing). However, some industries show significant development where competition in the market place and also competition among rules has been allowed to gain ground (insurance, pharmaceuticals).
- Hindrances to the development of a Single Market occur not only as a result of corporate conduct (leasing, retailing), but also as a particular consequence of the ways in which European Community legislation is implemented and enforced by national regulatory authorities (Majone 1996). There remains significant scope for variation in national implementation of Community measures that can create additional barriers to completion of a Single Market.
- There remain fundamental differences of culture, language, legal systems, accounting and financial systems within the European Community (retailing, leasing, insurance and pharmaceuticals). These seem likely to continue and will constrain the further development of a Single Market even if a common currency is adopted.

Note

This paper is based on the results of a project on 'The Role of the Firm in the Evolution of Rules for the Single European Market', funded by the Economic and Social Research Council (research grant no. R000233673) and conducted at the National Institute of Economic and Social Research in London. We would also like to thank those organisations and individuals that have participated and assisted in the research, but they are not responsible for shortcomings in it. A longer report on research findings will appear in the *International Journal of the Economics of Business* in early 1999.

References

Boleat, M. (1995) 'The European Single Insurance Market', *Geneva Papers on Risk and Insurance* 20(74): 45–56.
Boston Consulting Group (1995) *Strategic Study of the Machine Tool Industry*, Brussels: Commission of the European Communities.

Brazier, M., J. Lovecy, M. Moran and M. Potton (1992) 'Professional labour and the Single European Market: the case of doctors', *Journal of Area Studies* 1992 (1): 115–24.

Buigues, P., F. Ilzkowitz and J.-F. Lebrun (1990) 'The impact of the internal market by industrial sector', *European Economy Special Edition*, Brussels: Commission of the European Communities.

Butt, A. and M. Porter (1995) *Business, Border Controls and the Single European Market*, London: Royal Institute of International Affairs.

Cecchini Report (1988) *The European Challenge 1992*, Brussels: Commission of the European Communities.

Chinkin, C. M. (1989) 'The challenge of soft law: development and change in international law', *International and Comparative Law Quarterly* 38: 850–66.

Cox, A. (1993) 'Public procurement in the European Community: is a fully integrated market achievable?', *Public Money and Management* 13(3): 29–35.

Evers, P. (1995) *Pharmaceutical Regulation in Europe*, London: *Financial Times* Management Reports.

Fernandez Martin, J. M. (1996) *The EC Public Procurement Rules: A Critical Analysis*, Oxford: Clarendon Press.

Gold, M. (1993) *The Social Dimension. Employment Policy in the European Community*, Basingstoke: Macmillan.

Gold, M. and D. Matthews (1996) 'The implications of the evolution of European integration for UK labour markets', *Department for Education and Employment Research Series* no. 73, Sheffield: DfEE.

Gruchalla-Wesierski, T. (1984) 'A framework for understanding "soft law"', *McGill Law Journal* 30: 37–88.

Jacquemin, A. and D. Wright (1993) 'Corporate strategies and European challenges post-1992', *Journal of Common Market Studies* 31: 525–37.

Klepper, G. and P. Michaelis (1993) *Economic Incentives for Packaging Waste Management - the Dual System in Germany*, Kiel: Kiel Institute of World Economics.

Leaseurope/Arthur Andersen (1992) *Leasing in Europe*, Maidenhead: McGraw-Hill.

Majone, G. (1996) *Regulating Europe*, London: Routledge.

Matthews, D. (1997) 'The evolution of rules', in D. G. Mayes (ed.) *The Evolution of the Single European Market*, Cheltenham: Edward Elgar: 167–99.

Matthews, D. and D. G. Mayes (1992) 'The effect of "1992" on the machine tool industry in Britain and Germany', *National Institute of Economic and Social Research Discussion Paper* no. 30, London: NIESR.

—— (1994a) 'Towards a Single European Market? The evolution of the leasing industry', *International Journal of the Economics of Business* 1(2): 179–98.

—— (1994b) 'The role of soft law in the evolution of rules for a Single European Market: the case of retailing', *National Institute of Economic and Social Research Discussion Paper* no. 61, London: NIESR.

Matthews, D. and J. F. Pickering (1995) 'The role of the firm in the evolution of social policy rules: the case of the UK construction industry', *National Institute of Economic and Social Research Discussion Paper* no. 84, London: NIESR.

—— (1997) 'The evolution of rules for the Single European Market in insurance,' *National Institute of Economic and Social Research Discussion Paper* no. 115, London: NIESR.

Mazey, S. and J. Richardson (1993) *Lobbying in the European Community*, Oxford: Oxford University Press.

Neven, D., R. Nuttall and P. Seabright (1993) *Merger in Daylight*, London: Centre for Economic Policy Research.

Soper, D. and R. M. Munro with E. Cameron (1992) *The Leasing Handbook*, Maidenhead: McGraw-Hill.

Spencer Chapman, N. F. and C. Grandjean (1991) *The Construction Industry and the European Community*, Oxford: BSP Professional Books.

Tammes, A. J. P. (1983) 'Soft law', in *Essays on International and Comparative Law in Honour of Judge Erades*, The Hague: Nijhoff: 187–95.

Teague, P. (1989) *The European Community: The Social Dimension. Labour Market Policies for 1992*, London: Kogan Page/Cranfield School of Management.

Thompson, R. (1994) *Single Market for Pharmaceuticals*, London: Butterworth.

Weale, A. and A. Williams (1992) 'Between economy and ecology? The Single Market and the integration of environmental policy', *Environmental Politics* 1(4): 45–64.

Weidenfeld, G. (1996) 'The European internal insurance market. Expectations, assessment and consequences for business policy from the insurers' point of view: questionnaire results', *The Geneva Papers on Risk and Insurance* 21(78): 77–107.

Wellens, K. C. and G. M. Borchardt (1989) 'Soft law in European Community law', *European Law Review* 14(5): 267–321.

Wilks, S. (1992) 'The metamorphosis of European Community policy', *RUSEL Working Paper* no. 9, Exeter: RUSEL.

Wilson, C. and D. Matthews (1997) 'The Evolution of Rules for the Single European Market in Pharmaceuticals', *National Institute of Economic and Social Research Discussion Paper* no. 125, London: NIESR.

Woolcock, S. (1994) *The Single European Market: Centralization or Competition amongst National Rules?*, London: Royal Institute of International Affairs.

Woolcock, S., M. Hodges and K. Schreiber (1991) *Britain, Germany and 1992: The Limits of Deregulation*, London: Pinter.

7 Private sector international regimes

Virginia Haufler

Introduction

One of the prime activities of governments is to make and enforce the rules by which we live. In the realm of commerce, these rules are critical to the effective operation of the market. The problem is that the system of rule-making we have is divided among separate sovereign states. The rules have force within the domestic sphere, but have no relevance or authority over transnational or global issues that transcend national borders. Despite this lack of global governance, economic activity today operates at an international level which increases the demands by economic actors for a global framework for commerce. If governments cannot develop transnational institutions for rule-making, then new forms of international governance must be created. Typically we think of international governance as what emerges from state-to-state negotiations over international law and regulation, embodied in international organisations such as the United Nations. These laws, regulations, and institutions are not always effective, and do not cover all areas of international life. The demand for rules to govern commerce has given rise to a variety of sources of supply, and one of the most significant and growing sources of international governance is the private sector itself. We see emerging in many sectors and issues a set of international regimes that overlaps with and sometimes substitutes for the regimes established by governments.

Regime theory emerged in the late seventies as a contested but useful concept for understanding international relations (Krasner 1983, Rittberger and Mayer 1993). In a recent review of this literature, Hasenclever *et al.* separate its strands into three schools of thought: interest-based neo-liberalism, power-based realism, and knowledge-based cognitivism (Hasenclever *et al.* 1996). In an otherwise thorough discussion, these authors do not incorporate private sector actors into their analysis, and clearly argue that regimes are formed among states alone. In contrast, a number of other authors have argued that the regime concept is useful for understanding how and why firms cooperate to build institutions for self-governance (Porter 1993, Haufler 1993, 1997a, Cutler *et al.* 1999c). This chapter assumes the existence and importance of private international regimes, looks at them from an interest-based neo-liberal perspective, and tries to answer questions about the character and ubiquity of them.

The main argument of this chapter is that the globalisation of economic activity has produced a mis-match between markets and politics in terms of governance. One response has been the construction of private international regimes in many industry sectors as a form of self-regulation or rule-setting in the absence of an overarching global political regime. These private sector regimes address the problems of international efficiency, the security or stability of markets, the power and autonomy of firms, and the social embeddedness of economic actors. These will be explained more fully below.

The existence of business organisations that take on governmental functions is not an entirely new phenomenon. Just as non-governmental and intergovernmental organisations have experienced cycles of expansion and contraction, so too have the activities of private sector organisations (Charnovitz 1997, Murphy 1994). For instance, much of early commercial law was developed in the medieval era by merchants themselves, later to be codified by governments (Cutler 1999).[1] In the early stages of colonial exploration and domination, the East India Company, the Hudson's Bay Company, and other similar merchant companies carried out many of the functions of governments in peripheral areas of the world. By the nineteenth century, we see the emergence of the trade association, such as the International Chamber of Commerce, as a source of standards and best practice for businesses operating abroad. In the current era, private authority is expanding over a range of issues, contributing to the framework for commerce in the gaps between domestic and international public law.

One key element about the current era is the degree to which the private sector governance we see is based on international cooperation among competing firms. Their cooperation takes a variety of institutional forms, with 'institution' defined broadly to include both informal and formal modes of cooperation (Soltan *et al.* 1998):

- Informal industry norms and practices shape the behaviour of participants in a common direction by determining the limits of what is acceptable and appropriate; in the early years of the Eurobond market, for instance, a tacit norm developed restricting issuers to blue chip companies or governments, although there was no law mandating this.
- Coordination services firms, such as investment ratings agencies or insurers, facilitate the ability of other firms to engage in commerce by establishing common standards.
- International production alliances or network relationships among firms are formal, contractual cooperative arrangements to pursue mutual market opportunities; examples can be found in the complex relations among major car manufacturers and their suppliers.[2]
- International cartels represent an even more rigid, formal, and narrowly focused form of cooperation, in which market competition is restricted; they are most common in commodities.
- Transnational business associations organise a particular industry, in which the participants compete in the market but cooperate in setting standards, monitoring behaviour, and dealing with issues of mutual concern; these include

trade associations such as the International Council of Chemical Associations and business organisations such as the TransAtlantic Business Dialogue.

- Private international regimes can incorporate all of these in overlapping layers of formal and informal norms, principles, rules and decision-making procedures; they are particularly common in the financial services industries, such as insurance and banking (Cutler *et al.* 1999b, Porter 1993, Haufler 1997a).[3]

These categories are not mutually exclusive, and as the relationships among participants become more complex we tend to see many of these forms of cooperation overlapping and reinforcing each other.

Private international regimes govern broad areas of international commerce, operating both within and across industry lines. They incorporate informal norms about business behaviour, but also have explicit rules, decision-making procedures, and both informal and formal enforcement mechanisms. Private international regimes are often based on transnational business associations, such as industry trade associations, technical trade groups, and business lobbying organisations, representing the interests of a group of firms which negotiate over issues of common interest, and establish a framework of rules, standards and best practices guiding the behaviour of the participants. The regime as a whole may consist of multiple trade associations and business organisations, and the boundaries of the regime may not be distinct. While the literature on regimes tends to define these boundaries in terms of an issue area, private regimes generally are based on a particular industry sector and the issues it faces.

Why do businesses create regimes?

Why do businesses want to create a regulatory framework to rule themselves and others? Why would they want to self-regulate at the international level? Why not rely on the market to mediate all transactions, aside from the fundamental rules of contract and property that only government can provide and enforce? We typically believe that all businesses are against all regulation all the time, but in fact the market itself requires an underlying set of rules in order to function properly. The so-called 'invisible hand' only operates within a set of common constraints governing transactions, such as property rights and enforcement of contracts. Businesses themselves often demand regulation, in part to overcome market failures and in part to gain rents (Stigler 1968). Property rights, contract enforcement and even rents are difficult or impossible to assure at the international level, where there is no central government to which one can turn. As the complexity and interdependence of relations among market actors has increased over time, the number and character of the rules, norms, practices and standards needed to make markets function effectively have also increased. You can see this in the 'density' of institutions within domestic society which is notably lacking internationally.

We can analyse business motivations in terms of how they see a private regime as a means of achieving: efficiency, stability and security of transactions, power and autonomy, and responsiveness to social demands.[4] A group of firms may overcome the natural barriers to cooperation because they anticipate realising mutual gains in the form of enhanced efficiency for each member. Firms may cooperatively establish common rules for interaction, technical standards, and information collection capabilities to reduce transactions costs and help them establish and expand new markets.[5] For example, the banking system relies on a settlements system that today is critically dependent on high technology information systems that must be able to 'speak' to each other and interconnect across borders. The existence of rules, standards, and information are especially critical in overcoming the barriers to trade inherent in a system of divided political units, each with its own legal framework.

From the point of view of a firm attempting to penetrate new markets abroad or operate on a transnational basis, a private regime may be viewed as an important institution for establishing stability in international transactions. The regime lays out the important norms and principles of behaviour, and often establishes a dispute settlement mechanism. Regime members would all have similar expectations regarding appropriate behaviour and activities, no matter in which country they were operating. According to the economic historian Douglass North, the reduction of uncertainty in transactions is a key stimulus to the expansion of trade (North 1990).

Also, power and autonomy clearly are underlying motivations for business in constructing a self-regulatory regime. Business participants may create a regime to gain power over other businesses, or to prevent governments from being tempted to intervene and impose regulations of their own. The rules may benefit some firms over others, and may be used to exclude entry by new players. Regime theory typically assumes that these institutions serve the collective good by reducing conflict among states; this assumption cannot be easily made in the case of cooperative regimes among businesses. The outcomes of self-regulation may be beneficial by reducing the costs of commerce and expanding economic markets, but they also may be harmful by limiting competition and favouring narrow interests over larger public purposes (Strange 1983, Gale 1998).

The need to respond to public demands has been a notable spur to self-regulation at the domestic level, and it also is a significant motivation internationally. In order to demonstrate corporate citizenship, competing firms may decide it is in their intrest to constuct their own regulatory framework. In doing so, they may make it more difficult for governments to regulate, or they may make it easy for governments simply to legitimise what the private sector has already developed and incorporate it into legal and regulatory systems.

The role of governments and intergovernmental organisations

What is the role of government? The most minimal functions of a government are to establish the legal 'rules of the game', and to back them up with a judiciary and police force.[6] In the international political economy, these elements are missing, at least in some coherent and centralised form. Instead, we have a variety of governance mechanisms that apply to greater or lesser degree across state boundaries.

One set of such governance mechanisms is that of international regimes founded upon cooperation among states. However, as noted already, private sector international regimes can also establish some of the rules, standards, and adjudication of disputes in economic areas that governments typically provide. Why would governments allow the private sector to perform what is 'properly' the realm of governments?

One answer is that not all government leaders believe that government has a role in the economy, preferring a system in which most transactions are mediated by the market-place. In the past two decades in particular liberal free market ideology has come to dominate the discourse over the proper role of government in the domestic realm. This militates against public interference in the 'private' sphere of market transactions within and between states. Governments around the world have been shedding economic responsibilities, deregulating industries and privatising state-owned industries, and reducing the sphere of government authority (Yergin and Stanislaw 1998).[7] Political actors recommend market solutions to a range of problems, and when the market fails, either economic activity declines as potential transactions fail to be completed, or firms establish their own facilitating institutions by collaboratively establishing standards and rules among themselves.

Governments also allow and even encourage the establishment of private self-regulation at the international level because they themselves cannot cooperate to establish public regimes. Debates in the field of international relations theory, particularly the differences between realists and liberal institutionalists, centre on the likelihood that there will be long-lasting cooperation among states in an environment of anarchy and sovereignty. Given uneven cooperation among governments, combined with the globalisation of markets, private regimes may be viewed as a second-best alternative for promoting global trade, investment and economic growth.

Self-regulation appears to be particularly common in high-technology industries, where markets change rapidly and innovation is constant. Government leaders may view themselves as technically incapable of regulating effectively in these areas, domestically or internationally. The state today may simply be incapable of effective regulation, for a variety of technical, financial and political reasons. Fiscal constraints may make it difficult to hire sufficient expert staff to understand emerging issues raised by fast-changing technological developments in many economic areas. The fluidity of the global market and its increasing size relative to the size of any one state or group of states have led many observers to argue that the capacity of states is declining in general, and its effects can be seen in their retreat from regulation of the economy (Strange 1996).[8] The weakness of individual states may on the one hand push them to construct international institutions to do what they cannot do individually, but it is more likely that it simply makes it even more difficult to negotiate binding agreements that affect industrial interests. Under these circumstances, governments may encourage industries to develop their own regulations and standards, with the government monitoring the results, in the belief that firms have more capacity in this area. The result may further undermine government regulatory capacity.

Despite all these reasons for governments *not* to act, we know that in fact governments often do act, and even act collectively with other governments to establish and enforce law internationally. Few private international regimes are completely autonomous with respect to public authority. In many cases, governance of an area may be delegated to business associations by official bodies, domestic and international, with governments backing them up with their enforcement capability. In other cases, private regimes may be nested within larger public ones. This can make it quite difficult to disentangle all the levels and varieties of governance operative today at the global level. The contributions of the private sector to global governance have been neglected to date, and this chapter is an attempt to isolate private sector regimes as institutions which regulate international economic activity.

Efficiency, security, autonomy and social responsiveness

There exist numerous regimes today that are to a large degree based upon cooperation among firms, institutionalising their governance role. Industry self-regulation internationally is a growing phenomenon, especially in complex technical areas, reflected in the proliferation of computer industry alliances attempting to design standards. Another area where the private sector has taken the lead is in international arbitration, in which private sector bodies adjudicate a form of private law. The international shipping industry has long been governed by a private regime. The professions, such as law, engineering, accounting, medicine and higher education have a long history of self-regulation.

When we examine the self-regulatory phenomenon, four goals appear to predominate: the goal of establishing international standards driven by the need to increase efficiency in global transactions; the goal of ensuring the security of transactions; the goal of maintaining industry autonomy by pre-empting or preventing government regulation; and the goal of responding to societal demands and expectations of corporate behaviour. These four goals can be found to varying degrees across a range of examples of private sector international regimes.

The globalisation of commerce, in production but also in the distribution of services, has motivated different industries to seek standardisation in order to reduce the costs of doing business in many countries at once. There are two types of standardisation around which private regimes have formed: technical standards, and codes of conduct. The former is an area where we would not be surprised to see governments, limited by their lack of expertise, willing to turn over regulation to industry experts. The latter, however, gets into areas of social and political concern that tread more clearly on the territory typically staked out for resolution in the political process, and not for industry decision-making.

Clearly, the shift to an information economy in which telecommunications, computers, and information are all the basis of leading edge industries pushes businesses to become more global and, more importantly, to develop standards for interconnection. Efficiency is a concern in newly emerging sectors of the economy, such as computers, networking, and data services, and in sectors that make great use of the new technology, such as financial services and telecommunications. The lack of such standards, or the need to deal with conflicting standards in every country, reduces the efficiency of international trade in these areas. As one financial executive put it, 'The services industries in general, and the financial services sector in particular, compete on the basis of their ability to link together in a seamless and largely invisible way the data systems maintained by a large number of diverse participants in our economy, including merchants, lenders, credit bureaus, depository institutions, and others' (MacDonald 1997: 127). Such seamless linking requires standardisation across many different industries and individuals. This affects not just the computer industry, but every industry that utilises information technology of all sorts; and information technology is now being integrated into virtually every industry, no longer limited to just the leading edge sectors of the economy.

The international standards regime is composed of multiple overlapping sources of standards in both the public and private sectors. The main source of international standards today is the International Organisation for Standardisation (ISO), which is composed of representatives of member nations' national standards bodies. In some countries, these bodies are government agencies, and in others they are private. For instance, in the US the American National Standards Institute (ANSI) coordinates private sector standards and represents US industry interests in international fora such as the ISO. ANSI itself is a federation of representatives from industry, government, standards groups, labour, consumer unions and academia. Most industry associations participate in the ISO process, which sets voluntary international standards on a huge range of items. The ISO process is decentralised, with interested national bodies taking the lead in technical committees, where the details of standards are developed. These committees generally are dominated by industry representatives. Due to the significant industry participation in developing the standards, we can consider the ISO a quasi-public body or public-private regime.

The ISO is not the only international body for standards-setting, and faces competition from others. This competition often comes from transnational industry associations. For example, the American Society of Mechanical Engineers (ASME), although based in the United States, promulgates standards which are accepted internationally. The requirements for safety and commercial operation put forward by it are viewed as being appropriate standards in other countries and other contexts. The ASME, in a recent position paper, stated that an international standard must provide open and nondiscriminatory access to those affected by it and must meet the needs of the global market-place. As ASME industry executives point out, 'standards have a "massive" impact on a company's competitiveness in the global marketplace, and new stakeholders, including lesser-developed countries, are defining new rules for factors such as product life cycle and risk' (Hamilton 1997: 38).

In a bid to replace or supplement the ISO process, ASME recently has been pressuring the US government to support market-based international standards in addition to ISO standards as the US negotiates in the World Trade Organisation (WTO) over technical barriers to trade. According to the ASME, the ISO standards-

setting process is not based on consensus among the participants, and is not sufficiently representative of those affected by its decisions. Participation by US
standards developers can be difficult. The ISO process leaves some decisions to
later negotiation by governments, which ASME claims can politicise standards-
setting and undermine the international harmonisation of standards that ASME
supports. ASME prefers performance-based technical requirements and standards
that have been accepted by market actors, instead of imposed by governments or
intergovernmental organisations. According to the ASME, where no international
standards have been established by the ISO or other official body, industries that
already have established certain standards of behaviour regarding trade and
safety should continue to set the common standards (Hamilton 1997: 38).

When it comes to setting technical standards, efficiency is the primary driving
force. But many standards-setting organisations today also develop standards
which respond in part to societal demands for better environmental performance by
industry. For instance, governments and intergovernmental institutions now require
environmental performance standards by those with whom they do business.[9] The
International Organisation for Standardisation's most significant recent standards
are the ISO 9000 quality standards and the ISO 14000 environmental management
system standards. They each were developed within ISO technical committees
dominated by industry representatives. They were put forth as voluntary codes of
conduct to standardise the definition of quality in manufacturing and in environmental management systems. Significantly, however, both have now become *de
facto* requirements for doing business around the world as both businesses and
governments require ISO certification in order to assure the quality and performance
of their economic partners.

One industry heavily involved in developing global standards is the international
chemical industry. At the same time as it may adhere to the standards set by ISO
it also establishes self-regulatory mechanisms for its own members. Many
national chemical associations are now linked together in the International
Council of Chemical Associations (ICCA).[10] The ICCA and many of its member
organisations have been attempting to stay ahead of potential environmental
regulation via independent efforts to develop their own self-regulatory systems.
For instance, the United Nations Conference on Environment and Development
(UNCED) in 1992 laid the foundations of the new Intergovernmental Forum on
Chemical Safety (IFCS). Participants in UNCED were concerned about putting
particular categories of chemicals on the international negotiating agenda. In
response, the chemical industry has tried to forestall this by establishing its own
programmes. The ICCA launched a process of negotiation on chemical safety
among its members, and then developed a consensus on specific chemicals in
conjunction with, surprisingly, the environmental group Greenpeace.[11] A number
of experts have raised concern over persistent organic products (POPs), which are
toxic chemicals that accumulate in the environment, and the IFCS put them on their
agenda. Leading chemical industry representatives became concerned that environmental groups would lobby for government restrictions on chemical
components the industry views as vital. The ICCA, representing trade groups in

North and South America, Europe, and Asia, as well as major multinationals such as DuPont, began working with Greenpeace directly in order to formulate their own restrictions or standards, to which the chemical industry committed themselves to upholding. When the IFCS deadlocked on reducing or eliminating POPs, the ICCA and Greenpeace were able to negotiate a compromise. This reflects a complicated inter-relationship among the members of a private sector regime (ICCA), other non-governmental organisations (Greenpeace), and governmental institutions (IFCS and individual governments).

The chemical industry in general has persistently advocated self-regulation, and has created the institutions and programmes to support this process. Many firms adhere to the 'Responsible Care' programme first developed by the Canadian Chemical Manufacturers Association. The Responsible Care programme has been implemented by the US Chemical Manufacturers Association along with the Synthetic Organic Chemicals Association. Responsible Care establishes industry standards and best practices with regard to the handling of chemicals, and was a response to some major disasters within the chemical industry that threatened to place it under ever tighter government restrictions. Industry representatives often describe this kind of voluntary effort as a complement to government regulation, but it could also be viewed as an attempt by industry to pre-empt government intervention. Interestingly, developing country governments have become quite interested in the transfer of responsible care to chemical manufacturers within their jurisdiction, since the swift industrialisation of these countries is polluting their environment rapidly, yet their governmental institutions lack the capacity to address these problems. These governments hope that the ICCA will train local industry in the 'best practices' represented by the Responsible Care programme (Clapp 1998). This is already happening to a certain extent in developing countries in Asia and South America, where already existing strong national chemical associations are an institutional mechanism through which to transfer these standards (Farley 1997: 56–8).

Going beyond these regimes surrounding technical standards, a number of industries are now establishing international 'codes of conduct' in areas of social concern. They are often clearly designed to deflect the potential for regulation by governments or international organisations, and they deal with such issues as the environment and worker rights. Both the widespread adoption of the ISO 14000 voluntary standards and the Responsible Care programme in the chemical industry can be viewed as new codes of conduct and not just as technical standards. There are other initiatives, however, which represent an attempt to establish broader expectations about corporate behaviour.

One controversial area where industry has established an international code of conduct is in the textile and apparel industry. A number of businesses headquartered in the US but operating globally have established the Apparel Industry Coalition (AIC). This coalition has drawn up a list of worker rights that would apply to manufacturing plants both in the US and, more importantly, in all the factories that the businesses use for out-sourcing production and assembly. Global sourcing agreements lay out the rights of workers in such areas as health, safety, wages, child labour, union organising, and free speech, though not all cover every one of these issues. The AIC has established monitoring mechanisms to ensure that all foreign plants adhere to the company's code of conduct in their treatment of workers. The motivation of industry adherents was a combination of genuine concern and reaction to public outrage over sweatshop conditions, which could lead to a bad reputation, declining sales, and perhaps a consumer boycott. The AIC eventually was taken up by the Clinton administration, which helped set up the Apparel Industry Partnership as a forum for industry and non-governmental activists to resolve their disagreements and establish guidelines in this area.

Similar voluntary industry agreements exist in the soccer ball and rug manufacturing industries, generally involving not just industry participants but also the cooperation of non-governmental organisations and governments. This emerging voluntary industry regime for worker rights has been the subject of much scrutiny, accusations of whitewashing, and disagreements over the contents of different codes of conduct.[12] One of the most public debates occurred over Nike factories in Vietnam. Nike reacted by hiring an outside auditor, which reviewed Nike operations and declared that they met Nike standards, which led to severe criticism of the outside auditor.[13]

One of the important barriers to doing business across sovereign borders is the degree of both commercial and political risk this involves. Regimes to reduce risk may consist of industry members who regulate themselves and set standards designed to limit their risks directly. Another type of regime primarily consists of those firms that provide information about other firms. Information is one of the main tools for reducing risk. In both cases, these regimes address some aspect of the security of transactions and the stability of the industry. This type of security is not the same as the security more properly supplied by governments through policing and military protection. Instead, this security ensures that commercial transactions can be carried out despite high levels of uncertainty, or even despite weak or absent government-provided security.

Excellent examples of this can be found in the emerging information technology industries. Many of the industries involved in electronic commerce today are forming a new regime to standardise certain elements crucial to its success. One barrier to the expansion of buying and selling via the Internet, for instance, is that such commerce rests on a shaky foundation in terms of the security of the credit cards or bank drafts used to pay for merchandise or services. Fear of hackers obtaining individual credit card numbers or enough personal identifying information for 'identity theft' prevents widespread consumer and business acceptance of electronic commerce. In response, the major credit card companies, Visa and Mastercard, have allied with Web software developers such as Netscape, Microsoft, and IBM and others to establish a standard methodology to enhance the security of Internet transactions. The secure electronic transactions (SET), as it is called, will provide digital certificates that essentially hide an individual's credit card number from merchants while still linking the credit to the particular transaction. This is a technical fix established by a varied group of competing firms which are providing a new form of international security for a new form of commerce. The programme is still in its infancy, but it reflects the rush by private sector companies to provide the security upon which expanded Internet commerce must rest (Deterline 1997: 100). The information industries are well aware of the fact that another new information technology, so-called 'smartcards,' became ubiquitous in Europe only after the issuers developed a strict code of conduct that enhanced the security and privacy of the cards; the lack of privacy standards in the United States has inhibited the adoption of smartcards there.

The security of information is a key issue for both consumers and industry in many of the new applications of modern technology, particularly for the collectors and providers of personal information. Today, information is automatically collected on individuals and maintained in massive databases: health records, credit history, banking records, phone calls, TV/VCR rentals, cable TV records, records of Internet browsing, and purchases by mail, phone, or website (Swire 1997). There is rising consumer concern over the use of this information, particularly as it is sold or even made public. Consumers are losing control of the security of their personal information as it is collected and transferred among credit bureaux, insurers, medical agencies, and advertisers. Typically, governments in the past have responded to similar concerns with regulation and oversight. The European Union has established strict privacy standards that could limit the transfer of information between companies in the US and Europe, given that the Europeans are not confident in the self-regulatory system currently in place in the US. The US government is now debating privacy issues, and Vice-President Gore recently reiterated the administration's commitment to industry self-regulation. The decentralised, open, global character of one of the main transmission sources for personal data – the Internet – makes it difficult to design and implement effective regulations through top-down, government by government approaches (Mulligan and Goldman 1997).

In response, many of the businesses involved are establishing cooperative institutions to self-regulate. It is not to their advantage simply to leave this issue to the market, since that would invite government regulation. Their preference is to develop codes of conduct for all relevant industries, combined with technologies that are intended to help make the self-regulation work. While the main business associations organised in favour of self-regulation are based in the United States, many industry associations are deliberately establishing international links. The Internet Privacy Working Group, composed of the Center for Democracy and Technology, America OnLine, Microsoft, National Consumers' League, the Electronic Freedom Foundation and others are working feverishly to lobby against government private regulation while developing an alternative private sector international regime. They favour pressing forward with research and development to produce the software and hardware technology that would give consumers a means to convey to businesses that ask for personal information their preferences on how that information is handled. One such privacy standard is the platform for Internet content selection (PICs), which has not yet been widely adopted; other similar technological fixes are becoming available also. This group is working with a World Wide Web consortium to develop a means for both individuals and entire nations to choose the collection, use and disclosure standards appropriate for them (Mulligan and Goldman 1997: 69–70).

Another regime which addresses security and risk concerns is the international insurance industry. The insurance industry is, of course, a major vehicle for sharing the risks of commerce. Insurers have a long history of developing common practices and contract terms for insurers and have a number of national and international industry associations that promote industry best practices. This can be seen in the cooperative institutions established domestically and internationally within the insurance industry to develop common expectations about the conduct of business. The industry consensus on contract terms is designed in part to protect consumers by establishing common definitions, but it also protects the industry from some forms of competition. Most insurers agree on a set of exclusions for standard insurance contracts (such as that the contract is null and void in the case of nuclear war). Collective problems in the industry, such as how to handle salvage on insured ships, were long ago resolved through negotiation and institution building among themselves (Haufler 1997a). The insurance industry also functions as a source of information on the extent and nature of risk itself and in some sense protects the security of the transaction, or at least, the financial security of those involved in the transaction. In recent years, some industry participants have been attempting to establish criteria of risk regarding global climate change, its effect on insurers and investors, and the appropriate role of the industry in establishing new expectations regarding the conduct of business. By changing prices, terms and exclusions in insurance contracts, the insurance industry has great influence over the industries and individuals that buy its products (Haufler 1997b).

A related financial industry provides another kind of security for transactions. Financial rating agencies have developed common standards and expectations regarding the riskiness and value of investments. Their decisions about how to value, or rate, a given firm or country determines the ability to obtain credit and raise capital on good terms. These ratings can establish a reputation or completely undermine it. In response to a negative rating, a firm will feel compelled to change strategy and plans. A nation may find itself suddenly in a financial crisis, needing the help of the international financial institutions to recover. The securities ratings field is dominated by a few large corporations, such as Moody's and Standard and Poor's, which wield great influence despite the fact they do not always evaluate things accurately (Porter 1993, Sinclair 1999). Like insurers, rating agencies are part of an interdependent financial web that facilitates efficient transactions on a global basis, reduces uncertainty and increases security, and reflects the power of the players.

Conclusion

A number of interesting patterns emerge with regard to these regimes. First, many new standards regimes promoted by industry are in technical areas where governments are having difficulty determining what to do. These standards issues overlap with the need for security in transactions. In more socially oriented areas, such as the environment, privacy issues, and worker rights, it is clear that the private sector is acting strongly as a response to what they see as the threat of government regulation. If governance is all about legislation, enforcement and adjudication, then private regimes tend to specialise in the 'legislative,' or rule-making phase. Second, a large number of them involve negotiations between industry and NGOs, sometimes in combination with governments, sometimes parallel to international negotiations, and sometimes in the absence of government action. This reinforces the idea, presented in the introduction to this book, that governance today is a multifaceted phenomenon, with activity occurring at multiple levels with numerous different actors. Third, in terms of distribution, it is not always clear who is being counted in and who is being counted out by different standards and security regimes. The position of the developing countries on private sector regimes seems to vary between concern over their exclusion from the decision-making process to support for the transfer of beneficial standards. Certainly, some potential industry participants are probably being screened out of the market through these regimes, since standards-setting determines the barriers to entry in an industry. In some cases, these private regimes may raise concern over anti-trust and competition policies (Kattan and Shapiro 1997, Portnoy 1997).[14]

Further research should address a number of research questions raised here. First, we need to know more about the overall trends of expansion and contraction in private sector governance over time. We do not have a database or even a good historical collection of information that would draw attention to these trends and allow us to draw conclusions. The model for this kind of study could be Charnovitz's survey of NGOs, which surveys NGO activity from 1775 to the present (Charnovitz 1997). Second, we need to understand better how the character of private sector self-regulation has changed over time in terms of the goals or functions the regime must perform, and the style of its organisation. The scope and variety of private sector governance has evolved from private law and guilds, to colonisation and merchant companies, to market control and cartels, and finally, the mixture of organisations and institutions of the present era. Third, we need to develop more evidence on the effectiveness of private regimes, and this almost naturally will lead to examining the formal links between industry efforts and government monitoring and enforcement.

The existence of private international regimes must raise questions about the legitimacy of their goals, the accountability of their decision-making processes, and the distributional effects of the regime itself. Further research needs to be done to understand patterns in the relationship between private regimes and their outcomes. For instance, the WTO is concerned that various standards set by industry could distort trade patterns, yet data on this are difficult to assemble. The outcomes of particular regimes are felt by individuals, firms, and by the state itself. And, of course, the biggest question one might have about self-regulation in the form of private international regimes is about their effectiveness. Some of the literature on self-regulation at the domestic level indicates that it works best when the group is open to all and the industry participants have a common interest in maintaining a high reputation for their industry (Baker and Miller 1997). It is indeed clear that many of the cases discussed above involve situations where reputation is a critical market asset.

This short chapter has attempted briefly to discuss the nature and purposes of international private regimes, focusing particularly on industry motivation and the functions such regimes perform. The examples were not presented as systematic evidence of particular causal patterns, but as illustrations of the range of regimes in existence. Private international regimes emerge from cooperation among firms in pursuit of common interests. They often are based on transnational business associations, but almost always include less formal elements such as norms and practices. Most private regimes develop standards in conjunction with other relevant actors, such as governments and non-governmental actors. In general, although the industry often claims this is self-regulation, the voluntary nature of the agreements may leave them weak and ineffective. Private sector governance is an important element of the modern world economy, and the problems and opportunities it presents need to be explored in more detail.

Notes

1 Merchant law developed prior to the establishment of the inter-state system itself, during a period of time when the line between public and private realms was not as clearly drawn as it came to be during much of the twentieth century. The expansion of private regimes and other elements of civil society may indicate the emergence of 'neo-medievalism', as Kobrin has called it (Kobrin 1998).

2 There is now an increasing interest in structural associations, with a burgeoning literature on strategic alliances and networks in particular. Much of this research, however, comes out of a business school or industrial organisation perspective and thus does not focus on the governance elements involved (Hollingsworth and Boyer 1997, Nohria and Eccles 1992, Contractor and Lorange 1988).

3 This six-fold categorisation is described and explained in more detail in Cutler *et al.* (1999).

4 Efficiency and stability are often collapsed together, but stability or security of transactions is a separate factor driving much self-regulation in high technology industries. For an extended discussion that focuses on efficiency and power, see Cutler *et al.* (1999b).

5 The 'transactions costs' involved in any market interaction include the costs of designing and writing contracts, implementing them, and monitoring compliance. A number of scholars have analysed how transactions costs are involved in institutional development, with the most notable of them the Nobel economist Douglass North (1990). The most thorough application of transactions cost theory within a functionalist perspective on international regimes is Robert Keohane (1984).

6 The literature on the proper role of government is of course extensive, encompassing just about the entire field of political science. Here, I simply state the most obvious, fundamental functions of a government.

7 Philip Cerny (1990) contends that such deregulation is followed by re-regulation that seeks to make the state itself a competitive actor in world economic competition.

8 There is now an extensive literature on globalisation and its effects on the state, debating whether or to what degree the capacity of governments to govern has been undermined. Note, however, that by one measure the state is hardly retreating. The 1997 *World Development Report* published by the World Bank provides statistics showing that among OECD countries government expenditures have been rising as a percentage of GDP, demonstrating that states still have a large role in the economy after two decades of deregulatory fervour (World Bank 1997: 2).

9 Institutions such as the World Bank and the Eximbank of the US in the past few years have established environmental standards as a prerequisite for obtaining credit (Henderson 1995).

10 The ICCA consists of associations from North America, including the Canadian Chemical Producers Association, the Chemical Manufacturers Association (US), the Japanese Chemical Industry Association, the Plastics and Chemicals Industries Association (Australia), the European Chemical Industry Council, and others. The ICCA recently negotiated a Memorandum of Understanding between it and the World Customs Organisation, which represents customs agencies. This MOA covers some harmonisation of practices within the chemical industry to assist the customs agencies in tracking such things as illicit drugs and chemicals banned under the Chemical Weapons Convention.

11 Greenpeace has actively negotiated in recent years with a number of different industries, while maintaining a critical attitude towards most firms.

12 The standards set by the Apparel Industry Partnership conform in many ways to the conventions of the International Labour Organisation (ILO), an intergovernmental organisation with representation in its decision-making by governments, business, and labour. Critics are concerned that many corporate codes of conduct do not directly address the issue of whether the corporation pays a living wage.

13 The outside auditor was Goodworks, Inc., a firm headed by former US ambassador to the UN Andrew Young. Later, Nike hired an accounting firm, but that too back-fired.

14 Regulating such things as prices or selling territories clearly violates most anti-trust law, and is labelled cartelistic behaviour. But the activities of trade associations and the adoption of codes of professional conduct have also been subject to antitrust prosecution in the US (Kattan and Shapiro 1997).

References

Baker, D. and T. Miller (1997) 'Privacy, antitrust, and the national information infrastructure: is self regulation of telecommunications related personal information a workable tool?', in United States Department of Commerce/National Telecommunications and Information Administration June report *Privacy and Self Regulation in the Information Age*, Washington, D.C.: US GPO: 91–6.

Cerny, P. (1990) *The Changing Architecture of Politics: Structure, Agency, and the Future of the State*, London and Newbury Park, Cal.: Sage.

Charnovitz, S. (1997) 'Two centuries of participation: NGOs and international governance', *Michigan Journal of International Law* 18(2): 183–286.

Clapp, J. (1998) 'The privatization of global governance: ISO 14000 and the developing world', *Global Governance* 4(3): 295–317.

Contractor, F. J. and P. Lorange (eds) (1988) *Cooperative Strategies in International Business*, Lexington, Mass.: Lexington Books.

Cutler, A.C. (1999) 'Public and private authority in international trade relations: the case of maritime transport', in A. C. Cutler, V. Haufler, and T. Porter (eds) *Private Authority and International Affairs*, New York: SUNY Press.

Cutler, A. C., V. Haufler and P. Porter (1999a) 'Private authority and international affairs', in A. C. Cutler, V. Haufler, and T. Porter (eds) *Private Authority and International Affairs*, New York: SUNY Press.

—— (1999b) 'Conclusion: the contours and significance of private authority in international affairs', in A. C. Cutler, V. Haufler, and T. Porter (eds) *Private Authority and International Affairs*, New York: SUNY Press.

—— (eds) (1999c) *Private Authority and International Affairs*, New York: SUNY Press.

Deterline, B. (1997) 'Secure transactions', *Smartmoney* October: 100.

Farley, P. (1997) 'Ottawa forum shapes global regulation', *Chemical Week* 159(11): 56–8.

Gale, F. (1998) 'Cave cane! Hic dragones': A neo-Gramscian deconstruction and reconstruction of international regime theory', *Review of International Political Economy* 5(2): 252–83.

Hamilton, P. (1997) 'Debate begins on standards for international trade', *Mechanical Engineering* 119(6): 38.

Hasenclever, A., P. Mayer and V. Rittberger (1996) 'Interests, power, knowledge: the study of international regimes', *Mershon International Studies Review* 40(2): 177–228.

Haufler, V. (1993) 'Crossing the boundary between public and private', in V. Rittberger (ed.) *Regime Theory and International Relations*, Oxford: Clarendon Press: 94–111.

—— (1997a) *Dangerous Commerce: Insurance and the Management of International Risk*, Ithaca: Cornell University Press.

—— (1997b) 'Norms and the mobilization of inter-firm networks', paper presented at the International Studies Association conference, Toronto, April.

Henderson, D. (1995) 'Lending abroad: the role of voluntary international environmental management standards', *Journal of Commercial Lending* 77(11): 47.

Hollingsworth, R. and R. Boyer (eds) (1997) *Contemporary Capitalism: The Embeddedness of Institutions*, Cambridge: Cambridge University Press.

Kattan, J. and C. Shapiro (1997) 'Privacy, self regulation and antitrust', in United States Department of Commerce/NTIA June report *Privacy and Self Regulation in the Information Age*, Washington, D.C.: US GPO: 97–102.

Keohane, R. (1984) *After Hegemony*, Princeton: Princeton University Press.

Kobrin, S. J. (1998) 'Back to the future: neomedievalism and the postmodern digital world economy', *Journal of International Affairs* 51(2): 361–86.

Krasner, S. (ed.) (1983) *International Regimes*, Ithaca: Cornell University Press.

MacDonald, D. A. (1997) 'Privacy, self-regulation, and the contractual model: a report from Citicorp Credit Services Inc.', in United States Department of Commerce/NTIA June report *Privacy and Self Regulation in the Information Age*, Washington, D.C.: US GPO: 127–31.

Mulligan, D. and J. Goldman (1997) 'The limits and necessity of self-regulation: the case for both', in United States Department of Commerce/NTIA June report *Privacy and Self Regulation in the Information Age*, Washington, D.C.: US GPO: 65–74.

Murphy, C. (1994) *International Organization and Industrial Change: Global Governance since 1850*, New York: Oxford University Press.

Nohria, N. and R. G. Eccles (eds) (1992) *Networks and Organizations: Structure, Form and Action*, Boston: Harvard Business School Press.

North, D. (1990) *Institutions, Institutional Change, and Economic Performance*, Cambridge: Cambridge University Press.

Porter, T. (1993) *States, Markets and Regimes in Global Finance*, New York: St. Martin's Press.

Portnoy, B. (1997) 'Transnational networks and industrial order', paper presented at the American Political Science Association Annual Meeting, Washington, D.C., August 28–31.

Rittberger, V. and P. Mayer (eds) (1993) *Regime Theory and International Relations*, Oxford: Clarendon Press.

Sinclair, T. (1999) 'Bond rating agencies considered as coordination services firms', in A. C. Cutler, V. Haufler, and T. Porter (eds) *Private Authority and International Affairs*, New York: SUNY Press.

Soltan, K., V. Haufler and E. Uslaner (eds) (1998) *Institutions and Social Order*, Ann Arbor: Michigan University Press.

Stigler, G. J. (1968) *The Organization of Industry*, Chicago: University of Chicago Press.

Strange, S. (1996) *The Retreat of the State*, Cambridge: Cambridge University Press.

—— (1983) 'Cave! Hic dragones', in S. Krasner (ed.) *International Regimes*, Ithaca: Cornell University Press.

Swire, P. (1997) 'Markets, self-regulation, and government enforcement in the protection of personal information', in United States Department of Commerce/NTIA June report *Privacy and Self Regulation in the Information Age*, Washington, D.C.: US GPO: 3–20.

World Bank (1997) *World Development Report*, New York: Oxford University Press.

Yergin, D. and J. Stanislaw (1998) *The Commanding Heights: The Battle Between Government and the Marketplace that is Remaking the Modern World*, New York: Simon and Schuster.

8 Corporate political action in the global polity

National and transnational strategies in the climate change negotiations

David L. Levy and Daniel Egan

Climate change is a global environmental problem of potentially devastating proportions. Caused by the build-up of greenhouse gases, particularly carbon dioxide and methane, in the earth's atmosphere, climate change is a global commons issue requiring a coordinated international response. Because greenhouse gases are predominantly produced through activities associated with contemporary industrial economies, however, such a response is constrained by powerful economic and political forces which are unlikely to question the fundamental relationship between capitalism and ecological degradation. As capitalism and its ecological consequences become more universal, 'a *global* analysis of the power of capital is essential' (Gill and Law 1993: 102). Such a global analysis of the power of capital is essential for understanding the possibilities for and limits to international efforts to àddress global environmental issues such as climate change.

A major component of such an analysis is an understanding of how capital operates in the political arena. In the context of accelerating international economic integration and the growth of international institutions such as the World Trade Organisation, there has been growing concern that multinational capital has begun to turn to international fora to circumvent constraints from governments and social movements at the national state level. If the national state has historically been a site where the power of capital could be contested, the increased mobility of capital and interdependence of national economies within a system of international institutions defined by market rather than democratic values has, it is argued, eroded the autonomy and power of the national state and outmanoeuvred nationally-based social movements (Barnet and Cavanagh 1994; Korten 1995; Reich 1991; Strange 1996). The subsequent weakening of the national state's ability to manage national economies and construct nationally-defined social contracts, as well as the diffusion of state responsibilities to a variety of private and non-state actors, has resulted in 'a tendential "hollowing out" of the national state' (Jessop 1994: 251). The globalisation thesis sees the national state as 'look[ing] more and more like an institution of a bygone age' (Barnet and Cavanagh 1994: 19), as 'victims of the market economy' (Strange 1996: 14).

While this debate has focused on the ways in which the tripartite relationship among business, the state, and social forces is being reshaped at the national level, relatively little attention has been paid to the relationship between capital and international institutions. Proponents of the globalisation thesis generally assume that capital prefers to operate at the international level to avoid national regulation. In contrast to this monolithic understanding, we distinguish two major types of international institutions. *Enabling* institutions are those that provide the infrastructure of a neo-liberal world trade and investment regime and in which multinational capital is highly influential and supportive; *regulatory* institutions are those responsible for negotiating and promulgating social, labour and environmental policies. We argue in this paper that capital is far from uncontested in these arenas. More specifically, based on a case study of the climate change negotiations, we argue that many large companies fear the emergence of an international environmental regulatory structure beyond the channels of influence to which they are accustomed at the national level. This suggests that, in contrast to the globalisation thesis, capital is undertaking a contingent, multi-dimensional strategy relative to the national state and international institutions.

The growth of international regimes to address global environmental problems has been analysed extensively in the burgeoning literature on regime theory (Haas, Keohane and Levy 1993; Haggard and Simmons 1987; Young 1994). This literature, even in its more institutionalist variety, tends to focus on states as the primary actors in the international polity and neglects the role of corporate and social interests (Paterson 1996; Strange 1988). Perhaps more relevant and fruitful for the present question has been the emergence of transnational historical materialism (THM) (Cox 1993; Gill 1990 and 1993). Grounded in the Gramscian theory of hegemony (Gramsci 1971), THM posits the emergence of a transnational historic bloc, comprising a coalition of businesses, intellectuals, and state managers that transcends any one class and is bound together through common identities and interests by material and ideological structures. This process serves the interests of an emergent and newly conscious international elite which depends for its prosperity upon the continuation and extension of a secure international neo-liberal trade and investment regime. In this conception, 'international organization functions as the process through which the institutions of hegemony and its ideology are developed' (Cox 1993: 62). In contrast to the globalisation approach, capital's hegemony is not uncontested in the international sphere; rather, it secures legitimacy and consent through a process of compromise and accommodation that reflects specific historical conditions.

Although the THM school emphasises the role of capital in the emerging global polity, the national state plays a major mediating role in the construction of world hegemony. Van der Pijl (1989: 19), for example, points to the national state as 'support[ing] the existence of ruling classes in their particularity' and argues that capitalist internationalisation can take place only if capital 'succeed[s] in synthesizing their international perspective with a national one' (Van der Pijl 1989: 12). Cox, as well as Gill and Law, see internationalisation as a contradictory process, one which is not monolithic and absolute but rather one which provides opportunities for the development of a counter-hegemonic alternative. The emergence of such an alternative is 'likely to be traceable to some fundamental change in social relations and in the *national* political orders which correspond to *national* structures of social relations' (Cox 1993: 6 4). THM, in contrast to the globalisation thesis, thus accords the national state a more active role in the construction, reproduction, and possible subversion of internationalised capital.

While we believe that the Gramscian roots of THM offer a sophisticated theory of the material and ideological bases of the capitalist state (Boggs 1976; Showstack-Sassoon 1987), we also believe that THM would benefit from making more explicit the specific mechanisms and channels of capital's power relative to the state and international institutions. Thus, while our analysis of the role of capital in the international climate change negotiations is broadly located in the THM framework, we seek to integrate critical theories of the state with this framework. More specifically, our analysis is based on power elite or instrumentalist theories (Mills 1967; Domhoff 1990; Miliband 1969), structural dependence theories (Block 1987; Offe 1984; Poulantzas 1978), and cultural/discursive theories of the state (Foucault 1977; Habermas 1984; Hall *et al.* 1978). These theories are relevant to the question at hand because, in their fundamentals, they seek to explain how business influences politics within a capitalist system.

Although international institutions such as the UN are clearly not true states in that they are not sovereign supranational entities, Shaw (1994: 650) has observed that 'a *de facto* complex of global state institutions is coming into existence through the fusion of Western state power and the legitimization framework of the United Nations'. Our analysis of the climate change negotiations suggests that it might prove fruitful to reconstruct critical state theory to take account of the rise of extra-national bases of political power. We argue that international institutions are not mere epiphenomena created by dominant states, nor are they simply tools of international capital; rather, they possess significant resources, expertise, and regulatory initiative which they are able to deploy with some degree of organisational autonomy. In this context, critical theories of the state suggest a rich array of mechanisms by which capital might exert influence over these negotiations.

The increasing presence of social forces in the international arena has received growing attention in the literature on global civil society. Shaw (1994: 650) argues that 'civil society can be said to have become globalised to the extent that society increasingly represents itself globally, across nation-state boundaries, through the formation of global institutions'. The social movements engaged in such representation efforts are typically defined in terms of their common identity and interests, and their use of mass mobilisation as a prime form of sanction and power, though Peterson (1992) notes that international civil organisations tend to be decentralised, loose networks which typically lack coherence and common vision or goals. Wapner (1995) refers to the phenomenon of networks of associations actively working in international rather than national forums as 'world civic politics'. The relationships among civil society, social movements, the state and international institutions are subject to some debate. For Peterson (1992), civil society is autonomously organised public activity outside of the state. Shaw (1994: 648) articulates the Gramscian perspective in which civil society is both the 'outer earthworks of the state' and an arena in which social groups organise to contest state power. Some writers locate environmental organisations within the phenomenon of 'new social movements', which, it is argued, transcend class lines and are more concerned with personal identity than political conflict (Larana, Johnston, and Gusfield 1994). The climate change negotiations afford us an opportunity to witness the operation of global civil society.

Our extension of critical state theory to the international level will contribute to the development of the transnational historical materialist analysis of the relationship between capital, states, international institutions, and social forces. Where the globalisation thesis sees the withering and growing irrelevance of the state, we contend that developments in the international sphere serve to shift the ensemble of *national* relations in complex ways. If international economic integration erodes the access of nationally-based social movements to decision-making at the national level (Panitch 1994) and creates pressure for states to maintain 'economic competitiveness' by adopting measures favourable to mobile capital (Carnoy 1993; Picciotto 1991), this is likely to increase the political leverage of capital *within* the national state; indeed, it is the very division of the world into competing national states which provides global capital with its structural power (Gill and Law 1993). As a result, it is possible that the development of an international institutional infrastructure for a world neo-liberal economic order may contribute to a new relevance for the national state as capital's preferred arena for regulating social, labour, and environmental issues (Hirst and Thompson 1996). At the same time, social forces might attempt to coordinate internationally and press for the standardisation of environmental regulation through international governance structures. These preferences are the reverse of those for market-enabling institutions, where capital tends to prefer the international arena and social forces the national level. The international system is thus not supplanting or eclipsing the national state and its relations to national capital and social forces. Instead, these two spheres mediate and condition each other in a dialectical relationship. Our analysis of the development of international environmental policy on climate change illustrates this process.

The contention that business is running to the international arena in order to escape national social constraints is predicated on a more pluralist view of the relationship between business and the national state. Pluralists argue that sectoral divisions prevent business from acting in a unified way, and that the state can maintain neutrality and independence in mediating conflicting claims (Epstein 1969). By contrast, critical theories assert that the state actively serves business interests at the national level. Three major variants of these theories point to different sources of power that business wields over the state, despite the formal trappings of democratic and independent state institutions. The power-elite or instrumentalist perspective emphasises the ability of business to act cohesively in the political arena through a dense network of relationships between business and the state. Structural dependence theories acknowledge that the state enjoys a degree of autonomy from business power, but argue that in a market system, the state is structurally dependent on private sector profitability. State managers depend on popular support and legitimacy, which is a function of jobs and prosperity in the private sector and their ability to fund government programmes with tax revenue. These structural relationships cause state managers to act on behalf of, rather than at the behest of, business; indeed, the state needs to maintain its autonomy from any one business sector in order to resolve inter-sectoral conflicts and secure the system as a whole. Cultural or discursive theories emphasise the ideological and symbolic aspects of power. This loose collection of approaches has been applied to understand the state's relationship to business. Unlike power-elite theorists, who view cultural institutions such as schools and the media as subservient to business interests, discursive theories of the state see this sector as a relatively independent site of political struggle.

Corporate influence on the climate change process

Instrumentalist forms of power

The 1992 United Nations Conference on Environment and Development in Rio de Janeiro provided a setting for business to exert a very powerful influence over the direction of international environmental policy. Maurice Strong, head of the Canadian electric utility Ontario Hydro, was appointed to the position of Secretary-General of the conference; in turn, Strong appointed as his principal adviser the Swiss industrialist and multi-millionaire Stephan Schmidheiny, who organised the Business Council for Sustainable Development (BCSD), a group of industrialists representing forty-eight of the world's largest multinational corporations. Several scholars have argued that the conference structure gave companies special status and coherence that environmental NGOs lacked (Finger 1994; Kolk 1997). Despite the BCSD's professed commitment to achieving environmental goals through market measures such as green taxes (Schmidheiny 1992), it used its influence to help ensure that the Framework Convention on Climate Change (FCCC) agreed at the conference contained little commitment to concrete action (Mintzer and Leonard 1994; Hecht and Tirpak 1995). This example illustrates that when business does exert its power in international negotiations, it is often to keep regulation at the national level. Schmidheiny (1992:24) expressed his reasons for this quite candidly: 'Business has favored [national] regulation in the past because it also is more familiar with this approach, and feels it can influence it through negotiation. In addition, in many countries regulations are passed but rarely enforced.'

One important channel of influence at the domestic level in the US is the network of contacts maintained by large companies and their industry associations. For example, the Global Climate Coalition (GCC), the largest industry group active on the climate change issue, benefits from the personal connections of its director, John Schlaes, and of its member companies. Schlaes held a senior position in the executive office of the White House as director of communications under John Sununu, and still appears to exert significant influence on the Republican side of Congress. Financial donations to politicians represent a second channel of influence at the national level in the US. The oil industry alone provided $15.5 million in campaign contributions during the 1995–96 US election cycle, of which Republicans received about 80 per cent (Abramson 1997). Not surprisingly, recipients of this money tend to be people who are in a position to influence climate change policy (Makinson 1995). Industry associations opposing mandatory limitations on greenhouse gas emissions have been successful in securing the support of a key group of Republican Congresspeople in the 1994–6 House. The oil and automobile industries, which are major sources of greenhouse gases, are particularly powerful actors in the US domestic arena. A modest fuel tax proposed by the Clinton administration in 1992 was quickly dropped in the face of pressure from these industries. In more recent multi-party discussions sponsored by the White House on limiting emissions in the automobile sector, dubbed Car Talk, these industries appeared to be able to exert an effective veto. According to a representative of the Climate Action Network (CAN), an umbrella environmental organisation working on the climate issue, 'car companies would not discuss CAFE standards and oil companies would not entertain a gas tax. Without consensus, the process is dead.'[1]

In contrast to these points of leverage at the national level, industry's direct influence at the international negotiations since Rio has been more limited. Although groups such as the GCC have established good relationships with some national delegations, especially those from Canada, Australia, and oil exporting countries, these ties tend to based on a congruence of interests rather than personal or financial links. The international negotiations involve more than 100 countries, with whom the US-dominated industry associations share few social ties and whose politicians are beyond the reach of Political Action Committee (PAC) money. Most of the national delegations are drawn from the ranks of career civil servants and staff within each country's equivalent to departments of state, environment, energy, and commerce. Industry has not enjoyed the direct top-level influence provided at Rio through the Schmidheiny-Strong channel. Industry associations also have limited influence over less developed countries' (LDC) policies regarding climate change. The major industry associations active in climate change represent mainly larger multinational corporations based in North America and, to a lesser extent, Europe. Despite the potential leverage provided by their substantial investments in LDCs, the evidence suggests that industry has had little success in working with LDC delegations. Corporate managers report a degree of mistrust and suspicion, particularly from India and Latin America, which is partly a legacy of LDC hostility toward multinationals during the latter 1970s, and partly a function of the North–South divisions over climate change.

Industry groups have little direct influence over the UN environmental bureaucracy. Although the Conference of the Parties (COP), comprising delegates from more than 150 countries that are signatories to the Framework Convention, is formally the supreme decision-making body for the Climate Convention process, a number of UN-related bodies are more removed from national delegations susceptible to industry pressure. In January 1996 a permanent Convention Secretariat was established in Bonn, Germany. The Secretariat is based on a professional staff rather than country delegates, and, though it has no executive power, plays an important agenda setting role. Observers expect that the Secretariat will enjoy solid support from the host government, which is one of the leading advocates of a strong emissions treaty.

The COP process has a number of affiliated organisations that are widely regarded as relatively independent and committed to the process. The Conference Bureau, which organises the COP meetings, is staffed by a small group of country delegates who tend to be environmental professionals and staff from national environment ministries. The Ad-hoc Group on the Berlin Mandate (AGBM), with representatives from all the parties to the convention, is the main body that works between formal COP sessions to establish objectives for a protocol, study various options, and prepare recommendations for the next COP to adopt. Under the leadership of chairman Raul Estrada Oyuela of Argentina, the AGBM has steadily pushed towards a mandatory protocol. At AGBM-3, in March 1996, Estrada expressed his determination not to let oil producing countries delay AGBM activities, and 'declared that he would not tolerate obstruction from delegates who had tried to slow negotiations before' (ENB 1996: 19).

The convention process has been guided by the scientific and technical input provided by the IPCC, an international group of more than 2,000 respected scientists operating under the auspices of the World Meteorological Organisation and the United Nations Environmental Programme (UNEP). Despite efforts by the GCC to impugn the integrity of the IPCC process, the consensus reached in the IPCC's Second Assessment Report (1995) concerning the likelihood of greenhouse gas-induced climatic change has gained broad legitimacy and has been widely accepted by most national delegations and even centrist industry groups. Despite the vast resources available to business groups, most observers concur that their influence has not overwhelmed the voice of environmental NGOs at the international negotiations. Environmental NGOs have also been well organised. Indeed, according to Chris Flavin of the Worldwatch Institute, Washington D.C., 'the NGOs ran circles around the Global Climate Coalition in Berlin'.[2] The Climate Action Network has published an influential daily newsletter at post-Rio meetings that is distributed to delegates and around the world via e-mail and the web.

Critics of the instrumentalist position point to the diversity of industry interests as a source of weakness that prevents business from acting as a cohesive, conscious bloc. The climate change case is characterised by a plethora of industry associations representing different perspectives (Levy 1997a). Although pluralist theory suggests that this disunity would weaken the power of business in the negotiation process, it appears that the US administration is anxious to obtain the consent of *all* major affected sectors and to avoid steps that would be economically harmful to them (Wirth 1996). The desire for consensus in the face of these sectoral divisions provides the more intransigent industry associations such as the GCC with considerable leverage; it has been resolute in refusing to join the position of a more moderate industry group, the International Climate Change Partnership (ICCP), precisely because that could form the basis for a compromise agreement.

While this evidence suggests that industry associations are currently much more influential at the national than the international level, they are actively organising to broaden their geographic reach. Both the GCC and the ICCP are aggressively seeking more European, Asian, and developing country members. The International Chamber of Commerce has played a role in trying to coordinate international business responses to the climate change negotiations, although inter-sectoral differences have hindered its efforts. The International Chamber of Commerce, whose membership is primarily drawn from OECD countries, has a very active working party on climate change which met in London in January 1996 to plan strategy for the COP-2 negotiating session in Geneva in July 1996. Maurice Strong, having left Ontario Hydro in 1996, was appointed Deputy Secretary-General of the UN, and the UN is examining ways to formalise corporate input into its decision-making process.[3]

Structural dependency

Climate change has the potential to generate significant structural pressures on policy-makers because of the economic impact of measures to curb greenhouse gas emissions. Dependable access to cheap energy is often viewed by policy-makers as central to economic growth and prosperity, and a key strategic state objective (Newell 1997; Yergin 1991). Controls on emissions of carbon dioxide would affect not just the producers and refiners of oil and coal, but would significantly raise the price of these fuels for electric utilities and the transportation sector. Higher energy costs would also affect energy intense industries downstream on the value chain, such as chemicals, steel, glass, aluminium, cement, and paper. The GCC has been quick to point out the potential impact on growth and employment of curbing greenhouse gas emissions (WEFA 1996), and US officials have expressed concern about the sensitivity of American voters to fuel prices. In July 1997 the US Senate voted unanimously for the Byrd-Hagel resolution, which objected to any treaty measures that could hurt US competitiveness and employment. The US is not, of course, the lone champion of capital in international fora. European governments are extremely sensitive to the issue of unemployment, which has averaged more than ten per cent in the EU in recent years compared to around six per cent in the US. Structural dependence also extends to less developed countries, which have become increasingly eager to attract new inflows of private capital.

By contrast, the international institutions involved in the climate change negotiations are relatively insulated from structural pressures. The UN is not directly dependent for revenues on healthy national economies, nor does it have to compete with other entities to offer an attractive business climate. Indeed, the very lack of democratic accountability within international institutions that worries some observers also serves to insulate them from popular concerns about jobs and fuel prices. If curbing greenhouse gas emissions means higher fossil fuel prices, the UN might well be able to take actions that appear politically impossible in the US.

Those countries whose economic structures are most dependent on fossil fuels are the natural allies of industry groups opposed to emission limitations.

The Climate Council is known to have close links to Kuwait, Saudi Arabia, and other members of OPEC. The Global Climate Coalition has tried to exert its influence primarily with the JUSCANZ bloc of industrialised countries opposing strong measures.[4] This loose coalition shares economic interests that could be harmed by greenhouse gas controls. The US possesses substantial reserves of coal and oil, the value of which would decline if demand were curbed or substitutes developed. Perhaps more importantly, the US is home to five of the seven oil majors, and is also the home to large multinationals in energy intense user industries, such as automobiles, steel, and chemicals. The US relies heavily on fossil fuels for its energy needs; its carbon emissions are the highest in the world, both in total and in per capita terms (Brown 1996). The imposition of carbon taxes at approximately uniform rates across the world would cause much more serious adjustment effects in the US where energy taxes are very low. Canada and Australia, also major consumers and exporters of fossil fuels, have strongly opposed specific emissions limits.

An examination of the positions of various European countries also supports the structural dependence position, as they appear closely attuned to each country's specific economic and industrial structure. France has been relatively supportive of emission controls because it already obtains more than 60 per cent of its electricity from nuclear plants, and stands to gain export markets for its nuclear technology. Although Germany, the strongest European advocate of controls, relied on coal for about one-third of its primary energy needs in 1990, dependence on coal was already being reduced due to concern about acid rain and the cost of coal subsidies, which exceeded $4 billion a year. Germany has been able to reduce emissions through the closure of inefficient plants in the former East Germany, and is in the forefront of pollution prevention and renewable energy technologies. The UK, heavily dependent on coal, had followed the US position against controls until the early 1990s. The UK reversed its stance following the decision to end subsidies to the coal mining industry and close most of the coal pits (Boehmer-Christiansen 1995).

Much of the developing world has opposed any international agreement to limit emissions on the grounds that climate change is a rich country problem and that cheap energy is needed to fuel growth. China, with one-third of the world's proven reserves of coal, relies on coal for around 80 per cent of its energy needs, and in 1995 was already the world's third largest emitter of carbon dioxide. China planned to expand its coal production fivefold to three billion tons a year by 2020, which would increase global carbon dioxide emissions nearly 50 per cent (Grubb 1990). Brazil, Indonesia, and Malaysia, which are home to much of world's tropical rain forest, have expressed concern that a treaty might limit their ability to log and export timber, or to clear the land for agricultural use.

Although the broad correspondence between a country's negotiating position and its economic interests suggests that structural economic dependence is a powerful factor in the formation of policy, it does not illuminate which specific channels of influence are at work. Structural dependence can be translated into policy through instrumentalist mechanisms exerted by affected sectors, as discussed earlier, or discursively through the construction of 'competitiveness' as a primary goal of national policy. US government publications and interviews with US government officials reveal that US competitiveness is considered a high-priority issue of legitimate concern throughout government. A few government respondents expressed fear of the voters and the need to accommodate business concerns, but none gave any hint that dependence on tax revenues played any role. Rather, it was simply taken for granted that government policy-making should promote economic growth and avoid economic disruption to major sectors. This vision of the 'competition state' has been internalised as part of the construction of the public official and has been institutionalised in policy-making processes. The three forms of influence thus appear to be inherently intertwined and interdependent.

Discursive influence

If environmental policy formation is, at least in part, a struggle for discursive hegemony (Hajer 1995) it is important to examine corporate efforts to influence the discourse around climate change. In the US, corporate interests likely to be affected by climate change have made significant efforts to influence discourse over the issue. Fossil fuel interests have engaged in substantial public relations campaigns in the US, targeted to the public in general as well as policy-makers, to highlight scientific uncertainties concerning global warming and emphasise the high economic costs of curbing emissions. More broadly, they have attempted to construct global warming as the invention of anti-business environmental extremists, while the UN is often depicted as a threat to American freedom and prosperity. These themes find fertile ground because they resonate with existing discourses in American society, reflected in the growth of the Wise Use movement, a suspicion of federal, let alone international, authorities and a particular concept of freedom that is highly individualistic and symbolically related to automobiles (Rowell 1996).

Advertising and education are two channels through which industry associations have tried to influence public opinion. Western Fuels, a US utility association and member of the GCC, ran an advertisement in 1993 titled 'Repeal Rio' calling climate change a 'controversial theory' with 'no support in observations', and made the claim that 'CO_2 fertilization of the atmosphere helps produce more food for people and wildlife.' The association also spent around $250,000 to produce a video in 1991 called *The Greening of Planet Earth*, which carried the same message and was apparently influential in the Bush administration. One industry tactic has been to establish 'front groups' to mask the corporate interests involved. Coal, oil, and utility interests in the US established a group called The Information Council for the Environment in 1991, whose purpose, as stated in internal documents, was to 'reposition global warming as theory, not fact' (*Ozone Action* 1996). ICE developed a sophisticated print and radio media campaign directed at 'older, less educated men' and 'young, low income women', and set up a Science Advisory Panel which included three 'climate skeptics,' Robert Balling, Patrick Michaels and S. Fred Singer, all of whom have received funding from fossil fuel industries.

The GCC and its member organisations have engaged in a much more targeted effort to convince business leaders and policy-makers that measures to curb greenhouse gas emissions 'are premature and are not justified by the state of scientific knowledge or the economic risks they create' (GCC 1995). The GCC commissioned a series of economic studies that suggest that the US might suffer economic losses in the region of 3 to 5 per cent of GDP annually if it follows proposals to cut emissions 20 per cent below 1990 levels by 2005 (Montgomery and Charles River Associates 1995; WEFA 1996). In a September 1996 press release, the GCC warned that measures to curb emissions by 20 per cent 'could reduce the US gross domestic product by 4 per cent and cost Americans up to 1.1 million jobs annually.' As a result of these efforts, industry's concerns have permeated governmental discourse, in some cases almost literally; respondents at the Department of Energy talked in terms of the need to avoid 'premature retirement of capital', a term frequently used by fossil fuel and utility interests. Fossil fuel interests have also attempted to convince opinion leaders and policy-makers that the science of climate change is dubious at best. The Western Fuels Association has funded the publication and distribution of a monthly newsletter called the *World Climate Review*. Edited by Patrick Michaels of the University of Virginia, the newsletter is dedicated to debunking climate change science and is mailed to all the members of the Society of Environmental Journalists.

Despite the resources invested in influencing the scientific and policy debates, it is evident that the fossil fuel industry's point of view has not achieved hegemonic status, even within the US. The ICE programme was halted following a number of embarrassing media stories, and few familiar with the issue are as sanguine about climate change as the Western Fuels advertisements. Nevertheless, the 'climate sceptics' have succeeded in turning climate change into an apparently balanced 'debate' in the media. Moreover, they have played a key role in a number of state and Congressional hearings by providing some cover for politicians who, because of their ideological inclination or allegiance to certain business interests, want to delay any action on greenhouse gas emissions (Gelbspan 1997).

Industry associations have enjoyed much less influence over the scientific and policy discourse in the international negotiations. Although international networks of media ownership and distribution have expanded in recent years, the sophisticated public relations campaigns waged in the US are not easily duplicated in other countries, where corporate public relations departments are less experienced and more restrictions exist on commercial activities in educational institutions. An industry effort to challenge the integrity of the Intergovernmental Panel on Climate Change Second Assessment Report illustrates the difficulty faced by industry in affecting the scientific discourse within the UN process. The GCC and the Climate Council claimed that Benjamin Santer and Tom Wigley, two of the lead authors, had deleted passages that dissented or expressed uncertainty (ECO 1996). These accusations were quickly picked up by the mass media, including the *Wall Street Journal* (Seitz 1996) and the *New York Times* (Stevens 1996), but the allegations had little impact on the international negotiations, where officials were quick to express their support for the peer review process that resulted in the changes.

The primary reason for the failure of the GCC viewpoint to gain hegemony in the US is the emerging challenge from a competing discursive paradigm, that of ecological modernisation (Hajer 1995). The lure of this approach lies in the core assumption that being 'green' can also be good for business, and that addressing environmental problems can be a positive sum game (Levy 1995, 1997b; Russo and Fouts 1997). To generate these 'win-win' situations, ecological modernisation puts its faith in the technological, organisational, and financial resources of the private sector, voluntary partnerships between government agencies and business, flexible market-based measures, and the application of environmental management techniques (Cairncross 1991; Schmidheiny 1992). In the climate change context, this view has been embraced by industry associations representing companies in the renewable energy, gas, and energy efficiency sectors, by a number of major environmental organisations, especially the World Resources Institute and the Environmental Defense Fund (Dudek 1996), and increasingly by other sectors of industry, including members of the ICCP. The Clinton Administration's approach to Climate Change bears the clear imprint of this paradigm. The US Climate Change Action Plan (1993: 2) states that 'returning US greenhouse gas emissions to their 1990 levels by the year 2000 is an ambitious but achievable goal that can be attained while enhancing prospects for market growth and job creation, and positioning our country to compete and win in the global market'. The joint EPA/Department of Energy Climate Wise programme describes itself as 'a unique partnership that can help you turn energy efficiency and environmental performance into a corporate asset' (US DoE 1996).

This discourse has also permeated the international climate negotiations, partly due to the powerful position of the US and partly to the influence of Schmidheiny and the World Business Council for Sustainable Development. To coincide with the 1992 UN Conference on Environment and Development conference, Stephan Schmidheiny published the influential book *Changing Course* (1992), which championed the role of private capital and free markets in achieving 'sustainable development', while downplaying any possible contradictions between vigorous economic growth and environmental protection. The primacy of markets and private capital in addressing climate change is also reflected in the Second Assessment Report of the IPCC, particularly the section by Working Group III, which addressed social and economic policies.

Conclusions

Overall, the evidence does not support the notion that the international arena offers capital a safe haven from environmental regulations. For the case of a regulatory international regime such as climate change, business appears to prefer the well-charted and predictable waters of the national political economy. Indeed, the correspondence between national negotiating stances and economic interests provides testimony to the hegemony of corporate influence over national policy. The case study suggests that instrumentalist forms of power operate more effectively at the national level, and that international institutions are relatively insulated from these sources of pressure. US-based companies and industry associations have limited leverage over the climate policies of other countries, which tend to pursue what they perceive to be their own economic interests. In addition, the potential for greenhouse gas controls to cause substantial economic dislocation generates structural pressures at the national level, particularly in those countries most dependent on fossil fuels. International institutions themselves are removed from these pressures. Finally, business efforts to influence the science and policy discourse have also been much more prevalent and effective at the national than the international level. Even at the national level, the views advocated by the fossil fuel industry serve more to create the appearance of controversy than a hegemonic consensus. The more blatant attempts to discredit climate change science have fallen flat in the UN. Although a broad consensus has emerged about the central role of corporate solutions guided by market incentives in a future regulatory regime, the hegemonic nature of this discourse cannot be directly attributed to specific industry efforts; rather, it is related to the broader dissemination of the related discourses of neo-liberalism and ecological modernism.

The case highlights the importance of our distinction between regulatory institutions, such as those governing international environmental policy, and market-enabling institutions that provide the infrastructure for governance of global trade, investment, and financial flows. While capital might be highly supportive of international enabling institutions at the expense of national states, there is reason to be sceptical of the globalisation thesis in the case of regulatory institutions. This study suggests that capital does operate at the international level in an effort to influence emerging regulatory institutions, but that such action in this arena, rather than eclipsing the national state, is largely channelled through it, and is frequently directed toward blocking strong transnational action. In short, there are strong reservations against the claim of the neo-liberal global discourse (see introduction of this book) that transnational capital would gain authority at the expense of states due to globalisation.

Hirst and Thompson's argument that non-governmental organisations are more inclined to be transnational actors than are corporations is supported by the climate change case; environmental NGOs advocate for international regulation of greenhouse gas emissions because they recognise that many countries would not take strong action in the absence of an international agreement due to corporate pressures and the high cost of unilateral action. Moreover, they recognise the high status and influence of the international scientific community within UN-based institutions and the relative weakness of corporate pressures. This is the complete reverse of the case for international market enabling institutions such as the World Trade Organisation from which international civil society is largely excluded.

While our analysis provides support for the continued relevance of the national state within an internationalised capitalism, it also points to the changing relationship between capital, the state, international institutions, and social forces. Multinationals are developing more sophisticated transnational political capacities and are learning to coordinate their activities at the national and international level. As nation states lose some autonomy over economic policies and cede some responsibility for environmental regulation to international institutions, they are increasingly important as conduits of business power and as sites for the formulation and implementation of social, labour, and environmental policies. The international arena can thus be understood as a contested political field of increasing significance that inter-relates with and modifies relations in the national domain. Hegemony must be secured, but can also be contested, at both levels, opening up new possibilities for resistance.

Notes

The authors gratefully acknowledge funding for this research from the University of Massachusetts, Boston. This research is based on a series of interviews with representatives of industry associations, corporations, US government agencies, and environmental organizations, as well as extensive analysis of documentary and secondary materials.

1 Interview with Jennifer Morgan, 10 January 1996.
2 Interview with Chris Flavin, 11 January 1996.
3 On 24 June 1997, ten CEOs of transnational corporations, mostly members of the BCSD, met with fifteen government representatives, including three heads of state, the Secretary-General of the UN, and the Administrator of UNDP, to establish terms of reference for business sector participation in the policy setting process of the UN and partnering in the uses of UN development assistance funds (source: letter from David Korten, http://iisd1.iisd.ca/pcdf).
4 JUSCANZ comprises Japan, the US, Canada, and New Zealand.

References

Abramson, D. (1997) *The Oil Daily*, 24 February, 47(36): 1.
Barnet, R. J., and J. Cavanagh (1994) *Global Dreams: Imperial Corporations and the New World Order*, New York: Simon and Schuster.
Block, F. (1987) *Revising State Theory*, Philadelphia: Temple University Press.
Boehmer-Christiansen, S. A. (1995) 'Britain and the international panel on climate change: the impacts of scientific advice on global warming, part II: the domestic story of the British response to climate change', *Environmental Politics* 4(2): 175–96.
Boggs, C. (1976) *Gramsci's Marxism*, London: Pluto Press.
Brown, L. (1996) *State of the World, 1996*, Washington, D.C.: Norton/Worldwatch Institute.
Cairncross, F. (1991) *Costing the Earth*, Boston, Mass.: Harvard Business School Press.
Carnoy M. (1993) 'Multinationals in the changing world economy: whither the nation-state?', in M. Carnoy, M. Castells, S. Cohen, and F. Cardoso (eds) *The New Global Economy in the Information Age*, University Park: Pennsylvania State University Press:45–96.
Climate Change Action Plan (1993) Washington, D.C.: US White House.
Cox, R. W. (1993) 'Gramsci, hegemony and international relations: an essay in method', in S. Gill (ed.) *Gramsci, Historical Materialism and International Relations*, Cambridge: Cambridge University Press: 49–66.
Domhoff, G. W. (1990) *The Power Elite and the State: How Policy is Made in America*, New York: Aldine de Gruyter.
Dudek, D. J. (1996) *Emission Budgets: Creating Rewards, Lowering Costs and Ensuring Results,* New York: Environmental Defense Fund.
ECO (1996) *ECO Newsletter*, COP-2, Geneva, Issue no.1, 8 July.
ENB (1996) *Earth Negotiations Bulletin* 12(27), 11 March.

Epstein, E. (1969) *The Corporation in American Politics*, Englewood Cliffs, N.J.: Prentice Hall.

Finger, M. (1994) 'NGOs and transformation: beyond social movement theory', in T. Princen and M. Finger (eds) *Environmental NGOs in World Politics*, New York: Routledge: 48–66.

Foucault, M. (1977) *Discipline and Punish* (A. Sheridan, trans.), New York: Random House.

GCC (1995) *Global Climate Coalition press release*, February 9.

Gelbspan, R. (1997) *The Heat is On*, Reading, Mass.: Addison-Wesley.

Gill, S. (1990) *American Hegemony and the Trilateral Commission*, Cambridge: Cambridge University Press.

—— (1993) 'Gramsci and global politics: towards a post-hegemonic research agenda', in S. Gill (ed.) *Gramsci, Historical Materialism and International Relations*, Cambridge: Cambridge University Press:1–18.

Gill, S., and D. Law (1993) 'Global hegemony and the structural power of capital', in S. Gill (ed.), *Gramsci, Historical Materialism and International Relations*, Cambridge: Cambridge University Press: 93–124.

Gramsci, A. (1971) *Selections from the Prison Notebooks* (Q. Hoare and G. Nowell-Smith, trans.), New York: International Publishers.

Grubb, M. (1990) 'The greenhouse effect: negotiating targets', *International Affairs* 66(1): 67–89.

Haas, P. M., R. O. Keohane and M. A. Levy (eds) (1993) *Institutions for the Earth: Sources of Effective International Environmental Protection*, Cambridge, Mass.: MIT Press.

Habermas, J. (1984) *The Theory of Communicative Action*, Cambridge: Polity Press.

Haggard, S., and B. A. Simmons (1987) 'Theories of international regimes', *International Organization* 41: 491–517.

Hajer, M. A. (1995) *The Politics of Environmental Discourse: Ecological Modernization and the Policy Process*, Oxford: Clarendon Press.

Hall, S., C. Critcher, T. Jefferson, J. Clarke and B. Roberts (1978) *Policing the Crisis: Mugging, the State, and Law and Order*, London: Macmillan.

Hecht, A. D. and D. Tirpak. (1995) 'Framework agreement on climate change: a scientific and policy history', *Climatic Change* 29: 371–402.

Hirst, P. and G. Thompson (1996) *Globalization in Question*, Cambridge: Polity Press.

IPCC (1995) *Second Assessment Report of the Intergovernmental Panel on Climate Change*, Cambridge: Cambridge University Press.

Jessop, R. (1994) 'Post-Fordism and the State', in A. Amin (ed.) *Post-Fordism*, Cambridge: Blackwell: 251–79.

Kolk, A. (1997) *Forests in International Environmental Politics*, Atlanta: International Books.

Korten, D. C. (1995) *When Corporations Rule the World*, West Hartford, Conn.: Kumarian Press.

Larana, E., H. Johnston and J. R. Gusfield (eds.) (1994) *New Social Movements: From Ideology to Identity*, Philadelphia: Temple University Press.

Levy, D. L. (1995) 'The environmental practices and performance of transnational corporations', *Transnational Corporations* 4(1): 44–68.

—— (1997a) 'Business and international environmental treaties: ozone depletion and climate change', *California Management Review* 39(3): 54–71.

—— (1997b) 'Environmental management as political sustainability', *Organization and Environment* 10(2): 126–47.

Makinson, L. (1995) *The Price of Admission: Campaign Spending in the 1994 Elections*, Washington, D.C.: Center for Responsive Politics.

Miliband, R. (1969) *The State in Capitalist Society*, New York: Basic Books.

Mills, C. W. (1967) *The Power Elite*, New York: Oxford University Press.

Mintzer, I. M. and J. A. Leonard (eds.) (1994) *Negotiating Climate Change: the Inside Story of the Rio Convention*, Cambridge: Cambridge University Press.

Montgomery, D. W. and Charles River Associates (1995) *Toward an Economically Rational Response to the Berlin Mandate*, prepared on behalf of GCC, Washington, D.C.: Charles River Associates.

Newell, P. (1997) *The International Politics of Global Warming: A Non-Governmental Account*, doctoral thesis, University of Keele, England.

Offe, C. (1984) 'Theses on the theory of the state', in J. Keane (ed.) *Contradictions of the Welfare State*, Cambridge: MIT Press:119–29.

Ozone Action (1996) *Distorting the Debate: a Case Study of Corporate Greenwashing*, Washington, D.C.: Ozone Action.

Panitch, L. (1994) 'Globalization and the State', in R. Miliband and L. Panitch (eds) *Socialist Register 1994: Between Globalism and Nationalism*, London: Merlin Press: 60–93.

Paterson, M. (1996) 'IR theory: neorealism, neoinstitutionalism and the Climate Change Convention', in J. Vogler and M. F. Imber (eds) *The Environment and International Relations*, London: Routledge: 59–76.

Peterson, M. J. (1992) 'Transnational activity, international society and world politics', *Millennium* 21(3): 371–88.

Piccioto, S. (1991) 'The internationalization of the state', *Capital and Class* 43: 43–63.

Poulantzas, N. (1978) *Political Power and Social Classes*, London: Verso.

Reich, R. (1991) *The Work of Nations*, New York: Vintage Books.

Rowell, A. (1996) *Green Backlash: Global Subversion of the Environmental Movement*, London: Routledge.

Russo, M. V. and P. A. Fouts (1997) 'A resource-based perspective on corporate environmental performance and profitability', *Academy of Management Journal* 40(3): 534.

Schmidheiny, S. (1992) *Changing Course*, Cambridge, Mass.: MIT Press.

Seitz, F. (1996) 'A major deception on 'Global Warming', *Wall Street Journal*, 6 June: A16.

Shaw, M. (1994) 'Civil society and global politics: beyond a social movements approach', *Milllennium* 23(3): 648–55.

Showstack-Sassoon, A. (1987) *Gramsci's Politics*, London: Hutchinson.

Stevens, W. (1996) 'UN climate report was improperly altered, underplaying uncertainties, critics say', *New York Times*, 17 June: B6.

Strange, S. (1988) *States and Markets: an Introduction to International Political Economy*, New York: Blackwell.

—— (1996) *The Retreat of the State*, New York: Cambridge University Press.

US DoE (1996) *Climate Wise* DOE/EE-0071, EPA 230-K-95–003, Washington, D.C.: US Department of Energy.

US Office of the White House (1993) *US Climate Change Action Plan*, Washington, D.C.: US White House.

Van der Pijl, K. (1989) 'Ruling classes, hegemony, and the state system', *International Journal of Political Economy* 19: 7–35.

Wapner P. (1995) 'Politics beyond the state: environmental activism and world civic politics', *World Politics* 47, April: 311–40.

WEFA Group and H. Zinder and Associates (1996) *A Review of the Economic Impacts of AOSIS-type Proposals to Limit Carbon Dioxide Emissions* (prepared for Global Climate Coalition), Eddystone, Pa.: WEFA Group.

Wirth, T. E. (1996) Statement by Timothy E. Wirth, Under Secretary for Global Affairs, on behalf of the USA, at the Convention on Climate Change, second Conference of the Parties, July 17. Geneva, Switzerland: US Mission, Office of Public Affairs.

Yergin, D. (1991) *The Prize*, New York: Simon and Schuster.

Young, O. R. (1994) *International Governance: Protecting the Environment in a Stateless Society*, Ithaca, N.Y.: Cornell University Press.

Part III

Multinational companies and the international restructuring of production

9 Alliance capitalism as industrial order

Exploring new forms of interfirm competition in the globalising economy

Brian Portnoy

Introduction

This paper addresses an increasingly prominent phenomenon in the world economy: the coincidence of cooperation and competition among major private actors in the same sector at the same time. Sometimes referred to as the 'New Competition' (Best 1990), this duality reflects an ongoing redefinition of the competitive order in certain global industries such as pharmaceuticals, semi-conductors and automobiles. In these industries, large firms have been making cooperative arrangements for research, production and marketing while at the same time competing against one another in world markets. In this paper, I explore how such redefining occurs by investigating the international politics of industrial restructuring. My main argument concerns the governing of competition in global industries through the use of networks, especially transnational strategic alliances among multinational corporations (MNCs). The logic of this argument is straightforward: if networks are a distinct form of economic governance, and international strategic alliances are an important form of network organisation, then the growth in these alliances over the last couple of decades constitutes an increasingly important source of governance in the global political economy. Networks have by no means replaced other organisational forms, but their growth in prominence has been consequential for the character of competition. As such, business scholars such as John Dunning have referred to this current era of industrial restructuring as 'alliance capitalism'. In the semiconductor industry, the central industry case study of this paper, such alliances have been increasingly prevalent and consequential.

This paper is organised as follows. In the following section, I define globalisation as the restructuring of business organisation across national boundaries and introduce the debate on strategic partnering in the world economy. I also suggest that the idea of an industrial order helps capture the dynamic of international industrial restructuring. Alternative mechanisms of governance are central to identifying what type of industrial order exists. I highlight network (as opposed to market and hierarchy) modes of organisation. In the next section, I discuss the rise of alliance capitalism as manifested in the expansion of industrial networks beyond national borders, in particular transnational strategic alliances among

MNCs. Then I offer a case study of the global semiconductor industry in which the international politics of industrial restructuring are exemplary of the New Competition. Finally, I conclude by summarising the argument and briefly contrasting the present analysis based on the industrial order concept with liberal regime theory as developed in the international relations literature.

Globalisation, governance, and 'industrial order' as international organisation

The ongoing internationalisation of production and the emergence of strategic alliances among MNCs signal a qualitative shift in the operation of the world economy, which is not measurable in conventional terms, such as levels of trade or investment (Kobrin 1997: 147). Instead, the key shifts must be measured and analysed in organisational terms. According to business economist Stephen Kobrin, international strategic alliances, or 'post-modern global networks' mark 'the replacement of integrated transnational hierarchies by global networks, by a cooperative and reciprocal organization of economic transactions' (Kobrin 1997: 152). Whereas the scale of economic activity and organisation was once roughly congruent with the boundaries of the nation-state, now the scale of economic activity in certain (though not all) strategic industries necessarily stretches well beyond it.

If we are to draw attention to the qualitative dimension of economic activity, then it is useful to view industrial restructuring as an organisational problem.[1] Understanding industrial change, whether at the domestic or international level, involves examining what organisational frameworks emerge in particular strategic settings. As such, the puzzle for globalisation theory is, at bottom, one of institutional choice. What is often referred to as globalisation is simply an historical dynamic of industrial restructuring on a transnational scale. Since it requires the coordination of exchange, production, and distribution, we must inquire into institutional alternatives for such coordination: which are chosen, when, and why? For many observers, globalisation is viewed as 'the unleashing of the market' (Boyer and Drache 1996). Privatisation, deregulation, and liberalisation constitute the three definitional pillars of marketisation. Second, some stress the growth of the vertically integrated MNC, the rise of the 'global firm'. Finally, others like Kobrin and Dunning highlight the role of networks over markets and hierarchies.

This paper departs from the argument that the shape of globalisation is a mechanistic, technologically-determined process (cf. Kobrin 1995: 29). It argues instead that politics – broadly defined to include activity within industry itself – shapes the particular institutional configuration of the globalisation process. The interplay between production and politics – whether it occurs within the nation-state or across the state system – creates an historical process of destruction and construction of existing sociopolitical orders.

In this paper I aim to account for the political sources of alliance capitalism by studying states and firms through the conceptual lens of an 'industrial order'. By industrial order, I refer to the political and social conditions that support or promote particular patterns of industrial practice, while discouraging others (cf. Berk 1994; Herrigel 1994, 1996). Following in the tradition of Durkheim, Polanyi, and Weber, economic practice is not separated from its social and political context. How things are made, bought, sold, and learned is as much a function of social context as it is a function of strictly economic interplay.[2] Second, governance is central to the idea of an industrial order: it is 'the politically and socially constructed framework that creates the conditions under which particular repertoires of governance mechanisms emerge and are employed' (Herrigel 1994: 97). Amidst the endemic uncertainty in the context of industrial restructuring (Mytelka 1991), a governance structure is the particular arrangement employed to organise exchange among actors. The structures do not arise naturally from an underlying push toward efficient exchange, as the functionalist logic of neoclassical (and transaction cost) economics suggests. Instead, governance modes are strategic choices (Jarillo 1988; Stopford 1995; Sabel 1993: 5).[3]

Markets, hierarchies, and networks are the classic trio of governance structures.[4] For much of economic theory, markets are the natural fora for economic exchange. A market is the decentralised space where rational actors engage in exchange. Quickly, flexibly, and powerfully, prices rule behaviour, which are themselves the outcome of the inexorable laws of supply and demand. Also, prices are the means of communication, which then determine production and exchange. Decentralised order arises naturally through the rational pursuit of self-interest, as Smith's image of the 'invisible hand' memorably illustrates. Often, however, organisations are created to internalise market transactions. Put most simply, when exchange is risky, a hierarchically structured organisation can emerge to govern exchange (Coase 1937; Williamson 1975). For Alfred D. Chandler Jr. the 'visible hand' of managerial capitalism structures exchange. Within a firm, centralised authority determines behaviour by fiat and the creation of routines. The 'market versus hierarchy' debate is the centrepiece of modern institutional economics (Williamson 1975, 1985, 1996).

Networks are a distinct form of economic organisation. Several features distinguish them from markets or hierarchies (Grabher 1993: 8–12). First, networks are based on reciprocity among its members: there is the expectation that something of value given today will be repaid in the future. Second, actors in networks act strategically (i.e. with regard to what others have done and are expected to do), while markets are an impersonal arena in which individuals make parametric choices given certain conditions, and hierarchies are the locus of vertical authority and dependence.[5] Third, networks are marked by power relations, which emerge from the asymmetry of interdependence among the network's participants. This becomes especially evident when the network makes decisions or reshapes itself (Grabher 1993: 11). Moreover, there is debate over how the symmetry of capabilities and knowledge in the partnership affects the success of the network's stated goals. There is evidence to support the merits of either a symmetric or asymmetric partnership (Dussauge and Garrette 1995). In Table 9.1, I offer a summary comparison of the three governance modes along several dimensions.

Table 9.1 Making sense of governance

Key elements	Governance structure		
	Market	Hierarchy	Network
Normative basis	Contract/ property rights	Employment relationship	Complementary strengths
Means of communication	Prices	Routines	Relational
Methods of conflict resolution	Haggling/resort to courts for enforcement	Administrative fiat/ supervision	Norms of reciprocity/ reputational concerns
Degree of flexibility	High	Low	Medium
Actor preferences or choices	Independent	Dependent	Interdependent/ strategic
Mechanism	Prices	Authority	Trust; learning by monitoring
Type of order/ authority	Decentralised	Centralised	Multifocal
International economic transactions	Trade – production by national firms and arm's length, spot exchanges	MNC/FDI – internationalised, production, administrative hierarchy	Alliances, subcontracting, global commodity chains
Periodisation*	late 19th c.–1950s	1960s–1980s	1980s–

Source: adapted from Powell (1990a: 300) and Kobrin (1997).

Note:
* Kobrin denies a stage theory, but does claim that network organisational forms are superseding hierarchy (1997: 153).

Networks and the age of alliance capitalism

That networks of interfirm coordination are increasingly transnational signals the growing internationalisation of the world economy (Kogut, Shan and Walker 1993). Sometimes this coordination is arranged vertically into 'global commodity chains' in which different firms specialise in a distinct phase of the same production chain (Gereffi 1996). Other transnational networks are horizontal, to which the growth of alliances among MNCs attests.[6] The definition of an international corporate alliance (ICA) adopted here is 'interfirm collaboration in product development, manufacture, or marketing that spans national boundaries [which] is not based on arm's length market transactions, and includes substantial contributions by partners of capital, technology, or other assets' (Mowery 1988: 2–3).[7] In an ICA, the firms remain independent.[8] It is important to note that ICAs are rarely classic cartel arrangements, as interfirm cooperation is typically understood to be. The anti-competitive effects of ICAs are currently subject to debate – the rough consensus thus far is that most forms of ICAs do not restrict competition (Khemani and Waverman 1997).[9]

There are numerous motivations for such alliances, though many are related to the innovation process, such as capturing existing technologies and developing new ones.[10] The rising costs, risks, and complexity of technology have climbed steadily in the post-war era, accelerating even faster in the last fifteen years. Hagedoorn's (1993) evidence supports the increasingly shared idea that the greater the technological intensity of an industry, the more likely partnering will be. Alliances (as networks) have become a central location for learning among firms. Sometimes, more information will lead to better relationships between the partners, and thus to further collaboration. Search costs are reduced (Kogut, Shan and Walker 1993). Given the high costs associated with innovation and the scale necessary to recapture investments, many alliances are international. Indeed, the scale necessary to recapture investments has greatly expanded, exceeding even the largest national market. This leads to international partnering as well as consolidation through merger. Most ICA activity occurs among firms from the Triad (US, EU and Japan) countries (Khemani and Waverman 1997: 30).

In short, strategic alliances aim to govern and redefine competition. One of the more interesting elements of this phenomenon is *rivalry among alliances* where competition occurs on a project-by-project basis, rather than on stable interfirm competition, as is the traditional understanding of competition (Powell and Smith-Doerr 1994: 384). For example, in the telecommunications industry an alliance pattern featuring three major global coalitions is emerging, with each of the major American long distance carriers – AT&T, Sprint, and MCI – at the centre of an alliance. While few alliance patterns are as dramatic as in telecommunications services, the rival alliance phenomenon is increasingly evident in other sectors such as semiconductors, biotechnology, autos, and airline manufacturing. An important point is that these rival alliances alter the nature of capitalist competition. That is, cooperative alliances do not necessarily imply less competition, only a different form (cf. Powell and Smith-Doerr 1994: 384).

Through strategic alliances, MNCs are taking the lead in redefining the competitive order. Lynn Mytelka (1991) nicely details how the emergence of alliances changes (and is reflective of) the changing competitive dynamic in certain industries. Focusing on knowledge intensive industries, she argues that the increasing knowledge intensity has reshaped industrial dynamics in at least several ways. First, it has led to a significant increase in R&D expenditures. Innovations become increasingly costly over time since new discoveries are more difficult to come by. Second, this research intensity shortens the product cycle, increasing the pressure for firms to recapture their investments as quickly as possible. To recoup investment on a particular innovation before the next generation is discovered and produced greatly increases the risk of doing business.

The dynamic of investment is profoundly affected by these new risks. Firms are faced with a paradox because they often need to make enormous capital outlays for the discovery and production of knowledge intensive goods. Most of the time, such investments are too large for even the wealthiest firms, thereby spurring joint investment. The paradox is that these firms need to make large production runs in order to recapture costs and make profits for the next generation of research and production, but doing so can flood the market, thereby driving down prices, hurting (or even killing) the firms. The paradigmatic case of this dynamic occurs in the semiconductor industry.

The increasing research costs, shortening product cycles, and risks of investment produce a highly uncertain economic environment. More uncertainty (and more competition) drives firms toward flexible forms of industrial organisation, such as alliances. Cooperative interfirm relations are one solution that firms in computers, chemicals, pharmaceuticals, information technology, and so forth are employing to defeat the cycles of innovation, investment, and uncertainty. Competition, paradoxically, produces cooperation.

Critically, the mode of restructuring forces us to consider the broader political and social context within which it occurs. Indeed, often corresponding to the rise of networks is what Michael Best (1990) calls 'sector strategies' and 'sector institutions'. They address the long-term development and competitiveness of a sector, and are designed by the industry participants themselves: 'The creation of a sector strategy can emerge from private action by firms within a sector . . . [The firms] may also develop the capacity to adjust mutually to new challenges and respond collectively to new opportunities' (Best 1990: 18). This comes through dialogue and learning among the actors, as well as through the monitoring and enforcing of agreements. Thus, sector institutions can help move a group of self-interested firms to consider, and sometimes embrace, a common sectoral interest. Just as MNCs are responsible for reshaping the character of industrialisation, they are also concerned with governing that process. Clearly, this flags the potential rise of private authority structures in the international system.

I now turn to a brief study of the global semiconductor industry in which we can ground some of the ideas developed above.

Production, purpose and industrial order in global semiconductors

The global semiconductor industry is an appropriate industry in which to study alliance capitalism. Given the nature of technological innovation and inherent economic factors (e.g., the cyclical problems of surplus capacity associated with memory chip production), the industry has restructured itself over the last couple of decades.[11] In the early 1980s, it would have been impossible to predict the current industrial order that has emerged throughout the 1990s. Best's 'New Competition' framework helps illuminate this particular industrial order.

For most of the post-war era, American firms dominated the industry. When Japanese firms entered the market in the 1970s and 1980s, an older style of competition was in place: large hierarchical firms competing for market dominance.[12] International interfirm coordination was largely unheard of. But globalisation has changed that. The 1980s witnessed a redefinition of the competitive order, although not usually in ways that were as visible as the intense US–Japanese political rivalry over semiconductors. This redefinition has come largely through the advent of 'alliance capitalism' in the industry.

Recent evidence from the Electronic Industry Association of Japan (EIAJ) points out the extent and depth of interfirm cooperation over time. They note fifty major long-term international cooperative relationships among chip makers, such as IBM/Toshiba/Siemens, Goldstar/Hitachi, SGS Thompson/Mitsubishi, and Texas Instruments/Fujitsu/Hitachi/Sony. Moreover, they chart 117 examples of cooperative projects stemming from alliances between Japanese and non-Japanese semiconductor suppliers. Interestingly, seventy-nine of these projects were initiated after the 1991 US–Japan semiconductor arrangement became effective. Why we would witness a spike of cooperative business activity in the wake of a political bargain remains an interesting puzzle for investigation. There is also some evidence to support the claim that interfirm cooperation has become deeper. As the EIAJ put it:

> In the late 1980s, cooperative activities were largely limited to joint sales activity and information exchanges. [In the 1990s] the industry has witnessed a proliferation of full blown joint research and development and joint manufacturing projects among the industry's leading semiconductor manufacturers.
>
> (EIAJ 1995)

For instance, the number of production cooperation agreements increased from one in 1986 to four in 1990 to fourteen in 1993. Joint R&D projects followed a similar path. While there were only a total of four between 1985 and 1990, forty-one alliances were created between 1991 and 1994.[13] Moreover, 84 per cent of alliances were made between companies of different nationalities.[14] In short, the industry has become dominated by both global and local partnerships (Angel 1994: 3).

In line with Hagedoorn's (1993) assessment, the technological intensity of the semiconductor industry is at the core of why alliances are so prevalent. The semiconductor industry is one of the most capital-intensive, as well as R&D-intensive, industries in the world. The figure for R&D expenditures as a fraction of sales, a commonly used statistic to indicate research intensity of an industry, was 15.9 per cent for the semiconductor industry in 1990. Other research-oriented industries – for example, pharmaceuticals (8.0 per cent), electronics (5.8 per cent), or chemicals (4.9 per cent) – are less intensive than semiconductors. The average for all manufacturing industries is 3.4 per cent (EIAJ/MITI).

At the same time, the cost and risk of making chips has skyrocketed. Whereas the capital requirement to make 1MB memory (or DRAM) chips was around $300 million in the late 1980s, today it takes close to $2 billion to create the fabrication plant for 256M chips. This is 'lumpy' capital: it is invested or it is not. That makes for a huge gamble for even the wealthiest of chip companies. For instance, in the current research into 300mm wafer technology, no single company can afford the risk involved in such an investment. As a result, two rival consortia have been created recently. The Semiconductor Leading Edge Technologies (Selete) is comprised of ten Japanese chip makers, while an international consortium, the International 300 mm Initiative (I300I) is led by American firms and includes companies from Europe, South Korea, and Taiwan. Both groups have been evaluating the technologies necessary for the wafer manufacturing process, such as crystal cutters, wafer cassettes, and flatness testers.[15] This rival alliance pattern is a general feature of the industry. According to one study:

> The new institutional structure of innovation and technology development in semiconductors involves a complex array of international cooperative alliances and research agreements among US, Japanese, and European firms. To a significant degree, the primary axis of competition in the 1990s will no longer be between Japan and the United States, but between competing global networks of producers, such as that of IBM, Siemens, and Toshiba, or the alliance for longer technology development between AT&T and NEC.
>
> (Angel 1994: 7)

Cooperation and conflict have become inextricably intertwined. Indeed, the sector has been notoriously contentious over the last twenty years. The well-known American-Japanese dispute has been most prominent, although the Europeans, Koreans, and Taiwanese have all been party to the ongoing struggle over an industry whose current annual value is over $200 billion (measured in worldwide sales) and whose technology is at the core of a computer-based society. The pinnacle of the US–Japanese dispute came in 1985–86 when the US-based Semiconductor Industry Association (SIA) filed a Section 301 petition to the US government accusing the Japanese of 'unfair' trade practices. Compara-tively low levels of American access to the Japanese market and dumping of DRAM chips in the American market were the two central complaints. The USTR and Department of Commerce took the complaint to the Japanese, which resulted in bilateral negotiations among the governments (Cortell and Davis 1996: 459–64).

The dispute was 'resolved' through a 1986 interstate agreement – the Semiconductor Trade Agreement (STA) – in which the Japanese promised to allow more market access by foreign companies and to shore up DRAM prices.[16] Part of the deal was to officially revisit the case every five years. As a result, the STA was renewed in 1991, but because the proposed market share had almost been reached, and dumping was not as much a vital issue, the international politics were less contentious. In 1996, the STA was up for renewal again. As in 1991, there were some serious issues to be addressed, but not on the level of the 1986 talks. Also, by this point, the industry had changed substantially from only a decade before. For instance, by the early to mid-1990s, a Korean firm, Samsung, had taken the world lead in DRAM production. Still, the Americans, Japanese, and to some extent the Europeans, remain key players in the diverse semiconductor industry.

The most notable outcome of the 1996 STA renewal had little to do with the governments themselves. Rather, it was agreed by the respective participating industry associations – the SIA and the EIAJ – that the firms *via their industry associations* would take over much of the transnational management of the industry. This idea was largely supported by the governments, albeit with some concern from US antitrust regulators. The Japanese first suggested the idea of an international industry council. The EIAJ and the Japanese government both argued that the 1996 renewal of the STA was unnecessary since the goals of the earlier deals had been met. The Japanese reported that foreign market share had reached 30 per cent which, pursuant to an earlier agreement, eliminated the need for any more bilateral arrangements. (This figure was later found to be exaggerated.) The Americans disagreed, claiming that important market access issues had yet to be resolved. The Japanese suggested that a private multilateral forum would better manage global industry issues. At first, the SIA balked at the idea, arguing that it was simply a means to divert attention from persistent US–Japanese bilateral issues.

In the end, the 1996 deal was signed, but the World Semiconductor Council (WSC) was established as well. It was initiated by an agreement between the American and Japanese semiconductor industry associations. According to William Weber, Vice-Chairman of Texas Instruments, the aim of the WSC is to facilitate the prosperity and growth of the industry as a whole through the development of mutual understandings of common problems facing the industry. As Weber puts it, the WSC should be 'a forum in which to forge consensus on issues facing our industry.'[17]

What was most surprising to the SIA and EIAJ was the interest of other national industry groups in the WSC.[18] Both the European Electronics Components Manufacturers Association (EECA) and the Korean Semiconductor Industry Association (KSIA) clamoured for entrance into WSC.[19] Both groups wanted to avoid exclusion from discussion and planning of international industry issues. The EECA in particular wanted additional leverage to influence the Japanese, since the Europeans have only about 1 per cent of the Japanese market. However, the main criterion for entrance into the WSC, as established by the SIA and EIAJ, was the elimination of semiconductor tariffs. Unexpectedly, both the Europeans and Koreans did so in time to participate in the April 1997 meeting. Tariff elimination (or at least the process of eliminating tariffs) was a largely unexpected outcome of the WSC initiative.

Participating in the private inaugural conference were about twenty-five CEOs from major chip makers, plus staff members from the different industry groups. Numerous issues were discussed and several broad agreements were struck regarding, for instance, international environmental issues, market share, and the 300 mm wafer initiative. The Europeans and Japanese offered one controversial proposal to establish a sector-wide system for DRAM inventory monitoring. Given the large capacity swings on memory chips, which are commodities (and thus subject to major price fluctuations) inventory information would allow chip makers to plan in advance for expected price drops by tightening the supply of chips. The Americans (and their accompanying lawyers from the Antitrust Division) rejected such a system and the price controls such an arrangement implied. In June 1997, a joint industry session between the SIA and EECA was held in Brussels. More extensive US-European dialogue and cooperation on semiconductors is another unexpected outcome of the WSC process. Through the middle of 1998, the WSC continued to serve as a private forum for global industry management.

Beyond the WSC, other types of political cooperation have emerged among the firms in addition to research and development of new technology and products. For instance, the firms and industry associations have attempted to identify areas where the general health of the industry is at stake. A broad cooperative agenda includes collaboration on environmental, safety, and health (ESH) and intellectual property rights (IPR) issues. On the former, the industry has held several annual conferences to address problems such as reducing PFC emissions that contribute to global warming. Interfirm environmental cooperation is interesting because the industry itself defined the problem and took the initiative before a concerted effort by environmental groups to stem the problems. On the latter, the industry has worked closely with the software and pharmaceutical industries to construct a global IPR regime (Sell 1996).

The rise of a private regime in the industry does not necessarily indicate the end of government intervention. As outlined in the introduction of this book, the increasing importance of big corporations in global governance does not necessarily imply that states become insignificant. Public and private are not zero-sum categories. Indeed, government involvement remains important. First, part of the WSC process mandates that governments meet one month after the private sessions are held in order to review the issues discussed in the forum. Second, while American firms appear to have been taking the lead on helping to manage world semiconductor issues, the office of the US Trade Representative is still directly involved in the industry, which is much less contentious than it was a decade ago.[20] According to one SIA spokesman, 'When we need a policeman we know where to find one.' Of course, the close relationship between the EIAJ and MITI, and between the KSIA and the Korean government persists.

What is currently taking place in the global semiconductor industry exemplifies the 'New Competition'. The industry participants develop sector strategies with an eye toward the long-term prosperity of the sector as a whole. In Best's words, 'A common interest is identified and collectively pursued by inter-firm cooperation as opposed to government imposition' (Best 1990: 18). Within this sector strategy, sectoral (i.e. extra-firm) institutions are established, which facilitate the firms' capacity to understand their collective situation, and to mutually adapt to a changing competitive environment. Indeed, sectoral management often aims to reduce uncertainty. What is striking about the semiconductor industry is that such things have occurred at the *global* level. This makes the industry a 'hard case' for the New Competition paradigm, which has mostly focused on domestic settings. Furthermore, the ability to develop sector strategies and institutions relies in part on an appropriate division of labour within the industry itself. A diverse product line within the same industry facilitates specialisation. That is certainly true in semiconductors, where memory chips and higher-end microprocessors are mostly made by firms from different countries.[21] Specialisation into niches facilitates cooperation on general industrial management, such as opening national markets, improving sales, and solving standardisation-compatibility problems.

The WSC does not reflect a period of harmony in the industry. Nonetheless, within the context of a proliferation of international alliances, the WSC is one key indicator supporting the claim that the New Competition characterises industrial order in the semiconductor industry. That is, the point of the New Competition order is not that competition is dampened, but that it is being redefined.

The experience of the semiconductor industry gives us some insight into alliance capitalism and the politics of industrial restructuring in global industries where there are severe costs and risks in doing business in an increasingly global and competitive environment. In addition to suggesting further research into the shape and significance of ICAs, two other implications can be drawn.

First, the role of dialogue, especially among private actors, appears to be increasingly important. In many cases, it appears that firms themselves are better equipped to discuss and manage industry issues than are governments. One hypothesis that links the discussion of network forms of organisation and private cooperation is that as we see the networks among firms rising, we should also observe correlating broader sectoral agreements among the firms who recognise that common sectoral interests go beyond particular technological and production arrangements and spill over into broader political concerns.[22] This facilitates the view of MNCs as political actors in their own right, rather than merely constituents of the state (Strange 1996: 44–6). Take, for instance, the creation of the Transatlantic Business Dialogue, where numerous US and EU industries have established an ongoing framework in which to discuss and resolve sectoral issues, especially regarding standardisation and regulatory policy (Stern 1996). In addition, major pharmaceutical companies from the US, Europe, and Japan have convened several conferences in the 1990s that address the regulatory problems associated with the internationalisation of the drug industry (OECD 1996). Other more general discursive institutions have been created as well, such as the World Economic Forum.

Second, and relatedly, the role of industry associations appears to be increasingly relevant. Associations are a form of mesogovernance situated between firms and governments. There is some scattered evidence to suggest that the form of private coordination we are witnessing in the semiconductor industry occurs in other internationally organised industries. In the context of the European Union, this is already well documented (Pedler and van Schendelen 1994; Cowles 1997). But this sort of coordination occurs beyond the regional level. For instance, in the paper and forest products industry, there is regular consultation between the industry associations of the US, Canada, and the Scandinavian countries on general problems facing the industry. One such problem is persistent tariff barriers. As a result, the industry associations attempt to coordinate an industry-wide position on tariff policy and then revisit their home governments in order to lobby for changes.[23] One hypothesis that emerges from the study of networks is that we might expect tariff barriers to fall within networked segments of industries.[24] The logic is that barriers to trade will inhibit a well-functioning industrial network. The inclusion of industry associations into the story gives a political mechanism by which tariffs would actually fall.

Conclusion

The empirical focus of this paper has been, broadly conceived, the dynamic of industrial restructuring at the international level. I have focused on the duality of competition and cooperation in the same industry at the same time. Sometimes referred to as the 'New Competition', this duality has important and novel implications for how to understand order in the international system. I relied on the concept of an 'industrial order', drawn from economic sociology, to frame the historical dynamic. Within an industrial order, alternative forms of governance (such as markets, hierarchies or networks) are chosen in order to manage and reshape the competitive environment. In the current transnational industrial order – alliance capitalism – networks increasingly serve to govern industrial relations. In the global semiconductor industry, I attempted to show how the restructuring of global competition was defined by experimentation with new alliance-based organisational forms. I also demonstrated that such organisational practices were correlated with evolving forms of political management, such as the advent of the World Semiconductor Council and cooperation on pan-industry environmental concerns.

This paper has focused mostly on relations among firms in their aim to reconstruct the competitive architecture of transnationally organised industries. Virginia Haufler stresses the value of exploring such interfirm dynamics: 'It is hard to see how to gain a deeper understanding of the relationship between political authority and the increasingly global markets in which transnational corporations wield great power without understanding the relations among firms' (Haufler 1997: 30). Indeed, my approach, like Haufler's, advocates an exploration and elaboration of what Stopford and Strange have called 'triangular diplomacy', a nexus of bargaining relationships between states, between states and firms, and between firms (Stopford and Strange 1991; Dicken 1994). The first two dyads are relatively more explored than the latter: the first is the conventional focus of most international relations scholarship; the second is the subject of a rich literature on bargaining between states and MNCs.

The preceding analysis contrasts with liberal regime theory (cf. Krasner 1982). Though a durable framework that has inspired numerous valuable studies, liberal regime theory (LRT) does not provide much leverage on understanding evolving forms of business organisation. Yet, as I have suggested, business organisation itself becomes a form of international organisation, albeit not in ways conventionally discussed in the IR literature.[25] LRT suggests when regimes might emerge and fail, yet is largely silent on the institutional form of cooperation and thus on alternative modes of organisation. Thus, LRT is unable to capture the nuances in industrial change precisely because those nuances are best captured in organisational terms.[26] Often, LRT highlights the emergence of interstate 'market regimes' which are assessed as, first, essentially cooperative in nature and, second, largely a function of interstate relations (cf. Zacher with Sutton 1996). But descriptions of 'market regimes', while useful, are not precise enough to tell us about specific institutional forms and, in some cases, identifies the existence of markets when, in fact, other organisational forms are more prevalent.

The politics of industrial restructuring is not about the reconstruction of pre-existing markets that have 'failed' but about the strategic organisational choice of enterprises engaged in competitive struggle. Concerns about market failure reflect a liberal orientation toward the natural existence of markets. A business-oriented approach rejects this as a teleological assumption about the evolution of how economic activity is organised. It reflects what William Lazonick (1991) has called 'the myth of the market economy.' Of course, so much of political economy today is concerned about the liberalisation of national markets. But the two distinct ideas of markets-as-places *versus* market-as-governance mechanisms should not be conflated. The opening of markets to foreign business tells us little about the organisational forms that create the competitive architecture of international business. Moreover, establishing a 'market regime' tells us something about what role is played by the state but little about what the firms are doing. As a result, private organisation and authority in the international system remains underanalysed.

Notes

Earlier drafts of this paper were prepared for delivery at the conference on Non-State Actors and Authority in the Global System, University of Warwick, November 1997 and the Annual Meeting of the American Political Science Association, Washington, D.C., August 1997. I am grateful to Philip Cerny, David Deese, Gary Herrigel, John Kenny, Stephen Krasner, Keir Lieber, Susan Pratt, Daniel Verdier, and the editors of the volume for valuable comments.

1 As Walter Powell (1990b) puts it, 'solutions to economic problems are embedded in organisational policies and structures.'
2 Following in the tradition of economic sociology, it is important to understand markets as institutional choices, not as a default option that naturally arises in absence of other institutions. Markets are complex and constructed institutional forms, and not the only means of coordinating the economy. If such a universalistic understanding of markets were adopted, then the concept would lose its analytic leverage (Block 1990: 50; Boyer 1997).
3 The idea of an industrial order is applicable beyond the nation-state. Unlike Herrigel (1996), who analyses two forms of order within the boundaries of the German nation-state, I am concerned with *transnational* industrial order.
4 The following discussion draws heavily on the seminal contribution of Walter Powell (1990a). Like him, I treat these structures as discrete choices when, in fact, they are not always so. The point is to make a very complex reality simpler and more understandable: 'Stylized models of markets, hierarchies, and networks are not perfectly descriptive of economic reality, but they enable us to make progress in understanding the extraordinary diversity of economic arrangements found in the industrial world today' (Powell 1990a: 301).
5 Of course, in highly imperfect (i.e. oligopolistic) markets, strategic action is possible.

6 One comprehensive data base of technology-based alliances (MERIT/CATI) now holds over 13,000 entries covering a wide range of industries. John Dunning actually describes alliance capitalism in very broad terms: 'Within the framework of an innovation-driven market economy . . . there is room for a plurality of organizational arrangements. Indeed, in such an economy, cooperation, e.g. between firms and their suppliers, between the research and development (R&D) and manufacturing departments of a firm, between labor and management, and between the private and public sector, is often a critical ingredient of economic success' (Dunning 1997: 48).

7 According to Mowery (1988: 3), 'this definition excludes exports, FDI (meaning complete or near-complete control), and technology licensing.' The data problems of measuring and analysing alliances are notoriously difficult. Alliance data is sparse partly because how to count or measure alliances is controversial. Safarian (1997) and Khemani and Waverman (1997) elaborate on these problems.

8 However, there is often some cross-holding of shares among the firms, which can be thought of as 'hostages' in Williamsonian terms (Khemani and Waverman 1997: 134).

9 In Portnoy (1999), I investigate the internationalisation of antitrust issues, particularly how national regulators and firms have grappled with deciding which forms of business competition are legitimate (or not), and whether and how to regulate them.

10 For an extensive list of factors, see Cowhey and Aronson (1993) and Khemani and Waverman (1997: 134–5). Osborn and Hagedoorn (1997) provide a review of business and economics literature on corporate alliances.

11 'Semiconductors' include not only memory chips, but microprocessors, optoelectronic devices, and application-specific integrated circuits (ASICs).

12 To be sure, this is an oligopolistic industry, so it does vary from the classic competitive market.

13 Note that these figures refer only to alliances involving a Japanese partner, and therefore underestimate the degree of international cooperation.

14 DRI/McGraw-Hill, 'The Globalization of the Semiconductor Industry'.

15 'Mine's Bigger,' *Economist* 12 July 1997: 73.

16 Flamm (1996) offers an excellent industry overview.

17 Remarks by Weber at opening session of the WSC, Hawaii, 11 April 1997.

18 Interview with spokesperson from Semiconductor Industry Association, 1 August 1997.

19 More recently, Taiwan, Australia and Canada have sought entry into the group. The case of Taiwan is notable since its industry association has been explicitly denied admission into the group. Although Taiwanese firms are among the world's emerging chip producers, the prospect of angering the Chinese, whose huge market has yet to be tapped, has given the US and Japanese pause.

20 Plus, US–Japanese relations in the film, automotive, and airline industries are far more contentious in recent years; thus, more government attention is given to these industries.

21 The major makers of memory chips are the Japanese, Europeans, and Koreans, all of whom have clear interests in stable (and high) chip prices. The US chip makers focus on the higher end of the market, such as microprocessors.

22 The 1996 Information Technology Agreement, in which industry was closely involved, might be considered such a sector institution.

23 A similar dynamic of transnational coordination has occurred over intellectual property rights (Sell 1996).

24 Jacquemin (1991) hypothesises that 'a multiplication of strategic alliances among firms of different home nationalities makes protectionism in foreign markets less probable, given the high degree of interdependence resulting from such collaborations.'

25 If business organisation is absent from much of economic theorising, as William Lazonick (1991) forcefully contends, then we should only expect it to be even more so from liberal and realist IR theory.

26 The literature on transnationalism has long taken seriously the role of MNCs in the world political economy. But that literature, too, does not get us very far since it

usually analyses the relative bargaining power between states and firms. Furthermore, the focus on the MNC as powerful actor ignores the governance dimension of the vertically integrated firm. It also treats the firm as an ahistorical, static form of business organisation.

References

Angel, David P. (1994) *Restructuring for Innovation: The Remaking of the US Semiconductor Industry*, New York and London: Guilford Press.

Berk, Gerald (1994) *Alternative Tracks: The Constitution of American Industrial Order, 1865–1917*, Baltimore: Johns Hopkins University Press.

Best, Michael H. (1990) *The New Competition: Institutions of Industrial Restructuring*, Cambridge: Harvard University Press.

Block, Fred (1990) *Postindustrial Possibilities*, Berkeley: University of California Press.

Boyer, Robert (1996) 'The convergence hypothesis revisited: globalization but still the century of nations?', in Suzanne Berger and Ronald Dore (eds) *National Diversity and Global Capitalism*, Ithaca: Cornell University Press: 29–59.

—— (1997) 'The variety and unequal performance of really existing markets: farewell to Doctor Pangloss?', in J. Rogers Hollingsworth and Robert Boyer (eds) *Contemporary Capitalism: The Embeddedness of Institutions*, Cambridge: Cambridge University Press: 55–93.

Boyer, Robert and Daniel Drache (eds) (1996) *States Against Markets: The Limits of Globalization*, London and New York: Routledge.

Coase, Ronald H. (1937) 'The nature of the firm', *Economica* 4: 386–405.

Cortell, Andrew P. and James W. Davis, Jr (1996) 'How do international institutions matter? The domestic impact of international rules and norms', *International Studies Quarterly* 40(4): 451–78.

Cowhey, Peter and Jonathan D. Aronson (1993) *Managing the World Economy: The Consequences of Corporate Alliances*, New York: Council on Foreign Relations.

Cowles, Maria G. (1997) 'The changing architecture of big business,' paper presented at the 5th Biennial European Community Studies Association, Seattle, WA.

Dicken, Peter (1994) 'Global–local tensions: firms and states in the global space economy', *Economic Geography* 70(2): 101–28.

DRI/McGraw Hill 'The globalization of the semiconductor industry', htpp://www.eiaj.org /study/executive.html

Dunning, John H (1997) 'Governments and the macro-organization of economic activity: an historical and spatial perspective', *Review of International Political Economy* 4(1): 42–86.

Dussauge, Pierre and Bernard Garrette (1995) 'Determinants of success in international strategic alliances: evidence from the global aerospace industry', *Journal of International Business Studies* 26(3): 505–30.

EIAJ (1995) Electronic Industry Association of Japan, http://www.eiaj.org

Flamm, K. (1996) *Mismanaged Trade? Strategic Policy and the Semiconductor Industry*, Washington, D.C.: Brookings Institute.

Gereffi, Gary (1996) 'Global commodity chains: new forms of coordination and control among nations and firms in international industries', *Competition and Change* 1(4): 427–39.

Grabher, Gernot (1993) 'Rediscovering the social in the economics of interfirm relations' in Gernot Grabher (ed.) *The Embedded Firm: On the Socioeconomics of Industrial Networks*, London and New York: Routledge: 1–31.

Granovetter, Mark (1985) 'Economic action and social structure: the problem of embeddedness', *American Journal of Sociology* 91(3): 481–510.

—— (1994) 'Business groups', in Neil J. Smelser and Richard Swedberg (eds) *The Handbook of Economic Sociology*, Princeton: Princeton University Press: 453–75.

Hagedoorn, John (1993) 'Understanding the rationale of strategic technology partnering: interorganizational modes of cooperation and sectoral differences', *Strategic Management Journal* 14: 371–85.

Haufler, Virginia (1997) *Dangerous Commerce: Insurance and the Management of International Risk*, Ithaca: Cornell University Press.

Herrigel, Gary (1994) 'Industry as a form of order: a comparison of the historical development of the machine tool industry in the United States and Germany', in J. R. Hollingsworth, Philippe C. Schmitter, and Wolfgang Streeck (eds) *Governing Capitalist Economies: Performance and Control of Economic Sectors*, New York and Oxford: Oxford University Press: 97–128.

—— (1996) *Industrial Constructions: The Sources of German Industrial Power*, Cambridge and New York: Cambridge University Press.

Hollingsworth, J. Rogers and Robert Boyer (eds) (1997) *Contemporary Capitalism: The Embeddedness of Institutions*, Cambridge: Cambridge University Press.

Hollingsworth, J. R., Philippe C. Schmitter and Wolfgang Streeck (1994) 'Capitalism, sectors, institutions and performance', in J. R. Hollingsworth, Philippe C. Schmitter, and Wolfgang Streeck (eds) *Governing Capitalist Economies: Performance and Control of Economic Sectors*, New York and Oxford: Oxford University Press: 3–16.

Hollingsworth, J. R., Philippe C. Schmitter, and Wolfgang Streeck (eds) (1994) *Governing Capitalist Economies: Performance and Control of Economic Sectors*. New York and Oxford: Oxford University Press.

Jacquemin, Alexis (1991) 'Strategic competition in a global environment', in *Trade, Investment, and Technology in the 1990s*, OECD, Paris: OECD: 13–32.

Jarillo, J. C. (1988) 'On strategic networks', *Strategic Management Journal* 9: 31–41.

Khemani, Shyam and Leonard Waverman (1997) 'Strategic alliances: a threat to competition?', in Leonard Waverman, William S. Comanor, and Akira Goto (eds) *Competition Policy in the Global Economy: Modalities for Cooperation*, London: Routledge: 127–51.

Kobrin, Stephen J. (1995) 'Regional integration in a globally networked economy', *Transnational Corporations* 4(2): 15–33.

—— (1997) 'The architecture of globalization: state sovereignty in a networked global economy', in John Dunning (ed.) *Globalization, Governments, and International Business*, Oxford and New York: Oxford University Press: 146–71.

Kogut, Bruce, Weijian Shan and Gordon Walker (1993) 'Knowledge in the network and the network as knowledge: the structuring of new industries', in Gernot Grabher (ed.) *The Embedded Firm: On the Socioeconomics of Industrial Networks*, London and New York: Routledge: 67–94.

Krasner, Stephen D. (ed.) (1982) *International Regimes*, Ithaca: Cornell University Press.

Lazonick, William (1991) *Business Organization and the Myth of the Market Economy*, New York: Cambridge University Press.

Mowery, David C. (ed.) (1988) *International Collaborative Ventures in US Manufacturing*, Cambridge, Mass.: Ballinger.

Mytelka, Lynn K. (1991) 'Crisis, technological change and the strategic alliance', in Lynn K. Mytelka (ed.) *Strategic Partnerships: States, Firms, and International Competition*, Rutherford: Farleigh Dickinson Press.

OECD (1996) *Globalization of Industry: Overview and Sector Reports*, Paris: OECD.

Osborn, Richard N. and John Hagedoorn (1997) 'The institutionalization and evolution-ary dynamics of interorganizational alliances and networks', *Academy of Management Journal* 40(2): 261–78.

Pedler, R. H. and M. P. C. M. van Schendelen (1994) *Lobbying the European Union: Companies, Trade Associations, and Issue Groups*, Aldershot, England: Dartmouth.

Porter, Michael E. and Mark B. Fuller (1986) 'Coalitions and global strategy', in Michael E. Porter (ed.) *Competition in Global Industries*, Boston: Harvard Business School Press: 315–43.

Portnoy, Brian (1999, forthcoming) 'Constructing competition: antitrust and the political foundations of alliance capitalism', Ph.D. dissertation, University of Chicago.

Powell, Walter W (1990a) 'Neither market nor hierarchy: network forms of organization', *Research in Organizational Behavior* 12: 295–336.

—— (1990b) 'The transformation of organizational forms: how useful is organization theory in accounting for social change?', in Roger Friedland and A. F. Robertson (eds) *Beyond the Market Place: Rethinking Economy and Society*, New York: Aldine de Gruyter: 301–29.

Powell, Walter W. and Laurel Smith-Doerr (1994) 'Networks and economic life', in Neil J. Smelser and Richard Swedberg (eds) *The Handbook of Economic Sociology*, Princeton: Princeton University Press.

Sabel, Charles F. (1993) 'Constitutional orders: trustbuilding and response to change', in J. Rogers Hollingsworth and Robert Boyer (eds) *Contemporary Capitalism: the Embeddedness of Institutions*, Boulder: Westview Press: 154–88.

Safarian, A. Edward (1997) 'Trends in the forms of international business organization', in Leonard Waverman, William S. Comanor and Akira Goto (eds) *Competition Policy in the Global Economy: Modalities for Cooperation*, London: Routledge: 40–65.

Schmitter, Philippe C. (1990) 'Sectors in modern capitalism: modes of governance and variations in performance', in Renato Brunetta and Carlo Dell'Aringa (eds) *Labour Relations and Economic Performance*, New York: New York University Press: 3–39.

Sell, Susan (1996) 'Multinational corporations as agents of change: the globalization of intellectual property rights', paper presented at the Annual Meeting of the International Studies Association, San Diego.

Stern, Paula (1996) 'The transatlantic business dialogue: a new paradigm for standards and regulatory reform', in *Regulatory Reform and International Market Openness*, Paris: OECD: 155–64.

Stopford, John M. (1995) 'Competing globally for resources', *Transnational Corporations* 4(2): 34–57.

Stopford, John M. and Susan Strange (1991) *Rival States, Rival Firms*, Cambridge: Cambridge University Press.

Strange, Susan (1996) *The Retreat of the State: The Diffusion of Power in the World Economy*, Cambridge: Cambridge University Press.

Waverman, Leonard, William S. Comanor and Akira Goto (1997) 'Introduction', in Leonard Waverman, William S. Comanor, and Akira Goto (eds) *Competition Policy in the Global Economy: Modalities for Cooperation*, London: Routledge: 1–25.

Williamson, Oliver E. (1975) *Markets and Hierarchies: Analysis and Antitrust Implications*, New York: The Free Press.

—— (1985) *The Economic Institutions of Capitalism*, New York: Free Press.

—— (1996) *The Mechanisms of Governance*, New York: Free Press.

Zacher, Mark with Brent A. Sutton (1996) *Governing Global Networks: International Regimes for Communication and Transportation*, Cambridge: Cambridge University Press.

10 How global is Ford Motor Company's global strategy?

Maria Isabel Studer Noguez

Introduction

The view that Multinational Enterprises (MNEs) are actors that are gaining enormous power *vis-à-vis* nation-states and that, through their recently adopted global strategies, are creating a genuine global system of production is a popular one (see the global neo-liberal discourse outlined in the introduction of this book). This was, for instance, the prevailing view in the automobile industry during the 1980s, when the US Big Three automakers started to open new production plants overseas, to increase their imports of auto parts and small cars from South Korea, Taiwan, Japan or Mexico, and to establish joint-ventures with Asian vehicle producers. Given the automobile industry's reputation as a forerunner in the development of new systems of production and organisation processes, events in that industry were taken as examples of what would happen in other industries.[1] In spite of the popularity of this view, empirical analyses that prove that MNEs are indeed contributing to the emergence of a global system of production are scant. By analysing Ford Motor Company's global strategies, this article is an attempt at filling this gap.

Similarly, there is a great deal of conceptual ambiguity about the very meaning of the term 'global strategy'. This is partly due to the organisational complexity and the geographical scope of MNEs, which makes it difficult to create a simple standard to measure 'levels of globality' of MNEs' global strategies and operations. The objective of this article is to show that, like any other complex actors, MNEs struggle to introduce and implement changes in their structure and organisation. This explains that MNEs, at least those in the automobile industry, are not as mobile and flexible as they are generally portrayed. Indeed, the case of Ford proves that even if only its worldwide production operations are taken into account, these are regionally, not globally, integrated, and that the most significant change in those operations has taken place in North America.[2]

The paper is divided in seven sections. Section one presents a brief review of the debate over the meaning of global strategies. The following five sections are devoted to important areas of Ford's strategies during the past two decades or so, namely, production; sales, R&D and competition; trade; strategic alliances; and organisation and management. A final section is reserved for some concluding remarks.

What is a global strategy?

A great deal of conceptual ambiguity exists about the very meaning of the term 'global strategy'. The most basic definitions refer to the standardisation of a product to be manufactured and sold the same way throughout the world (Levitt 1983) or to the ability of the firm to build a broader product portfolio with many product varieties, so that investments on technologies and distribution channels could be shared (Hamel and Prahalad 1985). For Kogut (1985), a global strategy requires the flexibility to achieve multiple sourcing, shifts in production to low-cost location sites that result from changes in factor costs and exchange rates, and arbitrage to exploit imperfections in financial and information markets. By contrast, to other authors the key for a global strategy is the firm's ability to organise its integrated network, not whether MNEs spread their operations geographically or not (Stopford and Wells 1972; Hedlund 1986; Bartlett 1983). For Hamel and Prahalad (1985), two key elements of a global strategy are rather the cross-subsidisation of products and markets and the development of a strong distribution system, which may not require flexibility to shift to different production sites.

Another, perhaps more accurate, definition of a global strategy is a complex and efficiency-oriented approach that implies the rationalisation or reorganisation of the MNEs' value-added activities and the launching of production networks on a global basis (Doz 1986; Bartlett and Ghoshal 1989; Porter 1986). According to this view, global strategies consist of a dispersed geographical location of each or some parts of the value chain or company functions and a more centralised coordination of linked activities that are performed in different countries (Porter 1986: 23). Such strategies entail the division of the production process into discrete functions (assembly, procurement, finance, research and development), and the redistribution of these functions 'wherever they can be carried out most effectively in light of the overall needs of the firm as a whole.' As operations become dispersed across different national locations, the fragmented activities of MNEs are integrated into global production and distribution systems, being 'subject to one unified strategy that governs the entire corporate system' (UNWIR 1996: 98 and 138–40; Gereffi 1996: 64).

The operational value of this definition is, however, questionable. As complex organisations, MNEs face multiple options for where to locate different value-added activities in the production chain and for designing its organisational structure. For example, MNEs could disperse each or all activities of the value chain production, marketing and sales, service, technology, development and procurement (Porter 1986: 23–7). Research may not be integrated at all, while product development may be integrated at a worldwide level and manufacturing at a regional level, with marketing being integrated in certain aspects (pricing) but not in others (advertising). Furthermore, MNEs that choose a global strategy may rationalise their international operations in a number of ways, standardise some products and/or diversify others, and integrate manufacturing vertically or horizontally (Kobrin 1991: 18). Another problem is that some other variables that are critical for developing a global integration strategy, such as levels of effective inter-subsidiary coordination and communication, are difficult to measure.

For these reasons, alternative rankings could be used to assess the level of internationalisation or globalisation of MNEs strategies (for a discussion see Ruigrok and Van Tulder 1995: 152–75; UNWIR 1996). Ultimately, the levels of 'globality' for a given strategy are subjective, and depend upon the type and number of variables chosen for the analysis. Taking these conceptual and methodological problems into consideration, the present article focuses on one MNE, Ford Motor Company, and on a limited number of its value-added activities around the world. Ford was taken as a case study because, of all automakers, it has been considered the best prepared to face the industry's competitive challenges by means of a global strategy, due to its extensive network of international operations and the company's management experience in handling such operations.[3] Also, Ford has publicly announced the global integration of its operations as its strategic goal. Five areas of Ford's international operations are analysed: vehicle and parts production; competitive strategies, including sales and R&D; trade policies and defensive market strategies; competition through strategic alliances; and inter-subsidiary coordination or organisation.

Regionalism in Ford's production operations

Despite the fact that since the late 1970s Ford has launched three different 'world car' projects, the evidence does not support the belief that major shifts in vehicle production to low-wage sites in the developing world took place during the 1980s. As data in Figure 10.1 show, the bulk of Ford's vehicle production since 1979 has concentrated in the United States – accounting for about 45 and 50 per cent of Ford's total production – and does not show significant changes in its geographical distribution. In fact, Ford excluded developing countries, with the exception of Brazil and much later Mexico, from its world car programmes.

Traditionally, Ford had pockets of vehicle assembly in developing countries, locating the bulk of its vehicle production in industrialised countries (see Figure 10.1). Like other automakers, Ford's main interest in developing countries was securing or expanding market access. The lack of technical infrastructure (skilled labour, competitive auto parts suppliers, etc.) and small markets in those countries translated into higher production costs. Therefore, Ford established assembly or sales branches rather than manufacturing operations there. This situation changed after the mid-1980s, when Latin America, and to a lesser extent the Asia-Pacific region, increased their relative importance as production sites for Ford vehicles, as shown in Figure 10.1.[4]

While in the 1975–89 period the bulk of Ford's vehicles produced in the Latin American region were sold there, after 1987 a growing proportion of vehicles produced there were sold elsewhere in the world, as confirmed by a growing production-to-sales ratio, which reached 1.6 : 1 in 1993. It must be stressed, however, that the impact of this change on Ford's worldwide production operations is minor, considering that Ford's operations in Latin America represent less than 10 per cent of Ford's total vehicle production (as shown in Figure 10.1).

The argument could be made that the US Big Three did not shift 'vehicle'

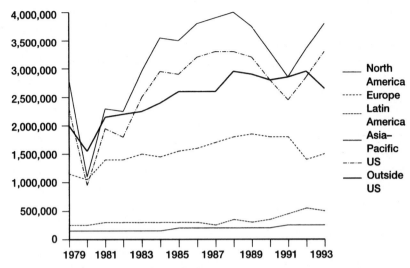

Figure 10.1 Ford production by region, 1979–93 (in units).
Source: Ford Motor Co. *Annual Report*, several years.

assembly to other countries as much as they increased their offshore outsourcing operations. Published information about auto parts operations is difficult to get, largely because there are hundreds of thousands of suppliers. US auto parts imports d outsourcing of parts. In the 1972–1993 period, those imports (largely from Japan and South Korea) increased from $2.5 billion to $35 billion dollars. Between 1985 and 1992, US auto parts imports from Mexico and Europe alone more than

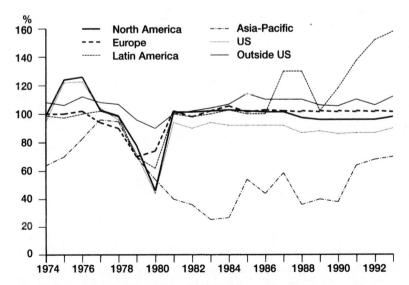

Figure 10.2 Ford production-to-sales ratio by region, 1974–93 (in per cent).
Source: Ford Motor Co. *Annual Report*, several years.

doubled, from $2.3 billion to $5.3 billion and from $1.6 billion to $3.6 billion respectively (*Industrial Outlook* several years). The figures could be higher if they included parts embodied in imported vehicles.

However, one could also argue that shifts in parts production necessarily followed shifts in vehicle production, simply because the Japanese system of production requires close coordination between suppliers and assemblers and, therefore, physical proximity between them and among different tiers of suppliers.[5] This system has been a key source of the Japanese competitive advantage (Hoffman and Kaplinsky 1988: 159; OSAT 1992: 100), and has been adopted by all other automakers.

In the absence of complete series data of Ford's parts production and trade by region, one proxy to measure the level of integration of Ford's worldwide production operations is inter-company sales. Ford's data on inter-company sales, taken from the company's annual reports, are presented in Figure 10.3. In absolute dollar values, those sales grew significantly between 1987 and 1994, but they remained, in average, at a 20 per cent of the company's total worldwide sales. This reflects Ford's strategy in the early 1980s of not outsourcing parts and small cars, at least not as much as GM and Chrysler did.[6] Ford's long-term strategies of revamping its in-house component operations and building a cooperative management-labour relationship restricted its outsourcing operations.[7] Nevertheless, by the mid-1980s, Ford was already facing a competitive challenge from other automakers, particularly GM and Chrysler, whose delivering cost of small cars in the North American market was substantially lower.

As Figure 10.3 shows, Ford inter-company sales outside of the United States shifted from about 20 per cent in the early 1980s to record highs of 49 per cent in 1985, then fell to 38 per cent in 1987, and thereafter remained at an annual average of 36 per cent between 1987 and 1993. Inter-company sales in Europe did not exhibit dramatic changes, but they did in 'other countries,' particularly after 1986. Data for Latin America are not published separately from 'other countries'

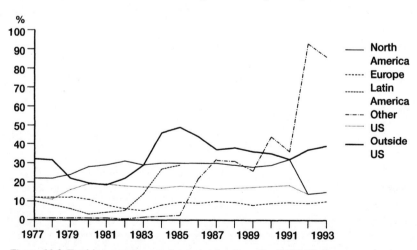

Figure 10.3 Ford intercompany-sales-to-total-sales ratio, 1977–93 (in per cent).
Source: Ford Motor Co. *Annual Report,* several years.

in Ford annual reports after 1985, but anecdotal evidence suggests that such changes reflect the integration of Ford's Latin American production operations into the company's regional/global strategy.

For instance, following GM's and Chrysler's leadership, in 1983, Ford built an engine plant in a Northern state of Mexico (Chihuahua) to produce four-cylinder engines for export. Ford established a company in Chihuahua to produce radios (Altec), a glass plant, and several joint-ventures with Mexican firms.[8] Ford's production operations in Mexico were not as extensive as those of General Motors. While in 1989 GM had twenty-five *maquiladoras* in Mexico (in-bond plants, or production-sharing established in the US–Mexico border region), employing more than 25,000 workers, Ford had only ten with 7,000 workers, compared to Chrysler's four plants with 5,000 workers (Rubenstein 1992: 244).

Data in Figure 10.2 also exhibit the regionalism of Ford's production operations. Except for the Asia-Pacific region, after 1981, most of Ford vehicles sold in each major regional market – North America, Europe, and Latin America – are produced within each region. As mentioned before, Latin America registered an important change in this regard, reflecting Ford's investments, first, in Mexico (during the 1980s and early 1990s) and, more recently, in Brazil and Argentina. It should be recalled that, in the early 1980s, the US automakers were at a disadvantage in the small car segment of the market. Therefore, they started to outsource those cars, that is, to import them from their own production facilities in other countries or from their joint-ventures with Asian manufacturers. Taken as a proportion of all small cars sold by Ford in the US market, Ford's outsourcing of those cars represented 40 per cent in 1993, compared to 23 in 1988. (Own calculations based on Ford Motor Co. *Annual Reports*, several years and *Ward's Automotive Yearbook 1995*). Ford's operations in Mexico helped to strengthen the company's small-car strategy. In fact, since 1988, Ford was producing more vehicles than those the company sold in Mexico, as shown in Ford's production-to-sales ratio of Figure

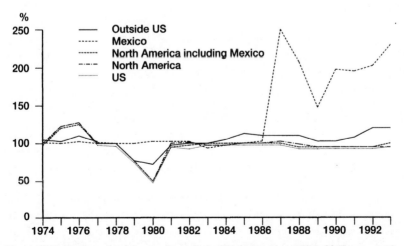

Figure 10.4 Ford production-to-sales ratio in North America, 1974–93 (in per cent).

Source: author's own calculations, based on Ford Motor Co. *Annual Reports*, several years.

10.4. Most of those vehicles came from Ford's plant in Hermosillo (Sonora, located in Northern Mexico), which produced, since 1987, the Mercury Tracer and the Ford Escort for the US market.

A regionally integrated system of production in North America

Ford's strategy of building regional systems of production. This strategy started in the 1960s, when opportunities for rationalisation emerged in Europe and North America with the establishment of the European Economic Commission (1968) and the signing of the US–Canada Automotive Trade Agreement (or Auto Pact) in 1965. The consolidation of a regional free market in Europe allowed Ford to coordinate its various European subsidiaries through a single European company, a functional organisation, 'with each subsidiary specialising in a particular component or model line' (Solvell 1988: 200). Ford of Europe became separate from the parent company, save financially, although it did not become fully integrated until the 1980s.

In Canada, the Auto Pact permitted Ford and the other automakers to overcome the inefficiencies in vehicle production that derived from the existence of a small market. After 1965, Ford began the integration of its Canadian operations with those in the United States. The new North American system of production provided automakers with the flexibility to allocate products at different plants (in the US or Canada) depending upon comparative advantages and changes in market demand in either country. In addition, the Auto Pact rules made it possible for Ford of Canada to outsource, from third countries, small cars as well as low-cost auto parts. Through those rules, throughout the 1980s, Ford of Canada was able to assemble large cars (the rear-wheel drive models, Grand Marquis and Crown Victoria, produced since 1985 in its St. Thomas plant, Ontario) with low-cost parts produced in third countries. Ford also got the extra benefits from selling these Canadian-built cars in the United States, because they were counted as imports to maintain US Corporate Average Fuel Efficiency standards. These regulations require that, in order to apply for those standards, domestic cars meet a 75 per cent of North American content. By sourcing at least 25 per cent of the components of large cars from third countries – which was possible through the Auto Pact – Ford could consider them 'imports' into the United States and, therefore, maintain its CAFE standards.

While during the 1980s Ford followed a strategy of minimum investments in Canada, between 1990 and 1994 it allocated a $2.4 billion dollar investment programme to expand, modernise, and introduce new products in that country. This programme confirmed the key importance of Ford Canada's operations in the parent company's global competitive strategies. With the programme, Ford of Canada specialised in the production of large cars, trucks and mini-vans: the new investments were used to produce Ford's new minivan (Windstar) at the Oakville assembly plant and the construction of paint facilities at the Ontario Truck Plant. Also, the St. Thomas plant was retooled for the production of the new 1992 Ford

Crown Victoria and Mercury Grand Marquis as well as the new 'global car' Contour, and the Windsor Engine Plant Two was overhauled for production of a new family of modular engines beginning in 1995 (Ford of Canada *Annual Report 1994*).

Despite the geographical proximity of Mexico to the US market, the opportunities to incorporate Ford's Mexican operations into a regional system of production did not emerge until the early 1980s, when the Mexican government started to liberalise its rules for the automobile industry. As a result of that liberalisation, in the early 1980s Ford invested in Mexico to boost its parts production there. Ford's Hermosillo plant, considered one of the most productive and modern in the world, represents the beginning of Ford's strategy of integrating Mexico into a North American system of automotive production. As mentioned before, the plant assembles small cars for the US and Canadian markets. Due to Mexico's liberalisation policies for the auto industry, more than two-thirds of the parts in those cars were produced in the United States, thus assuring the highest standards of quality and cost-efficiency. The plant was also an important breakaway from the traditional practice of establishing plants with obsolete technology in Mexico. By the late 1980s, Ford's plant was the only facility in North America to combine stamping, manufacturing and assembly, and it was linked to Detroit's Lincoln Mercury Division and Mazda's plant in Japan through computers and telecommunications, integrating it fully with decision-making centres (Morales 1994: 132). Geographical proximity of the plant to the US market also facilitated that integration.

In the early 1990s, Ford was leader in moving towards a rationalisation of its operations on a continental-wide basis (see ECLAC 1995: 23, Studer 1997: chapter 9). In Mexico, Ford started a $2 billion upgrading programme that included its engine plant in Chihuahua (to produce its most modern engine Zeta, which was also produced in Cleveland, Ohio), its Hermosillo assembly plant (for the production of a new Tracer model and the Escort), and its Cuautitlán plant in Mexico City (to start assembling the global cars – the Mercury Mystique and the Ford Contour, also produced in Kansas City). The North American Free Trade Agreement (NAFTA) strengthened Ford's strategy of creating a North American system of production.

Based on the Canadian model, implemented three decades earlier, Ford of Mexico became consolidated into Ford's North American operations in 1995. Like Ford of Canada, the Mexican subsidiary became responsible for sales and marketing, as well as labour, finance and industrial relations. Manufacturing is presently supervised by Ford Automotive Operations (*Automotive News* 23 June 1994). Also, Ford moved further towards the specialisation of vehicle assembly on a North American basis when it stopped the assembly of such luxury cars as the Cougar and the Thunderbird in Mexico. In 1994 Ford became, with GM, the largest importer of finished vehicles into that country.

In sum, the addition of Mexico into its North American system of production represents for Ford a key strategic move in its 'global strategy,' allowing for significant efficiency gains, cost reductions and overall competitive gains. The substantial investments that made possible this integration show that Ford, like the other US automakers, consider their Mexican and Canadian operations strategic in their competitive positions worldwide.

Global competition, managing cash flows

Implementing a global integration strategy implies managing the manufacturing cost-system worldwide, but also maintaining and strengthening a firm's presence in multiple national markets. Managing cash flows and strategic coordination is key, even if 'global integration across subsidiaries in terms of product flow does not take place' (Doz and Prahalad 1987: 39–40). Maintaining a presence in major markets has become increasingly difficult as competition has been intensified on a global scale. The Japanese aggressive export strategies and the protectionist policies adopted in North America and Europe have encouraged such competition. For instance, the imposition of Voluntary Export Restraints (VERs) in the United States encouraged the Japanese automakers to move from the small car to upgraded market segments, which represented for them higher prices on their cars and therefore a significant boost in profits.

Most importantly, those trade restrictions induced the Japanese to establish production operations in the United States, Canada, and to a lesser extent in Europe. In 1994, for instance, vehicles produced at Japanese plants located in the United States accounted for over 13 per cent of total sales in the US market, which added to 8 per cent accounted for their imports. This compares with 17 per cent of Japanese-built vehicle imports in 1990, the year when they started to produce vehicles in the United States (*Automotive News Market Data Yearbook* 1995). In this situation of higher levels of competition for automotive markets, automakers are forced to locate within the market for sale or cede that portion of the world vehicle market (Womack *et al.* 1990: 204; see also UNCTC 1982: 79 and Whitman 1981: 12).

This notwithstanding, the United States continues to be by far the largest market for Ford in terms of sales volume and value, accounting for over 60 per cent of the company's world sales in 1993 (Figure 10.5). Historically, Ford, like GM, has had a presence in major markets, with Europe representing its largest foreign

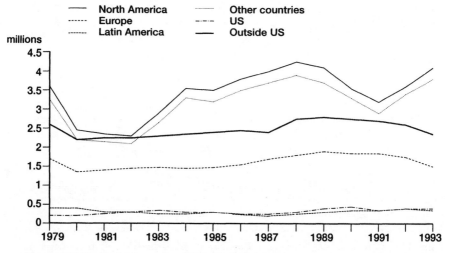

Figure 10.5 Ford sales by region, 1979–93 (in units).

Source: author's own calculations, based on Ford Motor Co. *Annual Reports*, several years.

market, selling in average one-third of the company's worldwide sales in dollar values. Ford's sales in Latin America reached record highs of over 10 per cent in 1980–1, and then declined continuously until 1987 (data for 1987–93 are not available in published form). In the 1990s, Ford's sales in dollar values outside Europe and the United States represented an average of 13 per cent of the company's worldwide sales.

In addition, operations outside North America have provided the cash flow needed by the parent companies to survive in difficult times. In the late 1970s, Europe generated excess cash flows that saved the companies from bankruptcy and supported Ford's North American automotive operations through the worst years of the industry's recession. As demonstrated in Figure 10.6, while between 1979 and 1982 Ford's operations in North America lost $5 billion, the company earnings outside North America were about $3 billion (or two-thirds of Ford's total capital expenditures in those years). Operations outside North America contributed with about one-fourth of the funds required to cover for Ford's worldwide capital expenditures (about $40 billion) for the 1980–91 period.

Trade: protecting regional markets

Contrary to commonly held beliefs, the Big Three have not been unconditional supporters of free trade, but rather of managed trade. In order to protect market shares against the Japanese automakers, since the late 1970s Ford and Chrysler have joined the United AutoWorkers' lobbying effort to protect the US market from Japanese competition. GM joined them in 1981, resulting in the VER agreements negotiated between the US and the Japanese governments. In the early 1980s, Ford of Europe commanded industry calls for the establishment of

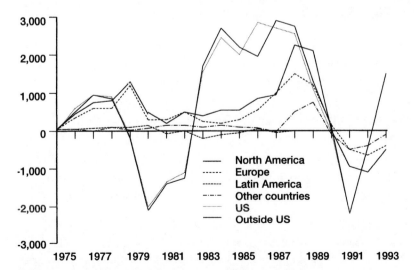

Figure 10.6 Ford net income by region, 1975–93 (in millions of dollars).

Source: author's own calculations, based on Ford Motor Co. *Annual Reports*, several years.

an 80 per cent local content rule in the European market, which could be explained by the fact that Ford's subsidiary depended mostly on trade of parts and components within the European region. By contrast, the US Big Three opposed the UAW demands for local content in the United States. 'As parts from Mexico and imported vehicles from Japan and South Korea became a more integral part of the Big Three's competitive response to Japanese-based firms, local content threatened to interfere with the US automakers' plants as well as their competitors' (Herzenberg 1991: 257).

The Big Three also favoured 'managed' free trade in the Canada–US Auto Pact of 1965, the Canada–US Free Trade Agreement of 1988 which granted them a 50 per cent rule of origin, and the NAFTA that raised that rule to 62.5 per cent. NAFTA removed a series of remaining obstacles to achieve a full integration of the production systems and the markets of the three countries, but also protected the North American market from non-regional competitors. While the Canadian duty-remission programmes and the Mexican local content and export-performance requirements were eliminated with NAFTA, the Big Three opposed a complete and immediate liberalisation of the Mexican auto industry as well as the removal of the Auto Pact. These actions were seen important to protect those domestic markets from Japanese competition.

Political considerations also played an important role in Ford's trade strategy. As long as trade balances are important to governments, MNEs operating in strategic industries have to consider the trade impact of their production, sales, and trade operations not only in foreign countries but also in their own home country. Considering that personal consumption for purchasing cars in developed economies is high – about $240 billion in North America alone – it appears difficult for MNEs to offset exports that could balance automotive trade among regions. This prevents automakers from supplying a major market from their own home country or from any other country. One example is Ford's decision in 1996 to incorporate Brazil into its new global organisation. The considerable expansion of the Brazilian market, that could reach two million units annually by the year 2000, prompted the company's decision to build new assembly and component plants there for the Fiesta minicar, the compact pickup and the European Escort (*Ward's Automotive Yearbook* 1995: 86).

Forging the global character of competition: strategic alliances

Like other automakers, Ford's alliances with Asian automakers represented a major change from past practices. One hundred per cent ownership and control of foreign and domestic operations had been a key principle in the US Big Three's strategies, one that in fact was the source of conflict and negotiations with a number of host countries. However, rising costs of R&D has encouraged the creation of joint-ventures with other automakers for the design and production of cars.

In the case of Ford, joint-ventures or joint-collaboration projects have multiplied in recent years, as shown in Figure 10.7. Ford's strategy of offshore sourcing small cars relied heavily on an alliance with Mazda, of which Ford has owned 25 per cent

Equity Arrangement

Company	Country	Holdings
AC Cars	UK	51%
Aston Martin Lagonda	UK	75%
Kia Motors Corp.	Korea	10%
Lio-Ho Motor Co. Ltd.	Taiwan	70%
Mazda Motors Corp.	Japan	25%
Jaguar plc.	UK	100%
Autolatina	Brazil / Argentina	49%
Associated Motor Ind. Sdn. Bhd.	Malaysia	30%
Iveco Ford Truck	UK	48%

Joint Ventures

Company	Country
Fiat	Italy
Toyota	Japan
Volvo	Sweden
Mazda	Japan
Nissan	Japan
Volkswagen	Germany

Technology Arrangement

Company	Country
Chrysler	USA
GM	USA
Mazda	Japan
Nissan	Japan

FORD MOTOR COMPANY

Joint Supplier Arrangement

Company	Country
Fiat	Italy
Renault	France
Mazda	Japan
Nissan	Japan
DeTomaso	Italy
Volkswagen	Germany

Marketing / Distribution Arrangement

Company	Country
Fiat	Italy
Kia	Korea
Suzuki	Japan
Mazda	Japan

Manufacturing Arrangement

Company	Country
BMW	Germany
Fiat	Italy
Kia	Korea
Mercedes Benz	Germany
Suzuki	Japan
Mazda	Japan
Nissan	Japan
Rover	UK
Volkswagen	Germany

Figure 10.7 International collaborative projects – Ford Motor Company.
Source: The International Automobile Industry in Canada, April 1992: 49.

since 1979.[9] By importing fully or partially assembled cars from Mazda, Ford was able to earn a high profit margin on those cars (Mazda could build a sub-compact car with 25 per cent fewer labour hours than Ford). With the Yen revaluation *vis-à-vis* the US dollar after 1986, Ford established alliances with Lio Ho Motors, a Taiwanese automaker, to produce the Mercury Tracer, and with Kia Motors in South Korea, to build the Ford Festiva. More recently, Ford established a joint-venture with Jinagling Motors, in China, to build a derivative of its Transit Van (*Ward's Automotive Yearbook* 1997: 148). Despite these projects, captive imports have not increased as much as predicted. For instance, Ford plans were to increase its captive imports to 350,000 a year by 1989 (Dyer *et al.* 1987: 170), but in that year Ford's captive imports amounted to 85,000 cars only, or about half of GM's captive imports and 80 per cent of Chrysler's (*Automotive News Market Data Yearbook* 1994). In the case of Ford, those imports had dropped to 60,000 and 37,000 in 1995 and 1996 respectively (*Ward's Automotive Yearbook* 1997: 209).

Those corporate alliances also sought to spread extraordinarily high design and engineering costs. In 1993, Ford's R&D costs were 5.3 times the company's automotive net income (although they dropped to 1.4 times in 1994), compared to a 92 per cent figure in 1978 (based on *Ford's Annual Reports*, several years). In the mid-1980s, Ford's goal was to create six or seven 'common-development programmes' with Asian vehicle companies. During its twenty-year association with Mazda, Ford developed and produced jointly a number of components and at least five vehicles to market in North America and the Pacific Rim: the Probe (based on Mazda's 626 platform), several models of the Mexican-built Ford Escort and Mercury Tracer (Mazda's 323 front-drive platform), and the 1990 Ford Laser, a sub-compact built and sold in the Asia-Pacific region. Another cooperative effort was the Australian-built Capri, with Ford's Ghia studios in Italy taking care of the design and Mazda of the mechanical engineering. Ford established a similar arrangement with Nissan, which designed and engineered the Villager minivans, supplied the powertrains and all major stampings, provided technical assistance to help Ford develop the assembly process, and even designed and built the plant's new body shop (*Ford Motor Company's Annual Report* 1991: 3 and 9; *Ward's Automotive Yearbook* 1992: 17).

As prospects of surplus global capacity in truck and passenger cars reached the 20 per cent mark, the nature of the Big Three's low-cost supply links with Asian automakers shifted to production-sharing agreements or transplants (production-sharing in US plants). GM had moved first in establishing those type of operations, with New United Motor Manufacturing Inc. (NUMMI), opened in 1984, followed by Diamond-Star Motors Corp., a venture between Mitsubishi and Chrysler, and then by Ford-Mazda's Auto Alliance International Inc. (AAII).[10] Ford also established a limited product-sharing relation with Nissan for the production of the Quest/Mercury Villager at Ford's Avon Lake, Ohio assembly plant.

Ford's co-production associations were not restricted to the United States, as illustrated by Ford's ventures with Volkswagen, one in South America (Autolatina, opened in 1986, although it was dissolved in 1995), which included production facilities in Brazil and Argentina, and one in Portugal to produce multi-purpose vehicles. While captive imports decreased in the early 1990s, from 3.7 per cent in 1988 to 0.8 per cent of the US market for passenger cars, production of cars at the Big Three transplants more than doubled, from 1.7 per cent to over 3.5 per cent of the US market for passenger cars (*Ward's Automotive Yearbook* 1995: 119). In that period, Ford accounted in average for about one-fourth of all sales of the Big Three's transplants.

Although those joint projects were the cornerstone in Ford's global integration strategy, they were not always successful. Ford cancelled its cooperative project with Mazda to jointly engineer and build Ford's Capri in Australia; as well as its co-production association with Volkswagen in South America (1995). Autolatina was envisioned under the rationale that both the Argentinean and the Brazilian markets were too small to support either company individually. The project was facilitated by Brazilian government regulations that, through lower duties and taxes, encouraged production of small cars. A declining market share for Ford during the Autolatina's lifespan, a change in the Brazilian government policy (increased duties on imports and raising taxes on popular cars), and expectations about a growing Brazilian market for vehicles prompted Ford to dissolve Autolatina.

The limits to globalisation: management and organisation

Ford has been considered a leader in achieving a high level of coordination in design and production facilities on a global basis (Doz 1986, 67; Womack *et al.* 1990: 213). However, management changes in corporate organisation have been very expensive. They have been implemented on a 'trial-and-error' basis and have not been totally successful.

The world car strategies

Since the late 1970s, Ford has launched three different 'world car' programmes. The first was the Ford Fiesta, which emerged as a response to the Japanese competitive challenge in the small car segment of the market. The rationale was that only enormous economies of scale and large sales volumes could produce the cost structures which would enable survival in the new competitive environment. The car would be built in production runs of millions of units, with one assembly plant or subsidiary being responsible for developing and engineering the car and other subsidiaries for manufacturing the completed design. This project seemed to fit the most simple definitions of a global strategy, referred to in the first section of this article, which implied the standardisation of a product to be manufactured and sold the same way throughout the world.

Ford of Europe was responsible for the development and production of that car. It was built in Spain, with parts from plants in Germany, England and France. The Fiesta soon achieved the highest unit sales of any new European car in history' (Dyer *et al.* 1987: 166), but the integration programme encountered major difficulties, mainly related to the company's failure to overcome cross-national logistical barriers. An integrated production system is extremely vulnerable to local disruptions; a labour strike in one single subsidiary could stop the entire operation. This actually happened in 1978, when a labour strike paralysed the Fiesta project in Britain.[11] This project was further compromised in the late 1970s, when shortages of the parent company's resources forced a difficult trade-off between sustaining a leading position in Europe through continued re-investments, or using cash flows from Europe to support ailing US domestic operations (Doz 1986: 155).

The 1980 Escort (or the Erica programme) was Ford's second 'world car' programme, which was jointly designed and engineered by several Ford's operating companies (Womack *et al.* 1990: 211; Doz 1986: 68). Rather than integrating production globally, Ford compartmentalised it by regions and kept component exchange between North America and Western Europe to a minimum. Despite this, problems related to market and product differentiation created tensions within the company. Ford of Europe and Ford's North American Automotive Operations specified so many changes in the Escort to accommodate European and US tastes and manufacturing preferences that, when introduced into their markets, the European and US Escorts 'shared only two parts: the ashtray and an instrument panel brace' (Womack *et al.* 1990: 212).

Since 1985, Ford started to work yet on another 'world car' project, the Mondeo lines of medium-sized cars (launched in the European market in 1992 and, as the Contour/Mystique models in North America, in 1994). By focusing on sharing design rather than production (as the earlier world car projects did) the new 'global car' project tried to avoid the problems that the world car projects of the 1970s faced, in particular the existence of different national consumer tastes and government production requirements in exchange for market access. A key goal at Ford has been achieving differentiation of the global cars, particularly for North America and Europe. Ford Europe has been responsible for product design, programme management and production engineering, along with the development of the new four-cylinder, multi-valve Zeta engine. North American Automotive Operations provided the distinctive design for the North American version and developed a new V6 engine, and the transmissions and steering components were produced in several US facilities. The programme has also involved the modernisation of nine major plants around the world that were going to produce those cars. In North America, the global cars are built at Ford's plants in Kansas City, Claycomo, Mo., at St. Thomas, Ontario (Canada) and at Cuautitlán, Mexico.

The development of the global cars however has been very expensive, costing about $6 billion, more than four times what Chrysler spent in its Dodge/ Plymouth Neon. The global cars also took too long to develop and have not had the expected market success. The goal for 1995 was to sell up to 800,000 cars annually in fifty-nine countries (Ford Motor Co. *Annual Report* 1993: 3 and 8–9). Ford actually sold 260,000 (*Ward's Automotive Yearbook* 1995: 114). These problems suggest the difficulties of integrating production on a global basis. It must be also stressed that the 'world car' programmes involved only one line of products.

Towards global integration: centralisation of design, engineering and R&D

Ford has tried different systems to coordinate its worldwide operations on a global basis, particularly in the areas of design, engineering and product development, and lately in marketing. In the late 1980s, Ford established Centres of Expertise (for product design), divided by regions, which specialised in specific products: Mazda (Hiroshima) in small cars; Ford North America (Dearborn) in mid-size and full-size cars; and Ford of Europe (Great Britain and Germany), in compact cars. Brazil concentrated on tractors and Australia on speciality cars. Coordination between subsidiaries and affiliates was facilitated by a computerised global communications network, the Worldwide Engineering Release System (WERS), which allowed 20,000 Ford people around the world to share design and manufacturing information as they developed new products (Ford Motor Co. *Annual Report* 1989: 8).

In 1994, Ford introduced other organisational changes that are expected to save the company about $2 billion to $3 billion annually by the end of the century. On the one hand, Ford's 2000 programme introduced a decentralised management scheme that sliced management layers from ten to seven, representing a 15 per cent reduction of its top 25,000 executives. On the other hand, the programme goal is to centralise key activities as design, engineering, and R & D of subsidiaries established in a handful of developed countries.[12] Ford's seven worldwide design operations (Michigan, California, Turin, England, Germany, Australia and Japan) were merged into one group called Ford Corporate Design (FCD). In 1995, Ford's North American and European Operations and its Automotive Components Group were also merged into a single operating unit, Ford Automotive Operations (FAO). Five Vehicle Programme Centres (VPC), four in the Ford Research and Engineering Centre in Dearborn and one split between the United States and Germany, were set up under FAO. Each VPC has a worldwide responsibility for the design, development and engineering of the vehicles assigned to it.[13] In 1996, this organisation faced yet another change: Ford consolidated those centres into three, one for small/midsize cars, a second for large cars and a third for light trucks (*Ward's Automotive Yearbook* 1997: 148).

Conclusion

In sum, the case of Ford Motor Company does not support the view, argued by the neo-liberal global discourse (see introduction of this book), that MNEs are creating a globalised system of production. The failure of Ford's 'world car' projects since the 1970s demonstrates a multiplicity of obstacles to move towards a fully globalised system of production. At most, Ford's production operations are regionally, not globally, integrated, specifically in Europe and in North America. Available information suggests that this also applies for auto parts production. The most important change in Ford's global production operations was the incorporation of Mexico in the North American system of production, as a producer of parts but most importantly as a site for one of Ford's global cars. Ford's worldwide sales operations reveal that the United States continues to be the most important market and that political considerations as much as different consumer tastes inhibited the company's attempts to seek standardisation of products across the Atlantic. The organisation of markets and production on a regional basis also explain Ford's demands to introduce regional trade policies that protect them from foreign producers through preferential access. R&D and design are the areas which Ford was able to move beyond transatlantic coordination. However, failures in maintaining some corporate alliances question the viability of such a strategy. Finally, changes in Ford's worldwide organisation have been expensive and difficult to implement, pointing to the social/national embeddedness of MNEs. Overall, Ford's production structure serves as an example for the third way of looking at globalisation, which argues that most of the big corporations are still firmly linked to home countries and/or regions (see introduction of this book).

Notes

1 Examples include Henry Ford's system of mass production and 'lean' or flexible production introduced by Toyota. Once new methods of production are adopted in the industry, these inevitably spread beyond, changing 'everything in almost every industry – choices for consumers, the nature of work, the fortune of companies and, ultimately, the fate of nations' (Womack *et al.* 1990).
2 For a complete analysis of Ford's strategies over the 1960–93 period, see Studer 1997.
3 Ford is the second largest vehicle manufacturer in the world, and the most transnational of all automakers, having operations in more than 200 countries and territories and employing about 350,000 workers. Its international network of operations has historically given Ford a competitive advantage over GM and Chrysler (see Whitman 1981: 14; UNCTC 1982: 85; and Studer 1997: chapter 3). Economies of learning and the ability to create linkages with host governments, local labour groups and suppliers allowed Ford to become a leader in complying with a range of host country regulations, facilitating its entry or gaining first-mover advantages in foreign markets.
4 The importance of Ford's production in the Asia-Pacific region also increased, doubling from about 2 to 4 per cent of Ford's total production between the mid-1980s and the early 1990s.
5 Japanese suppliers are committed to cost-reductions, to adapt their production and delivery schedules to their customer needs to deliver zero defect components. They are organised in a pyramid structure or systems of tiers, with each tier supplying the companies in the tier above it. Often automakers rely on one supplier as the sole source for a purchased part or component.
6 Before 1985, Ford had limited its offshore sourcing to manual transaxles, some automatic transmissions, and front-wheel-drive halfshafts from Mazda, as well as four-cylinder engines from Mexico.
7 According to one estimate, by 1985, imports of components made in Japan and Taiwan represented only 5 per cent of Ford's total manufacturing costs (Dyer *et al.* 1987: 170).
   The commitment to a cooperative relationship is found in all labour agreements between Ford and the UAW since 1982. In the 1987 agreement the company explicitly stated that 'no worker could be laid off due to a domestically made vehicle or component being replaced by an imported product...' (*Ward's Automotive Yearbook* 1988: 263; Ford Motor Co. *Annual Report* 1987: 7).
8 In 1981, Ford joined with Grupo Alfa to open Nemak, which is one of the largest suppliers of aluminum engine heads; in 1982, with Grupo Vitro and Grupo Visa to create Vitroflex and Carplastic which produce glass and plastic boards, respectively (Berry 1992: 17; Arjona 1990: 138–9). Ford bought Carplastic in 1988.

9 In 1979, Ford purchased a 25 per cent interest in this company (Rubenstein 1992: 157).
10 MUMMI is a 50–50 per cent GM–Toyota joint-manufacturing venture, located in Fremont, California. Today, Diamond-Star Motors Corp. is fully owned by Mitsubishi, but produces cars with a Chrysler badge. AAII is a 50–50 per cent joint venture, located in Flat Rock, Michigan.
11 The British unions made Ford a test case to challenge the Labour government's wage guidelines. Ford's willingness to compromise with the unions implied that it was opposing the government's wage control programme, therefore the government threatened Ford with various sanctions and reduced public orders of its vehicles (Doz and Prahalad 1987: 107; Ward's Automotive Yearbook 1979: 219). The strike affected all Ford operations in Europe and reduced worldwide scheduled production (Ford Motor Co. *Annual Report* 1978: 15).
12 Ford has also tried to integrate globally its marketing operations, by establishing brand managers, as well as its dealership networks through its Fordstar Dealer Communications Network.
13 The European Centre was responsible for small, front-wheel-drive cars, and the Dearborn Centre for large front-drive cars, rear-wheel drive cars, personal-use trucks and commercial trucks. Asia-Pacific and Latin American Operations were incorporated into the new global organisation in 1996.

References

Arjona, Luis Enrique (1990) 'La industria automotriz en México de la industria terminal a la industria de ensamble', in Jorge Carrillo (ed.) *La Nueva Era de la Industria Automotriz en México*, México: El Colegio de la Frontera Norte: 115–50.

Automotive News, 23 June 1994.

Automotive News Market Data Yearbook, several years.

Bartlett, Christopher and Ghoshal Sumantra (1989) *Managing Across Borders*, Boston: Harvard Business School Press.

Bartlett, Christopher (1983) 'MNCs: get off the reorganization merry-go-round', *Harvard Business Review* 61(2): 138–46.

Berry, Steven, Vittorio Grilli and Florencio López-de-Salines (1992) 'The automobile industry and the Mexico–US free trade agreement', *Working Paper* no. 4152, Cambridge, Mass.: National Bureau of Economic Research, Inc.

Doz, Yves L. (1986) *Strategic Management in Multinational Enterprises*, Oxford: Pergamon Press.

Doz, Yves L. and C. K. Prahalad (1990) 'How MNCs cope with host government intervention', *Harvard Business Review* March–April: 149–57.

—— (1987) *The Multinational Mission: Balancing Local Demands and Global Vision*, New York: Free Press.

Dyer, Davis, Malcom S. Salter and Alan M. Webber (1987) *Changing Alliances*, Boston, Mass.: Harvard Business School Press.

Economic Commission for Latin America and the Caribbean (ECLAC) (1995) *Restructuring and International Competitiveness: The Mexican Automobile Industry*, Santiago, Chile: Economic Commission for Latin America and the Caribbean.

Ford Motor Company *Annual Reports*. Washington, D.C.: Securities and Exchange Commission, several years.

Gereffi, Gary (1996) 'The elusive last lap in the quest for developed-country status', in James H. Mittleman (ed.) *Globalisation: Critical Reflections*, Boulder: Lynne Rienner: 53–82.

Hamel, Gary and C. K. Prahalad (1985) 'Do you really have a global strategy?,' *Harvard*

Business Review 63(4): 139–48.

Herzenberg, Stephen (1991) 'Towards a co-operative commonwealth? Labour and restructuring in the US and Canadian auto industries', Ph.D. dissertation, Massachusetts Institute of Technology.

Hoffman, Kurt and Raphael Kaplinsky (1988) *Driving Force. The Global Restructuring of Technology, Labour, and Investment in the Automobile and Components Industries*, Boulder: Westview Press.

Kobrin, Stephen J. (1991) 'An empirical analysis of the determinants of global integration', *Strategic Management Journal* Summer Special Issue, no. 12: 17–31.

Kogut, Bruce (1985) 'Designing global strategies: comparative and competitive value-added chains', *Sloan Management Review* 26: 15–28.

Levitt, T. (1983) 'The globalisation of markets', *Harvard Business Review* 61(3): 92–102.

Morales, Rebecca (1994) *Flexible Production. Restructuring of the International Automobile Industry*, Cambridge, Mass.: Polity Press.

Perry, Ross (1982) *The Future of Canada' s Auto Industry: The Big Three and the Japanese Challenge*, Canada: Canadian Institute for Economic Policy.

Porter, Michael (1986) *Competition in Global Industries*, Cambridge, Mass.: Harvard Business School Press.

Rubenstein, James M. (1992) *The Changing US Auto Industry. A Geographical Analysis*, London and New York: Routledge.

Ruigrok, Winfried and Rob van Tulder (1995) *The Logic of International Restructuring*, London and New York: Routledge.

Solvell, Orjan (1988) 'Is the global automobile industry really global?', in Neil Hood and Jan-Erik Vahlne (eds) *Strategies in Global Competition*, England: Croom Helm: 187–212

Stopford, John M. and Louis T. Wells Jr (1972) *Managing the Multinational Enterprise*, New York: Basic Books.

Studer Noguez, Maria Isabel (1997) 'Multinational global strategies and government policies: the case of Ford Motor Co. and the Mexican and Canadian automobile industries in the 1960–1993 period', Ph.D. dissertation, School of Advanced International Studies, Johns Hopkins University.

United Nations Centre on Transnational Corporations (UNCTC) (1983) *Transnational Corporations in the International Auto-Industry*, New York: United Nations Center of Transnational Corporations.

United Nations World Investment Report (UNWIR) (1996) *Investment, Trade and International Policy Arrangements*, New York: United Nations.

Ward's Automotive Yearbook. Michigan: Ward's Communications, several years.

Whitman, Marina (1981) 'International trade and investment', *Essays in International Trade and Finance*, no. 143, Princeton: Princeton University Press

Womack, James P., Daniel T. Jones, and Daniel Roos (1990) *The Machine that Changed the World*, New York: Basic Books.

World Motor Vehicle Data. Washington, D.C.: American Automobile Manufacturers' Association, several years.

11 Foreign capital, host-country-firm mandates and the terms of globalisation

Jochen Lorentzen

Introduction

In the 1970s and 1980s, the world knew desperate Latin American debtors, successful East Asian interventionists, and unsuccessful Soviet and East European planners. Each of these regions had its own economic problems and used its own institutions to try to solve them. By the end of the 1980s, Latin America had overcome the debt crisis through a mixture of structural adjustment and partial debt write-downs. The East Asian tigers continued to be so successful that the relative closure of their economies led to trade conflicts with the US and others, and ultimately forced them to gradually open up. Meanwhile, the Soviet Union and its satellites had largely planned themselves out of existence.

Since then, the international economic vocabulary has changed. Rather than distinguishing between Peru, the Philippines, and Poland, fund managers and policy-makers now refer to them as 'emerging markets' which is an undefined term except in so far as it implies certain economic (reform) policies and their result: high growth rates. The *Economist* regularly publishes a 'beauty contest' in which countries as diverse as Chile, China, Cameroon, and the Czech Republic are ranked according to unit labour costs, foreign capital inflows, or income per head and the like. Academics lost no time in giving their spin on globalisation. According to Jeffrey Sachs, both the worldwide scope of the changes in economic policy and the depth of economic integration hail the advent of a 'global capitalist world system' (Sachs 1995: 51).[1] That capitalism has extended its reach with the fall from grace of state-led development is not in dispute. It is also clear that globalisation is bringing benefits. What is not clear is *cui bono*, namely how exactly these benefits are being distributed between the advanced countries and the newcomers, and whether similarities rather than differences prevail in the way in which emerging-market countries operate in the global economy.

This question has no general answer which is one reason why the literature on the effects of globalisation is such a growth industry; answers can only be situation-specific. In what follows, the focus is on one region (Central Europe); one core economic reform of the last decade (openness to foreign direct investment (FDI)); and one benefit-creating relationship (the interaction between multinational enterprises (MNEs) and domestic firms). The heuristic interest is thus:

How does the role of the domestic firm (joint-venture partner or subsidiary) *vis-à-vis* the foreign investor determine the distribution of benefits between home and host country?

The chapter proceeds as follows. First, what is known about the impact of multi-national firms on host countries is briefly reviewed. This helps place the chapter in context. Second, changes over time in the organisation of international production are described. This is important for understanding developments in the relationship of foreign investors and local firms. Third, research into investor motivations in Central Europe is summarised. It introduces the significance of corporate networks. Fourth, a typology of the roles of domestic firms in international corporate networks is introduced, along with results from empirical work on subsidiary mandates in advanced economies. Fifth, the typology is used to examine three cases of interactions between foreign investors and domestic firms in a Central European country and to draw out differences between subsidiaries in advanced and in emerging markets. The final section concludes with recommendations for further research.

The effects of inward direct investment (IDI)

In international investments, there is a gap between economic analysis and public policy. The theoretical literature has focused primarily on why MNEs exist, and what impact they have on international trade. It is inconclusive about the welfare effects of FDI on both home and host countries (Caves 1996; see also Young *et al.* 1994: 659–61 for a discussion of virtuous *versus* vicious cycles of technological capabilities). By contrast, most countries have done away with restrictions on incoming foreign capital and indeed scramble to raise their share of available IDI. The empirical literature has paid attention to topics policy-makers are interested in, such as technology transfer, spill-overs, and the like. However, since there is no formal concept of linkages, economic reasoning provides no general basis for attracting FDI (Rodríguez-Clare 1996). In principle, a cost-benefit analysis of FDI should be simple: it hinges on whether the social rate of return from IDI is greater than the opportunity costs of the resources used. But in practice, this raises both conceptual (how wide a range of costs and benefits to include?) and measurement (with what time horizon?) problems (Radosevic, forthcoming). Evidently, if the analysis is extended to include non-economic criteria, it gets yet more complicated (Wells 1998). There is little hope that the study of the overall impact of FDI will ever yield a conclusive answer (cf. Caves 1996). For example, spill-overs seem to be sector-specific. Across countries, they differ with respect to a country's industry, market structure, and degree of technological development. High degrees of product differentiation and strong scale economies are less likely to lead to spill-overs because MNEs typically possess strong ownership advantages in these areas and may end up cornering the domestic market. Also, if the productivity gap between foreign and domestic firms is too high, the latter will be unable to exploit potential externalities.

Due to the theoretical impasse, it is more likely that the cumulation of narrow empirical analyses – on, for example, the balance of payments effect of intra-firm trade, export performance, location of innovation activity, profitability and productivity of foreign investment enterprises *versus* local firms – eventually will help understand the general impact of MNEs (for illustrations of work on Central Europe, see Altzinger and Winklhuber 1998; Eichengreen and Kohl 1998; Hunya 1998; Lorentzen *et al.* 1998; Rojec 1998). Until then, many of the earlier controversies that characterised the evaluations of the impact of foreign capital on developing host countries, which ultimately all imply a normative judgement of the effects of capital flows, are likely to be repeated for Central Europe.[2]

The available analyses of multinational behaviour in Central Europe generally agree that FDI raises efficiency. Questions that remain open are what kind of linkages are established between foreign and domestic firms; how local innovation potential is affected; and who captures the rents (for an overview, see Lorentzen 1998). In the absence of systematically collected information on the behaviour of affiliates of MNEs and on the structure and operation of host-country supplier industries, much work is in fact based on mere anecdotes, often rehashed from the same newspaper clippings and almost always about the same, world-class (and, thus, somewhat unrepresentative) firms, such as ABB. Aggregate analyses of trade data or firm balance sheets and income statements, while essential, are unable to identify linkages or track rent appropriation. Conversely, case studies of individual firms may manage to describe supply chain hierarchies and the scope and depth of local contributions to the global R&D agendas of MNEs. But, by definition, they are hardly ever representative. Therefore, the challenge is to reconcile the two, namely to undertake aggregate analyses at country or industry level for capturing general trends while doing sector and case studies to elucidate key features. How this might be done is the topic of the final section.

Multinational firms and integrated international production

Forms of international production have evolved over time. The literature distinguishes between three different types of strategies and associated organisational structures. They are, in turn, stand-alone; simple integration; and complex international production (UNCTAD 1993, chaps V-VI). Stand-alone affiliates resemble a smaller version of the parent firm with which they are linked by way of transferred technology and the supply of long-term capital. They are widespread in services whose non-tradability requires the duplication of the parents' production organisation in the host country.

Outsourcing is a prime example of simple integration. For cost reasons, multinational firms in manufacturing often locate labour-intensive production in economies with low unit labour costs. Since this implies an increase in intra-firm trade, simple integration presupposes decreasing trade barriers as well as relatively low transport costs. The parent firm may own the subsidiary or undertake non-equity arrangements with local firms. Likewise, some corporate functions are typically integrated while for others the component suppliers are on their own.

Complex integration strategies characterise firms who manage to locate almost any part of the value chain wherever it is most profitable. Whereas in the past certain productive activities such as R&D were limited to the parent's home country, they may now be transferred to especially skill- and innovation-intensive sites abroad. The same goes for corporate functions such as accounting or financial management. Technological advances in information and communication made this possible, while the worldwide liberalisation of trade and investment regimes heightened international competition, thus driving multinational firms to optimise the organisation of their value chains.

Stand-alone, simple, and complex integration strategies co-exist in international business. The latter are clearly of more recent vintage because their management depends on a degree of economic integration and technological development which began to characterise the world economy only in the 1980s. Complex integration strategies require complex organisational structures to handle coordination and control problems associated with global value chains. This leads to functional, product or geographical specialisations within a corporate group or to cooperative arrangements between unrelated firms. Where vertical intra-firm structures are combined with horizontal relationships such as strategic alliances, corporate networks emerge which may further increase organisational complexity.

This in turn has repercussions for the relationship between foreign investors and firms in the host country. For example, if a multinational firm moves from a multi-country to a global strategy, some corporate decisions that were previously the domain of the country manager will be centralised. The dismantling of a stand-alone role need not be negative for the host-country firm: it implies the danger of becoming a downsized organisation with little decision-making authority as well as the chance of acquiring broader international responsibilities (Moore 1998). Which of the two prevails depends in part on the motivations of foreign investors. Investor motivations in Central and Eastern Europe are reviewed in the next section. It also depends on the position a host-country firm occupies within a global value chain which is the topic of the section immediately thereafter.

The motivations of foreign investors in Central Europe

Openness to foreign direct investment is a key characteristic of emerging markets. It differentiates them from the suspicion or outright hostility with which many developing countries viewed foreign capital until about the first half of the 1980s. Although individual firms ventured into Central Europe prior to the system change, the area began to attract sizable inflows of FDI only from the early 1990s. In principle, foreign firms have one of two motivations for investing abroad: they either want to sell in the local market, and exports are not viable at all or only a second best alternative to producing locally. Or they want to take advantage of factor-cost differentials which in Central Europe would refer especially to cheap labour (for a full exposition of investor motives, see Dunning 1993).

Both market- and resource-seeking investments may benefit the host economy. Despite the uncertainties reviewed above, more often than not they are expected to increase competition, raise efficiency, upgrade technology, and generate spill-overs and linkages upstream and downstream (for an overview, see Blomström and Kokko 1996). But in terms of how they enable host-country firms to participate in the global economy, there are clearly differences between the two types of investments. To some extent, the effect of market-driven investments is comparable to the lowering of trade barriers. Local goods produced in plants with foreign participation compete against domestic producers and other foreign producers in the local market only.

By contrast, the output of resource-driven investments faces at least regional and possibly global competition. Consequently, the higher the degree of outward orientation, the more likely it is that the investment is accompanied by technology transfer, exacting quality control, sophisticated marketing channels, and the like. In fact, full foreign ownership is more typically associated with export supply projects than with local supply projects because in the former case the investment embodies intellectual property, skill intensity, production quality and sales strategies that it takes to be successful in international markets, and that the investor wants to protect (Lankes and Venables 1996). Thus, globalisation can be passive (opening up) or active (competing abroad). In the worst case, a market-seeking investor merely sets up a warehouse from which to wholesale imported or locally assembled goods. The benefits to the host economy are likely to be small (Reich 1998; see also Munday *et al.* (1994) for a test of the 'warehouse thesis' with respect to Japanese capital in Wales). In the best scenario, a resource-driven investor affords a subsidiary with worldwide responsibility for a globally distributed product.

Research shows that sales in the local market were primarily behind the decisions of foreign investors to locate production in Central Europe (Collins and Rodrik 1991; Creditanstalt 1992, 1993; Arthur Anderson 1994; Meyer 1995). When Central Europe first opened up, only a few manufacturing firms were found to be interested in local resources (NERA 1991). Over time, this seemed to be increasing (Deloitte Touche Tohmatsu International 1995). But even more recent in-depth studies concluded that factor cost considerations were less important than market motives (Altzinger and Winklhuber 1998). Only about one-third of all investments is resource-driven, and most of this went into the more advanced transition economies (Lankes and Venables 1996).

The problem with all these surveys is that they are inconclusive about the effects of FDI on the host economies. The fact that resource-driven investments are fewer and represent less incoming capital than market-seeking investments is an interesting finding. But it is surely more important to understand the relative impact on economic modernisation of these two types of investment in the transition countries. For example, the qualitative advances in the export performance of select Central European countries during the mid-1990s can be attributed in large part to FDI inflows (Eichengreen and Kohl 1998). Manufacturing firms with foreign ownership in Hungary, the Czech Republic, and Poland outperformed domestic firms in terms of exports growth, the technology intensity of exports, and labour productivity (ibid.). Industry-level comparisons across a number of

Central European countries demonstrate that foreign investment enterprises (FIEs) are more export-oriented than domestic firms, and that FIEs altered the export commodity structure upwards and promoted economic development (Hunya 1998). At the very least, this suggests that resource-driven investments warrant a closer look in order to understand whether the improvements benefited the host economy or were captured as rents by the foreign investors. Academic concern with this question is presented next.

Domestic firms in international corporate networks

Not by coincidence, much research on the position of domestic firms *vis-à-vis* their foreign partners or owners comes out of Canada or similar small economies (Taggart 1997: 54). The domination of Canada's manufacturing sector by foreign, mostly US firms gave rise to concern that local subsidiaries might turn into mere importing agents for their global parents. White and Poynter were among the first to design strategies for foreign-owned subsidiaries that would prevent Canadian firms from simply becoming a conduit for outside firms' production (White and Poynter 1984). They developed a typology of subsidiaries which was based on product scope (limited, unconstrained); market scope (local, global); and value-added scope (narrow, broad). They suggested that subsidiaries had to develop beyond a limited product and a narrow value-added scope in order to be successful in local or global markets. Their framework was subsequently modified and expanded; recently, Birkinshaw and Morrison summarised much of the relevant literature and simplified a common framework by identifying three types of subsidiaries: local implementers; specialised contributors; and world mandate (Birkinshaw and Morrison 1995).

Local implementers have a limited geographic and a severely constrained product or value-added scope. Specialised contributors have competence in specific, narrow functions or activities that are coordinated with the activities of other subsidiaries. A world mandate subsidiary has regional or global responsibility for a product line or an entire business, and unconstrained product and broad value-added scope (ibid.: 733–4). An empirical analysis of 126 subsidiaries in the US, Canada, the UK, France, Germany, and Japan produced the following results. First, world mandate subsidiaries enjoy more strategic autonomy than specialised contributors. Local implementers are most highly controlled by the parent firm. This is important in so far as strategic autonomy facilitates the creation and diffusion of indigenous innovations without hampering the acquisition of innovations from the parent company (Ghoshal and Bartlett 1988).

Second, linkages between local implementers or specialised contributors and other corporate affiliates are denser than those involving world mandate subsidiaries. In most cases, intra-firm trade balances are in favour of sales from the parent company to the subsidiaries, which suggests a relatively high level of one-way dependence from which the world mandate is unaffected. Third, the performance (in terms of return on investment) of specialised contributors is worse than that of the other two types. Perhaps this is due to their high degree of integration which means that they are cost rather than profit centres, with ample opportunity for transfer pricing (Birkinshaw and Morrison 1995).

Given the apparent desirability of world product mandates from the perspective of the local firm, Birkinshaw subsequently studied, this time with a small sample of Canadian subsidiaries, how mandates are gained, developed, and lost (Birkinshaw 1996). He used a broad definition whereby 'mandate' referred to any subsidiary responsibility that extends beyond its own market (ibid.: 468). He found, first, that mandates are gained through the entrepreneurial efforts of subsidiary management rather than given by parent management. The type of mandate gained depends in large part on the environmental and organisational context of the subsidiary. That is, market-seeking parent firms rely on a high level of subsidiary autonomy; the outcome is often a full-scope global mandate. Resource-driven subsidiaries exhibit lower levels of autonomy and typically acquire only manufacturing mandates, while product development and sales remain with the parent firm.

Second, mandate development is fundamentally subsidiary-driven as well. From the affiliate's perspective, this makes sense in that broader responsibility for product or business management gives the subsidiary more control over its destiny than managing a single function. Third, whether a mandate continues or is lost does not depend on subsidiary autonomy as such (contrary to Birkinshaw and Morrison 1995) or on the degree of integration between subsidiary and parent. Rather, the key factors are a high internal competence as well as the specificity of the business to the host country. In other words, if both firm- and country-specific advantages are strong, it is less likely that the mandate is contested by other entities, which enhances its sustainability (Birkinshaw 1996). The prominent role identified for subsidiary management suggests the nature of entrepreneurship in MNE affiliates as a fruitful area for further research (cf. Young *et al.* 1994: 666).

Birkinshaw then developed a framework of mandate types which is depicted in Figure 11.1. The sustainability of a mandate depends on the degree of strategic relatedness between the activity of the subsidiary and the rest of the firm. It furthermore depends on the level of distinctive value-added the subsidiary realises. The problem of a commodity mandate is that it is short on competence; in the long run, its activity may be performed more effectively by another corporate entity. The result could be divestment or mandate decline. An isolated mandate

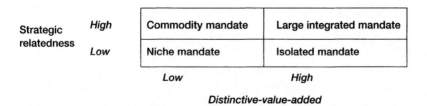

Figure 11.1 Framework of mandate types.
Source: Birkinshaw (1996: 487).

may not be seen as a strategic priority for the group and lead to phasing out. A niche mandate is the worst even though many subsidiaries start out that way. The only sustainable position is that of a large integrated mandate. Hence, autonomy by itself is not sufficient; it is the underlying capabilities of subsidiaries that are key to their long-term growth.

This framework is helpful for thinking about corporate networks but it has some drawbacks. First, it only looks at subsidiaries and does not include joint ventures or independent suppliers. In a number of high-risk emerging markets, foreign firms prefer joint ventures over majority acquisitions. A joint venture deal gives them access to tangible and intangible assets of the local firm. Majority ownership gives them control over proprietary assets whose protection would be difficult to specify in a contract (Lankes and Venables 1996; for a theoretical treatment, see Møllgaard and Overgaard 1998). So joint ventures seem to be better equipped to deal with information problems which typically characterise countries at the early stage of transition. Therefore, excluding them implies not to understand corporate networks in a whole set of significant countries, including Russia.

Second, while Birkinshaw's research describes the situations in which mandates are gained, developed or lost, it does not explain the process by which the relationship between a parent company and the domestic firm is structured in a certain way. The interaction involves mutual influence between the two sides plus possibly other stakeholders such as the government. How this plays out depends on the control of resources and, ultimately, bargaining (Ruigrok and Van Tulder 1995, chapter 4). For example, automobile industrialisation in Malaysia, the Philippines, Indonesia, and Thailand happened despite the opposition by Japanese investors in the sector (Doner 1991). This is because certain local firms managed to expand activities at the expense of foreign capital and to exploit the intense rivalry of Japanese car manufacturers to their benefit.

Thus, it is important to analyse host-country capabilities in bargaining, look at differences between local firms, and investigate coalitions between local public officials and entrepreneurs *vis-à-vis* foreign firms. Research on joint venture negotiations in Hungary and Romania demonstrated that key stakeholder influence – in this case through the agencies in charge of privatisation – was both frequent and extensive in strategically important industries. It also showed that interventions occurred mostly in the pre- and post-negotiation phase (Brouthers and Bamossy 1997). This is clearly relevant for how mandates are gained or developed.

Foreign investors and domestic firms in Central Europe

This section discusses data on a few case studies of foreign direct investments in Central Europe drawn from a multi-country and -sector study (Lorentzen *et al.* 1998; Møllgaard 1997; Møllgaard and Schröder 1997). The data was developed by surveying, with company executives, the ownership structure, the production and sales profile, the degree of vertical organisation, the quality of intra-firm integration, the investment motives and the subsidiary performance of pairs of home- and host-country firms. Only three cases from two sectors (electrical engineering and telecommunication equipment) in one country (Slovenia) are discussed here. But, together with automobiles, these sectors have been the prime targets of foreign investors. The foreign firms either belong to the world's most R&D-intensive companies (Siemens and Bosch) or are otherwise considered world-class competitors (Danfoss) (Cookson 1998; Jackson 1997). Hence, in principle, there is scope for the decentralisation of R&D, technology, and skills which are among the most critical components of subsidiary status and, indirectly, of host-country benefits. The cases suffice to show that subsidiary mandates differ even within countries, let alone across the entire region. This means that in order to understand the distribution of benefits between parent companies and affiliates, analyses need to be located at the level of individual relationships between foreign and domestic firms.

The cases are summarised in Table 11.1. Danfoss is a wholly-owned subsidiary of Danish Danfoss and produces compressors. They are sold all over the world although the EU is the major market. The affiliate manufactures only one product line; the parent firm has responsibility for product development, sales, purchases,

Table 11.1 Subsidiary typologies of three case studies

Type/Firm	Danfoss	MGA	Iskratel
Market scope			
local			
regional		Europe	license production
global	mainly Europe		own system
Product scope			
limited	only compressors	only appliances	license production
unconstrained			all other production
Value-added scope			
narrow	mature industry	no new products	
broad			new products/processes
Subsidiary type			
local implementer			license production
specialised contributor	manufacture only	no development	buy-backs
world mandate			own system
Scope for mandate development			
low			
high	relocation from Denmark	competence centre	*
Potential for mandate loss			
low	*	*	*
high			

Source: Lorentzen *et al.* (1998).

and long-term strategy. Compressors are a homogeneous product in a mature and highly competitive industry, thus value-added scope is narrow. From the perspective of the parent company, Danfoss is a specialised contributor in the sense that it is one of several affiliates involved in the manufacture of compressors. Due to its limited functional responsibilities, it is currently no more than that. The prospect of mandate development is quite likely because Slovenia is an ideal site to progressively relocate production from high-cost plants in Germany and Denmark. However, the offshored production is always prone to be at the tail end of the product cycle. And mandate development will not affect a graduation of subsidiary type to world mandate: the parent company plans to retain R&D and advanced production in Denmark and Germany. Barring extremely adverse real wage developments, the danger of mandate loss seems remote.

MGA is a fully-owned subsidiary of Bosch-Siemens Hausgeräte. MGA manufactures small household appliances which are sold through the parent firm which is Europe's second biggest white goods producer. The product scope is not unconstrained though less limited than in the case of Danfoss. MGA is currently mainly active in established products and as such a specialised contributor. However, the scope for mandate development is relatively high. While the affiliate still depends on headquarters for design and advanced technologies, it has been designated a 'European Competence Centre' which suggests an extension of its functional responsibilities. MGA may also assume product responsibility for the manufacture of thermic appliances, a new product line. In time, it could acquire a world mandate. The potential for mandate loss appears low.

Iskratel is a joint venture between a group of domestic investors and Siemens in which the latter holds a minority share. The company mainly produces switching devices for telecommunication systems and associated equipment and software. Its sales are mainly to Germany, Eastern Europe, and the CIS. The product scope is unconstrained because roughly half the firm's output represents a system developed in-house. Iskratel also produces a Siemens switching device under licence, for which it agreed to honour limits on market and product scope. The company has the capability to develop new products and processes which indicates a broad value-added scope. It is a local implementer (for the Siemens system), a specialist contributor (by selling software solutions to Siemens), and a world mandate subsidiary (because of the global potential of its own system). Mandate development already happened when Siemens began sourcing customised switching equipment on a buy-back basis, in part to compensate for the demise of the market of the former Yugoslavia. Thanks to Iskratel's specific competencies, the potential for mandate loss is low.

All three investors were, to different degrees, resource-driven. Siemens initially pursued primarily a market-seeking strategy although access to skilled labour, manufactured inputs, and technological knowhow was important as well. For Bosch-Siemens and Danfoss, low-cost, high-skilled labour was the prime motive for their acquisition. Despite these similarities, the affiliated domestic firms have different mandates. Using the terminology introduced in Figure 11.1, Danfoss and MGA have a commodity mandate but, thanks to its higher distinctive value-added, MGA is closer to being an integrated-mandate subsidiary. Danfoss's strategic relatedness to the parent company is relatively low because compressors are neither an input to what the group produces nor likely to generate spill-overs for new product developments in other areas. Iskratel, due to its strong R&D performance in software customisation and its key presence in the difficult eastern markets, has a high distinctive value added and is strategically related to Siemens. Therefore, of the three it comes closest to having a large integrated mandate.

What is different about these cases in comparison with the literature briefly reviewed above is that the evidence suggests a much more passive role for domestic firms.[3] In other words, mandates are given rather than earned. This probably reflects dramatically different situations between the transition economies and places like Canada. In Central Europe, many of the companies that were put up for sale had close to no output; Danfoss is one such example. An urgent need for capital often lowered their bargaining power, even if they originated in strategic industries. Nonetheless, it is self-evident that local capabilities, as suggested by Birkinshaw (1996), influence what kind of a mandate a parent company sees fit for a subsidiary or joint venture partner. These observations do not necessarily imply that affiliates in transition economies differ systematically from those in more mature economies or from those in other emerging markets with a longer track record of reform and, hence, older subsidiaries. But this possibility certainly exists. At present not enough time has passed in Central and Eastern Europe's transition record to comprehensively judge the potential of the initiative of local management.

What does this mean for the distribution of benefits between home and host country? A subsidiary with a large integrated mandate has more influence over its own destiny than those that score low on value added, strategic relevance, or both. This is because its bargaining power is enhanced by occupying a key part of a global value chain. Therefore, rent extraction by foreign firms becomes more difficult. The framework helped to distinguish among three firms in a host country, and between them and firms in advanced host economies. It certainly did not help to remove concerns about the distribution of benefits.

Conclusion

The sample is too small to afford generalisations. But it is large enough to show where generalisations undertaken elsewhere are way off the mark. The 'global capitalist world system' does not make old differences between how firms in rich and poor countries operate in international markets disappear. Although subsidiary strategies are an under-researched topic, especially regarding emerging markets, what partial evidence there is suggests that affiliates in advanced economies may well be at a structural advantage over those in transition countries when struggling to define their mandate. Therefore, the global market does not necessarily hold equal prospects for its participants.

Furthermore, it is doubtful that the growing group of emerging market economies is easier to characterise by their similarities than by their differences.

The *World Investment Report 1995* argued that FDI would have the same effect on Central Europe as it did on East Asia (UNCTAD 1995: 262–4). Such sweeping comparisons hide more than they reveal. Multinational firms clearly do exploit factor-price differentials regardless of where they operate. But that does not mean that the comparative advantages of countries, let alone regions, are useful units of analysis. Figure 11.2 shows that investments in Central Europe take place in labour-intensive and in capital-(including human-capital-) intensive sectors, and that the produced goods are both standard and highly specialised. In fact, investments are not even firm- or sector-specific but case-specific. Investments by the same multinational in the same product in different countries can be structured very differently and thus have a differentiated impact on the host economy. Also, investments in different products by the same company and in the same country need not have the same effect because, for example, the subsidiary mandate varies (for evidence, see Lorentzen *et al.* 1998; cf. Blomström and Kokko 1996). Thus, the power of MNEs *vis-à-vis* countries differs from investment to investment and cannot be considered to be generally predominant as done by the neo-liberal global discourse (see the introduction of this book).

Which way forward for research on the effects of globalisation on the reform economies? The significance of case studies such as those presented above would be greatly enhanced if they were embedded in sectoral analyses. A group of scholars associated with the Berkeley Roundtable of International Economics (BRIE) suggested that MNEs may create cross-national production networks (CPNs) in Central Europe in much the same way as US electronics firms did in Asia. There, so-called systems firms such as Intel, with control over product market standards – rather than over the final product itself – outsourced most of the manufacturing activity to local firms with which they established a closer than arms-length relationship though often without sharing equity links. Therefore, CPNs could come into being in the absence of FDI. The logic behind this division of labour among heterogeneous economies was not principally based on lower wages, or access to resources and markets. Instead, it hinged on local technical specialisations (Borrus and Zysman 1997). The advantage of CPNs to US system firms was they could concentrate on product definition and market strategies, thus conserving capital and gaining product flexibility. Ultimately, this is what explains the astonishing revival of the US electronics industry for which many

		Factor proportions	
		Labour-intensive	*(human) capital-intensive*
Product characteristics	*Standard*	Danfoss, Bosch-Siemens/MGA	e.g. automobiles
	Specialised	e.g. electrical engineering	Siemens/Iskratel

Figure 11.2 FDI and the division of sectors.

pundits had already composed post-mortems in the mid-1980s (ibid.). More interestingly from a Central European perspective, the 'new competition' creates market opportunities where previously giant, oligopolistic assemblers dominated. Furthermore, CPNs provide small producers with cost-effective production strategies to exploit the new market opportunities. A key feature of CPNs is their complementary architecture. More precisely, Central European firms would not need to master the full package of managerial and technological resources that it would take to compete head-on with West European firms (Zysman *et al.* 1997). Instead, it would suffice to build up and maintain a specific competence. Borrus and Zysman predict that CPNs will come into being outside the electronics sector because their success will lead to the assimilation of best practices elsewhere (1997).

This proposition awaits verification. Interesting sectors would be automobiles and electrical engineering. Their analysis would reveal how typical a network form of production organisation is (see Pearce and Papanastassiou 1997 for work that goes partially in this direction). Case studies would show at what level MNE affiliates or suppliers are associated with these networks, and who captures the benefits. Finally, it would be possible to evaluate aspects of equity and distribution of international production for home and host countries.

FDI was generally promoted for economic restructuring in Central Europe. Therefore, openness to foreign capital benefited the transition economies. Firms which locate production in Central Europe because they want to make the region an integral part of their European or global strategies are on the rise relative to market seekers. For Central Europe's future in the global economy it is arguably more important how its firms in sectors such as automobiles, engineering, consumer electronics, and telecommunications participate in worldwide corporate networks rather than whether its dishwashing liquid is imported, or produced locally by a domestic or foreign-owned firm. Thus, the dynamics of resource-seeking investments merit serious attention.

This brief analysis has shown why it is problematic to generalise about the distribution of the resulting gains between parent and host-country firm, or between home and host country. Whether firms in the transition economies manage to occupy strategic parts of global value chains rather than just doing simple assembly operations depends on the development of specific competencies. The latter, in turn, relies prominently on capturing the benefits from the interaction with the advanced technology that foreign capital embodies. The key is what kinds of assets each side controls when the acquisition or joint venture takes place, and how the two sides bargain about the contract that formalises their relationship. The analysis of the relationship between the organisational strategies of foreign investors and the business mandates of local firms is what transition research should turn to; it would help to understand the terms of globalisation for newcomer countries.

Notes

1 Whether increased economic integration and accelerated technological innovation – perhaps the most commonly accepted definition of globalisation – has created a

genuinely new world economic situation is in dispute. See Julius (1997) and Strange (1996) for evidence in favour, and Hirst and Thompson (1996) for a contrary view. It is beyond doubt, however, that today's emerging markets, in terms of their share in world output, trade, and capital flows, are more important than they have ever been, and that their significance is going to rise further.

2 See Ellingstad (1997) for a critique of Central Europe's maquiladora prospects; Carson (1998) for a positive evaluation of the chances implied in maquiladora development; and Reich (1998) for an argument about differential development potential depending on MNEs' country of origin.

3 Note, however, that Birkinshaw (1996) found that resource-driven investments typically acquire less autonomy compared with market-driven subsidiaries.

References

Altzinger, W., and R. Winklhuber (1998) 'General patterns of Austria's FDI in Central and Eastern Europe and a case study', *Journal of International Relations and Development 1, 1–20*: 65–83.

Arthur Andersen (1994), 'Assessing investment opportunities in the economies in transition', quoted in Lankes and Venables (1996).

Birkinshaw, J. (1996) 'How multinational subsidiary mandates are gained and lost', *Journal of International Business Studies* 27(3): 467–95.

Birkinshaw, J. and A. J. Morrison (1995) 'Configurations of strategy and structure in subsidiaries of multinational corporations', *Journal of International Business Studies* 26(4): 729–53.

Blomström, M. and A. Kokko. (1996) 'Multinational corporations and spillovers', Discussion Paper no.1365, CEPR, London.

Borrus, M. and J. Zysman (1997) 'Wintelism and the changing terms of global competition: prototype of the future?', in *Foreign Direct Investment and Trade in Eastern Central Europe*, Final Report coordinated by the Bruno Kreisky Forum for International Dialogue, Vienna [mimeo].

Brouthers, K. D. and G. J. Bamossy (1997) 'The role of key stakeholders in international joint venture negotiations: case studies from Eastern Europe', *Journal of International Business Studies* 28(2): 285–308.

Carson, I. (1998) 'Meet the global factory', Survey of Manufacturing, *Economist* 20 June: 1–22.

Caves, R. E. (1996) *Multinational Enterprise and Economic Analysis*, Cambridge: Cambridge University Press.

Collins, S. M. and D. Rodrik (1991) *Eastern Europe and the Soviet Union in the World Economy*, Washington, D.C.: Institute for International Economics.

Cookson, C. (1998) 'Advantage to the scientists', *Financial Times* 25 June: 11.

Creditanstalt (1992, 1993) 'East European Investment Survey', quoted in Lankes and Venables (1996).

Deloitte Touche Tohmatsu International (1995) 'Investment experience in Central and Eastern Europe', quoted in Lankes and Venables (1996).

Doner, R. (1991) *Driving a Bargain: Automobile Industrialization and Japanese Firms in Southeast Asia*, Berkeley: University of California Press.

Dunning, J. (1993) *Multinational Enterprises and the Global Economy*. Wokingham: Allison Wesley.

Eichengreen, B. and R. Kohl (1998) 'The external sector and development in Eastern Europe: the determinants of differential performance', *Journal of International Relations and Development* 1, 1–2: 20–45.

Ellingstad, M. (1997) 'The *maquiladora* syndrome: Central European prospects', *Europe–Asia Studies* 49(1): 7–21.

Ghoshal, S., and C.A. Bartlett (1988) 'Creation, adoption and diffusion of innovations by subsidiaries of multinational corporations', *Journal of International Business Studies* 19(3): 365–88.

Hirst, P. and G. Thompson (1996) *Globalisation in Question: The International Economy and the Possibilities of Governance*, Cambridge: Polity.

Hunya, G. (1998) 'FDI penetration in Central European manufacturing industries: an introduction and some findings', paper presented at a Phare-ACE project workshop, Vienna Institute for International Economic Studies, 29–30 May [mimeo].

Jackson, T. (1997) 'World beaters of tomorrow', *Financial Times* 8 December: 12.

Julius, D. (1997) 'Globalization and stakeholder conflicts: a corporate perspective', *International Affairs* 73(3): 453–68.

Lankes, H. and A. J. Venables (1996) 'Foreign direct investment in economic transition: the changing pattern of investments', *Economics of Transition* 4(2): 331–47.

Lorentzen, J. (1998) 'Foreign capital, Central Europe's catch-up, and EU enlargement: policy issues and analytical problems', *Journal of International Relations and Development* 1, 1–2: 8–19.

Lorentzen, J., P. Møllgaard and M. Rojec (1998) 'Globalisation in emerging markets: does foreign capital in Central Europe promote innovation?', Working Paper no.1–98, Department of Economics, Copenhagen Business School.

Meyer, K.E. (1995) 'Foreign direct investment in the early years of economic transition: a survey', *Economics of Transition* 3(3): 301–20.

Møllgaard, H. P. (1997) 'Danfoss Compressors' investment in Slovenia: motives and obstacles', Working Paper no.7-97, Department of Economics, Copenhagen Business School.

Møllgaard, H. P. and P. Overgaard (1998) 'Temporary partnerships as an information transmission mechanism: foreign investment in emerging markets', Centre for Industrial Economics, University of Copenhagen [mimeo].

Møllgaard, H. P. and P. Schröder (1997) 'A Siemens investment in Slovenia: motives and obstacles', Working Paper No.8-97, Department of Economics, Copenhagen Business School.

Moore, K. (1998) 'How subsidiaries can be more than bit players', *Mastering Global Business*, Part 4, 14–15. Supplement to the *Financial Times* [no date].

Munday, M., J. Morris and B. Wilkinson (1994) 'Factories or warehouses? A Welsh perspective on Japanese transplant manufacturing', *Regional Studies* 29(1): 1–17.

NERA (1991) 'Foreign direct investment to the countries of Central and Eastern Europe', quoted in Lankes and Venables (1996).

Pearce, R. and M. Papanastassiou (1997) 'European markets and the strategic roles of multinational enterprise subsidiaries in the UK', *Journal of Common Market Studies* 35(2): 243–66.

Radosevic, S. (forthcoming) *International Technology Transfer and 'Catching-Up' in Economic Development*, London: Edward Elgar.

Reich, S. (1998) 'Globalization and changing patterns of foreign direct investment: the lessons for Central and Eastern Europe', *Journal of International Relations and Development* 1, 1–2: 358.

Rodríguez-Clare, A. (1996) 'Multinationals, linkages, and economic development', *American Economic Review* 86(4): 852–73.

Rojec, M. (1998) 'The effects of foreign direct investment on restructuring and efficiency upgrading in Slovenia's manufacturing sector', *Journal of International Relations and Development* 1, 1–2: 46–64.

Ruigrok, W., and R. Van Tulder (1995) *The Logic of International Restructuring*, London: Routledge.

Sachs, J. (1995) 'Consolidating capitalism', *Foreign Policy* 98: 50–64.

Strange, S. (1996) *The Retreat of the State*, Cambridge: Cambridge University Press.

Taggart, J. H. (1997) 'Autonomy and procedural justice: a framework for evaluating subsidiary strategy', *Journal of International Business Studies* 28(1): 51–76.

UNCTAD (1993) *World Investment Report 1993*, New York: United Nations.

—— (1995) *World Investment Report 1995*, New York: United Nations.

Wells, Jr, L.T. (1998) 'Multinationals and the developing countries', *Journal of International Business Studies* 29(1): 101–14.

White, R. E. and T. A. Poynter (1984) 'Strategies for foreign-owned subsidiaries in Canada', *Business Quarterly* 48(4): 59–69.

Young, S., N. Hood, and E. Peters (1994) 'Multinational enterprises and regional economic development', *Regional Studies* 28(7): 657-77.

Zysman, J., E. Doherty and A. Schwartz (1997) 'Tales from the "global" economy: cross-national production networks and the reorganization of the European economy', *Structural Change and Economic Dynamics* 8(1): 45–85.

Part IV

Globalisation and inter-governmental and non-governmental organisations

12 Private authority, scholarly legitimacy and political credibility

Think tanks and informal diplomacy

Diane Stone

Introduction

Think tanks are non-state actors that have mobilised expertise to contribute to policy thinking. These organisations are independent policy research institutes but are not simply learned societies. Instead, many act as policy entrepreneurs within both domestic and international policy domains proffering policy advice on cross-national problems of pollution, pandemics, trade and so forth. Furthermore, some institutes contribute to processes of global and regional governance. They supply information and expertise, and encourage consultation and exchange between official and other private actors. Through their scholars, research reports and intellectual advocacy, think tanks provide input to international conferences, the monitoring of international agreements and project development in organisations such as the World Bank. Some provide a venue for 'closed discussions' or a prestigious non-governmental forum for international conferences and visiting dignitaries. Accordingly, the think tank phenomenon warrants greater attention not only because there has been a massive proliferation of these organisations across the globe but because they appear to represent an important component of burgeoning transnational policy elites.

The first section of this chapter outlines the international spread of these organisations and the transnationalisation of their activities. The second section analyses how many think tanks attempt to construct their authority as independent non-state actors by attributing value to their scholarly mission and status as non-profit civil society organisations. The third section addresses the policy relevance of think tanks. Ideas by themselves are rarely persuasive but require individuals and organisations to act entrepreneurially. Through the networks that think tanks seek to participate in, they are brought closer to policy-making fora. Finally, to illustrate one type of governance role that think tanks perform in global and regional affairs, the fourth section focuses on informal diplomacy. Think tanks exercise authority because of the scholarly legitimacy and intellectual expertise they claim, or are perceived, to hold. However, their political credibility and scholarly legitimacy is finely tuned and can be called into question by ideological advocacy and politicisation which undermines their reputation as providers of objective information or neutral expertise.

The worldwide think tank boom

Although well entrenched in the lexicon of politics, the term 'think tank' is slippery. It is applied broadly to a range of organisations undertaking policy related, technical or (social) scientific research and analysis. Such organisations may be independent non-profit organisations, or they may be policy units that operate within government, or yet again, they may be attached to a profit-making corporate entity or a pressure group. This chapter focuses on policy research organisations that are primarily non-profit organisations that act with significant autonomy from other actors. These non-profit think tanks may be created initially by government and then 'spun off' as an independent entity or established by policy entrepreneurs outside the state.

Think tanks are usually categorised as non-governmental organisations (NGOs) or as non-state actors by international relations scholars; and sometimes as civil society organisations by scholars working in the field of democratisation. None of these labels is entirely satisfactory for think tanks. NGO is a 'blanket' term for a vast range of quite different organisations. Unlike most NGOs, think tanks are not membership bodies with extensive roots in civil society and nor do they adopt the strategies generally associated with pressure groups. They often disdain advocacy. More often than not they are elite bodies; some institutes have much in common with university centres and others have close ties to government. Indeed, some are best described as governmentally organised or manipulated NGOs (that is, GONGOs or MANGOs) which posit some qualifications in automatically designating think tanks as civil society organisations. Accordingly, despite being a broader and more diffuse category than NGO, 'non-state actor' is more appropriate in that it is a label that accommodates the absence of a sharp distinction between public and private actors which operate both below and above the level of nation-states.

Private policy institutes were a relatively unusual phenomenon prior to World War Two and limited to a few industrialised democracies. In general, the first generation were few in number, elite in composition, idealistic in motivation and scholarly in style. Foreign policy institutes emerged as increasing interdependence brought about by trade and technological advances along with the crises of war, regional instability and ethnic or nationalistic tensions generated a new interest in knowledge about international affairs. Domestic policy institutes emerged to confront the policy problems concerning rapid industrialisation, urbanisation, poverty and illiteracy. In this early period, the creation and concentration of a pool of expertise in these private organisations was often of comparable quality and sophistication to that found within both government and university departments.

Very few institutes operated on a global or regional level. The Institute for Pacific Relations was exceptional as an international research institute (albeit with autonomous national councils) established in 1925 for the study of the conditions of the Pacific peoples with a view to the improvement of their mutual relations (Woods 1991). For a brief period post-Versailles, the newly established institutes with an interest in defence or foreign policy had tenuous relationships with overseas counterparts (Wallace 1994). In the final days of the British empire, the think tank model was spread to the former colonies. For instance, sister institutes of the Royal Institute of International Affairs (also known as Chatham House) were based in Australia, Canada, New Zealand, and at later dates in India, Nigeria, Trinidad and Tobago. In general, however, policy institutes did not cultivate foreign ties but sought to penetrate domestic policy circles.

The intellectual climate in Europe and North America after and as a consequence of World War Two was very different from the forty years prior to the war. The idealism of many of the foreign policy institutes, often founded on a belief or aspiration that dialogue and discussion would contribute to peace, tolerance and understanding, was counterpoised by the realist understandings and rationalist frameworks of a new breed of strategic studies institutes. To name a few: the RAND Corporation, the Hudson Institute and the Center for Strategic and International Studies in the USA and the International Institute of Strategic Studies (IISS) in Britain. Institutes were often established to address security issues with government backing or military support. The Institute for Defence Studies and Analyses in India, established in 1965, receives most of its funding from the Ministry of Defence. Addressing national security and India's foreign relations, it has been described as 'hawkish' in orientation, a supporter of Indian nuclear capacity and critical of US foreign policy (Chipman 1987: 29).

Development studies institutes and peace research bodies also emerged. The World Peace Council in Finland was created in 1950. Identified with Soviet-bloc priorities until the 1980s, the Council was concerned to promote international peace, the prevention of nuclear war and general disarmament. Similarly, policy institutes addressing domestic policy issues burgeoned in the USA while a creditable number were established in other countries, especially in Britain where think tanks corresponded in style and organisation to those in the USA, and in smaller numbers in Australia and Canada; the large and relatively well-resourced party-connected institutes of Germany and the Netherlands; and government-supported institutes throughout Scandinavia and parts of the developing world. These second generation institutes primarily addressed domestic policy communities.

Since the 1970s, there has been first, a massive proliferation of think tanks worldwide; second, increasing competition, diversity and styles of operation with the emergence of third generation institutes; and third, the transnationalisation of think tanks. It is beyond the scope of this chapter to outline the extent of think tank development around the world. Suffice it to say that it has been propelled by factors such as the break-up of the former Soviet Union, the demise of authoritarian regimes in many Latin American nations, the increasing availability of foundation support and development aid for such organisations and the worldwide phenomenon of 'third sector' associational growth (Salamon, 1994) alongside greater numbers of policy entrepreneurs and intellectuals willing to establish think tanks (see Stone, Denham and Garnett 1998; McGann and Weaver 2000).

As a consequence of the international boom in think tanks, this industry is characterised by increasingly diverse organisational forms and styles. There are significant differences between think tanks that are scholarly in focus and geared towards publication of books and reports such as the Carnegie Endowment for International Peace, compared to think tanks like the Institute for Development Studies in Malaysia that are more activist and engage in grass-roots activity, training and 'people development'. Some institutes – including SIPRI (Stockholm International Peace Research Institute) and the Conference Board of Canada – have substantial resources with large in-house professional staff whereas others are small, with limited budgets and few personnel. Some institutes are technocratic – the Korea Development Institute or *IFO* (Institute for Economic Research) in Germany – whilst others, like the proliferating free market liberal policy institutes in Eastern and Central Europe and Latin America are often more ideological and advocacy oriented. Increased competition in the think tank industry has encouraged specialisation; that is, environmental think tanks (*Instituut voor Europees Milieubeleid* in Arnhem), institutes focused on tax policy (Institute of Fiscal Studies in Britain) or a specific region or community (*Groupement d'Etudes et de Recherches sur la Mediterranée* in Morocco). Another tendency has been an increased propensity for policy advocacy and the politicisation of research and analysis, most particularly in the USA.

A further trend since the late 1980s has been the growing number of think tanks operating beyond their home states. The Trilateral Commission and the Institute of South East Asian Studies (ISEAS) in Singapore are perhaps two of the oldest extant examples of an international and a regional think tank but other think tanks are transnationalising their activities (see Stone 2000). For example, the Tocqueville Foundation was incorporated in the USA in 1985 but is based in Brussels and promotes free market ideas in French speaking countries. Some American institutes have opened offices abroad; the Heritage Foundation in Hong Kong and the Urban Institute in Russia. The increasing pace of European Union activity has seen the emergence of regional institutes which do not adhere to any specific national identity: the Centre for A New Europe and the European Policy Centre, both in Brussels, and the Research Institute for European Studies in Greece. International research collaboration and interaction has become extensive and is reflected in the web-sites and Internet directories of think tanks. Formal international networks of think tanks are more common. The Institute for African Alternatives was established in London in 1986 with a network of branches in Nigeria, South Africa, Tanzania, Senegal, Zimbabwe. Similarly, the *Instituut voor Europees Milieubeleid* is formally linked to environmental institutes in four other European nations.

Think tanks are also being pushed into global and regional fora by the expansion of international agendas and the range of trans-border policy problems. Think tanks established to address domestic policy issues are adopting broader research agendas in recognition of compromised state sovereignty. Furthermore, just as academic groups, professional associations and policy communities become transnational, so think tanks are carried along by the same dynamics. There are significant sources of demand at global and regional levels for think tank services. International organisations such as the United Nations or the World Bank are contracting think tanks to provide expert evaluations of their programmes. Other non-state actors – business associations as well as advocacy groups such as Greenpeace or Amnesty International – find the substantive analytic work undertaken by think tanks useful in bolstering policy recommendations and normative positions. Many development or human rights NGOs do not have the resources, in-house expertise or access to data to substantiate arguments opposing government or corporate positions, or to develop policy alternatives. Think tanks are specialised organisations supplying such argumentation. Accordingly, think tank transnationalisation has paralleled developments in their social, political and intellectual environment.

These developments are matched by a proclivity of think tank entrepreneurs to initiate international think tank meetings to exchange views on policy issues or management concerns. The Atlas Foundation organises an annual international conference for free market policy institutes to help promote their spread and consolidation. 'Global ThinkNet' is an *ad hoc* elite gathering of the heads of the world's largest and most prestigious think tanks to discuss ways of influencing policies. The World Bank in 1998 sponsored a number of regional and international meetings of think tank executives as part of its broader agenda of promoting 'knowledge development'. These factors have helped create a transnational community of think tank experts. These experts interact in think tank networks but also in other transnational policy networks.

There are constraints that prevent many think tanks becoming global actors. Many organisations do not seek to interact at a global or regional level but direct their research and analysis to domestic constituencies in government departments, business groups or other national and local bodies. Other constraints concern resources. The majority of think tanks around the world are very small operations and do not have the funds to devote to networking at a global or regional level. This kind of activity also requires leadership skills and vision as well as expert personnel to carry forward the organisation into these new fora. Accordingly, the ability of think tanks to interact at global levels is also a function of size and command over material and ideational resources. This does not mean that smaller or lesser known institutes are of no consequence. They analyse and articulate policy positions, and act as a 'sounding board' for new ideas for policy-makers. Furthermore, they provide services such as ethics training to government employees involved in international affairs. They are essential in broader social processes that educate the 'attentive' or 'educated' public in the downward or domestic flow of information. Similarly, they perform an informal service of leadership recruitment of new generations of policy experts. However, they tend to lack the size, stature, recognised experts and funding of institutes in the global realm. Even those think tanks that have acquired a high international profile still speak to local and national audiences. Institutes engage in a multi-level effort to secure their policy relevance and organisational survival and expansion.

Whilst the global expansion and diversification of think tanks has contributed to an increasingly diverse and plural NGO community it has also created new hierarchies. The internationally prominent institutes tend to be Western organisations, or at least, those institutes based in OECD countries. Asian, Latin American or African institutes may acquire regional stature but few gain the global reputation of the Brookings Institution, SIPRI or the Trilateral Commission. Partly, this is due to the longer history of the think tank in Western political systems as well as their superior resources, whether it be funding, professional personnel or entrée to transnational policy networks. Yet, these Western think tanks are often regarded by think tanks in the 'south', as well as by their home governments, as disseminating ideas or norms that bolster the prevailing liberal hegemonic order of free market economies and liberal democratic polities. From such vantage, certain think tanks are viewed as one organisational component of a transnational grouping of global norm-setting elites (Kowalewski 1997).

Private authority and scholarly legitimacy

The authority and legitimacy for think tank involvement in global affairs is not naturally given but has been cultivated and groomed through various management practices and intellectual activities. The private authority of think tanks rests in large degree with their establishment as non-profit organisations or charities. Think tank managers can argue on the one hand that they are not compromised by the need to generate profits in tailoring the policy analysis to the needs of clients, and on the other hand, that they have independence or autonomy from bureaucracies and political leaders. Another strategy to enhance their legitimacy is rhetorical resort to the professional and scientific norms of scholarly discovery and intellectual investigation. Think tanks set themselves apart from other non-state actors as independent knowledge organisations, and often cultivate a reified image as public-minded civil society organisations untainted by connection to vested interest or political power. Such authority and legitimacy is a necessary component in effectively diffusing ideas and propelling them into official domains.

The non-profit form of most think tanks is advantageous. The non-profit label 'is a signal of trust' (Kingma 1997: 144). According to 'trust theory', one reason non-profit organisations are created is to provide goods – such as health care, education or day care – which consumers do not trust profit-making organisations to provide in sufficient quality or quantity because of information asymmetries. As they do not seek to maximise profits, these organisations are supposedly more trusted as altruistic entities. The non-profit status of most think tanks confers social status; they acquire an image of charitable endeavour. Think tanks are presented as public interest organisations producing information and analysis as a public good. They are often founded and staffed by committed individuals or by scientific experts and social scientists who subscribe to professional codes and epistemic values. Accordingly, the non-profit status and intellectual standing of an institute is an important source of its authority.

Related to their non-profit status, many think tanks adopt the rhetoric of being civil society organisations. That is, that they contribute to the enhancement of a tolerant, plural, educated and democratic citizenry. Think tanks provide services and perspectives needed by the public that are not produced by either the state or the market. Not only do policy research institutes supposedly provide a distinctive service in raising the standard of debate or broadening the agenda but they can present the views of minority groups. It is not unusual to see think tanks adopt the mantle of protectors of the principles and philosophies underlying democratic societies. Furthermore, it is often in their interests to do so, especially when seeking grants or aid from foundations or foreign donor agencies keen to promote civil society development.

Yet, it is the think tank image as relatively objective knowledge actors that is perhaps their most significant source of authority. They have social status as expert, research and analysis organisations. In general, think tanks distinguish themselves from bodies such as Greenpeace and Amnesty International which are relatively high profile activist organisations engaged in lobbying, pressure tactics and advocacy of norms. By contrast think tanks are *usually* perceived as more scholarly, dispassionate and scientific and the analysis emanating from them is often *assumed* to be based on expert knowledge. Attributed as public-spirited and with a steadfast commitment to independence, objectivity and scholarly enterprise bestows authority on think tanks in a dynamic that also boosts the reputations of the individuals associated with it. These groups (and often the media in its quest for expert commentary) legitimate their members as 'serious' and 'expert' persons capable of public service, dispassionate judgement and selfless pursuit of the general interest.

In some cases, however, the think tank scholarly 'aura' and independence may be misleading. Think tanks cast themselves above politics and profit, but in reality ideas become harnessed to political and economic interests. Expertise has been politicised by interest groups and NGOs and used as ammunition in partisan policy battles (Rich and Weaver, 1998). Furthermore, the ideological character of many new think tanks and management practices that emphasise advocacy, attracting media attention and political commentary rather than solid policy analysis and adherence to the norms of social science undermines the reputation of all institutes for balanced, impartial and highly credible research and analysis.

Nevertheless, to maintain their reputation and repudiate accusations of politicisation, advocacy and lobbying or ideological polemic, think tank managers often encourage engagement with academic communities. Those institutes that are most highly regarded tend also to be the institutes that have long-standing interaction with universities and scientific establishments, and participate in academic peer review processes. In short, many individuals associated with think tanks adopt the professional norms associated with academia to secure scholarly legitimacy. Indeed, there is often a considerable degree of mobility between think tanks and university departments. For example, the Tasman Institute in Australia has a formal affiliation with Melbourne University and the Director of this Institute teaches in the Economics Department. Furthermore, institutes are a means to incorporate the perspectives of practitioners – former military personnel, government officials or NGO leaders who would not easily qualify for appointment to a university – in scholarly developments. In general, most think tanks attempt to provide a forum which links the academic world with decision-making domains.

The research of leading institutes is in some ways analogous to that in universities. Furthermore, the publications of bodies such as Brookings, SIPRI, ISEAS and Chatham House are often to be found on student reading lists in social science subjects whilst RAND has its own doctoral programme. Many think tanks produce journals which are often found in university libraries. The academic standing of these publications is cultivated through refereeing not only to protect a think tank's independent standing but also to attract academic contributors. Other institutes also offer the equivalent of post-doctoral fellowships for younger scholars. Some institutes are able to compete with traditional university centres for public research funds. For example, the scholarly status of IISS in London was more widely recognised when the Economic and Social Research Council awarded IISS stewardship of the Pacific-Asia Programme. However, think tanks are not engaged in purely academic study of international relations but are focused on policy-driven questions. As such, they occupy a political and cultural space between academia and government. Whilst the scholarly credentials of many think tanks boost their authority as non-state actors, this does not equate with policy relevance. Scholarly interest in ideas, publication and seminars is not sufficient to see think tank ideas and policy recommendations adopted and institutionalised. Think tanks need to form alliances and build coalitions with representatives from state and international organisations as well as with other non-state actors.

Political credibility, policy relevance and networks of influence

As they are usually recognised authorities in their field of expertise, think tank experts can provide a range of services for official consumers such as informed judgements and analysis of existing programmes as well as acting as independent agents monitoring progress on adherence to international treaties and agreements. The North-South Institute in Canada provides a good example of the kinds of interaction that think tanks can develop with international organisations and government agencies. Two years after its founding in 1976, one of the Institute's first cooperative projects was to co-host an international conference with the World Bank. In 1985, former Canadian Prime Minister Brian Mulroney appointed the Institute's Director, Bernard Wood, as his personal representative on a fact-finding mission to Southern Africa. During 1986, Institute staff testified before the Special Joint Committee on Canada's trade relations in the Asia-Pacific, and in 1989 appeared before committees of the House of Commons to discuss the Brady Plan for the global debt crisis. Finally, the Institute has a long-standing cooperative relationship with the Canadian International Development Agency.

On other occasions, think tanks aspire to provide intellectual leadership in policy communities. In the words of the President of the Carnegie Council on Ethics and International Affairs, Joel Rosenthal:

> The Carnegie Council does not preach. Rather we provoke. We provoke substantive discussion on urgent issues of international concern, and we do

so in ways that will be constructive to all those who believe, as we do, that ideas matter. We also provide leadership by shaping debates and setting out challenging intellectual agendas. Perhaps most important, we provide a home for all who are interested in this work, including those from government, business, media and the academic community.

(*Ethics and International Affairs Newsletter*, Spring 1998)

These organisations are not weighed down by the bureaucratic weight of government agencies. Consequently, they have a capacity for direct action and immediacy not always available to official agencies in mobilising intellectual resources via conferences, study groups and research networks. However, the impact of these organisations on the global order is not subject to ease of analysis. It is extremely difficult to find examples of think tank research having an independent impact. Establishing a causal nexus between think tank policy research or norm-promotion and the establishment of new regimes or institutions is fraught with methodological problems. The agenda-setting capacity of a think tank (if any) is intangible. One example would be the civilian strategists found centring around RAND which influenced Pentagon thinking on nuclear deterrence in the late 1950s and 1960s (Gray 1971). However, this was a time-specific example of a think tank acting as the organisational centre of an influential epistemic community (Adler 1992). Most of the time, think tanks do not have extensive paradigmatic influence over official thinking. If it is used at all, think tank analysis may only be adopted by decision-makers to help legitimate policy positions by reference to so-called 'independent' policy analysis.

Whilst there are limits to influence, there also numerous opportunities for think tanks. These organisations are routinely used by political leaders to announce foreign policy initiatives or to clarify policy positions. For example, most American Presidents and a host of distinguished international leaders have delivered presentations at the Council on Foreign Relations in New York. Other foreign policy institutes such as the *Institut Français des Relations Internationales* in Paris, and the Polish Institute of International Affairs perform similar roles organising seminars and closed discussions as well as hosting foreign delegations. Ministries and international organisations occasionally prefer dealing with a think tank rather than with NGOs active on a particular issue. Sometimes NGOs are deemed to be arrogant, demanding and intransigent in policy consultations. Because of their professional image and scholarly aspirations, think tanks are viewed as a more benign or cooperative alternative when compared to the relatively more critical stance and occasionally disruptive lobbying adopted by many NGOs. Accordingly, a few think tanks have built stable relationships with official actors. Think tanks get access to information and entry to official policy communities while state agencies can legitimise their policy position by arguing that they are interacting with and consulting independent or neutral civil society organisations. These interactions raise the issue of think tank independence and questions of capture and cooption. If think tanks, or other organisations, are state sponsored and coopted, they are no longer recognisable as civil organisations. Instead, they become MANGOs if they are not already GONGOs. The distinctions between state and non-state actors become blurred.

Nevertheless, the network arrangements and strategic alliances that link think tanks to other global actors are a key component in their power to influence policy agendas. Networks enable think tanks to operate beyond their domestic context and networks are the means by which think tanks individually and in coalition can project their ideas into policy thinking across states and within global or regional fora. However, think tanks are involved in different kinds of networks. These can range from non-political cross-national research collaboration with academics, foundations and scientific associations as well as formal partnership with various community groups, schools and so forth to provide educational resources or training. Policy networks also differ in composition, tactics and style. Accordingly, think tanks can be incorporated into official policy communities (such as represented by informal diplomacy), participate in broad 'transnational advocacy coalitions' (Keck and Sikkink 1997) that accommodate a range of NGOs and activists; or they can be incorporated in the more elite 'epistemic communities' (Stone 1996) which are primarily composed of knowledge actors. In short, think tanks are immersed in multi-layered networks characterised by dense exchanges of information, personnel and funding.

Informal diplomacy

As noted, think tank social status as independent, expert organisations bestows intellectual authority and scholarly legitimacy. Consequently, select think tanks are often deemed within official circles to represent a respectable forum to stage events for visiting diplomats. Furthermore, they can act as intermediaries or brokers between policy actors because of their image of neutrality, objectivity and non-partisanship relative to other organisations. This 'informal diplomacy' is an important factor in explaining the increasing visibility of think tanks in global fora. This kind of diplomacy entails activities or discussions involving academics and intellectuals, journalists, business elites and others as well as government officials and political leaders 'acting in their private capacity'. The suggestion that bureaucrats and politicians are acting in their private capacity is to be treated as a 'polite fiction'. Various official and non-governmental participation in seminars, conferences and organisations is 'mixed' or 'blended' suggesting that the demarcation between official and unofficial involvement is unclear. Informal diplomacy is a useful mode of negotiation in circumstances such as, for example, where new international or regional arrangements are being flagged, requiring coordination, information, analysis and discussion (Hocking 1996). Informal 'track-two' dialogues are also valuable at times when, for whatever reason, official dialogues are stalled or official relations strained.

Relatively few think tanks achieve the incorporation into decision-making processes which informal diplomacy represents. It often involves a high degree of trust whereby think tanks are unofficially encouraged to take the initiative in overcoming communication lapses by starting dialogues. They provide 'a middle ground' where new forms of cooperation or approaches to regional conflicts can be explored 'in an off-the-record setting'. For example, the Argentinean Council for International Relations and the Chilean Council for International relations played an important role in ameliorating tensions over the Chilean-Argentine border (Sherwood Truit 1998: 15). Such an activity is useful to governments if the think tank is a prominent organisation, of which foreigners have heard, and more importantly, if it can draw upon a network of distinguished statespeople, business leaders, diplomats, military officers, and scholars. It is, however, rare to see NGOs included in discussions that involve sensitive issues. Furthermore, officials are often only willing to patronise track-two dialogues on the implicit understanding that think tanks 'screen' the non-state participants. The price of political credibility is often conformity to official considerations and closure to outside groups.

The London-based IISS is one organisation that has played an early leadership role in think tank track-two activity in the post-Second World War era. For example:

> After a series of false starts over the past eighteen months, the IISS finally arranged a track-two meeting with North Koreans in April. Given the Institute's close relationship with South Korea, and its long-standing work on regional security issues in North-east Asia, the IISS felt it necessary to establish contacts with North Korea. Because of its leading role in the European Council for Security and Co-operation in the Asia-Pacific (ECSCAP), the Institute was especially anxious to help draw North Koreans into new forms of dialogue about regional issues. It was therefore delighted to receive a small delegation, notionally from the Institute of International Affairs in Pyongyang, but in practice from the Foreign Ministry.
>
> The delegation was led by the Director of the Europe Department of the North Korean Foreign Ministry Mr Chun Guk Kim, and the main purpose of the meeting was to explore possibilities for improving European relations with North Korea. . . . The main events of the visit were two meetings at the IISS. These took place under the rules of strict confidentiality so essential to the track-two process, and included officials from various European governments and journalists in their private capacities.
>
> (*IISS Newsletter*, Summer 1996: 8)

Through think tanks, informal channels of communication remain open and can be utilised as and when necessary by governments. However, the value and impact of track-two activity is not clear. On the negative side, governments can use the track-two process and think tanks for the purposes of public symbolism. Realists, for instance, are likely to argue that think tank fora are no more than 'talking shops'. At worst, the various think tank gatherings may offer little more than an amenable social and intellectual exercise for participants. If this were the case, however, such arrangements would not persist. Instead, the pace of informal dialogues has accelerated.

Think tanks represent neutral ground and can provide a private venue for closed meetings, but at the same time, informal diplomacy allows think tanks to facilitate the flow of policy information. When operating at a domestic level, think tanks facilitate the downward flow from national decision-makers and foreign policy elites to local levels of decision-making, as well as to the 'educated public'. When operating at global or regional levels, think tanks facilitate the horizontal flow of information between transnational policy elites as well as to other non-state actors. It encourages the development of common or shared understandings of policy problems or tension, and consensus-building. For example, the EuroMeSCo network of policy institutes parallels the EuroMediteranean Partnership process, complementing the Euro-Med ministerial meetings with intellectual interaction and 'unconstrained brain storming' to nurture 'mutual understanding and respect' beyond the official level amongst the wider community (*EuroMeSCo News*, September 1997). The benefits of such 'track-two' dialogues are often intangible but occasionally, as in South East Asia, the outcomes of informal diplomacy are substantive.

The Association of South East Asian Nations' Institutes for Strategic and International Studies (ASEAN-ISIS) was an important research and policy network establishing political support for new ideas about security in the region, and central in the initiation of a new multilateral forum, the ASEAN Regional Forum. Founded in 1988 by five institutes, ASEAN-ISIS sought to strengthen and increase regional cooperation in the development of research on strategic and international problems and issues in ASEAN countries and intensify communication between and coordination among members of the Association. The Association built a set of processes to discuss security issues on a multilateral basis and as such, the 'ASEAN-ISIS initiative was somewhat ahead of the official position' (Kerr 1994: 403). The role played by the ASEAN-ISIS was that of policy entrepreneur in which it was very effective as all the national institutes possessed a route of formal access to policy-makers as well as strong informal connections to political leaders.

The Council for Security Cooperation in Asia Pacific (CSCAP) has since been created to help coordinate track-two activities in the region and is also characterised by a high degree of think tank involvement (Evans 1994). This involves both improved communication among like minded states as well as more ambitious objectives of instituting 'cooperative security approaches' that transcend ideological divisions and existing alliance structures. It provides a more structured process for regional confidence building. CSCAP 'aims to be one step ahead of governments by sponsoring dialogues on sensitive issues (that officials may prefer to avoid), conducting technical studies' and to 'provide a mechanism for linkage and mutual support between the second track and official regional cooperation processes' (Ball quoted in Khong 1995: 52). Like ASEAN-ISIS, CSCAP performs an intangible function of building a history among participants encouraging loyalty and a common identity.

These dialogue venues are characterised by informality, personal relationships, consensus-building and have been important in generating trust and respect among participants through a 'habit of dialogue'. In short, 'talking-shops' such as CSCAP or EuroMeSCo facilitate social learning. Think tanks help socialise specific norms such as those associated with security cooperation but have also been one set of actors engaged in broader processes to define and refine collective identity. However, as ideas of security cooperation have coalesced into a new institution – the ASEAN Regional Forum – the agenda-setting impact of informal dialogue conducted through regional think tanks is likely to diminish. In the case of the Regional Forum, a policy community emerged in which political and economic interests became dominant rather than the looser network arrangements of think tanks. Furthermore, informal diplomacy can be undermined by other events, such as the unfolding Asian economic crisis or the persistence of fundamental conflict amongst many of the Southern Mediterranean countries of EuroMeSCo.

Conclusion

The preceding discussion may give the impression that think tanks are important non-state actors. This is not usually the case. Few think tanks make key contributions to decision-making in global or regional fora, or exert paradigmatic influence over policy thinking. Instead it is more appropriate to view them as cogs in the machineries of governance. Furthermore, it is dangerous to generalise about think tank influence given the vast differences in size and resources of think tanks and the range of activity in which they are engaged. However, this is not to suggest that these organisations are without authority, legitimacy or influence.

Think tanks appropriate authority first on the basis of their scholarly credentials as quasi-academic organisations focused on the rigorous and professional analysis of policy issues; and second, their establishment as non-profit organisations independent from both the state and market that strengthens their reputation as civil society organisations beholden neither to the interests of market nor the state. These endowments give think tanks some legitimacy in seeking to intervene with knowledge and advice into global and regional policy processes. This image is reinforced by the public relations efforts of these organisations as well as the media exposure of the leading institutes. Think tanks are frequently perceived by publics, bureaucracies and other political actors as having scholarly status and intellectual authority in providing expert opinion and analysis. It is another matter, however, whether such analysis is incorporated into policy or negotiations. Furthermore, think tank research and reports do not escape challenges or criticism from other knowledge actors, whilst they may be ignored or patronised at will by governments, corporations and international organisations.

Nevertheless, although think tanks are not really part of those actors which share authority in the global system (see introduction of this book), these organisations acquire political credibility by performing services for states and for other non-state actors. Think tanks respond to demand for high quality and reputable research and analysis, ideas and argumentation. They also contribute to governance and institution building by facilitating exchange between official and other private actors via informal diplomacy. In general, think tank activity in the global system tends to be based on a complex interweaving of network interactions. Sometimes, these are loose, *ad hoc* relationships with other like-minded policy institutes, NGOs, university centres and government agencies, in a given issue area to exchange information, ideas and keep abreast of developments. At other times, think tanks act as policy entrepreneurs within tighter networks such as an epistemic community. Networks are important to think tanks both in embedding them in a relationship with more powerful actors, and in increasing their audience or constituency, thereby potentially amplifying their impact. However, such relationships also pull think tanks towards advocacy and ideological polemic or partisanship and politicisation. Too close an affinity with government, a political party, or NGOs can seriously undermine their authority and legitimacy as objective (or at least balanced) knowledge providers, and potentially dissolve important distinctions between the research institute and advocacy group.

Note

Research for this paper was supported by the award of a Fellowship from the Economic and Social Research Council (ref. no.: H52427008094).

References

Adler, Emanuel (1992) 'The emergence of cooperation: national epistemic communities and the international evolution of the idea of arms control', *International Organization* 46(1): 101–45.

Chipman, John (1987) *Survey of International Relations Institutes in the Developing World*, London, International Institute for Strategic Studies.

Day, Alan. J. (1993) *Think Tanks: An International Directory*, Essex: Longman Group.

EuroMeSCo News, September 1997.

Evans, Paul (1994) 'Building security: the Council for Security Cooperation in the Asia Pacific (CSCAP)' *Pacific Review* 7(2): 125–39.

Gray, Colin (1971) 'What RAND hath wrought', *Foreign Policy* 7: 111–29.

Hocking, Brian (1996) 'The woods and the trees: catalytic diplomacy and Canada's trials as a "forestry superpower"', *Environmental Politics* 5 (3 Autumn): 448–75.

Keck, Margaret and Kathryn Sikkink (1998) *Transnational Issue Networks in International Politics*, Ithaca: Cornell University Press.

Kerr, Pauline (1994) 'The security dialogue in the Asia-Pacific', *Pacific Review* 7(4): 397–409

Khong, Yuen Foong (1995) 'Evolving regional security and economic institutions', *Southeast Asian Affairs 1995*, Singapore, Institute of Southeast Asian Studies.

Kingma, Bruce (1997) 'Public good theories of the non-profit sector: Weisbrod revisited', *Voluntas* 8(2): 135–48.

Kowalwski, D. (1997) *Global Establishment: the Political Economy of North/Asian Networks*, Basingstoke: Macmillan.

McGann, Jim and Weaver, R. Kent (eds) (2000) *Think Tanks and Civil Societies: Catalysts for Ideas and Action*, Washington, D.C.: Brookings Institution and the World Bank.

Rich, Andrew and R. Kent Weaver, (1998) 'Advocates and analysts: think tanks and the politicization of expertise', in Alan J. Cigler and Burdette Looumis (eds) *Interest Group Politics* (fifth edition), Congressional Quarterly Press: 235–53.

Salamon, L. M. (1994) 'The rise of the non-profit sector', *Foreign Affairs* 73: 109–18.

Sherwood Truitt, Nancy (1998) 'Think tanks in Latin America', paper presented to the Conference on Think Tanks and Civil Societies: Catalysts for Ideas and Action, Economic Development Institute of the World Bank, Barcelona, 29 June – 1 July 1998.

Stone, Diane (2000) 'The policy roles of think tanks in global governance', in Karsten Ronit and Volker Schneider (eds) *Private Organisations, Governance and Global Politics*, London: Routledge, forthcoming.

Stone, Diane (1996) *Capturing the Political Imagination: Think Tanks and the Policy Process*, London: Frank Cass.

Stone, Diane, Andrew Denham and Mark Garnett (eds) (1998) *Think Tanks Across Nations: A Comparative Approach*, Manchester: Manchester University Press.

Wallace, William (1994) 'Between two worlds: think tanks and foreign policy', in C. Hill and P. Beshoff (eds) *Two Worlds of International Relations: Academics, Practitioners and the Trade in Ideas*, London: Routledge and London School of Economics: 139–63.

Woods, Lawrence T. (1991) 'Non-governmental organizations and Pacific cooperation: back to the future?', *Pacific Review* 4(4): 312–21.

13 International trade rules and states

Enhanced authority for the WTO?

Gilbert Gagné

Introduction

The role of non-state actors and authority in a globalising system deserves to be studied carefully. Ever-increasing socio-economic interdependence implies greater competition among states and firms, which in turn leads almost inevitably to an increased potential for conflicts. Among non-state actors on the international scene, traditional intergovernmental institutions and regimes are called to play a leading role in ensuring the conditions for a mutually beneficial global system, as they provide the rules which preside over international exchanges as well as a forum for the settlement of disputes between states.

Yet a fundamental question which comes to mind is whether such institutions have the necessary authority to arbitrate (growing) conflicts and clashes of interests between states. With a view to responding more adequately to such issues and challenges in the field of international trade, a World Trade Organisation (WTO), superseding the General Agreement on Tariffs and Trade (GATT), was established in 1995 and provided with broader and more stringent rules, notably with regard to the settlement of disputes.

This paper revolves around three main related issues. The first is the ability of the newly established WTO and its strengthened dispute settlement provisions to ensure the conditions for a smooth functioning of the world trading regime. Another crucial issue concerns state compliance with international rules, and the attitude of major powers, most especially the United States, towards the WTO and actions with which the US may disagree. Finally, the impact of globalisation on nations is to be considered in the light of states', mostly US, attitude towards the international trading regime.

This paper argues that the advent of the WTO and strengthened dispute procedures enhance the authority of such an international institution to preside over world trade and tackle potential conflicts among states. Even though state cooperation, and notably that of powerful ones, remains essential to ensure the viability of international rules, the WTO's and the Uruguay Round's extensive provisions are both eloquent testimonies to states' commitments and to the legitimacy of those provisions. These factors, coupled with the ever-increasing impact of the globalisation process, both concur to make it constantly harder for states, both in economic and political terms, not to observe international trade obligations.

The structure of this paper is as follows. First, I will discuss the GATT, the WTO, and the dispute settlement procedures, pointing the relevant rules. Second, I will turn to some basic considerations on international provisions and compliance by states with those provisions. Third, I will consider the attitude of major powers towards the WTO, essentially that of the United States, reviewing elements as to US stances *vis-à-vis* the world trading system. Fourth, I will stress the impact of globalisation in the light of US attitude towards international rules. Finally, I will conclude on WTO's authority over the international trading system.

The GATT/WTO and dispute settlement procedures

The GATT and the WTO

The GATT, now superseded by the WTO, has constituted the main international organisation established to promote order and cooperation in world trade relations. It is the only institution which provides a worldwide system of rules – of rights and duties voluntarily accepted by its signatories – governing international trade. Around 90 per cent of world trade today takes place within this single set of rules.

The GATT at its inception in 1948 comprised twenty-three state signatories, whereas the WTO counted, as of May 1998, 132 member states and some thirty-one states seeking accession, including Russia and China. Hence, with its effective coverage of more than 130 nations, with a number of other countries showing interest in the WTO, and with the remainder of the world's states indirectly affected through its most-favoured-nation rule, the WTO clearly represents the central institutional basis of the present world trading system.

The world trading regime has been extended over the years, principally as a result of successive 'rounds' of multilateral trade negotiations. The eighth and latest of such rounds, the Uruguay Round, was launched in September 1986 and concluded in December 1993. The Final Act of the Uruguay Round was signed in April 1994 and, following submissions to national governments for formal approval, entered into force on 1 January 1995. It was the most comprehensive ever trade round, some would indeed say the largest and most complex negotiation ever. The results of the Uruguay Round include detailed schedules of tariff reductions, and subjects as diverse as anti-dumping, subsidies, technical standards, customs valuation and agricultural trade, the latter of which proved the main stumbling block in the negotiations. The Uruguay Round has also brought new areas into the ambit of world trade rules, namely, services, trade-related investments and intellectual property. Comprised in the Round agreements are two main institutional measures: the Charter for a WTO, and a new set of dispute settlement procedures, both designed to assist in the effective implementation of the substantive provisions agreed as a result of the Uruguay Round.

If succeeding GATT rounds significantly expanded the scope of international trade rules, the Uruguay Round has been the only such negotiation to strengthen the institutional foundation of the world trading system. The 1947 GATT Geneva negotiation led to a 'Protocol of Provisional Application', awaiting the Havana Charter as the basis of the proposed International Trade Organisation (ITO) which never came into being. It was the Final Act of the Uruguay Round which transformed the GATT into a permanent international institution, the WTO, responsible for the conduct of trade relations among its members. The 'Agreement Establishing the World Trade Organization' can best be described as a mini-charter.[1] The text of the WTO Charter itself does not include substantive rules, but rather establishes a legal framework which ties together the various trade pacts negotiated under the GATT. Hence, most of the provisions of the WTO Agreement involve institutional and procedural rules governing the activities of the organisation.

The WTO consists of a single institutional framework encompassing the GATT, as modified by the Uruguay negotiation, all agreements and arrangements concluded under its auspices, and the complete results of the Uruguay Round. It is headed by a Ministerial Conference meeting once every two years, while a General Council oversees the operations of the organisation and its ministerial decisions, and acts as a dispute settlement body and a trade policy review mechanism. The General Council counts three subsidiary bodies: a Council for Trade in Goods, a Council for Trade in Services, and a Council for the trade-related aspects of intellectual property rights. Such a framework is designed to ensure a single undertaking approach to the results of the Uruguay Round. In contrast to GATT previous practice, WTO members must accept all the results of the Round. There are still two plurilateral agreements, relating to government procurement and civil aircraft, whose membership remains optional, two others on dairy products and bovine meat having been terminated at the end of 1997.[2]

The evolution of GATT dispute settlement

An important part of the GATT/WTO framework consists of its provisions for consultation, conciliation and dispute settlement, as contained in Articles XXII and XXIII of the GATT. States are required to consult with other member governments, particularly when one government feels that benefits due to it under GATT are being 'nullified or impaired' by the conduct of another. In case bilateral consultations fail to settle a problem, GATT/WTO may offer its good offices and act as a conciliator. Should the dispute still not be resolved, dispute settlement procedures come into play under which a panel of three neutral experts examines the factual and legal aspects of the conflict, helps the disputants find a solution acceptable to both sides, and if no such solution can be reached, makes findings and recommendations for adoption by the GATT/WTO Council.

Panel reports, as for virtually all measures in GATT, were adopted by consensus, that is, when they did not raise objections from any state. This was the GATT 'consensus approach' or practice. When the reports were adopted, in case the recommendations were not carried out, the Council could, as a last resort, authorise retaliation by allowing the impaired party to withdraw trade concessions to the offending member. However, in practice, cases were settled before that point was reached.[3] If the GATT process of dispute settlement were initially a relatively informal one, as time went on, it evolved more towards a 'rule oriented' system, and gradually developed not only procedural but substantive legal concepts. It became more formal with the use of objective third party panels from the late 1950s. Before that, disputes had been considered in broader working parties comprised of government representatives.

The GATT 'contracting parties' came to utilise the panel process more and more. Panels were established well over 100 times during GATT history, and, by the end of the Uruguay Round, more frequently than ever before. Many countries, including the United States which had been the largest single applicant for dispute settlement procedures in GATT, found it useful to take issues to panels as part of their broader approach to trade diplomacy. Increasingly, panel reports focused on more precise and concrete questions of 'violations' of treaty obligations. At the end of the Tokyo Round in 1979 an understanding on dispute settlement was adopted which embraced some of these concepts and embodied dispute settlement procedures which had developed during the previous decades (Jackson 1995: 19–20).[4]

The Uruguay Round negotiations sought to remedy the main problems in the dispute settlement procedures which had plagued the GATT system, notably delays in the establishment of a panel and in the conclusion of dispute panel proceedings, the ability of disputants to block the consensus needed to approve panel recommendations and authorise retaliation, and the difficulty in securing compliance with GATT rulings.

Reforms adopted at the mid-term review of the Uruguay Round, which became effective in 1989, established notably a new optional arbitration procedure whereby disputing parties could agree to abide by the arbitration award, and confirmed the authority of the GATT Director-General to form a panel when the parties to a dispute could not agree on its composition. As a result, there has been greater automaticity in decisions on the establishment, terms of reference, and composition of panels, so that such decisions have no longer been dependent on the consent of disputing parties. There has also been a provision whereby a panel procedure must be completed within nine months. However, as to the all-important question of Council adoption of panel reports, the possibility for a losing party to block consensus has continued (GATT 1989: 61–7).

The WTO dispute settlement understanding

In the Final Act of the Uruguay Round, the Dispute Settlement Understanding (DSU) provides for an integrated mechanism to settle disputes under all trade agreements covered by the WTO (Article 1 and Appendix 1 of the DSU).[5] Authority is exercised by the WTO Council acting as a Dispute Settlement Body (DSB). The new mechanism extends the greater automaticity agreed in the 1988 mid-term review to the whole decision-making process, including the adoption of panel reports, and strict time limits are set out. It also institutes a new standing Appellate Body, to review panel rulings, as well as new procedures to ensure compliance with WTO decisions, including the monitoring of compliance actions and automatic retaliation in case of non-compliance.

Of fundamental significance are new rules which remove, at US insistence, the ability of any one state to block the adoption of a panel or Appellate Body report. Such a report is automatically adopted unless the DSB decides by unanimous consensus against adoption (Articles 16 and 17:14).[6] This is referred to as the reverse consensus rule and represents a complete shift from previous practice when a single member state (often the losing party in a dispute) could prevent the adoption of a panel report and then any possibility of action for GATT.

The whole dispute process should not take more than twenty months, from the time of a request for consultations to the authorisation of counter-measures in case of non-compliance, and less if the panel decision is not appealed. The process is more expeditious in the case of certain issues, such as subsidies and countervailing measures, where the time allotted for the conclusion of a panel review is shorter than for other WTO disputes.

Under existing provisions in GATT Article XXIII, the DSU can adjudicate disputes involving measures which nullify or impair benefits accruing to a WTO member, but do not violate any provision of the WTO agreements. In such 'non-violation' cases, a panel report cannot require the withdrawal of the disputed measure, but instead makes a non-binding recommendation as to a mutually satisfactory adjustment of the dispute (Article 26: 1).

If panel recommendations, which may be approved or modified as a result of an appeal, have not been fully implemented within a reasonable period of time (agreed to by the disputants or imposed by an arbitrator), and subsequently no satisfactory compensation has been agreed, the complaining party could retaliate by suspending the application of WTO obligations to the offending state (Article 22:2).[7] Here again, under the new reverse consensus rule, retaliation is automatically authorised unless the DSB decides by consensus against such action (Article 22:6). Under the previous rule, where the application (as against now the non-application) of sanctions had to be approved by the Council, GATT authorised retaliatory measures only once, in 1952, and in that case, which involved dairy quotas, the target country, the United States, essentially gave consent to the counter-measures meted out in the form of a quota on wheat flour to be applied by the Netherlands (Hudec 1990: 181–200).

As the DSU integrates the various trade agreements under the umbrella of the WTO, cross-sector retaliation is possible. Even though the rules prescribe that retaliation should normally entail suspension of concessions or obligations which affect the sector subject to the dispute (Article 22: 3), when that is not practicable or effective, concessions or obligations may be suspended in other sectors under the same agreement. Ultimately, if that is still not satisfactory, the suspension of concessions or obligations under another covered agreement may be allowed, namely, cross-retaliation (Schott 1994: 125–9).

As Whalley and Hamilton have observed, great hopes are pinned on the ability of the WTO to generate an elevated joint commitment to a strengthened focal point for the international trading system with stronger enforcement of system rules, to weaken those forces which have eroded the system, to lessen the risk of trade wars, and generally to lead to yet stronger global economic performance (Whalley and Hamilton 1996: 123).

In order to assess the ability of the WTO to achieve such results, some primary notions about international provisions and state rule compliance must be stressed. These relate notably to the standing of international rules with regard to state power, and the character and implementation of international provisions.

International rules and state compliance

There is a fundamental problem concerning the relationship between law and norms on the one hand and power and interests on the other. If it is true that many international rules reflect the influence of powerful governments, rules may also make a difference as states may not like to be seen to contravene the provisions and principles of the international organisations to which they belong. Clearly a good deal of the compliance pull of international provisions derives in this respect from the relationship between individual rules and the broader pattern of international relations: states follow specific rules even when inconsistent with short-term national interest because they have a longer-term interest in the maintenance of a law-impregnated international community (Hurrell 1993: 51–4, 59–61, 66–7).

Yet, a crucial question and probably the most important issue of international law, but which has nevertheless been given little systematic attention by governments and scholars, is how to achieve a reasonable degree of compliance with international obligations (Jackson 1969: 163; Levy *et al.* 1995: 278, 315–16). It should first be stressed that international rules, as opposed to domestic law, cannot be enforced automatically and are not self-executing. Neither do dispute panel rulings automatically become part of national laws. Such rulings are also binding only on case participants and do not necessarily have strict precedential effects on future cases. In other words, international obligations have to be translated in national laws by state governments. International rules and decisions thus cannot be enforced against an unwilling sovereign state. As a result, international institutions or regimes do not establish binding or enforceable legal liabilities in any strict or reliable sense. However, this has not prevented the development of extensive provisions at the international level, and in the case of a far-reaching regime such as the European Union, some of the rules tend to acquire near-enforceable features.

With regard to the GATT/WTO, implementing or enforcement mechanisms are part of dispute settlement procedures which only seek to settle conflicts between states. This means that apart from the notification to the WTO of certain trade measures on the part of state authorities and reviews of national trade policies, WTO interventions are limited to cases of complaints brought to its attention. Obviously, a rarity of dispute instances may not necessarily reflect overall rule observance, but rather a reluctance from states to object to others' practices, presumably because they employ similar measures. In the same logic, a large number of conflicts may not reflect widespread disregard for international rules, but maybe a desire on the part of member states to ensure strict compliance with international provisions. Finally, the existence of a dispute settlement system, especially a strengthened one under the WTO, can act as a deterrent against conflicts and play a crucial role in pressing states to solve their differences.

Under GATT, recourse to dispute settlement, while accelerating during the Uruguay Round, remained relatively uncommon. Developing countries, for instance, rarely invoked dispute settlement procedures. A 1985 study of the GATT dispute mechanism prepared for the US International Trade Commission found that only eight developing countries had ever filed GATT complaints. Another study showed that, from 1948 to 1993, the United States, the European Union and EU members, Canada, and Australia filed 73 per cent of the complaints, and that the large majority of GATT members had never participated in the dispute settlement process. Japan filed its first formal request for a GATT panel only in 1990. Furthermore, disputes may be addressed outside WTO auspices. Indeed, trade disputes between major powers sometimes escalated outside the GATT process, and were often resolved bilaterally (Whalley and Hamilton 1996: 133-4, 138). In such cases, conflicts may be settled without due regard to international provisions. The WTO dispute settlement procedures then should not be confused with a 'real' enforcement mechanism, as in domestic law. For the most part, 'enforcement' of GATT/WTO provisions takes the form of self-discipline or retaliation.

As anticipated, the number of dispute cases has increased with the advent of the WTO in January 1995. As of May 1998, 131 requests for consultations have been notified. These have covered a whole range of matters, including issues which have just become part of international trade rules, such as intellectual property. About one-quarter of the disputes have been resolved by the parties themselves at the consultation stage, and all panel reports so far have been brought to the Appellate Body for final ruling. When different panel requests involve similar issues, often a single panel has been set up.

In the first case where a panel report was reviewed by the Appellate Body, which concerned a complaint by Venezuela and Brazil over a US regulation regarding gasoline composition, the panel report was modified after the appeal while its results were left intact. On May 1996, both the Appellate Body report and the panel report as modified by it were adopted by the DSB. The United States was required to bring its regulation into conformity with GATT, essentially that it did not discriminate against imports, which the US did within an agreed time frame of fifteen months.

A major case where the panel report was also appealed relates to the complaints by Ecuador, Guatemala, Honduras, Mexico, and the United States against the European Union's regime for the importation, sale and distribution of bananas. The Appellate Body mostly upheld the panel's findings that the EU regime was inconsistent with WTO rules. The DSB adopted both reports on 25 September 1997. As determined by an arbitrator, the EU had a fifteen-month period from September 1997 to implement the WTO recommendations and rulings. The EU reaffirmed its attachment to the WTO DSU and stated that it would fully respect its international obligations. This is to be contrasted with EU's attitude under the 'old GATT' when in the first half of the 1990s it prevented the adoption of two panel reports on its banana regime.

Among dispute cases resolved through a mutually agreed solution, one involved a request for consultations from Japan in May 1995 on announcement by the United States of 100 per cent import duties on luxury cars from Japan, amounting to almost $6 billion in sanctions, in retaliation for what the US considered regulatory barriers and restrictive practices in the Japanese auto parts aftermarket. This was the US-Japan auto dispute, a major conflict which served as a 'test case' for the newly established WTO. In this case, the knowledge that both sides were to refer their respective grievances to the WTO dispute system apparently pressed them towards a deal. Yet, it must also be emphasised that the deal was struck on the day the US threat of unilateral tariffs was to become effective, which would of course have violated GATT obligations.

There were, as of May 1998, nineteen active panels and eleven completed cases. In a marked change from the past, both developed and developing countries are actively using the WTO to settle their trade conflicts. Hence, the United States has been involved in forty-nine disputes as a complainant and been the subject of twenty-three complaints, while developing nations have filed thirty-five complaints and been involved in forty-eight disputes as respondents. This is perceived as a sign of increased confidence in the impartiality and effectiveness of the WTO and its dispute settlement system. In short, the WTO and its DSU have been described as a success story. The Ministerial Declaration issued after the WTO first Ministerial Conference held in Singapore in December 1996 noted the role that several WTO bodies played in helping to avoid disputes.

For its part, the second Ministerial Conference which took place in Geneva in May 1998 focused on implementation of existing WTO agreements and on the future work programme. The Ministerial Declaration did not specifically refer to dispute settlement. Although, as agreed during the Uruguay Round, a review of the dispute settlement rules and procedures was to take place in 1998, WTO members are reluctant to make major changes to the DSU in the near future. As the 'bedrock' of the WTO's ability to enforce rules, members prefer to wait for clearer evidence over a longer period of time than the four years it has been in place. As of the end of 1997, no WTO member had chosen to test the DSU provisions which allow for the negotiation of compensation instead of complying with a panel ruling. Also, until the US requess for retaliation over the 'revised' EU banana regime, authorised by the OSB in April 1999, there had been no case in which a WTO member asked the DSB to authorise retaliation because another member had not fully complied (WTO 1996: 5–6, 88, 132–8; WTO 1997b: 1–5).

The attitude of major powers towards the WTO: the US case

One of the main open questions over the authority and effectiveness of the WTO relates to the attitude of major powers with regard to a strengthened organisation overseeing world trade. In the United States notably, concerns have been raised about potential loss of national sovereignty to the WTO, particularly with respect to the dispute settlement procedures. The attitude of the United States *vis-à-vis* the WTO is more worrisome than is the case with other trading powers in view of the fragmentation of the US trade policy-making process.[8] One could only recall the role of the US Executive in the negotiations for the ITO and the refusal from Congress to ratify its charter.

Following the US Constitution, foreign trade is the responsibility of the Congress. The American Congress has then not only been a focal point for pressures to gain relief from foreign competition, but, given the structural relationship between Congress and powerful private interests, has been more responsive than the US Executive to demands for protection (Goldstein 1988: 192). If the strengthening of the GATT dispute settlement procedures were one of US key negotiating objectives at the start of the Uruguay Round, as the United States increasingly became a defendant as well as a plaintiff in GATT disputes, Congressional support for stronger multilateral procedures became more ambivalent. From the beginning of the Uruguay Round through May 1993, the United States was taken to the GATT thirty-one times and filed fifty-two complaints against foreign trade practices. Along with the EU, the US had also been the main laggard in delaying panel procedures and implementing panel decisions (Schott 1994: 129). Within the WTO, the United States has also been an active complainant and defendant, but the compliance record has seemingly improved.

With regard to US attitude towards the WTO, a first main issue pertains more specifically to the drafting of the legislation translating in US law the results of the multilateral trade negotiations. Gary Horlick has noticed that the US implementing legislation, the Uruguay Round Agreements Act (URRA), departs from the text of the Uruguay Round agreements in at least thirty-eight instances (Horlick 1995). This could be seen as a first disquieting factor whether the US Congress would be willing to respect the terms of the Uruguay Round agreements (Moyer 1996: 75).

Most fear over possible US unilateralism has focused on the so-called Section 301 of US trade legislation. This consists of a procedure allowing the US government, as well as firms to compel the US government, to enforce US rights under international trade agreements and to respond to alleged harmful or unfair foreign practices, which could lead to retaliatory action, notably under the form of import restrictions. Since Section 301 calls for dispute cases to be taken to the relevant international dispute settlement process, the US has insisted that Section 301 is integrally linked to the WTO dispute settlement mechanism. Indeed, since the entry into force of the WTO, all US Section 301 actions involving WTO members have been conducted under the DSU. For as long as it is considered relevant for the United States to make use of the WTO DSU to pursue its national interest, this is to give credibility and strength to the world trading regime. In this respect, it has been argued that Section 301, if appropriately used, could represent a constructive measure not only for US trade policy, but also for world trade policy.

However, it is also clear that US Section 301 actions may disregard WTO rules. In the US–Japan auto dispute, the US threatened to impose unilateral sanctions before bringing the matter to the DSU. In its Statement of Administrative Action

(SAA) accompanying the URRA, the US Executive explicitly stresses that it would be willing to take action under Section 301 which has not been authorised by the WTO, even if it might face WTO-authorised counter-retaliation. Furthermore, as happened in the case of intellectual property rights, which the US sought to enforce unilaterally using 'Special 301' before they were included within the realm of international trade rules, there remains the question of how to integrate into the WTO realm new or emerging issues, such as environment and trade rules.

Moreover, section 129 of the URRA specifies procedures to be followed in the event of adverse decisions by WTO bodies, and then Congress would decide whether to bring US practice to conformity with such WTO decisions. An even more ironic declaration of potential US unilateralism is through the 'WTO Dispute Settlement Review Commission', which systematically reviews every final WTO dispute panel that finds against the United States to determine notably if the WTO panel exceeded its authority or acted outside the agreement (Moyer 1996: 76–9).

A further source of concern relates to the main US agencies with responsibilities for international trade, namely the Department of Commerce, the International Trade Commission, and the Office of the US Trade Representative, the way they implement the Uruguay Round agreements through their regulations, and the way they respond to WTO panel decisions. Their responses to decisions of binational panels under the US–Canada Free Trade Agreement (FTA) and later the North American Free Trade Agreement (NAFTA) do not provide an encouraging preview. In a series of cases, US agencies openly resisted complying with binding decisions of FTA/NAFTA panels, while in a few instances they did so defiantly, disparaging panel decisions. There are also fears of a 'politicisation' of administrative agencies and processes in case of certain controversial trade matters as a result of strong pressures exerted by Congress and lobbies representing specific interests (Moyer 1996: 64–9, 79–80).

Finally, the United States has a strong tradition of exercising leadership in international economic affairs by acting unilaterally. Even though US unilateral measures have sometimes brought about changes in multilateral rules, in many respects the Uruguay Round agreements could be cited as instances of multilateral standards following developments in US law, aggressive unilateral action may not be as effective in the case of the WTO and particularly dispute settlement. US leadership in securing new strengthened dispute settlement rules is expected to be accompanied by a commitment to play by those rules as well. Should it not be the case, the 'leading' image of the United States may be diminished, as well as US credibility in the international community (Moyer 1996: 82–3).

Although WTO members, among them the United States, agreed during the Uruguay Round negotiations to resort to the multilateral dispute settlement understanding to deal with international trade conflicts, and not rely on unilateral trade measures, whether the United States can respect this commitment remains doubtful, especially considering the nature of the American political system. As is the case with international law, a state always has the option of not complying, leaving itself subject to retaliatory measures. A large country with a diversified economy and an important internal market, such as the United States, is obviously in a stronger position to take this route in comparison with smaller ones, which in addition are often heavily dependent on external trade. The weight of the United States appears to enable such a country to take whatever route best suits its interests and to abide by WTO rules only when they happen to coincide with US interests.

However, on the basis of the first four years of the working of the WTO dispute settlement system and the trade matters being referred to the organisation, it seems that the United States on the whole has subscribed to the rules of the new broader and strengthened world trading regime.

Regimes, states and globalisation

In a global system, unilateral actions on the part of a major power such as the United States can obviously have a strong impact on the conduct of states as well as on the trade regime as a whole. Yet, the globalisation process works both ways, and major powers have themselves become more exposed to the trading system. For instance, US dependence on exports of goods and services as a percentage of GDP passed from 7.4 per cent in 1985 to 10.3 per cent in 1993. More generally, the ratio of US trade to GDP has increased from 17.2 per cent in 1985, to 20.6 per cent in 1990, and to 23.6 per cent, that is nearly 25 per cent, in 1995 (United Nations 1996: 175; WTO 1997a: xxv). Another element likely to refrain US unilateralism pertains to the adoption by states of provisions and standards similar to those so far found in the United States.

As we know, the United States has been a pioneer with regard to trade policy and law, and in fact many notions now embodied in GATT/WTO rules have originated from the US. This is notably the case of the provisions dealing with so-called 'unfair trade', mostly dumping, subsidies, and anti-dumping (AD) and countervailing duties (CVDs). These involve what are probably the most contentious of the 'rules of conduct' clauses of the world trading regime. Many of these notions were used by the United States before they were even translated in international law in order to secure protection against 'unfair' practices and to put pressure on states to adopt similar measures. The protectionist bias of such actions should of course be borne in mind. Indeed, the term 'contingency protection' has been used to refer to such actions.

These factors largely explain why the United States has been the nation which has used such instruments most extensively. For instance, from 1980 to 1993, the United States initiated 345 CVD actions, among which 137 led to the application of definitive duties. During the same period, Canada initiated twenty actions, with eleven cases of duties, the EU only six actions leading to three duties, and Japan, only one CVD action with no imposition of duties. US CVDs have been imposed against products from a vast array of countries. Those most affected have been Mexico with fourteen duties, followed by Canada and Spain, ten duties each, and Brazil and Thailand with nine. For its part, the United States has not been much implicated in (the few) CVD actions from other trading powers. Yet, we mentioned that, as a result of the Tokyo and even more the Uruguay Rounds, states have adopted similar legislations. Hence, since the 1990s, Brazil has started to initiate CVD actions, nine so far, and interestingly the United States has counted among the target countries.[9] The WTO 1996 Annual Report also mentions that since the use of non-tariff measures (e.g. quotas) has declined, contingency measures have proliferated. AD measures have been widely applied in industrial countries, but are increasingly used in developing countries, particularly Mexico and Brazil (WTO 1996: 32, 37).

As a result, there could be observed a concern on the part of major US exporters that new 'unfair trade' laws in other countries may well become market barriers to US exports. Some countries have already targeted American exports in retaliation for US AD laws being used against them (Moyer 1996: 84). This fear of reciprocity, as a result of globalisation and the adoption at the multilateral level of trade notions along US lines, signals that although protectionist pressures in the United States from import-competing interests may remain strong, counter-forces are gaining strength, which could limit the extent of US trade unilateralism. It will become ever more difficult, indeed unlikely, for the United States to safeguard its national interest while disregarding international obligations and other states' interests. The US then would not only expose itself to WTO-authorised counter-measures, but also to the threat of unilateral retaliation from increasingly significant trading partners.

Conclusions

As the economic cooperation scheme overseeing world trade, the GATT was, and remains with the WTO, an intergovernmental organisation with hardly any element of supranationality. Notably with respect to dispute settlement, only retaliatory measures in the form of withdrawal of concessions or obligations taken by the complaining state could be allowed in case of non-compliance with WTO decisions. Yet the need to strengthen multilateral trade provisions was clearly recognised by the international community. As a complete shift from GATT previous practice, panel recommendations and counter-measures may now be adopted almost automatically, unless there is consensus to reject them.

Such provisions may definitely contribute to bring about increased compliance by states with international trade commitments. States do not normally like to be seen to contravene the principles of the organisations to which they belong. They are then likely to avoid being singled out for not complying with a decision adopted at the multilateral level. Thus, WTO rules make it more costly for states, both in terms of finance and prestige, to disregard international trade rules.

As international rules and decisions cannot be automatically enforced on states, their continuing willingness to make such provisions effective remains essential. The cooperation of major powers in this respect is of particular significance to ensure the credibility and the viability of the world trading regime. Following the first five years of WTO existence, major powers, including the United States, on the whole have abided by the international rules they have themselves greatly contributed to adopt in the pursuit of their trade interests. Generally, the dispute settlement system has functioned as anticipated. The number of disputes has increased, in part reflecting the new broader scope of multilateral trade rules, and the increased reliance on the system from developing countries.

Such considerations allude to the difficult issue of state compliance with international rules. We have emphasised that provisions of international regimes may exert a compliance pull of their own, as states may perceive a higher interest in observing rules with which they may not entirely agree. In an increasingly interdependent world, international rules, however unsatisfactory, are likely, even for major powers, to prove better than an anarchical situation characterised by a series of major trade conflicts and escalating retaliation.

Yet there remains the possibility that states, and again especially major ones, may prefer to disregard some international rules which they find unsatisfactory in order to exert pressure on other states if, as a result, provisions closer to their views could be adopted. Such kind of 'illegal' pressure has manifested itself in the past, notably on the part of the United States through the non-observance of GATT recommendations or unilateral initiatives disregarding the spirit of international provisions. More than in the case of any other major power, there remains concern over US unilateralism, which is related to the fragmentation of the trade policy-making process and a seemingly ambivalent attitude towards the WTO.

We emphasised that the global system also affects major powers. As far as the United States is concerned, the adoption by WTO members of trade legislations along US concepts as a result of the Uruguay Round has led to worries that such notions may in turn be used as barriers to US exports. The globalisation process is making states more and more dependent on international exchanges, to the extent that even for powerful states the benefits from an effective world trading regime may outweigh any possible short-term gains stemming from unilateral initiatives.

Hence, although the cooperation of major powers remains essential to ensure the credibility of international rules, and indeed the smooth functioning of the world trading system, broader and strengthened rules about dispute settlement and the ever-increasing impact of globalisation on nations combine to make it increasingly hard for states, including powerful ones, to act without regard to international trade provisions. The Uruguay Round results and particularly the dispute settlement provisions, through the commitments they entail on the part of member states and their ensuing legitimacy, significantly expand the ability and the authority of a non-state actor such as the WTO to preside over world exchanges and tackle potential trade conflicts among states. Overall, this provides an example for the general claim made in the introduction of this book that authority in the global system is nowadays shared by states and non-state actors such as International Governmental Organisations.

Notes

1 Agreement establishing the World Trade Organization' (hereafter cited as WTO Agreement), in *Final Act Embodying the Results of the Uruguay Round of Multilateral Trade Negotiations,* 15 April 1994 (hereafter referred to as the *Final Act*), pp. 9–21.

2 On the GATT, see notably Jackson (1989). On the WTO, see Jackson (1995). On the history and outcomes of the Uruguay Round, including the WTO and dispute settlement, see Croome (1995); Stewart (1993). For an assessment of the WTO and the Uruguay Round agreements, see also Schott (1994); and Whalley and Hamilton (1996).

3 For a history of GATT dispute settlement, see Hudec (1990).

4 Understanding regarding notification, consultation, dispute settlement and surveillance', in *GATT* (1979: 210–16).

5 Understanding on rules and procedures governing the settlement of disputes', in *Final Act:* 353–77.

6 Presumably, such negative consensus can be defeated by any major objector (Jackson 1995: 20).

7 n principle, parties should comply immediately with a panel's rulings and recommendations. If that is considered impracticable, compliance must occur within a 'reasonable' time, which is determined in one of three ways: as proposed by the member concerned and approved by the DSB; as agreed between the parties concerned within forty-five days after adoption of the panel or appellate report; or as determined through binding arbitration within ninety days after adoption of the panel or appellate report. In the case of arbitration, a guideline is provided which recommends that the reasonable period of time to implement a panel or appellate report must not exceed fifteen months from its adoption (DSU Article 21).

8 For an analysis of US trade policy, see Destler (1995).

9 Annual reports of the Committee on Subsidies and Countervailing Measures, in GATT, *Basic Instruments and Selected Documents*, Supplements nos 28 to 39.

References

'Agreement establishing the World Trade Organization' (1994), in *Final Act Embodying the Results of the Uruguay Round of Multilateral Trade Negotiations*, 15 April: 9–21.

Croome, John (1995) *Reshaping the World Trading System. A History of the Uruguay Round*, Geneva: WTO.

Destler, I. M. (1995) *American Trade Politics,* third edition, Washington: Institute for International Economics.

General Agreement on Tariffs and Trade (1989) *Basic Instruments and Selected Documents,* 36th Supplement, Geneva: GATT.

Goldstein, Judith (1988) 'Ideas, institutions, and American trade policy', *International Organization* 42(1): 179–217.

Horlick, Gary (1995) 'Anti-dumping and subsidies agreements and US AD/CVD laws', Panel Presentation, Uruguay Round Program Series, American Bar Association Section of International Law and Practice, 31 January.

http://www.wto.org/anniv/press.htm

http://www.wto.org/anniv/50th index.htm

http://www.wto.org/wto/dispute/bulletin.htm

Hudec, Robert E. (1990) *The GATT Legal System and World Trade Diplomacy,* 2nd edn, London: Butterworth.

Hurrell, Andrew (1993) 'International society and the study of regimes: a reflective approach', in Volker Rittberger (ed.), *Regime Theory and International Relations*, Oxford: Clarendon Press: 49–72.

Jackson, John H. (1995) 'The World Trade Organisation: watershed innovation or cautious small step forward?', in Sven Arndt and Chris Milner (eds), *The World Economy. Global Trade Policy*, Oxford: Blackwell: 11–31.

—— (1989) *The World Trading System: Law and Policy of International Economic Relations,* Cambridge, Mass.: MIT Press.

—— (1969) *World Trade and the Law of GATT,* Indianapolis: Bobbs-Merrill.

Levy, Marc A., Oran R. Young and Michael Zürn (1995) 'The study of international regimes', *European Journal of International Relations* 1(3): 267–330.

'Major changes to WTO dispute settlement unlikely during 1998 review' (1997) *Inside US Trade,* 26 December.

Moyer Jr., Homer E. (1996) 'How will the Uruguay round change the practice of trade law in the United States? US institutions, not the WTO, may hold the answer', *Journal of World Trade* 30(3): 63–85.

Schott, Jeffrey J. (assisted by Johanna W. Buurman) (1994) *The Uruguay Round: An Assessment,* Washington: Institute for International Economics.

Stewart, Terence P. (ed.) (1993) *The Uruguay Round: A Negotiating History,* Deventer: Kluwer.

'Understanding on rules and procedures governing the settlement of disputes' (1994), in *Final Act Embodying the Results of the Uruguay Round of Multilateral Trade Negotiations,* 15 April: 353–77.

'Understanding regarding notification, consultation, dispute settlement and surveillance' (1979), in GATT, *Basic Instruments and Selected Documents,* 26th Supplement, Geneva: 210–16.

United Nations (1996) *Statistical Yearbook,* forty-first issue, New York.

United States, Congress (1994) *Uruguay Round Agreements Act.*

United States, Executive (1994) *Uruguay Round Agreements Act, Statement of Administrative Action,* H.R. Doc. 316, 103d Cong. 2d Sess.

Whalley, John and Colleen Hamilton (1996) *The Trading System After the Uruguay Round,* Washington, D.C.: Institute for International Economics.

World Trade Organization (1996) *Annual Report 1996,* volume I, Geneva.

—— (1997a) T*rade Policy Review. United States 1996,* Geneva.

—— (1997b) *WTO Focus No. 21,* Geneva.

14 The World Bank, the World Trade Organisation and the environmental social movement

Marc Williams

Introduction

This chapter examines the interactions between the World Bank, the World Trade Organisation (WTO) and the environmental social movement (ESM). Specifically, it explores the demands made by environmentalists on the global economic institutions (GEIs) and the reaction of the GEIs to this new constituency. In the first part of the chapter the outlines of the environmental social movement are sketched. The aim of this section is to provide an introduction to the various actors which comprise the ESM, and also to raise some of the key issues attendant on the role played by non-state actors in global politics. The second part of the chapter focuses on the troubled history of the World Bank's relationship with environmental activists. The third section of the chapter explores the demands made by environmentalists of the WTO and the organisation's response. In both these sections the relationship between the GEIs and other social movements forms an important part of the context in which discussions between the international organisation and the ESM is conducted. The final part of the chapter attempts to derive some general conclusions about the relationships examined.

The environmental social movement and global politics

Social movements and an emerging global civil society

The 1990s have witnessed a renewed interest in both social movement theory, and the concept of civil society in a number of academic disciplines. These trends can be traced to a number of factors. First, the revival of academic debate on the meanings and boundaries of democracy attendant on the global spread of democracy and democratic politics. Both social movements and civil society have been rediscovered and re-evaluated as means towards cementing new democratic forms of governance. Second, theorists of world politics have stressed the fact that there is a serious disjuncture between increasingly globalised structures of power and processes of representation and accountability that remain locked within territorial boundaries. It can be argued that in the context of globalisation, state and governmental authority no longer fulfil the roles they once did. In this respect authority relations are fractured, consensus is difficult to achieve and modes of legitimation increasingly subject to contestation. Within this new global political space specific attention is given to the role of social movements as a democratic alternative and harbinger of a new politics (see, for example, Shaw 1992; Otto 1996). Third, recent transformations in Eastern and Central Europe alerted many scholars to the role played by social movements in the (largely) peaceful transformations that took place at the beginning of the decade. The strength of the regimes in the Soviet bloc having been extolled for many years, and the importance of social movements undervalued, tremendous attention is now given to these movements.

International social movements have important implications for governments and international governmental organisations. Although the setting of international norms usually arise from processes dominated by states and international organisations the question of how discourses change over time and who plays a role in the debate should not be confined solely to states or organisations composed of states. The emergence of international social movements with objectives aimed at transforming regimes, for example, those pertaining to development assistance and the environment, has implications for the theoretical and practical aspects of policy formulation and implementation. The concept of global civil society reorients attention to the role played by non-state actors in world politics. Global politics (unlike international politics) is clearly a terrain occupied by actors other than states. Analysts who focus on social movements tend to start from a viewpoint which admits the existence of an international society composed of states and non-state actors. The distribution of power in this model is varied among a number of actors. And the sources of power include both traditional and non-traditional sources. The agenda is unlimited and the various actors can influence the agenda in a number of diverse ways.

The environmental social movement

The environmental social movement is commonly perceived as a new social movement, one which arose within post-industrial society. It is widely recognised to be a significant transnational force despite being a diverse movement consisting of a range of actors with differing strategies and goals. However, differences in size, orientation, aims, ideology, resources, organisational forms, organisational culture, and range of activities makes it difficult to conceive of a single movement. Many writers, for example, distinguish between northern and southern environmental groups. This distinction reflects asymmetries in power, and different value systems. Nevertheless, it has become commonplace to write of an environmental movement articulating and espousing an alternative development paradigm from the conventional socio-economic one, and challenging the conventional political systems of Western democracies (Dalton 1994; Lipschutz 1992).

Initially, environmental activism was principally focused at the local and national levels. It was a response to local awareness of environmental degradation and the efforts of activists to resist environmental damage. Since the 1980s, however, environmental non-governmental organisations (ENGOs) within civil society have grown in size, scaling up their operations in order to influence states and international organisations (Princen and Finger 1994). Although the vast majority of environmental groups remain rooted in their activities and focus at the local, regional or national levels, many ENGOs attempt to exert influence in global politics. In international environmental politics the main representatives of 'civil society' are the various ENGOs active in lobbying national governments and international organisations. Within the new politics of the environment NGOs have emerged as prominent and significant actors. The composition of the ESM varies from large, well-known NGOs like Greenpeace and the International Union for the Conservation of Nature (IUCN) to varying grassroots environmental groups. The world of the professional environmental activist who meets with representatives of national and international bureaucracies is, on the one hand, significantly removed from the activities of grassroots actors but on the other hand, diverse environmental networks create alliances and link unlikely partners in specific campaigns (Nelson 1996; Keck and Sikkink 1998). At the forefront of lobbying efforts directed towards either the World Bank or the WTO or both are leading American and European based NGOs including the IUCN, World Wide Fund for Nature (WWF), Environmental Defence Fund (EDF), World Resources Institute (WRI), International Centre for Trade and Sustainable Development (ICTSD), and the Centre for International Environmental Law (CIEL).

The World Bank and the environmental movement

The World Bank is not a monolithic organisation, and change in the Bank is as much driven by internal considerations as external pressures. Moreover, important constituencies and individuals in the organisation can slow the pace or effectively block reform. Not all sections of the Bank have embraced the increasing contacts between civil society associations and the Bank with the same degree of enthusiasm. The public output of the organisation may often mask internal disagreements, and policy implementation frequently is uneven across sectors because of the absence of consensus. Many of the social movement representatives in Washington recognise the plural nature of the organisation, and therefore attempt to cultivate informal linkages with sympathetic Bank staffers. In a similar vein, neither the NGO Liaison Unit nor the Environment Department perceive the ESM as a single entity, and formal and informal contacts with movement representatives are based on this recognition of difference.

In the past two decades the World Bank's contact with social movement organisations has expanded considerably. It is generally recognised that the environmental movement was pivotal in securing increased linkages between NGOs and the Bank. Moreover, the environmental movement has apparently achieved the greatest success of all groups lobbying the Bank. It is helpful to assess the relations between the environmental movement and the Bank in the context of the general increase in the Bank's contacts with social movements given the reciprocal nature of the interactions.

The World Bank and social movements

The Bank's recognition of diverse groups in civil society in practical terms amounts to the development of policies towards NGOs. The 1970s witnessed an explosion in NGO activity in the development sector. Increasingly OECD governments began to channel resources through NGOs. This transformation has continued, for example in 1994 more than 10 per cent of official development assistance was channelled through NGOs (Gordenker and Weiss 1996: 25). The rise of NGOs as significant actors in the development regime in the 1970s inexorably brought them into contact with the World Bank, the leading multilateral development bank. At the beginning of the 1980s the World Bank recognised the importance of the NGO sector through the creation of the NGO-World Bank Committee in 1982. By the end of that decade the expansion, developing professionalism and increased stridency of NGOs led to greater attention to NGOs within Bank policies. Between 1973 and 1988 only 6 per cent of World Bank projects had some kind of NGO involvement. In 1989 NGO participation reached 20 per cent and has been over 30 per cent in every year in the 1990s attaining a peak of 50 per cent in 1994 (World Bank 1995: 2). Since 1988 the Bank has placed greater emphasis on engaging local NGOs in the operations it finances. In 1995 for example 81 per cent of projects with NGO involvement included national (indigenous) NGOs, 42 per cent incorporated grassroots organisations, and only 18 per cent involved international NGOs. (World Bank, 1996: iii)

From the perspective of the World Bank, NGOs are defined as, 'groups and institutions that are entirely or largely independent of government and characterised primarily by humanitarian and cooperative rather than commercial activities' (Operational Directive 14.70, August 1989). Specifically, NGOs refer to private organisations that pursue activities to relieve suffering, promote the interests of the poor, protect the environment or undertake community development. Currently, the World Bank distinguishes between operational NGOs and advocacy NGOs. Operational NGOs are defined as those 'whose primary purpose is running or funding programs designed to contribute to development, environmental management, welfare or emergency relief' (World Bank1996: 1). In contrast advocacy NGOs are defined as those whose primary purpose is advocating a specific point of view or concern and which seek to influence the policies and priorities of the Bank, governments and other bodies' (World Bank 1996: 2). This definition is not one accepted by many NGO activists who see it as inaccurate and divisive.

The linkages between the Bank and NGOs cover a wide spectrum of the organisation's activity. The Bank analyses these interactions according to a three-fold categorisation: operational collaboration, economic and sector work and policy dialogue. Operational collaboration refers to the inclusion of NGOs in the design and execution of Bank financed projects. This has been a major growth area in the past decade, and is seen by the Bank as the centrepiece of its activities in relation to NGOs. Economic and Sector Work (ESW) comprises a broad range of research and analysis undertaken by the Bank. The activities undertaken under

ESW provides a framework for the World Bank's lending policies. The third area of collaboration, often referred to as broader policy dialogue, is the one given most coverage by political scientists. This covers the exchange of information between the World Bank and NGOs on the Bank's development policies. The official site of policy dialogue between the World Bank and NGOs is the NGO-World Bank Committee.

The World Bank and the environmentalists

The World Bank is the largest lender for environmental projects in the developing world, a co-agency for the Global Environmental Facility, and environmental considerations notably in the form of environmental assessments (EAs) have become integrated within its development portfolio. Although the first mention of environmental considerations was made by the then President of the Bank Robert McNamara in a speech to the United Nations Economic and Social Council (ECOSOC) in November 1970, environmental considerations were not given serious attention in the organisation until 1987. The Bank, until that point, appeared unwilling to address the ecological impacts of its lending policies. The pursuit of economic growth at the expense of the environment symbolised an institution confident of its intellectual rationale, policy mandate, and project implementation. Traditional Bank lending often had serious environmental consequences such as acceleration of deforestation and destruction of natural resources and biodiversity. Bank officials were not accountable to the affected populations and neither were they concerned for the environment. The key goals were the promotion of economic development conceived almost solely to mean an increase in GNP, and the maximisation of the rate of return on the loan. In May 1987, Barber Conable, the Bank's President, admitted that the organisation had made serious errors in its environmental policy and announced organisational reforms including the creation of an Environment Department. Since 1987 the Bank has expanded its focus on environmentally sustainable development and has striven to incorporate environmental concerns into policy-making. It is widely acknowledged that environmental NGOs played a pivotal role in the reform process in the Bank. This story has been told on numerous occasions and I will not replicate it in great detail.

There is little doubt that the Bank responded to the pressure exerted by the environmental movement. No agreement, however, exists on the extent to which the Bank has become a 'green' institution. The official Bank version (World Bank, 1995a) presents a picture of an organisation committed to environmentally sustainable development in which environmental considerations have been incorporated into the mainstream of its operations. Critics from academia (Wade, 1997), and the environmental community (Rich, 1995; Horta 1996) remain unconvinced about the scope and depth of the reforms. Whether convert or agnostic, something has changed and at the very least the Bank has been forced to address an issue that it had long ignored.

The standard account of the success of the environmental movement in shifting the Bank's agenda focuses on the role played by NGOs in shaping US policy towards the Bank (Bramble and Porter 1992: 325–36). The campaign launched in 1983 by a coalition of US environmental organisations against the environmental policies of the multilateral development banks reaped its first success with the creation of the Environment Department in 1987. The coalition's decision to target the US Congress was eventually successful for a number of reasons. The intensification of the NGO campaign, and the widening of the movement from its largely US base to encompass NGOs from the developing world and other industrialised countries were crucial factors in persuading more members of Congress to support the demands of the environmentalists. These US NGOs were assisted in their campaign by Southern peoples and organisations. A number of civil society associations in the developing world in regions directly affected by Bank projects with adverse environmental consequences provided first-hand information about the local situation (Bramble and Porter 1992: 332–4). But Congressional pressure supplemented by sympathetic media coverage was not sufficient in itself to alter the policies of the Bank. The support of the US Treasury and the replacement of Tom Clausen by Barber Conable as Bank President were key changes in 1986 and 1987. The US Treasury moved from a position of indifference to one of support for reform of the Bank because it needed Congressional approval to expand the Bank's capital base to enable it to increase its role in the debt crisis. Conable as the new Bank president recognised the political importance of the environment issue (Wade 1997: 21–3).

But the 'success' of the environmental movement in 1987, and continued pressure on the Bank is not solely attributable to the role played by actors in the US political process. Four further developments helped to shape (and continue to do so) the ability of environmental groups to influence Bank policy. First, the Big Dam controversies provided not only powerful evidence of the Bank's failure to pursue environmentally sustainable policies but concrete issues around which campaigns could be built. Second, over the past decade a framework of consultations has developed between certain NGO personnel and Bank staff. This raises questions of equity within the environmental movement since these contacts are limited to Washington insiders, thus effectively marginalising those groups without any representation in Washington. Third, high level research disseminated by environmental actors to the public, legislators and the Bank in an attempt to create epistemic communities has been instrumental in shifting perceptions. Fourth, the Bank is still sensitive to public campaigns and the efforts of the '50 Years is Enough' movement proved more than an irritant to Bank officials who devised strategies to counter what they perceived as ill-informed publicity.

Environment (and development) groups remain unconvinced by the rhetoric of the Bank. Certainly considerable change has taken place; namely the official promotion of sustainable development and the existence of formal and informal channels of access for environmental activists to Bank staff. The climate of hostility, suspicion and distrust evident in the early years of the exchange has been replaced by one of cooperation. But the Environment Department is not the entire Bank, and for many the problems arise from the loan culture of the Bank and its organisational structure (Wappenhans 1992).

The aims of the ESM can be seen in terms of four broad demands (Horta 1996). First, the demand for increased transparency and participation. The aim is to improve the quality of projects by making them environmentally sound and socially beneficial. Representatives of the environmental movement argue that in order to meet these aims the active participation of local communities and their local or regional governmental structures is necessary. The demand for greater transparency and participation has achieved some success in eroding the Bank's tradition of secrecy and withholding of information concerning its projects from the public. The new information disclosure policy which became effective in January 1994 is a striking success. The Bank decided to declassify a number of documents and established a Public Information Center in Washington with further offices planned in Tokyo, Paris and London.

The second demand is for social assessment and participation. Civil society representatives campaigned for increased participation of stakeholders in social assessments carried out by the Bank. A key area covered by this demand is the World Bank's dialogue on sustainable development. In September 1994, the World Bank approved a Participation Action Plan based on social assessment guidelines, but little concrete results have to date been forthcoming. Third, the ESM has insisted that the Bank's lending to the environment should be increased. The Bank has responded to this in both the brown agenda (projects designed to address pollution in urban areas) and green agenda (projects concerned with natural resource management in mostly rural areas). The focus tends to be on forestry, fisheries and agriculture. In 1995 the Bank supported more than 100 environmental projects representing a commitment of $5 billion and a total investment of more than $13 billion. The green agenda has formed the central part of the Bank's efforts with issues grouped in this portfolio representing $3.2 billion of the $5 billion commitment. Environmental groups have also campaigned for more widespread use of environmental assessments (EAs). They are a valuable tool for understanding the environmental consequences of proposed new development projects. Since 1989 EAs have become a formal requirement for all World Bank projects that are expected to have significant adverse environmental impacts. But EAs are frequently used to legitimise previously established project concepts. The lack of follow-through, absence of controls and high use of foreign consultants serves to diminish the impact of EAs. The appearance suggests tremendous change but the reality of implementation suggests otherwise.

Finally, environmental NGOs have expressed reservations concerning the accountability of the Bank. A major response by the Bank was the creation of an Inspection Panel in September 1994. Community organisations or NGOs representing citizens harmed by World Bank projects can request a full-scale investigation of the situation if there are indications that the Bank is ignoring or violating its own policies and procedures. The first case investigated by the Inspection Panel was the Arun III hydro-electric dam project in Nepal. The investigation began in November 1994 and a report published in December 1994 called for further investigation. The project was finally cancelled by James Wolfensohn in August 1995.

The story of the World Bank and the environmental movement is one of increasing linkages between the Bank and environmental NGOs, and the appearance that NGO pressure was successful in changing Bank policies and priorities. A note of caution should be entered on both counts. First, a quantitative increase tells us very little about the quality of the interactions. However, it would be rather narrow and short-sighted to conclude that no change has occurred. The very fact that the Bank has felt the need to address and respond to the demands of this new constituency is a sign of a change in the operation of the organisation. Moreover, increasing integration of environmental NGOs into the Bank's work shifts the relations between the international organisation, governments and civil society. Second, it is very difficult to measure influence. This dialogue is a continuing process and any conclusions can be only tentative.

In terms of access to the World Bank a clear difference in resources exists between Northern, especially US based, NGOs and their Southern counterparts. Much of the policy dialogue between the Bank and NGOs is conducted informally (for example, the Tuesday Group meetings) and Southern NGOs are therefore excluded from this process. Representation from the developing world is greater in respect of the more formal channels such as the World Bank-NGO Committee and consultations such as those on forest, water, and energy.

The WTO and the environmental social movement

The WTO was established on 1 January 1995 as a result of the decisions taken by the Contracting Parties to the GATT at the conclusion of the Uruguay Round. The Final Act signed in Marrakesh in April 1994 concluded a process begun at Punta del Este, Uruguay in September 1986. The WTO as the successor to the GATT provides the legal and institutional foundation of the global trading system. It replicates but also extends the mandate of the GATT. As an organisation the WTO has three main dimensions. It is, first, a legal agreement which provides a framework of rules, norms and principles to govern the multilateral trading system. In other words, it is the legal and institutional foundation of the world trading system. Second, it is a forum for multilateral trade negotiations. Multilateral trade agreements specify the principal contractual obligations determining trade negotiations and trade legislation, and the Trade Policy Mechanism facilitates the evolution of trade relations and trade policy. Third, it acts as a centre for the settlement of disputes. The WTO dispute settlement procedures provide the machinery for settling members' differences on their rights and obligations. The extension of the WTO beyond trade in goods into intellectual property protection, surveillance over investment issues, and the strengthening of the dispute settlement procedures (see the contribution by Gagné in this book) opens up a wider debate concerning the role of a multilateral trade organisation.

The WTO and social movements

The WTO is an intergovernmental institution, and no formal provision exists for social movements to engage with the membership of the organisation. Although the WTO has created no institutional mechanisms which provide for contact between the organisation and social movements, it was suggested by President Clinton at the Second Ministerial Meeting (May 1988) that in future the organisation should reach out to business, consumer, environmental and labour organisations. Currently the General Council of the WTO is empowered by Article v.2 to review relations between the organisation and NGOs.

In July 1996 the Secretariat was given prime responsibility for liaison with NGOs, and was empowered to engage in an expanded dialogue with the non-governmental sector. The Secretariat provides briefings on its work programme, and receives representations from NGOs. Apart from these contacts the Secretariat has organised symposia with social movement representatives. Furthermore, the General Council agreed to de-restrict documents. Under the procedures most WTO documents will be circulated as unrestricted, some will be de-restricted automatically after a sixty-day period, others can be de-restricted at the request of a member but others, especially those pertaining to important current policy decisions, will remain restricted.

Interest in the activities of the WTO has been evinced by NGOs and other organisations representing environmental, development, and consumer interests. A number of NGOs call for increased access to the WTO decision-making machinery and outline a set of reasons for increased public participation. Public participation, it is argued, is vital for balanced policy input and the promotion of sustainable development.

The WTO and the environmentalists

The relationship between trade and the environment has given rise to two broadly competing positions (Williams 1993: 87–92). On the one hand, proponents of free trade argue that no inherent incompatibility exists between the goals of environmental sustainability and trade creation and expansion. On the other hand, environmentalists of different persuasions contend that a liberal trade regime automatically creates the conditions conducive to environmental degradation. This conflict between free traders and environmentalists has been labelled a clash of policies and a clash of cultures.

The central contention of liberal economists is that trade liberalisation promotes growth which enables states to tackle environmental degradation. This position is admirably summed up in the World Development Report 1992 which stated *inter alia* that, 'using trade restrictions to address environmental problems is inefficient and usually ineffective. Liberalised trade fosters greater efficiency and higher productivity and may actually reduce pollution by encouraging the growth of less polluting industries and the adoption and diffusion of cleaner technologies' (World Bank 1992: 67).

This view was echoed by the GATT Secretariat Report on Trade and the Environment (1992) which argued that GATT was neutral in the formation of policies necessary to promote sustainable development; that the solution lies in assigning prices and values to environmental resources so that the environmental effects of economic activity can be identified and valued; and that if the policies necessary for sustainable development are in place, trade promotes development that is sustainable.

Within the liberal economic paradigm trade liberalisation is not seen as the primary cause of environmental degradation. Here it is argued that unsustainable economic growth arises from market failure and the inability of governments to engage in adequate environmental pricing. The presumption is that restrictions on trade are not only inadequate but also positively dangerous since under the cloak of environmentalism the dangers of protectionism are ever present. Although empirical evidence and developments in trade theory cast strong doubt on the shibboleth of free trade, the underlying truth of the law of comparative advantage and the superiority of market-based solutions remain articles of faith for many economists and policy-makers.

Environmentalists call for trade restrictions to prevent the spread of pollution by trade. Moreover, they argue that trade should be restricted because a liberal trading regime provides incentives to expand production and trade whilst disregarding pollution. Environmentalists believe that trade liberalisation in encouraging economic growth damages the environment. Production for export markets is more environmentally damaging than production for home consumption; for example, 'putting agricultural resources at the service of export markets, in countries that are not self-sufficient in food, enormous pressures are created for local peoples to over-exploit other resources simply to eke out the barest existence.' (Shrybman 1990: 31).

The immense task faced by those who challenge the prevailing orthodoxy has been concisely summarised by David Pearce (1991). He argues that the environmentalists' case must pass three tests before trade can be restricted for environmental reasons. First, environmentalists need to show that free trade, rather than some other factor, does in fact cause degradation. Furthermore, that the loss in welfare resulting from environmental degradation is greater than that which would result from trade restriction. Second, environmentalists need to provide a convincing defence for the imposition of extra-territoriality. That is, import of a good should not be restricted because of the environmental damage caused in its production unless it can be shown that importers lose something through the production process, thus making it a legitimate concern of the authorities and traders in the importing country. Third, environmentalists need to show that the most effective means of changing the production process giving rise to the externality is through resort to trade controls. In regard to the first test, since it is not possible at the present to calculate the monetary values of environmental losses from trade, environmentalists can exaggerate the damage accruing from trade. The second test raises political issues surrounding the exercise of sovereignty. Where producers damage global heritage the solution should be through existing multilateral treaties rather than the resort to unilateral action. He concludes that the environmentalists' case is weak with regard to the third test because trade restrictions may not be the least cost policy.

Discussion of the environmentalist challenge to the organisation responsible for monitoring developments in the world trading system usually begin with the dolphin-tuna controversy, but to understand the development of the debate concerning the greening of world trade it is necessary to establish the historical context within which the trade and environment issue arose in the GATT, and to trace (briefly) the organisational response to this new issue. This story is a good example of agenda-setting. It shows us how a topic defined as an issue made its way on to the formal agenda but was effectively blocked from active consideration until circumstances changed. In November 1971, immediately prior to the United Nations Conference on the Human Environment (the Stockholm Conference), the GATT Council established a Group on Environmental Measures and International Trade (GEMIT) to examine 'upon request any specific matters relevant to the trade policy aspects of measures to control pollution and protect the human environment, and report back to the Council' (GATT 1993a). However GEMIT, a political response to the Stockholm Conference, never met since the strength of opposition to merging trade and environment interests was very strong. In the run up to UNCED new pressures arose for an examination of the trade/environment nexus. At the Uruguay Round Ministerial Meeting in Brussels in December 1990 the European Free Trade Area countries requested that the GEMIT be convened to examine the relationship between trade and environmental policies. This led to an inconclusive debate in May 1991 at the GATT Council Meeting. The opposition of a number of delegations was sufficient to stymie the calls for a GEMIT meeting. Immediately after UNCED, and following the first dolphin-tuna ruling, it was apparent that the trade and environment issue occupied a place on the agenda, and that UNCED issues were not adequately covered in GEMIT's remit. GEMIT was re-convened in July 1993 to discuss the results of UNCED.

At this time it became clear that leading advanced industrialised countries, and developing countries felt that the time had come for GATT to take up the trade and environment debate. These views were sometimes defensive. For example, the US delegate stated that environmental issues should not be left to environmental experts given the overlap between trade and the environment; and the Indian representative expressed the view that it was imperative for GATT to counter the false propaganda that the organisation was indifferent to environmental concerns. Some delegations adopted a more positive approach; for instance the Brazilian delegate argued that Agenda 21 should be fully integrated into GATT since poverty is the worst polluter in the developing world (see GATT 1993b).

The standard GATT, and later WTO, position on the environment was adopted at this time. The viewpoint expressed by the majority of member governments was that environmental concerns could be fully accommodated within a flexible interpretation of GATT rules. Moreover, it was stressed that an open non-discriminatory system can facilitate environmental conservation and protection by helping to encourage more efficient resource allocation to generate real income growth. Three key policies were identified: multilateral environmental agreements, transparency, and eco-labelling.

The Uruguay Round was launched in Punta del Este, Uruguay in September 1986 before environmental issues became prominent on the international agenda. In this context it is interesting to note that John Croome's official history of the

Uruguay Round published by the WTO contains no reference to the environment either in the table of contents or index (Croome 1995). Although the preamble to the WTO includes direct reference to sustainable development the push for integrating environmental concerns into the structure of the organisation through the creation of a Committee on Trade and Environment was unsuccessful. Opponents of the establishment of an environmental committee based their argument on two considerations. The first was precedent. It was argued that it had never been GATT practice to create institutional frameworks before matters of a substantive nature had been settled in a particular area. The second argument appealed to political realities. Those opposed to the mainstreaming of environmental issues in the new organisation argued that the issue was so divisive that attempts to resolve it would further delay the ratification of the WTO. It was therefore decide to consider the institutional structure in consultations prior to Marrakesh. The Marrakesh Ministerial Meeting (April 1994) which led to the creation of the WTO decided to create a Committee on Trade and Environment (CTE). In the interim before the WTO began work on 1 January 1995 a sub-committee of the GATT was created to handle environmental matters.

Concerted pressure on the GATT by environmentalists first surfaced as a result of the 1991 GATT Panel ruling in respect of the dolphin-tuna dispute between the United States and Mexico. The Panel's decision which upheld Mexican sovereignty and rejected the extra-territorial expansion of American law appeared to many environmentalists to be fundamentally flawed. The ensuing debate was frequently portrayed as a clash between free trade economists on one hand and green protectionists on the other. Differing perceptions of the impact of the liberal trading system on environmental degradation, the potential of market-based solutions for environmental harm, and commitment to continued economic growth produced divergent and conflicting policy proposals from liberal economists (and the GATT Secretariat) and the environmental movement. Relations between environmentalist groups and the WTO have changed from one of incomprehension to the beginnings of some accommodation, at least as far as the Geneva-based environmental NGOs are concerned.

At the outset both groups mistrusted the economic arguments put forward by the other side and little real dialogue was possible. Both groups are now aware that the existing knowledge on trade-environment links is very tentative and in the past two years both the WTO Secretariat and NGOs like WWF and the IUCN have been prepared to examine the evidence in a manner unlikely to maintain the previous degree of polarisation. Other environmental groups, e.g. Greenpeace, are less prepared to engage in these discussions.

Environmental issues arise throughout the WTO's organisational structure but it has been in the Committee on Trade and Environment (CTE) that discussions have centred on the interrelationship between trade and the environment. The CTE is a deliberative rather than a policy-making body which, between its first meeting in February 1995 and the Singapore Ministerial Meeting, concentrated on clarifying the relationship between trade and the environment. The first Ministerial Conferences of the WTO (Singapore 9–13 December 1996) provided the environmental movement with its first opportunity to address the achievements of the WTO in a comprehensive manner. Environmental NGOs were strongly critical of the failure of the CTE to make any substantive progress in its deliberations (WWF 1996; IISD 1996). The CTE, instead of addressing the crucial issues on trade and the environment, had been sidetracked into discussions on technical issues. Moreover, environmental NGOs were sharply critical of the manner in which environmental issues had been shifted to the CTE. Sustainable development touches on the WTO's work programme in a number of ways, and environmental NGOs argue that this realisation should influence WTO policy. This environmental critique was reiterated at the time of the second Ministerial Meeting (Geneva, May 1998). And it appears that the failure of the CTE has now been accepted by major Western governments.

Environmental activists have also campaigned for increased accountability in the WTO. Although the WTO has achieved a degree of openness unprecedented under GATT environmentalists argue that an increased scope for participation exists. It has been pointed out that access to information and participation in decision-making is vital for democracy and will also improve the policy outputs of the WTO (Esty 1996). This is not a claim for an open access regime since the activists based in Geneva are sensitive to the secrecy necessary for successful trade negotiations. Nevertheless, environmental NGOs argue that an increased scope for participation exists. For example, the WTO can be reformed in ways which do not impinge on the need for secrecy in bodies like the Trade Policy Review Mechanism. The membership of the CTE should be expanded to include NGOs. The Dispute Settlement Mechanism should make greater usage of independent experts. On the issue of transparency, NGOs are very critical of the existing arrangements for the de-registration of documents. They argue that if crucial documents can be kept restricted until six months after being issued the monitoring functions of NGOs will be handicapped. At the Second Ministerial Conference, Ruggiero pledged to consider how moves towards greater transparency could be taken further *(Bridges Weekly Trade News Digest,* 18 May 1998).

Conclusion

It is mistaken to think that the ESM represents solely voices from the periphery. At the level of interactions with GEIs the ESM is characterised not only by diversity but also by a highly sophisticated policy elite which shares more than access to modern technology with those who run the institutions. In order to be heard, representatives of social movements of necessity must enter into a dialogue (and speak the language) of the holders of power. This paper has documented two different case studies. Both the World Bank and WTO have taken cognisance of civil society actors, increased the public dissemination of information and altered substantive policy in response to the demands of environmental activists. However, these changes and the significance to be attached to them vary between the two GEIs. While the WTO remains relatively closed to representatives from social movements, the World Bank has engaged in an expansion of formal and informal linkages with the environmental movement. Unlike the WTO, the Bank has gone some way towards institutionalising contact with social movement representatives.

A number of points emerge from the narratives developed here. The contrasting reactions of the World Bank and WTO to the environmental movement suggests caution in drawing conclusions about the impact of the environmental movement on international organisations. Learning curves and the development of a global democratic politics appear to be specific to the organisation rather than part of a general trend. Second, it is very difficult to assess influence. We can certainly trace the linkages which have developed but the importance of these lines of communication are not easily established. Nevertheless, although a shift from the old to a new multilaterlism (see introduction of this book) has not occurred yet, some change is taking place, and NGOs have been accepted as legitimate actors (at least as far as the Bank is concerned). Moreover, NGOs are clearly a permanent feature of a new global politics.

Note

This paper was written as part of the Economic and Social Research Council's Global Economic Institutions Programme. It is part of a project titled 'Global Economic Institutions and Global Social Movements'. I would like to thank my colleagues on that project, Robert O'Brien, Jan Aart Scholte and Anne Marie Goetz, and the participants at the Non-State Actors and Authority in the Global System Conference for helpful comments.

References

Bramble, B. J. and G. Porter (1992), 'NGOs and the making of US international environmental policy', in A. Hurrell and B. Kingsbury (eds) *The International Politics of the Environment*, Oxford: Clarendon Press: 313–53.

Bridges Weekly Trade News Digest (18 May 1998) 'Clinton endorses call for high-level WTO meeting on trade-environment and calls for WTO openness', 2(18): 2.

Croome, J. (1995) *Reshaping the World Trading System*, Geneva: World Trade Organisation.

Dalton, R. J. (1994) *The Green Rainbow: Environmental Groups in Western Europe*, New Haven and London: Yale University Press.

Esty, D. (1996) *Why the World Trade Organization needs Environmental NGOs*, Geneva: International Centre for Trade and Sustainable Development.

GATT (1992) *Trade and Environment Report*, Geneva: GATT Secretariat.

GATT (1993a) *Bulletin Trade and Environment Geneva*: GATT Doc TE.001.

GATT (1993b) *Bulletin Trade and Environment Geneva*: GATT Doc TE.002.

Gordenker, L. and T. G. Weiss (1996) 'Pluralizing global governance: analytical approaches and dimensions', in T. G. Weiss and L. Gordenker (eds) *NGOs, the UN and Global Governance*, Boulder and London: Lynne Rienner: 17–47.

Horta, K. (1996) 'The World Bank and the International Monetary Fund', in J. Werksman (ed.) *Greening International Institutions*, London: Earthscan: 131–47.

IISD (1996) *The World Trade Organization and Sustainable Development*, Winnipeg: IISD.

Keck, M. E. and K. Sikkink (1998) *Activists Beyond Borders*, Ithaca and London: Cornell University Press.

Laferrière, E. (1994) 'Environmentalism and the global divide', *Environmental Politics* 3(1): 91–113.

Lipschutz, R. D. (1992) 'Reconstructing world politics: the emergence of global civil Society', *Millennium* 21(3): 389–420.

Nelson, P. J. (1996) 'Internationalising economic and environmental policy: transnational NGO Networks and the World Bank's expanding Influence', *Millennium* 25(5): 605–33.

Otto, D. (1996) 'Nongovernmental organizations in the United Nations system: the emerging role of international civil society', *Human Rights Quarterly* 18(1): 107–41.

Pearce, D. (1991) 'Should the GATT be reformed for environmental reasons?', *CSERGE Discussion Paper*, GEC 92–101.

Princen, T. and M. Finger (1994) *Environmental NGOs in World Politics*, London: Routledge.

Rich, B. (1995) 'Statement of Bruce Rich on behalf of the Environmental Defense Fund, National Wildlife Federation, Sierra Club, Greenpeace' before The House Committee on Banking and Financial Services Subcommittee on Domestic and International Monetary Policy Concerning The World Bank: effectiveness and needed reforms, 27 March.

Shaw, M. (1992) 'Global society and global responsibility: the theoretical, historical and political limits of international society', *Millennium* 21(3): 421–34.

Shrybman, S. (1990) 'International trade and the environment: an environmental assessment of the General Agreement on Tariffs and Trade', *Ecologist* 20(1): 30–4.

Wade, R. (1997) 'Development and environment: marital difficulties at the World Bank', *ESRC Global Economic Institutions Working Paper* No.29.

Wappenhans, W. A. (1992) *Report of the Portfolio Management Task Force*, Washington, D.C.: The World Bank.

Williams, M. (1993) 'International trade and the environment: issues, perspectives and challenges', *Environmental Politics* 2(4): 80–97.

World Bank (1992) *World Development Report 1992*, New York: Oxford University Press.

World Bank (1995) *NGOs and the World Bank: incorporating FY94 progress report on cooperation between the world bank and NGOs*, Poverty and Social Policy Department, Washington, D.C.: World Bank.

World Bank (1995a) *Mainstreaming the Environment*, Washington, D.C.: World Bank.

World Bank (1996) *NGOs and the World Bank: incorporating FY95 progress report on cooperation between the World Bank and NGOs*, Poverty and Social Policy Department, Washington, D.C.: World Bank.

WWF (1996) *The WTO Committee on Trade and the Environment – Is It Serious?* Geneva, December.

15 'In the foothills'

Relations between the IMF
and civil society

Jan Aart Scholte

Formally, and also largely in practice, multilateral institutions deal in the first place with states. However, in the post-Westphalian circumstance that has arisen in the contemporary globalising world, multilateral governance is not a question of the states-system alone. Since the 1970s, most of the main global regulatory agencies have experienced a major expansion of exchanges with actors in civil society. Global governance has thereby become at least a triangular affair, with complex relationships between national governments, multilateral institutions, and civic associations (see further Scholte 1997, 1999b).

This general shift from Westphalian 'international organisation' to post-sovereign 'global governance' is clearly seen in the recent history of the International Monetary Fund (hereafter IMF, or 'the Fund'). The IMF has since the 1970s experienced major growth in its competences, resources and authority. In the late twentieth century the Fund has not only been shaped by its member states (stronger governments in particular), but has also exerted considerable influence over them (weaker governments in particular).

Not surprisingly, given the far-reaching significance of IMF activities for much contemporary public policy, numerous civil society organisations across the world have over the past several decades developed keen interest in the Fund. Many of these non-state actors (including business associations, academic institutions, trade unions, non-governmental organisations (NGOs), religious groups, etc.) have by-passed national governments to seek direct contact with the IMF. Concerned citizens have wanted to understand and interrogate this new major player in governance. Interest groups have wanted to lobby and perhaps to extract advantage from this important locus of policy-making.

This chapter examines these burgeoning, yet so far little studied, relations between civil society and the IMF (see also Scholte 1998, 1999b). The first section below sets the context by elaborating on the expansion of the Fund in the globalising political economy of the late twentieth century. The second section surveys the range of contacts that have developed between the IMF and civil society. The third section reviews the aims that the Fund and the various civic associations have pursued *vis-à-vis* each other. The next two sections examine the strategies and tactics that the parties have employed in their interactions. The sixth section discusses the impacts that civil society has had on both the substantive policies and the operating procedures of the IMF. The seventh section highlights several major limitations to these relationships, in terms of biased access, general shallowness, and the frequent absence of a veritable dialogue. The eighth section lays out the main forces which have to date hindered a fuller development of exchanges between the Fund and civil society. A further section suggests several reforms which could enhance the contributions of IMF-civil society relations to more effective and democratic global economic governance.

The issues at hand here are important. Both the IMF and civic organisations are players of growing significance in world politics. Current dynamics of globalisation suggest that the involvement of civil society in global governance is for the time being irreversible and, indeed, likely further to expand. If conducted well, contacts between the Fund and civic groups can make substantial contributions to more effective and democratic regulation of macro-economic affairs. A healthy dialogue can increase information flows, stimulate policy debates, involve stakeholders in policy-making, advance civic education, and help to legitimate Fund activities. However, if handled badly, IMF-civil society relations can undermine policy efficacy and undercut democracy. For example, the exchanges could be highly exclusive and favour the privileged; or they could be poorly informed and disrupt policy processes; or they could be treated merely as public relations exercises. A key challenge for global governance in the twenty-first century is therefore to design and execute exchanges between multilateral institutions and civil society in ways that minimise their possible pitfalls and maximise their potential benefits.

To date, links between civil society and the IMF have remained underdeveloped. As an Executive Director of the Fund has acknowledged, 'When it comes to managing "participation", the IMF is only in the foothills; and some people want us back in the valleys' (interview with author). It is hoped that the present research may help IMF-civil society relations to reach higher elevations.

Growth of the IMF

The International Monetary Fund emerged from the Bretton Woods Conference in July 1944. During its first quarter-century of operations, the Fund was mainly concerned to establish and manage the international regime of fixed (but adjustable) exchange rates. Its interventions with member governments were relatively infrequent and brief; they were generally limited to countries of the North; and they were mainly restricted to monetary and trade policies.

The IMF lost much of its old role with the end of the dollar-centred fixed-rate system in 1971; however, the rapid globalisation of money and finance since the 1960s has prompted the Fund to reinvent itself with a much expanded agenda (Vries 1986; James 1996). For one thing, the IMF has since 1978 exercised so-called 'surveillance', scrutinising both the economic policies of individual member-states and the performance of the world economy as a whole. Second, the Fund has since the 1970s intervened more intensely with many client governments by designing for them not only traditional stabilisation measures for short-term corrections of the balance of payments, but also structural adjustment packages for medium- and long-term economic reconstruction. IMF-sponsored structural adjustment programmes began in the South during the 1970s and extended to the East in the 1990s with the transition in those countries from state socialism to a market-based economy. In the process the scope of Fund conditionality (i.e. the policies that a state must follow in order to use IMF resources) has widened to encompass liberalisation, privatisation, fiscal reform and more. Third, the 'second generation' IMF has undertaken major training and technical assistance activities, largely in order to provide poorly equipped states with staff and tools that can better handle the policy challenges of contemporary globalisation. Fourth, the Fund has pursued various initiatives to promote stability in global financial markets, including several major rescue operations.

To handle this enlarged agenda, the IMF has undergone substantial institutional growth. Its Executive Board now meets in at least three (long) sessions each week. Staff numbers have more than tripled, from 750 in 1966 to about 2,600 in 1998 (IMF 1966: 133; http://imf.org/external/np/ext/facts/glance.htm). Since the 1970s the Fund has developed its own 'diplomatic service', with resident representatives stationed in sixty-eight countries by 1998. From 1970 the IMF has had its own money form, the Special Drawing Right (SDR). Quota subscriptions to the Fund have grown from the equivalent of twenty-one billion SDRs in 1965 to 212 billion SDRs in 1999. Various other sources (gold stocks, the General Arrangements to Borrow, etc.) have given the IMF potential access to tens of billions of additional SDRs for lending purposes (IMF 1995a; GAO 1998).

Given this growth in competences and resources, the IMF has in the late twentieth century become a major site of economic governance. Its voice carries far in global markets, in national economic policies, and eventually in local and household budgets. In these circumstances it is hardly surprising that the Fund has since the 1970s attracted progressively more attention from civil society.

Range of contacts

The IMF has since its creation maintained at least sporadic contacts with certain parts of civil society (such as academic associations). However, the number and impact of its links with civic groups were on the whole negligible until the 1980s. The main growth in the frequency, range and sophistication of interchanges between civil society and the Fund has occurred during the 1990s.

All manner of actors in civil society have developed contacts with the Fund. For example, national bankers' associations in most IMF programme countries have held periodic meetings with Fund officials, as has the Institute of International Finance with its 1999 membership of over 300 financial services providers headquartered in fifty-six countries (http://www.iif.com). Many national industrial associations and chambers of commerce have likewise regularly exchanged views with IMF staff. A wide range of think tanks like the Institute for International Economics (IIE) and the Cato Institute in Washington and the Overseas Development Institute (ODI) in London have often contributed to discussions of IMF approaches to macro-economic policy. The labour movement has actively engaged the Fund through both national and transborder trade union coalitions. The International Confederation of Free Trade Unions (ICFTU) has figured especially importantly in this regard (ICFTU 1988: 50–1; ICFTU 1992: 43–8; ICFTU 1996: 66–8). A multitude of development NGOs in both the South and the North have lobbied the IMF at its headquarters and in the field. Prominent examples include the Washington-based Development GAP, the Brussels-based European Network on Debt and Development (EURODAD), the various Oxfam groups across the world, and the Swiss Coalition of Development Organisations. A few environmental NGOs like the United States branch of Friends of the Earth (FOE-US) have campaigned actively on the Fund since the late 1980s. Meanwhile other NGOs (e.g. concerned with human rights, the status of women, corruption and peace) have had sporadic interchanges with the global monetary institution. Finally, the IMF has maintained contacts with a number of Christian churches and orders as well as certain religious NGOs like the Washington-based Center of Concern.

These various parts of civil society have engaged the IMF at a number of different points in the institution. Especially since the early 1990s, the present Managing Director (MD), Michel Camdessus, has given considerable priority to cultivating links with business circles, trade unions and churches. Since the mid-1990s, the three Deputy Managing Directors have also increased their contacts with civic groups. The twenty-four Executive Directors (EDs), who represent national governments at IMF headquarters, have (with varying mixes of enthusiasm and reluctance) in the 1990s held increasing numbers of interviews with civil society representatives. Within the staff, the Fund has greatly expanded its External Relations Department (EXR), first established in 1981. A Public Affairs Division has existed in EXR since 1989, *inter alia* to handle the IMF's day-to-day relations with civil society groups. More exchanges with civic associations have also taken place in the 1990s through the operational departments of the Fund, especially Policy Development and Review (PDR) and the Fiscal Affairs Department (FAD). For the rest, contacts between IMF officials and civic circles have transpired in the field, through staff missions and resident representatives.

In sum, then, a complex web of relations has developed since the 1980s between civil society and the IMF. On the side of civil society, the exchanges have involved a host of business associations, academic institutes, trade unions, NGOs and religious organisations. On the side of the Fund, the exchanges have involved management, external relations officials, operational staff in Washington, and missions and resident representatives in the field.

Aims of engagement

As might be expected, given the variety of constituencies just described, civic organisations have pursued diverse objectives in their lobbying of the IMF. For example, business associations have primarily aimed to advance the commercial interests of their members, both specifically (through the promotion of particular policy measures) and generally (through the support of business-friendly macro-economic policy frameworks). Mainstream think tanks like the IIE and the Brookings Institution have engaged the Fund in the hope of improving its performance, usually within the existing broad lines of policy.

In contrast, various other voices in civil society have challenged the reigning policy frameworks at the IMF. For example, trade unions have sought to reverse the claimed negative effects of Fund-sponsored policies on employment levels and working conditions. A host of NGOs, religious organisations and reform-minded academic institutes have aimed to halt the purported adverse consequences of IMF-supported structural adjustment on the poor (Watkins 1995: chapter 3). Many of the same circles have urged the Fund to support major reductions in the external debt burdens of the South. A few environmentalist groups like FOE-US and the World Wide Fund for Nature have hoped to place issues of ecological sustainability at the heart of the IMF agenda (Reed 1996). Other critics in civil society have argued that Fund policies should be changed to remove their disproportionately greater costs to women (Woestman 1994). Several NGOs have moreover demanded that IMF conditionality be reformulated to promote human rights, reductions in military spending, and an end to corruption.

Along with these desired changes in substantive IMF policies, some civic groups have aimed to alter certain of the Fund's operating procedures. For example, a number of campaigners have argued for changes in the voting system at the IMF in order to reduce the dominant voice of a handful of governments. In addition, under the slogan of 'ownership', advocates of increased democracy in Fund operations have also urged greater participation by client governments and civil societies in the formulation and implementation of IMF-supported programmes. With reference to 'transparency', many advocates of change have demanded greater openness about policy-making processes at the IMF: e.g. what decisions have been taken; by whom; from among which options; and on the basis of what information. On the theme of 'accountability', various activists have pressed the Fund to establish comprehensive, systematic and transparent mechanisms of policy evaluation.

As for the IMF, it has sought increased contact with civil society in the 1990s mainly in the hope of building support for the macro-economic policies that the Fund sponsors. Both management and staff at the IMF have become convinced that overtures to business associations, labour unions, religious groups and NGOs can help to construct a popular base for worldwide economic restructuring on the neo-liberal lines which the Fund has favoured. Many an IMF official has in recent years declared that 'a broad-based social consensus is needed to sustain a Fund programme' or that 'we have to persuade the population that an adjustment package is legitimate' (interviews with the author).

In addition, the IMF has taken some of its initiatives *vis-à-vis* civil society with the aim of securing its resource position. In particular, the Fund has learned that a poor public image can complicate the approval of quota increases and other requested monies, especially by the United States Congress. In another episode, the IMF created its Visitors' Center in 1986 when the municipal government of

Washington, D.C. threatened otherwise to deny permission for an extension of the headquarters building. (It is a sign of changed times that the Fund needed no outside pressure a decade later to decide on a substantial expansion of the Visitors' Center.)

Strategies

In pursuing the aims noted above, civil society organisations have adopted one or a mixture of three broad strategies: conformism, reformism and radicalism. Those who have taken what might be called a 'conformist' approach to the IMF have broadly accepted the institution's existing premises, policy frameworks and operating procedures. A conformist strategy implies working through the Fund's own terms: that is, the promotion of liberal capitalism; the methodology of neoclassical economics and so on. In contrast, reformers and radicals have challenged the status quo at the IMF, though they are divided on how this challenge should be mounted. Whereas reformers believe that the existing Fund can be reconstructed so that it produces more effective and democratic policy, radicals see the organisation as incorrigible and pursue its contraction or outright abolition (Jordan 1996). Reformers usually welcome opportunities to meet, debate and work with the IMF, while radicals tend to regard any collaboration as a recipe for cooptation.

This threefold categorisation of strategies is of course a simplification; nevertheless, it remains an analytically useful characterisation of the range of approaches taken in civil society *vis-à-vis* the IMF. Broadly speaking, business associations have tended to fall towards the conformist end of the spectrum. Trade unions, NGOs and religious bodies have generally operated somewhere in the reformist and/or radical realms. Meanwhile research institutes have worked across all bands. Thus, for example, the Brookings Institution has taken a conformist line, the Washington-based Overseas Development Council (ODC) has taken a reformist approach, and the Heritage Foundation has taken a radical outlook.

As for the IMF, its overall strategy in relations with civil society has followed two main strands: one proactive and the other reactive. On the proactive side, the Fund has since the late 1980s pursued concerted public relations efforts to win friends and influence people. IMF officials have sought to retain their existing backers in civil society and, more importantly, to 'educate' and 'correct' their critics. Firmly convinced of the merits of Fund-sponsored policies, management and staff have presumed that once people 'understand' the IMF, everyone will support its activities.

On the reactive side, the Fund has sought to contain criticism in civil society, especially from radicals, in order that such opposition does not harm the IMF's work and reputation. In the late 1980s Camdessus declared that the Fund would no longer stay silent in response to attacks on its performance. Subsequently IMF officials have quickly and emphatically defended their organisation against critical academic studies, editorials, press reports, conference resolutions and so on.

Tactics

Both civic groups and the IMF have in the 1990s become considerably more sophisticated in dealing with each other. In earlier years, civic activists tended to hold *ad hoc* street protests against the Fund, to submit petitions, to write letters to the Managing Director, and to publish journal articles. A few of these initiatives attained impressive proportions, such as the marches that accompanied the 1988 Annual Meetings in Berlin, the 'IMF riots' in Venezuela in February 1989 that left over 300 dead, and a 1989 petition to the Fund from Save the Rainforest that held nearly 28,000 signatures from five major member countries. However, on the whole these initiatives were not designed and executed in ways that would shift IMF policy. Before 1990 only a few business and academic organisations such as the Institute of International Finance (IIF), the Japan Center for International Finance (JCIF), the IIE and ODI held face-to-face meetings with Fund officials on detailed policy questions.

Some civic associations have continued to this day to sponsor demonstrations, letter-writing campaigns and the like in respect of the Fund, but other more precisely targeted and sustained activities have developed as well. For example, several civil society campaigns to influence the IMF have hired professional lobbyists, consultants and/or information officers. Certain organisations based outside the USA (e.g. the ICFTU and Oxfam International) have set up bureaux in Washington *inter alia* to monitor the Fund. Increasing numbers of deputations from business associations, trade unions, religious organisations and NGOs have called at IMF headquarters for interviews with EDs and officials from relevant functional and area departments. On other occasions, civic groups have invited management and staff of the Fund to their own events. For instance, the IIF, the JCIF and the ICFTU have frequently included participation from the IMF in their seminars on topics such as global finance and structural adjustment. The ED from Switzerland has accompanied staff from the Swiss Coalition of Development Organisations in joint fact-finding missions to Ghana in 1993 and Bangladesh in 1996.

Civic associations have also developed political sophistication with their use of indirect pressure on the Fund, for example, via national governments. The most advanced tactics of this kind have developed in the USA, where lobbies have since the late 1970s intervened with some effect variously to promote, oppose or attach conditions to congressional approval of increased monies for the IMF. Other civil society engagement of national legislatures on issues concerning the Fund has transpired during the 1990s in Britain, Ireland and programme countries like Haiti where a structural adjustment package requires the approval of the representative assembly. In Germany, the Netherlands, Switzerland and the USA, certain civic associations have discussed IMF policies with the national ministry of finance and central bank.

Civil society groups have also indirectly pursued influence on the IMF via other global governance agencies. In this vein the ICFTU has linked up with the International Labour Organisation to advocate a larger social dimension in Fund programmes. On similar lines EURODAD has engaged with the European Commission, in particular the Structural Adjustment Unit of Directorate General VIII. Meanwhile many activists have hoped that campaigns for change targeted at the World Bank might reverberate on the Fund.

Turning to non-official circles, a number of lobby groups have in the 1990s given increased attention to civic education about the IMF. To this end they have issued popular information packs, organised symposia, and produced several films concerning the Fund (e.g. Torfs 1996; Maryknoll n.d.). NGOs have since the mid-1990s maintained half a dozen listservs on the Internet with continually updated information about the IMF. Some organisations like Oxfam have cultivated links with the mainstream press in the hope of reaching the wider public via newspapers and the broadcast media.

Finally, civic associations have in the 1990s advanced their tactics *vis-à-vis* the IMF with improved communications among themselves. For example, NGOs have held a Forum alongside all IMF/World Bank Annual Meetings since 1986. NGOs and trade unions have (separately) also convened a number of regional gatherings where Fund-related issues have been discussed. Lower telephone charges, faxes, electronic mail and the World Wide Web have enabled activists with access to these technologies to develop closer day-to-day contacts with one another. With such means a substantial network has grown since 1994 around the theme of '50 Years Is Enough'. By 1998 this coalition to limit the powers of the Bretton Woods institutions encompassed over 200 US-based associations plus 180 partner organisations in sixty-five countries (http://www.50years.org).

As for the IMF, it has pursued its strategies of self-promotion and self-protection on the largest scale through publications. A Pamphlet Series was started already in 1965, and the biweekly *IMF Survey* was launched in 1972; however, the Fund did not issue any popular information booklets until 1988 (Driscoll 1988a, 1988b; Landell-Mills 1988). In the 1990s the External Relations Department has greatly expanded the IMF publications programme with books, reports, brochures and regularly updated fact sheets. The Public Affairs Division has accumulated a worldwide mailing list of some 700 addresses and distributes materials to these individuals and groups in three languages. EXR has also produced several films about the IMF and has made the organisation publicly accessible on the Internet since 1995 (http://www.imf.org/).

The Fund has also given increased attention in the 1990s to cultivating its image in and through the mass media. The institution has expanded its flow of press releases, news briefs and public information notices to scores per year. IMF officials have also regularly issued rejoinders on the letters pages to what they regard as inaccurate reporting of Fund activities and their consequences. Meanwhile the Managing Directors and Executive Directors of the IMF have in recent years granted newspaper, magazine and broadcast interviews on a scale unheard of in an earlier generation. Management has likewise encouraged IMF mission chiefs and resident representatives to cultivate links with the press in programme countries. In 1993 EXR initiated media training courses for Fund staff, which had by 1996 involved over 325 employees (IMF 1994: 186; IMF 1996: 193).

Many other IMF outreach activities have taken the form of face-to-face meetings. For instance, Camdessus and his three deputies have during the 1990s given dozens of speeches to civic associations and other audiences. The Managing Director and the First Deputy MD, Stanley Fischer, have on various occasions met privately with representatives of civil society both in Washington and on their frequent travels abroad. In 1996, delegations of Executive Directors met with business organisations, trade unions and other civic associations during tours of the Middle East and Eastern Europe. Meanwhile EXR has since 1990 organised a number of external relations missions abroad, where IMF staff have met with civic groups in selected countries including China, India, South Africa and Ukraine. More routinely, IMF mission chiefs and resident representatives have given briefings on Fund policies and procedures to a variety of civic associations in programme countries. Scores of civil society organisations have in the 1990s received invitations to attend the IMF/World Bank Annual Meetings, where the hosts have *inter alia* provided an NGO Room with full communications facilities.

The IMF has also pursued some tactics of indirect influence on civil society. In particular, the Fund has repeatedly argued – both in public declarations and in private urgings – that national governments should take the lead in forging popular support behind IMF-sponsored policies. On a few occasions (e.g. in Venezuela in 1996), Fund staff have worked closely with a government to 'sell' a structural adjustment programme to business groups, political parties, labour unions and church leaders. IMF officials have also engaged civil society through the United Nations, for instance, at UN-sponsored global conferences on environment and development in 1992, on social development in 1995, and on women also in 1995.

Impacts on IMF policy

To recapitulate the preceding sections, since the 1980s multifarious actors in civil society have engaged the IMF with a variety of aims, through diverse strategies, and with increasingly sophisticated campaign tactics. Concurrently, multiple parts of the Fund have developed relations with civil society, normally with fairly focused aims and strategies, and likewise employing increasingly sophisticated tactics. Yet what significance have relations between civil society and the IMF acquired in terms of policy impacts?

Needless to say, it is impossible to determine exactly the degree to which civic associations have affected IMF behaviour. The Fund's actions result from a complex interplay of circumstances of which inputs from civic groups are but one. Yet although the effects cannot be precisely measured, it is clear that civil society has over the last two decades had noteworthy influences both in reinforcing the primary lines of IMF policies and in shifting some of their secondary aspects.

Organisations pursuing conformist strategies towards the Fund have often played an important role in bolstering the IMF's existing policy frameworks. Bankers' associations, chambers of commerce and mainstream economic research institutes have rarely pushed the Fund to depart from its prevailing assumptions, modes of analysis and broad prescriptions. When these circles have exerted pressure, they have normally urged the Fund to make minor amendments or to perform better, that is, within established policy lines. To be sure, such criticisms have sometimes been sharply worded: e.g. on how the IMF might have miscalculated a target indicator; or how the Fund might have failed to anticipate a financial crisis. However, conformist groups have not attacked the primary Fund prescriptions, namely, for stabilisation, liberalisation, deregulation, privatisation, tax reform, a streamlined civil service, etc. On the contrary, mainstream business associations and think tanks have usually explicitly or implicitly endorsed these neo-liberal formulas. Contacts with conformist circles in civil society have thereby had an important effect of reinforcing the confidence of Fund officials in their established approaches to surveillance, conditionality, debt problems, and so on.

At the same time, civic associations pursuing changes at the IMF have made some impact in shifting both substantive policies and operating procedures in the institution (see further Scholte forthcoming). On the substantive side, inputs from trade unions, NGOs, development studies institutes and other critics have encouraged the Fund to reconsider its approach to conditionality in certain respects. Most prominently, IMF-sponsored programmes have since the mid-1990s given greater attention to the so-called 'social dimension' of structural adjustment. 'Safety nets' are now regularly incorporated into the package to protect, for example, health and education services (IMF 1995b; Chu and Gupta 1998). In addition, Fund research and policy have since the mid-1990s occasionally given attention to issues of environmental degradation, gender consequences of macro-economic policy, and corruption (Gandhi 1996; Stotsky 1996; Mauro 1997). On the question of external debt, persistent pressure from a variety of religious bodies and NGOs have helped to nurture a recognition in the Fund that these burdens form a hindrance to development in the South. Indeed, in 1996 the IMF together with the World Bank launched the Highly Indebted Poor Countries (HIPC) Initiative, a programme which has for the first time included modest relief on repayments to the two multilateral institutions (Boote and Thugge 1997).

With regard to operating procedures, inputs from civic associations have encouraged the IMF to adopt a number of steps in the 1990s toward greater transparency, accountability and participation. In respect of openness, the Fund has not only massively increased its production of public relations material (as noted earlier), but it has also since the mid-1990s released substantial numbers of policy documents and other details about its advice to governments. In addition, the IMF has answered calls for greater accountability in its operations with (hesitant) moves to develop a policy evaluation programme (Wood and Welch 1998). Finally, Fund management and staff have become more sensitive to a need for greater participation by client governments and civil societies in the formulation of IMF-supported policies.

In relation to the aims for change specified earlier, the shifts in policies and *modus operandi* just described constitute fairly modest alterations. Labour protection, poverty eradication, ecological sustainability, gender equity and human rights have not become central planks of IMF conditionality. The Fund has not come close to endorsing debt write-offs for the South. Some IMF operations continue to be cloaked in secrecy. Evaluation mechanisms for Fund policies remain underdeveloped. IMF officials are often still unclear how to move from the rhetoric of 'ownership' to the practice of participation.

On the other hand, none of these issues figured on the Fund agenda at all before the 1990s. Seen in this light, the IMF has undergone some reform in the broad directions that many civic activists have advocated. More generally, critics in civil society have stimulated searching debates in the 1990s about the desirable shape of global economic governance.

Limitations

As the preceding sections have indicated, contacts between the International Monetary Fund and civil society have become more numerous, more intricate and more influential than many observers of global economic governance appreciate. Nevertheless, the links remain in important respects underdeveloped. On three major counts, the relationships have manifested dangers for policy efficacy and democracy through the IMF.

The first key limitation concerns bias. The various parts of civil society have had unequal access to a dialogue with the Fund. In a rough ranking, academic institutions and business associations have tended to have easiest entry to the IMF. Trade unions have generally occupied second place. (Christian) religious groups, development NGOs and environmental NGOs have broadly come third, while many other groups including smallholder associations and women's organisations have had almost no contact with the IMF. Other biases in the relationships have favoured associations based in the North over groups located in the South and the East. In class terms, the great majority of contacts have involved university-educated, computer-literate, (relatively) high-earning English speakers. Owing to an urban-rural divide, organisations based in towns (especially national capitals) have usually had greater access to the Fund than groups in the countryside. Women have been severely under-represented both in the professional staff of the IMF and in the civic associations with which the Fund has had most contacts (i.e. business groups, economic research institutes and trade unions). Given these various biases, IMF-civil society relations have often poorly represented the various constituencies with a stake in the Fund's activities. The contacts have to this extent tended to reproduce or even enlarge structural inequalities and associated arbitrary privileges in the world political economy.

The second major shortcoming in IMF-civil society relations to date has been their overall shallowness. On both sides, most participants in these interchanges have remained inadequately informed about each other and have not given sufficient priority to developing their relationships. In spite of the many initiatives described earlier, links between civic associations and the Fund have on the whole been only weakly institutionalised and haphazardly sustained. The Executive Board has not yet formally articulated what purposes contacts with civil society should serve; nor has management carefully considered what institutional mechanisms would best advance the dialogue. In civil society, only a few associations like the IIF, the ICFTU, FOE-US and the Cato Institute have pursued sustained, focused, carefully researched campaigns to influence Fund policies. Many activists advocating change in the IMF have struggled *against* with only vague ideas about what they are struggling *for*. In these circumstances of overall superficiality on both sides, the Fund has missed many potentially valuable inputs from civic partners, while many initiatives from civil society toward the IMF have been ill-informed and misdirected.

The third core problem in IMF-civil society relations has concerned shortfalls in reciprocity. That is, the parties have tended to enter discussions with inadequate readiness to listen to, learn from, and be changed by the other side. A dialogue of the deaf has arisen especially when the general public relations strategy of the Fund has clashed with the reformist and radical strategies of many civic associations. On the whole, exchanges between these civic groups and the IMF have involved insufficient negotiation of differences. Civic organisers have complained that 'the IMF won't have a frank discussion about the problems of its policies', that 'you cannot critique in a dialogue with the Fund', and that 'if you're too insistent in expressing a different point of view, IMF people tell you to keep quiet' (interviews with the author). For their part, Fund officials have frequently objected that '[NGOs] spend the whole time telling us we're wrong', that 'it's hard to get a dialogue going with such people', and that 'some NGOs are just rabid' (interviews with the author). These difficulties have often prompted the IMF to focus its contacts with civil society more on conformist groups, to the relative neglect of challengers. Such a marginalisation of critics (whether deliberate or unconscious) could give the Fund an exaggerated sense of popular endorsement of its policies and might at some point generate a backlash against the institution.

Constraints on relations

The underdevelopment of relations just described has rarely resulted from ill will on the part of either IMF officials or civil society organisers. If blame is to be allocated, then it has lain principally with: (a) the limited resources that the parties have had to hand; and (b) certain deeper structures (e.g. related to institutional culture and the organisation of the world political economy) that the parties have inherited.

Neither civil society nor the Fund have had sufficient resources to realise the full potential of their relationships with each other. In terms of personnel, for example, the IMF staff has included no 'civil society experts' beyond a handful of public affairs officers in EXR. Other Fund officials have usually been overstretched with other responsibilities that are accorded a higher priority than dialogue with civic groups. Likewise, most civic organisations have lacked personnel with expertise regarding the IMF.

As for finances, the Fund has in the late 1990s allocated just 3.6 per cent of its fairly modest operating budget to cover all external relations activities (IMF 1997: 225). Meanwhile, apart from a few well-endowed think tanks and business lobbies, most civic groups have struggled on small budgets. NGO campaigns on the IMF have usually depended on small short-term grants from a handful of donors.

With regard to information, the IMF has accumulated but a meagre store of data concerning civic organisations. On the civil society side, although increased transparency at the Fund in the 1990s has improved matters, much crucial information regarding policy substance and process in the institution remains inaccessible to the public. As one experienced civic organiser from Africa has objected, 'How can we ever influence the IMF if we barely know it?' (interview with the author).

Both civic groups and the IMF have done little to compensate for their limited personnel, funds and information by coordinating their efforts. For example, the Fund has rarely drawn on the greater expertise and information regarding civic contacts which is available from the World Bank and various United Nations agencies. In civil society, although new technologies have helped to improve communications between associations in the 1990s, the various organisations have often failed to share intelligence and coordinate initiatives.

In addition to – and compounding – these resource shortfalls, several structural conditions of the world political economy have also hampered a fuller development of IMF-civil society relations in the late twentieth century. One of these barriers has related to the particular institutional characteristics of the Fund. As an organisation, the IMF has been highly monolithic and tightly run under a hierarchical, interventionist management. This institutional context has arguably discouraged Fund staff from developing more extensive and open discussions with civic groups.

Difficulties of access to the IMF for civil society have also resulted from the culture of secrecy that has traditionally enveloped all of monetary and financial regulation. To be sure, there are sound arguments for discretion in some Fund activities. For instance, devaluations, interest rate changes and the like clearly should not be publicised in advance. However, institutions of macro-economic policy-making like the IMF have tended to drape the cloak of secrecy over much more than sensitive matters. As noted earlier, the Fund has in the 1990s shifted its views on the balance between the need to know and the need for confidentiality in favour of the former. All the same, an embedded culture of secrecy does not dissolve quickly.

A third structural circumstance of the late twentieth century, namely, the power of neo-liberalism, has helped to produce both biased access and shortfalls in reciprocity in IMF-civil society relations. The neo-liberal paradigm has prescribed liberalisation, deregulation, privatisation and liberal democracy as a universal formula for the good society in the contemporary globalising world. Following the stagnation of post-colonial socialism in the South, the collapse of central planning in the East, and the retreat of corporatist welfarism in the North, neo-liberal ideology has reigned supreme across the world in the 1980s and 1990s. Alternative visions propounded in some civic circles – such as neo-mercantilism, Keynesianism, socialism, feminism and environmentalism – have in these times been readily marginalised. The structural power of neo-liberalism has enabled the IMF readily to reject unorthodox talk and to concentrate its contacts with civil society on sympathetic quarters like business associations and mainstream think tanks. Indeed, some campaigners for IMF reform have – deliberately or unconsciously – shifted their language in the direction of neo-liberalism in order to obtain a more serious hearing from the Fund.

Meanwhile embedded social hierarchies have played an important role in creating uneven access to the IMF for the different parts of civil society. In other words, the previously noted unequal entry has not been accidental. Social structures in the contemporary world political economy have systematically favoured the North over the South and the East, propertied and professional classes over poorer and less literate circles, urban centres over rural areas, and men over women. Such inequalities are easily (indeed, usually unconsciously and inadvertently) reproduced; they are but rarely (usually only with deliberate and persistent efforts) counteracted.

Another structural hierarchy – namely, that which has favoured the state over other social actors – has helped to keep most relations between the IMF and civil society shallow. True, as highlighted at the start of this chapter, states are far from the sole players in emergent post-Westphalian politics. Governments have lost sovereignty in its traditional sense of supreme, absolute, comprehensive and unilateral control over a territorial jurisdiction. On the other hand, states have become anything but powerless, and they have clung jealously to the *claim* that they always have the final say in governance. By the letter of international law, in the mindset of IMF staff, and also among many civic organisers, the Fund is seen to be responsible first and foremost to states and only secondarily, if at all, to civil society. Both the Fund and civic groups have usually limited their direct contacts to levels that national governments would tolerate.

Finally, IMF-civil society contacts have to date remained under-developed owing to insufficient attention on the part of civic organisations to their democratic credentials. Many of these groups – including some which have pressed hardest for a democratisation of the Fund – have not done enough to secure their own representativeness, consultation processes, transparency and accountability (see Bichsel 1996). These shortcomings have dented the credibility of many NGOs in particular and have allowed the IMF and states to take these associations less seriously than they might otherwise have done.

In sum, some very powerful social forces have hindered the development of a wider and deeper dialogue between civic groups and the Fund. Given the major resource limitations and inauspicious structural conditions reviewed above, it is not surprising that IMF-civil society relations have often had a partial, shallow and troubled character.

Towards the future

How might current shortcomings in relations between civil society and the IMF be overcome? They are by no means inevitable and incorrigible. After all, the contacts have over the past two decades already become more extensive and richer than any observer in 1980 might have imagined. True, major increases in resources and fundamental transformations in world structures would be required for exchanges between the Fund and civil society to realise their full potential to enhance efficacy and democracy in global economic governance. However, more modest and immediately feasible steps could substantially improve the situation in the short and medium term.

For one thing, both the IMF and civic associations could clarify their objectives in engaging with one another. On the side of the Fund, the Executive Board could formulate explicit general aims for the organisation's relations with civil society. Drawing on these guidelines, department heads could issue specific instructions to mission teams, resident representatives and other relevant staff. Many civil society groups could also establish more explicit, specific and practicable goals for their initiatives *vis-à-vis* the IMF.

The dialogue between the Fund and civic groups could also benefit from further development of institutional mechanisms. For example, the IMF's Articles of Agreement could be amended to 'legalise' the Fund's contacts with civic associations. More concretely, the IMF could at national level join with government, civil society actors and perhaps other global governance agencies like the World Bank to establish a consultative framework regarding Fund and other multilateral involvements in the country concerned. In addition, the IMF could include on its staff specifically designated 'civil society liaison officials' who would, with the consent of the governments concerned, be included in the Fund teams for designated countries. In civil society, meanwhile, many associations could alter their institutional procedures with a view to enhancing their democratic credentials.

Tight budgetary constraints for the time being preclude major increases in resources for IMF-civil society relations; however, it is to be hoped that, given the stakes involved, donors and managers might see fit to enlarge financial allocations at least somewhat. For civil society, such funds could be used in the first place to build capacity regarding the Fund, particularly in programme countries. Such capacity building would require a commitment of multiple years' funding rather than one-off short-term grants.

The Fund could use a modest expansion of allocations *inter alia* to hire the previously mentioned civil society liaison officials. In addition, monies could be used to give relevant IMF officials short training courses on cooperation with civil society. The Fund could furthermore use extra funds to increase its distribution of information to civic groups (particularly in the South and the East) which do not have access to the Internet. The IMF could also at limited expense expand and systematise a data base on civil society organisations. This task would probably be done most efficiently in collaboration with other multilateral institutions, for example through the Non-Governmental Liaison Service of the United Nations.

Finally, relations between civil society and the IMF could benefit from a number of shifts in attitude. For example, all parties could accord a higher priority to developing their mutual relations. IMF officials could go further in shifting their general approach from one of selling policies to one of discussing options. Civic organisers could do more to move beyond criticisms of the Fund to concrete suggestions for improvement. To encourage greater participation of marginalised circles, all parties in the IMF-civil society dialogue could make a habit of regularly asking 'who is missing'? Finally, both civic associations and the Fund could nurture greater sensitivity to questions of their accountability. In post-Westphalian times, non-state actors can no longer shift all responsibility for policy outcomes on to governments.

Conclusion

As seen from the preceding discussion, IMF contacts with civic associations illustrate the general contemporary trend whereby 'international organisation' of the Westphalian system has mutated into 'global governance' involving complex interlinkages of states, multilateral institutions and civil society. The Fund has since the 1970s grown into a major regulatory agency with some relative autonomy from its member governments. Over the same period, increasing numbers of civic groups have sought to learn about and influence the IMF, often by-passing states to establish direct links with the multilateral agency. Both civic organisations and the Fund have in their mutual relations pursued a variety of (progressively more sophisticated) aims, strategies and tactics.

Although a shift to a new multilateralism from below, identified in the introduction of this book, has not yet materialised, these interchanges have made some notable policy impacts at the IMF. On the one hand, inputs from business associations and mainstream think tanks have often reinforced the Fund's established policies. These conformist circles have underwritten and helped to fine tune orthodox approaches to stabilisation, neo-liberal prescriptions for structural adjustment, and conventional responses to external debt problems. On the other hand, inputs from trade unions, religious organisations, NGOs and reform-minded academic institutes have helped in the 1990s to induce marginal shifts in IMF conditionalities, first steps toward relief on multilateral debts for poor countries, and substantial moves toward greater transparency in Fund operations.

Yet relations between the IMF and civil society could, with further development, offer much more for effective and democratic global governance. The interchanges need to be more sustained and better informed. The dialogue needs to be more open, reflexive and creative. Access needs to be geared toward wider participation on equal terms. A number of immediately practicable steps are available to advance these ends, for example in terms of policy clarifications, institutional innovations, new resource allocations and attitudinal shifts. Such moves can help to ensure that emergent global governance through the IMF contributes to prosperity, equity, democracy, social cohesion and ecological sustainability.

Note

Research for this chapter has been supported through a grant under the Global Economic Institutions Programme of the Economic and Social Research Council in the United Kingdom (award no. L120251027). I am grateful to more than 130 persons in civil society, the IMF and other official circles who have shared with me their experiences of and reflections on relations between the Fund and civic groups. Interviews and correspondence were conducted on condition of non-attribution.

References

Bichsel, A. (1996) 'NGOs as agents of public accountability and democratization in intergovernmental forums', in W. M. Lafferty and J. Meadowcroft (eds), *Democracy and the Environment: Problems and Prospects*, Cheltenham: Edward Elgar.

Boote, A. R. and K. Thugge (1997) *Debt Relief for Low-Income Countries: The HIPC Initiative*, Washington: International Monetary Fund, Pamphlet Series no. 51.

Chu, K.-Y. and S. Gupta (1998) *Social Safety Nets: Issues and Experience*, Washington, D.C.: International Monetary Fund.

Driscoll, D. D. (1988a) *What Is the International Monetary Fund?* Washington, D.C.: International Monetary Fund.

—— (1988b) *The IMF and the World Bank: How Do They Differ?* Washington, D.C.: International Monetary Fund.

Gandhi, V. P. (ed.) (1996) *Macroeconomics and the Environment*, Washington, D.C.: International Monetary Fund.

GAO (1998) *International Monetary Fund: Observations on Its Financial Condition*, Washington, D.C.: United States Government General Accounting Office.

http://www.50years.org

http://www.iif.com

http://www.imf.org

ICFTU (1988) *Report of the Fourteenth World Congress*, Brussels: ICFTU.

—— (1992) *Report on Activities/Financial Reports 1987–1990*, Brussels: ICFTU.

—— (1996) *Report on Activities/Financial Reports 1991–94*, Brussels: ICFTU.

IMF (1966) *Annual Report 1966*, Washington, D.C.: International Monetary Fund.

—— (1994) *Annual Report 1994*, Washington, D.C.: International Monetary Fund.

—— (1995a) *Financial Organization and Operations of the IMF*, Washington, D.C.: International Monetary Fund, Pamphlet Series No. 45, fourth edn.

—— (1995b) *Social Dimensions of the IMF's Policy Dialogue*, Washington, D.C.: International Monetary Fund, Pamphlet Series No. 47.

—— (1996) *Annual Report 1996*, Washington, D.C.: International Monetary Fund.

—— (1997) *Annual Report 1997*, Washington, D.C.: International Monetary Fund.

James, H. (1996) *International Monetary Cooperation since Bretton Woods*, New York: International Monetary Fund and Oxford University Press.

Jordan, L. (1996) 'The Bretton Woods challengers', in J. M. Griesgraber and B. G. Gunter (eds), *Development: New Paradigms and Principles for the Twenty-First Century*, London: Pluto.

Landell-Mills, J. (1988) *Helping the Poor: The IMF's New Facilities for Structural Adjustment*, Washington, D.C.: International Monetary Fund.

Maryknoll (n.d.) *Banking on Life and Debt*, film by Maryknoll World Productions.

Mauro, P. (1997) *Why Worry about Corruption?* Washington, D.C.: International Monetary Fund, Economic Issues Series No. 6.

Reed, D. (ed.) (1996) *Structural Adjustment, the Environment and Sustainable Development*, London: Earthscan.

Scholte, J. A. (1997) 'The globalization of world politics', in J. Baylis and S. Smith (eds), *The Globalization of World Politics: An Introduction to International Relations*, Oxford: Oxford University Press.

—— (1998) 'The IMF meets civil society', *Finance and Development* 35, 3: 42–5.

—— (1999a) 'Civil society and a democratisation of the International Monetary Fund', in P. Yeros , S. O. Vandersluis and and S. Owen (eds), *Poverty in World Politics: Whose*

Global Era? London: Macmillan.

—— (1999b) 'Globalisation and governance', in P. Hanafin and M. S. Williams (eds), *Identity, Rights and Constitutional Transformation*, Aldershot: Ashgate.

—— (forthcoming) 'Social movements and the International Monetary Fund', in R. O'Brien *et al.*, *Contesting Global Governance: The Global Economic Institutions – Social Movement Nexus*, Cambridge: Cambridge University Press.

Stotsky, J. G. (1996) *Gender Biases in Tax Systems*, Washington, D.C.: International Monetary Fund, Discussion Paper 96/99.

Torfs, M. (1996) *The IMF Handbook: Arming NGOs with Knowledge*, Brussels: Friends of the Earth Europe.

Vries, M. de (1986) *The IMF in a Changing World, 1945–85*, Washington, D.C.: International Monetary Fund.

Watkins, K. *et al.* (1995) *The Oxfam Poverty Report*, Oxford: Oxfam UK and Ireland.

Woestman, L. (1994) *Male Chauvinist SAPs: Structural Adjustment and Gender Policies*, Brussels: EURODAD/WIDE.

Wood, A. and C. Welch (1998) *Policing the Policemen: The Case for an Independent Evaluation Mechanism for the IMF*, London and Washington: Bretton Woods Project and Friends of the Earth-US.

16 Transnational environmental groups, media, science and public sentiment(s) in domestic policy-making on climate change

Susanne Jakobsen

Students of international relations (IR) with an interest in global environmental politics (GEP) have tended to reach mainly for books on games theory and regimes. As a result, the study of GEP has become the study of intergovernmental negotiations, institution-building and regime effectiveness. This has left the sub-discipline with a rather narrow focus, implying that states are the principal agents of GEP, while the activities of non-state actors are mostly ignored or explained as marginal phenomena. The interest of the state, moreover, is perceived as systemic, as being based merely on positioning in the international system, and case studies, while resting more on theoretical assumptions than actual empirical investigations, have largely evolved around the participation of industrialised countries.

This paper presents the findings of a study carried out from a somewhat unusual approach to GEP from within IR. The study explores policy-making on climate change in Brazil and India from 1988 to 1997. To this end, the intergovernmental has been replaced with the domestic and the transnational.[1] Second, non-state as well as state actors have been scrutinised in terms of their interests and actions. Third, the study is based on empirical fieldwork rather than theoretical assumptions.[2] Fourth, it is focused on developing rather than industrialised countries.

The parallel study of policy-making processes in Brazil and India in relation to climate change scrutinises interests and roles of two federal bureaucracies. In India, these are found to have relied heavily on domestic non-state actors, while the process in Brazil has been tightly closed off to outsiders. The study goes on to explore the activities of non-state actors. Domestic environmental groups and research communities in India are found to have had a crucial impact on the government's policy-making in relation to climate change, mainly through their application of knowledge and insights gained through transnational networking and aided by overseas funding. In Brazil, on the other hand, where domestic non-state actors have been less influential, indeed mostly absent, it has been campaigning by North American and European environmental groups that has directed much of the agenda facing the government in this area. This campaigning has been reinforced by abstract forces of public sentiment and media coverage in North America and Western Europe.[3] The promotion of specific items of knowledge on tropical deforestation and its importance to global climate change by foreign researchers has further added to a situation where the Brazilian government has been left merely responding and performing on the international stage regarding the environment.

Hence I suggest that, in addition to intergovernmental negotiations, GEP is characterised by transnational networks of non-state actors such as environmental groups and research communities who apply particular sets of knowledge in order to promote specific interests. Further, diffuse non-state actors such as the media and public sentiment(s) appear to have important agenda-setting roles. Capturing GEP as a matter of intergovernmental bargaining resulting in a convention created in a compromise between North American, European and developing country governments and their exogenously defined preferences is too simplistic. Empirical policy analysis of the domestic processes shaping the Brazilian and Indian national positions on climate indicates that multiple state and non-state interests interact on the domestic and transnational levels to shape the positions presented at the intergovernmental negotiation table. This paper is therefore also arguing that we begin at the beginning, with the study of the interests that enter those intergovernmental negotiations.

Brazil and India at the International Convention on Climate Change

International negotiations on climate change culminated in 1992 with the agreement on the United Nations Framework Convention on Climate Change (UNFCCC). The convention is unambiguously rooted in a context that differentiates North and South, not only in requiring developed countries to take the lead in combating global changes in climate, but also in its repeated references to the differing circumstances and responsibilities of developed and developing countries. The UNFCCC notes that 'the largest share of historical and current global emissions of greenhouse gases has originated in developed countries, that per capita emissions in developing countries are still relatively low and that the share of global emissions in developing countries will grow to meet their social and development needs' (IEA/OECD 1996: 67).

Major developing countries, such as India, Brazil and China, played a crucial part in the insertion of such statements in the UNFCCC, repeatedly being at the forefront of the G77 in demanding 'new and additional funding' and technology transfers for developing countries to participate in the UNFCCC.[4] The Indian government in particular has played a considerable role in promoting such common positions among the G77. At the second meeting of the Intergovernmental Negotiating Committee (INC) in 1991, the Indian delegation drafted a proposal for a convention that suggested a per capita approach to the handling (stabilisation, growth or mitigation) of national carbon dioxide emissions. In the words of India's chief negotiator: 'If per capita emissions of all countries had been on the same levels as that of developing countries, the world today would not have faced the threat of global warming'.[5]

While India's position has been fairly stable over the years, Brazil's has undergone extensive modifications. The initial Brazilian position on climate change developed out of intense international attention in the late 1980s to the government's development and deforestation activities in Amazonia. Overseas attention from the media, politicians and environmental groups provoked a series of immediate, defensive statements concerning the international threat to Brazil's 'sovereign right to use its own territory' from President José Sarney.[6] Months of rhetoric, resistance and denial were followed by gradual acceptance and confusing signals in 1988–9 that 'we understand that the international community has a right to be concerned by the . . . damage done to the environment wherever it may occur . . . Brazil shoulders its responsibilities.'[7] This was followed up with the application to the United Nations to host the forthcoming Conference on Environment and Development (UNCED). From 1990 to 1992, the newly-elected President, Fernando Collor de Mello, sought to remove any remaining doubts on the international scene with respect to Brazil's environmental image by introducing vigorous domestic environmental reforms and constructive engagement in the international preparations for UNCED. Government rhetoric moved away from denunciations of outside interference and towards demands for external assistance. With the hosting of UNCED in 1992, the Collor government took to favouring a strong convention on climate change founded on the shouldering of 'common but differentiated responsibilities'. Subsequently, this activity evaporated into a period of political passivity with regard to the problem (1992–4), but in recent years (1995–7) new aspirations and scientific consolidation have been used to reinforce the claim that Brazil is 'making efforts to preserve the environment and promote sustainability because we are aware of the importance of the Amazon for us and for the world'.[8]

Exploring policy-making and interests within the state

The early (1988) Brazilian position on deforestation in Amazonia, which eventually evolved into a position on climate change, was the result of immediate reactions emanating from enclosed, secretive meetings of the military sector and the Presidential office. Brazil had barely returned to democracy from a period of military rule which had linked the concept of national security to national development, particularly in the economic sphere (Allen 1992).[9] Following the military coup in 1964, the government had begun a systematic policy of development in the Amazonia region (Allen 1992; Guimarães 1992; Hall 1992; Hurrell 1990). The military had tended to perceive Amazonia not only as of source for national development and thus an abstraction of national sovereignty, but also as a vast territory of unoccupied land that had to be physically occupied in order to secure the national territory in a frontier region which had undefended borders with seven neighbouring states (Browder 1989; Goldstein 1992; Goodman and Hall 1990: 4–8; Hall 1992: 6). The military administration was thus heavily involved in the government-sponsored development of Amazonia, not only under the military regime itself (1964–86), but also in the years of the *Novo Estado* (1986–90) (Allen 1992; Henberg 1994), and the 1980s actually saw a resurgence of military interest in the region (Hurrell 1991). Foreign attention to the government's activities in Amazonia in the late 1980s was consequently perceived as 'subversive manoeuvres' threatening national sovereignty.

The gradually more cautious responses of the later Sarney government (1989–90) were increasingly dominated by the more conscious efforts of the Ministry of External Affairs (Itamaraty) to intervene and create an actual foreign policy on the environment. While most governments in North America and Western Europe had experienced the gradual introduction of climate change as an issue from their domestic civil societies, the Brazilian government had the completely different experience of being abruptly awakened to the ecological crisis and the subsequent public demands for action by external actors and forces. Before even having a national policy on the environment, Brazil had to build a position on deforestation and climate change. As international attention increased, the shaping of the national position came to be a concern primarily of officials within Itamaraty.

Under Collor de Mello (1990–2) military involvement in federal policy-making became much more ambivalent and less obvious (Henberg 1994) and foreign policy became primarily the domain of Itamaraty. Its immediate interest with respect to the climate was largely a variant on the concerns for national sovereignty uttered by the military. The ministry had interacted closely with the military during the 1970s and 1980s over Amazonia, and thus came to assist the military and the Presidential office in the initial shaping of responses to foreign pressure concerning Amazonian deforestation and climate change. Throughout the life of the Collor government, Itamaraty remained a conservative backstop to domestic forces such as the President, who was eager to soften the international image of the Brazilian government. Collor, in need of foreign investments for his ambitious economic programme, saw UNCED as a unique opportunity to revise North American and West European perceptions of his government. Part of Collor's 'green image' had been to appoint environmental activist José Lutzenberger as his Minister of Environment. Itamaraty, however, had Lutzenberger dismissed a few months prior to UNCED.

In the post-UNCED period, Itamaraty is fully in charge of the national position. The Ministry of Science and Technology (MCT) manages the national emissions inventory, but it has little political input. Itamaraty's monopoly hardly signals any specific interest of the ministry in climate change but is more likely the result of a domestic impasse in relation to climate change which creates little concern or interest today among federal bureaucrats. International attention regarding deforestation in Brazil has somewhat evaporated from the negotiations on climate change, and climate change as a topic thus survives in the corridors of Itamaraty largely because of continuing negotiations under the terms of UNFCCC. The military shows little interest in these as perceptions of national security have shifted from physical occupation to satellite monitoring, and neither the Ministry of the Environment nor the MCT have shown any interest in becoming involved in the shaping of the national position.

In India, on the other hand, the government has left the national position to the Ministry of Environment and Forests (MOEF). In the preparations for UNCED, the Ministry of Foreign Affairs showed some concern and disputed the decision-making power of the MOEF. Today, external affairs officials participate in national delegations but seem disinterested, their major focus being to streamline the MOEF position in accordance with general foreign policy objectives. Generally, climate change seems to attract little concern or controversy within the bureaucracy.

The MOEF receives technical support from a wide range of federal ministries, but there is little exchange of opinion on the political aspects of the position. Many interviewees outside government suggested that the national position hardly exists on paper but only in the heads of the delegation officials; consequently it is hard for other parties in the government bureaucracy to comment on the position. Individual researchers and activists outside government have nevertheless suc-ceeded in being major sources of input for the initial shaping of the position. The government did not activate itself on climate change until 1990, when domestic researchers and activists sounded alarm bells on the political consequences that were at stake for India and other developing countries. A 'learning period' followed where MOEF officials relied extensively on non-state actors to explain and advise them on the issue. In recent years, as in the case of Brazil, climate change survives as a topic with the government primarily because government officials have to attend ongoing negotiations under the UNFCCC.

In both countries, and throughout the research period, politicians, business interests and political parties have been largely absent from domestic policy-making processes on climate change.[10] National positions remain in the hands of government technocrats. However, this does not mean that positions merely reflect the interests of the bureaucracy. Rather, a complex web of actors and diffuse forces outside government bureaucracies have been paramount in shaping the framework within which Brazilian and Indian government officials have had to respond and perform. The interests, positions and reflections of environmental groups, climate-change researchers, the media, public sentiment(s) and 'triggering events' shaped the contours and had tremendous impact on the contents of govern-mental decision-making on climate change in both countries.

Environmental groups, researchers and policy-making processes

The impact of various non-state actors on government policy-making has taken very different routes. In Brazil, it has been external, largely coincidental, indirect and often rather diffuse. In India, it has been domestic and mostly the result of direct and focused lobbying.

Domestic environmental groups and researchers have had little impact on the Brazilian position, as only a handful of individual activists have shown any interest in the issue. Rather, foreign groups have been highly influential in their campaign-ing in the 1980s against deforestation activities in Amazonia, a campaign which has had considerable effect on the contours of the Brazilian position, then and now. In the mid-1980s, American environmental groups transformed Amazonia into a 'global' issue as they began campaigning on the American government's support of World Bank lending and its environmental effects.[11] The first stage of this campaign became that of getting the American government to play a leading role in examining the environmental policies and procedures of multilateral development banks (MDBs). In order to achieve this, American environmental groups linked up with local groups in order to bring eyewitnesses from the borrowing countries before Congress (Bramble and Porter 1992). From 1983 to 1986 seventeen hearings were held before Congress into projects funded by MDBs in Brazil, India, Indonesia and Africa (Arnt 1992).

In subsequent years, American groups were joined by their West European counterparts.[12] On both continents grass roots organisations issued certificates to buy up areas of the Amazon rain-forest, rock-stars staged concerts to 'save the rainforest', and television footage of the fight between landless poor, Amazon Indians and large cattle-ranchers over tracts of land entered the living-rooms of many Americans and Europeans. To the rest of the world, the Brazilian forest came to represent an exotic last wilderness, the 'lungs of the earth', while the Brazilian government, responsible for much of Amazonia's deforestation and general socio-economic problems, accordingly became the environmental villain of the world.

Increasingly, overseas campaigning translated into an uneasy international political situation for the Brazilian government, with the Amazonia question intruding into talks and negotiations on trade and financing. The World Bank, having sustained much international criticism throughout the 1980s, eventually responded by setting an example in 1986, when negotiations with the Brazilian government on an energy investment plan for Brazil comprising a series of large dams in Amazonia were suspended with reference to environmental concerns (Kasa 1994). North American and West European groups, by mobilising domestic politicians against MDB lending and its environmental effects, have thus been paramount in provoking actual bilateral (American government) and multilateral (World Bank) pressure on the Brazilian government in relation to deforestation. In the end, with deforestation and climate change being closely related, such non-state, external pressure came to constitute a political framework constraining policy-making on the national position.[13] The Brazilian government, having suffered numerous attacks on its Amazonia policies, was left with little option but to acknowledge the importance of the climate and Brazilian responsibility for a 'common future'.

Until recently, Brazilian researchers had little knowledge of or training regarding climate change-related matters or the importance of tropical deforestation for the calculation of global carbon dioxide. In any case, domestic political demand for scientific inputs on the question has been limited. In recent years, under the Cardoso government, there have been attempts to coordinate and strengthen domestic research on climate change. The tendency is, however, for scientific inputs and political positions to be treated separately. Researchers themselves seem reluctant to issue comments on the political aspects of the national position.

The shaping of India's national position has been much more directly influenced by domestic environmental groups and climate change experts. Researchers within the Tata Energy Research Institute (TERI) and activists from the Centre for Science and Environment (CSE) were highly influential in the initial shaping of the MOEF's preference formation. A process evolved in which researchers and activists advised MOEF officials on the political issues at stake. As Kamal Nath, Minister of Environment (1991–5), said in my interview with him, 'TERI and CSE came to be my major arms of input in the UNCED negotiations'. Post-UNCED, the MOEF has become more self-reliant. TERI officials appear to have maintained a fairly close exchange on the topic with MOEF officials. Although they have been less active than in previous years, CSE officials have also influenced MOEF officials, though mostly in respect of last-minute decisions on positions during the actual international protocol negotiations.

Domestic cooperation between non-state actors has generally been minor. Only a few domestic researchers and activists beyond TERI and CSE have shown any interest in climate change, and TERI and CSE have differed widely in their perception of the issues at stake. Further, given the absence of an exotic, tropical rainforest, foreign popular attention to the Indian government's environmental policies has been minimal and of little importance.

Science and knowledge-based gateways

Non-state impacts, although differing in aim and direction in the two cases, have rested primarily on the application of specific patches of scientific knowledge and political insights.

In the case of Brazil, North American and West European environmental groups produced a variety of scientific claims on the extent of deforestation, its environmental effects and ultimately its role in global climate change. The production of Brazilian witnesses before the American Congress and the added effect of captive media footage transformed such scientific claims into public sentiment, political actions and a general international situation with which the Brazilian government could do nothing but comply.

In 1990, the prestigious American World Resources Institute (WRI), in collaboration with UNDP, published its influential second annual *World Resources* report. There, the WRI claimed that developing countries were just as responsible for climate change as developed countries. The report characterised Brazil as a key contributor to global warming, as it ranked Brazil third in a global greenhouse gas index (1987 figures), its total emissions (deforestation as well as fossil fuel related emissions) outstripping the fossil fuel emissions of the United States. Concluded WRI: 'even developing countries can emit large quantities of greenhouse gases to the atmosphere' (World Resources Institute 1990: 15–17, 345–9).

The WRI index was one of the first attempts to compare national emissions across the world and was therefore widely discussed in the international negotiations as a potential tool for a global agreement. The scientific results produced by this external, non-state actor came to provide a crucial element in the global political setting within which Brazilian policy-makers had to form a position on climate change. In addition to external concern over deforestation and its socio-ecological effects at a local level, the Brazilian government now had to respond to concerns on global atmospheric effects. The Brazilian government was now suddenly perceived as a key actor in any intergovernmental agreement on this issue.[14]

India was ranked just below Brazil as the fourth contributor to global greenhouse gas emissions. In a counter-report (Agarwal and Narain 1991), the Delhi-based CSE challenged the WRI results as 'based less on science and more on politically motivated mathematical jugglery'.[15] The CSE report became a real eye-opener, not only for the Indian government, but also for the delegations participating in the INC preparations for UNCED. The CSE report was possibly the first attempt to bring considerations of equity into the emerging negotiations, and it was the first serious questioning of the responsibility of developing countries in combating global emissions. The debate between the WRI and the CSE, right at the beginning of the negotiations on a convention, significantly fuelled the North-South debate on climate change.

In India, the dispute received wide press coverage. The MOEF adopted firmer action on the shaping of its position and gradually turned away from the initial reaction of then Minister of Environment, Maneka Gandhi, that (in the light of the WRI conclusions) 'India should stop producing rice'.[16] MOEF officials picked up the CSE discourse that there is a difference between the 'survival emissions' of the poor (from cows and rice fields) and the 'luxury emissions' of the rich (from fossil fuel burning), and the Minister switched her position from one of India being equally responsible to one pointing to a 'methane conspiracy' that attempted to focus attention on India's emissions rather than Europe's or North America's.

Generally, domestic climate change researchers have had considerably easier access to the policy-making process in India than in Brazil. In 1990-1, Indian activists (in the CSE) and researchers (in TERI) had significantly greater knowledge and insight into climate change-related matters than many of the government officials who were to form the initial Indian position. Thus it was in response to informal request from the MOEF that TERI and the CSE began advising the Ministry on these matters in 1990. The MOEF issued a specific grant to TERI to provide analytical support on the issue. The CSE, being more of a traditional 'watchdog' organisation, did not receive any such funding, but a situation developed where both organisations became essential advisors to the Indian government on its strategy and foreign policy concerning climate change. The more knowledge and insight that domestic groups possessed, the more government officials seemed to adopt their preferences.

Transnational gateways

Transnational networking has been a second major gateway providing influence to non-state actors in the case of both Indian and Brazilian government policy-making on climate change. In the case of Brazil, foreign groups, partly through their networking with local Amazonian groups, were able to pressure North American and West European politicians and thus the World Bank, whereby they indirectly established the framework for the Brazilian government's position. Initially, the transnational agenda facing Brazil was more about deforestation,

Amazonian Indians and the rural poor. However, as scientific findings on tropical deforestation and its role in the global carbon cycle prevailed in media coverage, intergovernmental negotiations and public sentiment in North America and West Europe, the Brazilian government could no longer disclaim responsibility for Amazonian deforestation, nor fail to voice concern over global changes in climate.

In the case of India, transnational contacts were of paramount importance to the impact exerted by domestic activists and researchers. By employing their transnationally derived knowledge of climate change, domestic non-state actors gained fairly direct access to government policy-making in this field. In 1988, TERI had received funding from the Rockefeller Foundation in the United States, the International Development Research Centre (Canada) and the Ford Foundation (USA) to set up a Research Centre for Global Warming and Climate Change, and the CSE, although having little affiliation with the issue initially, enjoyed rapid access to information through their overseas contacts. Such transnational contacts and networking, in some cases involving sponsorship, might have contributed to the Indian delegation's change of position during the Second Conference of the Parties (COP2) in 1996 from years of resistance into acceptance of a pilot phase of Assisted Implementation Jointly (AIJ).[17] Through the years of government resistance to any kind of market-based implementation mechanisms, TERI as well as the Bombay-based Indira Gandhi Institute for Development Research (IGIDR) have been involved in a striking number of transnational research projects and programmes on tradeable permits and AIJ. Most of these projects are directly sponsored by or paid for by Northern research institutions and funds.

Essentially, then, policy-making by non-state actors has been neither purely domestic nor international, but transnational. Researchers and environmental groups, through their transnational activities and connections, have framed the agenda, shaped the contours of and laid down the foundations for government policy-making. Consequently, the national position, beyond simply reflecting the 'national interest' of the state, is also a transnationally shaped construct of non-state preferences and interests. Such non-state interests have found their way to government decision-making in a variety of ways. Non-state channels of impact on the Brazilian position have been mainly external, but they depend to some degree on internal, that is, domestic non-state sources of information. The opposite is the case with the Indian position, where non-state channels of impact have been largely domestic, but relying heavily on external sources of information and funding.

These patterns of transnational policy-making have brought with them the agendas, discourses and interests of researchers and activists from the industrialised North. Research on climate change has been dominated largely by North American and West European scientists (Sagar and Kandlikar 1997; Smith 1994).[18] In both India and Brazil, it remains consistently underprioritised, underfunded and marginalised, relying extensively on financial and institutional collaboration with European and North American research institutions and programmes. As a result, Brazilian and Indian researchers are, at least to some extent, likely to produce preferences and interests developed by researchers and political priorities in the North. The Indian government in particular, by relying heavily on the insights and advice of transnationally informed domestic researchers and activists, came indirectly to lock themselves into a policy-making process where the response to a largely Northern government agenda would be shaped with the help of Northern-dependent domestic knowledge.

Media, public sentiment(s) and 'triggering events'

Finally, in the largely transnational policy-making process with its state and non-state actors, more elusive agents, such as the media, public sentiment(s) and 'triggering events' have contributed to the shaping of the national positions, especially in the case of Brazil.

Until the late 1980s, Amazonia was of little interest to the North American and West European media, and then mostly as the 'River Wonderland' (*New York Times* 16 March 1986, vol. 135: 65), where one could find 'Amazing Amazon tin' (*Economist*, 7 December 1985, vol. 297: 78) in a forest of 'exotic abundance' (*New York Times*, 19 March 1987, vol. 136: 10).

With the assassination of Chico Mendes in December 1988 and the February 1989 meeting of the Kayapó Indians in Altamira to protest against the building of the Kararao Dam on the Xingu river, there was a sharp, almost hysterical increase in international press coverage of Brazil.[19] The assassination was the lead story in the *New York Times* the following day ('Brazilian who fought to protect Amazon is killed') and headlines shifted drastically from romantic perceptions of a fertile tropical forest to that of 'Amazon ablaze' (*New York Times*, 24 December 1988, vol. 138: 1). Burning of the rain forest' (*Christian Science Monitor Monthly*, February 1989 Vol. 2, No. 2: 20), 'Murder in the Amazon' (*Discover*, January 1990, Vol. 11, No. 1: 30), 'Beauty endangered' (*Maclean's*, 21 May 1990, Vol. 103, No. 21: 60) and 'One of the great tragedies of history' (*Time*, 18 September 1989, Vol. 134, No.12: 76). Old footage of Chico Mendes' struggles to protect the rubber-tappers was transformed into a fifty-minute documentary covering his life and assassination and the later attempts to find his murderer ('*Murder in the Amazon*').[20]

Such media coverage is likely to have triggered a number of popular events, which in turn led to more media coverage. Ilzamar, Chico Mendes' wife, sold the rights to his story for more than a million US dollars and a number of producers competed for the rights to make a film on his life.[21] The year after, Senator Al Gore travelled to Amazonia with two delegations from the Congress. In New York City, pop star Madonna helped organise a benefit concert entitled 'Don't Bungle the Jungle', which also featured other popular names, such as the B-52s and the Grateful Dead's Bob Weir. Meanwhile, a sequence of events in 1988 – an extremely dry and hot summer on the American and European continents, a giant forest fire in the popular American Yellowstone National Park, hurricane Gilbert in the Caribbean, tens of thousands of flood victims in Bangladesh, and prolonged drought in the American Midwest – provoked public concern in North America and Western Europe about global warming. The statement by NASA scientist James Hansen to the American Congress that very same summer, 'that the evidence is pretty strong that the greenhouse effect is here', is likely to have been another defining moment in the triggering of public concern and political awareness in relation to climate change.[22]

Eventually, such 'triggering events' and the earlier described media coverage came to reinforce and focus public sentiment on Brazilian Amazonia, a sentiment that had earlier been initiated by the MDB campaigning of North American and West European environmental groups. It was this complex web of agents and diffuse forces outside the state that gradually came to force upon the Sarney and Collor governments directions for their performance on the international environmental scene in the late 1980s and early 1990s. The Brazilian rainforest, as Andrew Hurrell (1991) has earlier pointed out, became a particularly powerful focus for protest and campaigning for environmental movements in North America and West Europe, as the drama and visibility of deforestation, with pictures of huge palls of smoke, bulldozers at work, vast areas of jungle being flooded, the existence of clear villains (a fairly undemocratic government, multilateral banks) and the tragedy of the victims (Indians and the rural poor) easily lent themselves to media coverage.

Conclusion

In this paper, I have explored global environmental politics (GEP) from a somewhat different angle than contemporary norms dictate within this subdiscipline. I have deliberately chosen to investigate the formation of the state's national interest before it enters into those very intergovernmental negotiations that have otherwise been heralded as our focus for analysis. This has involved the analysis of government bureaucracies and their sometimes contradictory interests and preferences. More importantly, the study has incorporated analysis of the activities and interests of a multitude of non-state actors in policy-making processes. In order to grasp fully the extent of the political activities carried out by non-state actors, the analysis has taken place at the level of domestic and transnational rather than international politics.

Given the fact that the empirical observations on policy-making concerning the Brazilian and Indian national positions on climate change are at least to some extent representative of contemporary GEP, it becomes obvious that IR theory on the environment has run into stalemate. The majority of IR-GEP studies, while focusing on the state as the principal agent of international politics, have contributed little to the actual analysis of the state. Consequently, we know the state merely as a black box with given preferences. This assumption falls short of recognising the identified subsets of bureaucratic interests in this study that have engaged in shaping the national positions of Brazil and India in relation to climate change. Further, non-state actors have generally attracted little analytical attention among IR-GEP scholars, who tend to rely heavily on neo-liberal institutional approaches. In this study, however, the frame of analysis has been expanded to include domestic and transnational politics and consequently a myriad of interests and agents outside the state were disclosed. Through a variety of channels, environmental groups, scientific communities and diffuse forces of media and public sentiment not only influenced, but in some cases directed the policy framework of government decision-making. In other words, in contrast to established IR theory, this study has been able to account for the range of non-state actors which nowadays share authority with states at the global level (see introduction of this book).

Overall, the analysis of the Brazilian and Indian governments' preparations for the intergovernmental negotiations on climate change shows that GEP takes place not merely between governments in international regimes but also in the interface between domestic and transnational politics. Both governments have at times been mere puppets in a show outlined by the transboundary campaigning of environmental groups, the release of selected data by scientists, catching media coverage and public sentiment(s) in the industrialised North. Non-state actors are thus important facets of our study of GEP, not only in terms of their interaction with and impact on states, but also in their own right as important political actors who set the agenda, selects the issues at stake and colour the discourse of intergovernmental bargaining. Contemporary GEP consists not only in the immediacy of intergovernmental cooperation or the conspicuous actions of the state in the international system, but also in the complex interactions and competing interests of media, public sentiment, environmental groups and scientific communities.

Finally, most studies have ignored developing countries as an object of study when it comes to GEP. The tendency has been to pigeonhole them as 'slackers' and to argue, in overly moral tones, that all nations must get together to solve the problems. This analysis has instead indicated the necessity of attending to the varying definitions, understandings and calculations of 'our global common'. Government officials, as well as environmentalists and researchers in developing countries, disagree considerably with their peers in the industrialised North over matters of concern and the issues at stake. Moreover, the developing country government administration, unstable and fractured as it often is, is likely to be subject to the influence of transnational non-state actors more easily. In simple terms, the investigation of non-state actors and their transnational networking might be more accessible from an angle that is focused on developing country politics.

Notes

1 Risse-Kappen (1995) has slightly modified the original definition of 'transnational relations' to cover (3): 'regular interactions across national boundaries when at least one actor is a non-state agent or does not act on behalf of a national government or an intergovernmental organization'.

2 Interviews with more than forty individuals in each of the two countries took place in 1996 (Brasilia, São Paulo and Rio de Janeiro) and 1997 (New Delhi and Bombay). Among those interviewed were high-level government officials, former ministers, politicians, researchers and representatives of environmental groups and private industry. In addition, the research builds on secondary sources of information such as academic texts, newspapers and the Internet.

3 I have employed the concept 'public sentiment(s)' to replace the more commonly used, but rarely defined, 'public opinion'. One can hardly speak of a single, cognisant public opinion. Nor is it possible to know the exact character of a single or

more 'sentiment(s)'. The employment of sentiment, however, is an attempt to charac-terise a loose sense of feelings, perceptions and emotions that run through a number of people in a given society on a given issue.

4 The Group of 77 is a coalition of developing countries in the United Nations' system established on 15 June 1964 by seventy-seven developing countries. Membership has since increased to 132 countries.

5 Chandrasekhar Dasgupta, chief Indian negotiator to INC2 in 1991; quoted from *The Statesman* (New Delhi), 23 June 1991.

6 *The Times*, 8 March 1989 quoted in Hurrell (1991) and *Journal do Brasil*, 18 March 1989.

7 *Brazilian Positions on Environment and Development,* Brasilia, Brazil: Ministry of External Relations, General Secretariat for Foreign Policy, Division for the Environment, 1991.

8 President Cardoso in a press release, two weeks before the Third Conference of the Parties (COP3) in Kyoto. *Climate-List,* 26 November 1997.

9 Brazil returned to democracy in 1985 after twenty-one years of authoritarian rule; transition was slowed substantially when Neves, the winner of the first democratic presidential election, died shortly before his induction and vice-president José Sarney took over the presidency. The new republic was established on the institu-tional foundations of the authoritarian regime rather than on its ruins, allowing most of the political and bureaucratic elites of the former regime to remain in control. The strong state apparatus built up by the military remained intact and military influence in civilian policy-making went largely uncontested (Hagopian 1990; Henberg and Zirker 1994; Sznajder 1996; Wirth *et al.* 1987: 2).

10 Business interests have been almost totally absent from the policy-making process in India. In Brazil, financial interests and large ranchers in Amazonia mobilised around the issue of deforestation in the late 1980s. They have, however, shown little interest in later positions on climate change.

11 In 1983, the National Wildlife Federation and the Environmental Policy Institute initiated a 'Bank Rolling Disasters' campaign. In 1985, they were joined by the Environmental Defence Fund, the Sierra Club and the Rainforest Action Network (Bramble and Porter 1992). Kolk (1996) adds Friends of the Earth and Cultural Survival to this list.

12 Contacts were made with groups in the United Kingdom, Germany, the Netherlands and Scandinavia to bring similar pressure for reform to bear on other governments with large voting shares on the World Bank's Executive Board (Rich 1994).

13 Deforestation leads to release of the primary greenhouse gas carbon dioxide. On a global scale, the Intergovernmental Panel on Climate Change (IPCC) puts the contribution of deforestation at 18 per cent of total greenhouse gas in the 1980s with an uncertainty range of between 9 and 26 per cent (IPCC 1990 cited in Paterson 1996: 174).

14 In the following years critical examinations of former deforestation estimates in Amazonia unveiled methodological problems in the interpretation of remote-sensing images. In the 1992 WRI index, Brazil dropped to number five in the world of total GHGs, and number forty-four from a per capita perspective (World Resources Institute 1992: 201–3; 345–9).

15 The CSE challenged the WRI claims on three grounds: first, WRI had assessed the emissions from every single country, ignoring the size of a country or its population; second, there was no differentiation between the 'luxury emissions' of the rich (fos-sil fuel emissions) and the 'survival emissions' of the poor (emissions from paddy fields and dairy cattle); third, the CSE called into question the WRI's extrapolation of methane measurements from paddy fields in Europe and the USA to those in Asia. From this the CSE concluded that developing countries could only be held accountable for 33 per cent of global greenhouse gas emissions (Agarwal and Narain 1991).

16 Paddy fields emit methane, which is a greenhouse gas.

17 An AIJ pilot phase was agreed at the first Conference of The Parties in 1995. The

pilot phase is voluntary and the investing country cannot claim credit for reduced emissions in the recipient country where emission reduction is taking place due to the joint project.

18 International scientific networking is also dominated by scientists from North America and Western Europe. The International Geosphere-Biosphere Programme, which IPCC relies on heavily for information, is comprised of 36 per cent of scientists from Western Europe, 33 per cent from the USA and Canada, 7 per cent from Eastern Europe, 6 per cent from Australia, 6 per cent from Latin America, 4 per cent from Japan, 4 per cent from Africa, 2.6 per cent from China and India, and none from the Middle East (Smith 1994).

19 Chico Mendes organised unions among the Amazonian rubber-tappers (called *'seringueiros'* in Brazil) in the 1970s and 1980s. The rubber-tappers were losing access to much of the land they had been living on for decades, as large-scale cattle-ranching began to encroach upon many regions in Amazonia with the help of government subsidies. Often the rubber-tappers suffered terrorism and violence from local ranchers in fights over land. In 1987 Mendes presented a plan for 'extractive reserves' to the International Development Bank that would secure reserved areas of forest for the rubber-tappers, where they could tap rubber and collect Brazil nuts. Ranchers would have no rights to clear these reserves. http://www.earlham.edu/www/polisci/17Fall96/inneske/grassroots.HTM

20 *Murder in the Amazon.* 1989. Central Independent Television; produced and directed by Adrian Cowell; distributor: Bullfrog Films; publisher: McNabb and Connolly; 51 minutes.

21 *Time* 17 December 1990, Vol. 136, No. 26: 76.

22 Hansen's statement is quoted in Paterson 1996.

References

Agarwal, Anil and Sunita Narain (1991) *Global Warming in an Unequal World*, Delhi: Centre for Science and Environment.

Allen, Elizabeth (1992) 'Calha Norte: military development in Brazilian Amazônia', *Development and Change* 23: 71–99.

Arnt, Ricardo Azambuja (1992) 'The inside out, the outside in: pros and cons of foreign influence on Brazilian environmentalism', in *Green Globe Yearbook 1992*, Oslo: Fridtjof Nansen Institute, 15–23.

Bramble, Barbara J. and Gareth Porter (1992) 'Non-governmental organizations and the making of US international environmental policy', in Andrew Hurrell and Benedict Kingsbury (eds) *The International Politics of the Environment. Actors, Interests, and Institutions*, Oxford: Clarendon Press, 313–53.

Browder, John O (1989) 'Public policy and deforestation in the Brazilian Amazon', in Robert Repetto and Malcolm Gillis (eds) *Public Policies and the Misuse of Forest Resources*, New York: Cambridge University Press, 247–97.

Christian Science Monitor Monthly, February 1989, vol. 2 no. 2.

Climate-List, 26 November 1997.

Discover, January 1990, vol. 11 no. 1.

Division for the Environment, General Secretariat for Foreign Affairs, Ministry of External Relations (1991) *Brazilian Positions on Environment and Development*, Brasilia.

Economist, 7 December 1985, vol. 297.

Finger, Matthias (ed.) (1992) *Research in Social Movements, Conflicts and Change. The Green Movement Worldwide*, Greenwich and London: JAI Press.

Goldstein, Karl (1992) 'The Green movement in Brazil', in Finger (ed.) 1992.

Goodman, David and Anthony Hall (eds) (1990) *The Future of Amazonia. Destruction or Sustainable Development?*, London: Macmillan.

Guimarães, Roberto P (1992) 'Development pattern and environment in Brazil', *CEPAL Review* 47 (Aug.): 47–62.

Hagopian, Frances (1990) 'Democracy by undemocratic means? Elites, political pacts, and regime transition in Brazil', *Comparative Political Studies* 23 (2):147–70.

Hall, Anthony (1992) *Making People Matter: Development and the Environment in Brazilian Amazonia*, London: Institute of Latin American Studies, Working paper no. 4.

Henberg, Marvin and Daniel Zirker (1994) 'Amazonia: democracy, ecology, and Brazilian military prerogatives in the 1990s', *Armed Forces and Society* 20 (2): 259–81.

Hurrell, Andrew (1990) 'Brazil and the international politics of Amazonian deforestation', in Hurrell and Kingsbury (eds) *The International Politics of the Environment*, Oxford: Clarendon Press, 398–429.

—— (1991) 'The politics of Amazonian deforestation', *Journal of Latin American Studies* 23: 197–215.

Hurrell, Andrew and Benedict Kingsbury (1992) *The International Politics of the Environment*, Oxford: Clarendon Press.

International Energy Agency and Organisation for Economic Co-operation and Development (1996) *Climate Change Policy Initiatives, 1995/96 Update, Vol. II: Selected Non-IEA Countries*, Paris: IEA/OECD.

Kasa, Sjur (1994) 'Environmental reforms in Brazilian Amazonia under Sarney and Collor: explaining some contrasts', *Ibero Americana, Nordic Journal of Latin American Studies* 24 (2): 42–63.

Kolk, Ans (1996) *Forests in International Environmental Politics. International Organizations, NGOs and the Brazilian Amazon*, Amsterdam: International Books.

Maclean's, 21 May 1990, vol.103 no. 21.

New York Times, 19 March 1987 and 24 December 1988, vol.137/138 no.1.

New York Times Magazine, 16 March 1986, vol. 135.

Paterson, Matthew (1996) *Global Warming and Global Politics*, London and New York: Routledge.

Repetto, Robert and Malcolm Gillis (eds) (1989) *Public Policies and the Misuse of Forest Resources*, New York: Cambridge University Press.

Rich, Bruce (1994) *Mortgaging the Earth. The World Bank Environmental Impoverishment and the Crisis of Development*, London: Earthscan.

Risse-Kappen, Thomas (ed.) (1995) *Bringing Transnational Relations Back In. Non-State Actors, Domestic Structures and International Institutions*, Cambridge: Cambridge University Press

Risse-Kappen, Thomas (1995) 'Bringing transnational relations back in: introduction', in Risse-Kappen (ed.) *Bringing Transnational Relations Back In. Non-State Actors, Domestic Structures and International Institutions*, Cambridge: Cambridge University Press: 3–33.

Sagar, Ambuj and Milind Kandlikar (1997) 'Knowledge, rhetoric and power. international politics of climate change', *Economic and Political Weekly* 6 December: 3139–49.

Smith, Thomas B. (1994) 'Global climate change in Asia: the politics of public policy-making and science agenda setting', *Science and Public Policy* 21 (4): 249–59.

Sznajder, Mario (1996) 'Transition in South America: models of limited democracy', *Democratization* 3 (3): 360–70.

Time, 18 September 1989 and 17 December 1990, vol. 134 no.c 12.

Wirth, John D., Edson de Oliveira Nunes and Thomas E. Bogenschild (eds) (1987) *State and Society in Brazil. Continuity and Change*, Boulder and London: Westview.

World Resources Institute (1990) *World Resources 1990–91*, New York and Oxford: World Resources Institute in collaboration with UNDP and UNEP; Oxford University Press.

World Resources Institute (1992) *World Resources 1992–93*, New York and Oxford: World Resources Institute in collaboration with UNDP and UNEP; Oxford University Press.

Index